JEWISH
PRIORITIES

JEWISH PRIORITIES

Sixty-Five Proposals for the Future of Our People

EDITED BY DAVID HAZONY

WICKED SON
BOOKS

A WICKED SON BOOK

An Imprint of Post Hill Press

ISBN: 979-8-89565-085-1

ISBN (eBook): 978-1-63758-745-4

Jewish Priorities: Sixty-Five Proposals for the Future of Our People

© 2023 by David Hazony

All Rights Reserved

Published in cooperation with the Z3 Project. For more information visit Z3Project.org

Epigraph: Abraham Isaac Kook, "A Love for the World," in *Abraham Isaac Kook: The Lights of Penitence, Lights of Holiness, the Moral Principles, Essays, Letters, and Poems,* trans. Ben Zion Bokser (New York: The Paulist Press, 1978), pp. 227-228.

Book designed by Mark Karis

Post Hill Press

New York • Nashville

WickedSonBooks.com

Published in the United States of America

1 2 3 4 5 6 7 8 9 0

"When they confront their own people, to whose happiness, continuity and perfection they feel committed in all the depths of their being, and find it splintered, broken into parties and parties, they cannot identify themselves with any particular party. They desire to unite themselves with the whole people, only with the all-embracing whole, in all its fulness and good."

—ABRAHAM ISAAC KOOK, *LIGHTS OF HOLINESS*

CONTENTS

INTRODUCTION 1
A New "Torah" for Our Time
DAVID HAZONY

1 TOWARD A GREEN ZIONISM 7
Rediscovering Herzl's Environmentalist Vision
YOSEF ISRAEL ABRAMOWITZ

2 CULTIVATING COMMITMENT 17
A Four-Point Plan for Stronger Personal Ties with Israel
SALLY ABRAMS

3 TIKTOK AND THE TALMUD 24
How to Connect Young People with Our Ancient Wisdom
MIRIAM ANZOVIN

4 THE POLITICS OF THE MIZRAHI MOTHER 33
A Proven Path to Living with Our Differences
AVISHAY BEN HAIM

5 CONFRONT THE NEW COSSACKS 43
A Jewish Political Survival Guide
DAVID L. BERNSTEIN

6 THE TYRANNY OF "IDENTITY" 51
Why DIY Judaism Is No Substitute for Tradition
MIJAL BITTON

7 STAY SEXY 60
How to Rediscover Jewish Intimacy
CHANA BOTEACH

8 THE NARROW BRIDGE 66
Embracing the In-Betweens that Make Us Human
NESHAMA CARLEBACH

9 PROUD JEW IN THE NBA 71
How Keeping Kosher Made Me a Better Basketball Player
OMRI CASSPI

10 RESCUE OUR RECIPES 77
Cultivating Jewish Joy Through Our Culinary Traditions
JAKE COHEN

11 TOWARD A UNITED FRONT 81
Why We Still Need Consensus-Building Institutions
WILLIAM C. DAROFF

12 THE POWER OF SOFT WORDS 88
Relationships, Rather than Public Campaigns, Repair the World
SHLOMO ELKAN

13 SAY YES TO TRIBALISM 94
The Need for Solidarity in an Atomistic Age
RACHEL FISH

14 MOVE TO ISRAEL 103
A Third Way for the Anxious Diaspora Jew
BLAKE FLAYTON

15 OUR BIBLICAL BIRTHRIGHT 110
Reclaiming the Land-of-Israel Narrative
YISHAI FLEISHER

16 TEACH THE IDEA OF THE JEWISH PEOPLE 119
Protect Young Jews from the Intellectual Assault on Their Identity
DAVID GEDZELMAN

17 REINVENT JEWISH GIVING 129
The Case for "Return on Investment" Philanthropy
MARK GERSON

18 WE ARE ALL REFUGEES 139
Jewish Lessons for a World on the Move
ROYA HAKAKIAN

19 HOW TO FIX "TIKKUN OLAM" 146
Why Judaism Can't Be Reduced to Universalist Activism
AMMIEL HIRSCH

20 PRAISE THE LIVING JEWS 155
An Alternative to Holocaust Education
DARA HORN

21 THE KEY TO CONTINUITY 163
How to Forge New Links Across Generations
LAURA JANNER-KLAUSNER & ALLY GOLDBERG

22 NEEDED: MORE JEWS 168
Why We Should Actively Promote Conversion
TAL KEINAN

23 THE MOUNTAIN OF SPICES 174
Recovering the Erotic Core of Judaism
BENJAMIN KERSTEIN

24 THE JEWISH SPIRITUAL QUEST 183
Finding God in the Twenty-First Century
YOSSI KLEIN HALEVI

25 ARGUE LIKE A JEW 188
Rediscovering the Rabbinic Art of Disagreement
WILLIAM KOLBRENER

26 SEPARATION OF CHALLAH 194
An Ancient Ritual Opens the Door to Our Mothers' Wisdom
LIHI LAPID

27 EMBRACE THE CHAOS 199
Affirming the Edgy, Creative, Crazy Side of Being Jewish
NOLAN H. LEBOVITZ

28 AGAINST PRESTIGE ADDICTION 206
Stop Seeking Validation from Those Who Hate Us
LIEL LEIBOVITZ

29 TO DIE AS A JEW 212
Living Well in the Face of Mortality
MELANIE LEVAV

30 WHY EXILE MATTERS 218
How to Rebuild Diaspora Culture Without Using Israel as a Crutch
SHAUL MAGID

31 THE VIRTUE OF INCLUSIVITY 228
We All Have Something to Contribute to the Mosaic
MANISHTANA

32 AN END TO ASHKENORMATIVITY 234
Let's Put Bagels-and-Lox Jewishness Behind Us
HEN MAZZIG

33 AN AGGADIC JEW 241
Liberate the Power of Jewish Storytelling
RUBY NAMDAR

34 UN-HIJACK HUMAN RIGHTS 248
How a Movement Founded by Jews Can Be Restored
HILLEL C. NEUER

35 DEEP ROOTS MAKE STRONG BRANCHES 258
Build Our Future by Investing in Our Common Heritage
IRINA NEVZLIN

36 EXPAND THE ABRAHAM ACCORDS 263
Cracking the Code of Coexistence
HOUDA NONOO

37 MAKE FUN OF EVERYTHING 268
Why Humor Is the Key to Jewish Pride
CLAUDIA OSHRY

38 STRONG INDIVIDUALS MAKE STRONG COMMUNITIES 274
Why We Can't Have One Without the Other
FANIA OZ-SALZBERGER

39 TZEDAKANOMICS 284
The Power of the Haredi Social Safety Net
ELI PALEY

40 SAVING THE JEWISH-PROGRESSIVE ALLIANCE 293
Why We Must Fight for the Soul of the Left
CARLY PILDIS

41 STUDY THE TALMUD THE OLD-FASHIONED WAY 302
Forget Viral Videos. Find a Teacher. Open a Book.
URI PILICHOWSKI

42 WHY JEWS NEED A COMMON LANGUAGE 309
A Plan for Universal Hebrew Literacy
VARDIT RINGVALD

43 ONLY THE JEWS CAN SAVE EUROPE 319
Why We Shouldn't Quit the Continent
SIMONE RODAN-BENZAQUEN

44 THE SATMAR ART OF NOT GIVING A F*CK 327
Hidden in Brooklyn, a Surprisingly Vibrant Communal Model
ARMIN ROSEN

45 ZIONISTS ARE MADE, NOT BORN 337
The Fight for Israel's Image Can Be Won. Here's How.
ROZ ROTHSTEIN

46 RAISING INQUISITIVE CHILDREN 346
Educate Kids to Ask Better Questions
JODI RUDOREN

47 THOU SHALT BE BEAUTIFUL 355
The Forgotten Jewish Ideal
LIZZY SAVETSKY

48 DON'T TAKE DEMOCRACY FOR GRANTED 363
Why We Must Not Be Politically Complacent
DAHLIA SCHEINDLIN

49 WANTED: A JEWISH TOLKIEN 371
Why We Need a New Mythology
JOE SCHWARTZ

50 STRENGTHEN THE CHRISTIAN-JEWISH ALLIANCE 380
The Urgency of Overcoming Our Prejudice
FAYDRA L. SHAPIRO

51 THE RIGHT WAY TO COMMEMORATE THE HOLOCAUST 386
By Using It to Reclaim Our Nationhood
NATAN SHARANSKY & GIL TROY

52 THE JEWEL IN THE CROWN OF JEWISH EDUCATION 396
The Power of History to Shape Our Kids' Identity
LAURA SHAW FRANK

53 LET'S GET BACK TO SMASHING IDOLS 405
The Worship of Power Is More Dangerous Than Ever
SCOTT A. SHAY

54 A WESTERN WALL FOR EVERYONE 413
Why Was I Arrested for Praying at the Kotel?
HALLEL SILVERMAN

55 LIBERATE OUR INSTITUTIONS 418
A New Organizational Paradigm
ANDRÉS SPOKOINY

56 A NEW PANTHEON OF HEROES 427
Without Stories of Courage and Sacrifice, We Can't Have Jewish Pride
MICHAEL STEINHARDT

57 THE POWER OF "NO" 435
Judaism Began with an Act of Refusal. We Still Have a Lot More Refusing to Do.
BRET STEPHENS

58 THE CASE FOR JEWISH GUILT 440
Why Feeling Bad About Our Non-Observance Is Crucial for Passing the Torch
DAVID SUISSA

59 HOW TO BEAT THE NEW ANTISEMITISM 446
It's Not About Human Rights. It's About Soviet Propaganda.
IZABELLA TABAROVSKY

60 IGNORE THE GLOBALISTS 456
Why Jewish Nationalism Drives Them Up a Wall
GADI TAUB

61 ZIONISM AS THERAPY 465
How the Movement's Founding Texts Offer an Answer to Today's Bullies
EINAT WILF

62 ON MORAL CONFIDENCE 473
How the Diaspora Lost Its Jewish Spine, and How to Get It Back
RUTH R. WISSE

63 RESPECT YOUR OPPONENTS 479
In Great Disputes, There Is No Solitary Truth
DAVID WOLPE

64 A CURE FOR DIASPORA DELUSIONS 484
What We Can Learn About Ourselves from Soviet Immigrants
ALEX ZELDIN

65 THE CITY OF OUR DREAMS 489
Why Tel Aviv Is the Model for Jewish Life in the Twenty-First Century
NERI ZILBER

AFTERWORD 498
Is This a Jewish Book? A Jewish Publisher's Priorities
ADAM BELLOW

Acknowledgments 508
About the Author 510

INTRODUCTION

A New "Torah" for Our Time

DAVID HAZONY

WHAT IS A JEWISH PRIORITY? Who gets to say? How do we agree on what our priorities should be? What does it even mean to ask this question?

In the essays that follow, each contributor was asked a simple question: If you could stand before the Jewish people and advocate for a single priority for our collective future, what would it be?

When Adam Bellow, publisher of Wicked Son books, first raised the idea of this volume, an immediate question arose: How do we keep it from becoming a collection of boring, conventional arguments about things most Jews already agree on, like "fighting antisemitism" or "remembering the

David Hazony is an award-winning editor, translator, and author. He is the former editor-in-chief of the journal *Azure* and was the founding editor of TheTower.org. His book *The Ten Commandments* (Scribner, 2010) was a finalist for the National Jewish Book Award. His translation of Uri Bar-Joseph's *The Angel* (HarperCollins, 2016) was a winner of the National Jewish Book Award. He has edited two previous anthologies: *Essential Essays on Judaism* by Eliezer Berkovits (Shalem, 2002), and, with Yoram Hazony and Michael B. Oren, *New Essays on Zionism* (Shalem, 2007). He has a Ph.D. in Jewish Philosophy from the Hebrew University and lives in Jerusalem.

Holocaust"? In order to be worth the effort, we agreed, such a book would need to be filled with *new* ideas, provocative and timely, controversial and creative. Ideas that spark debate and turn our focus to hard questions while also being, on some level, intellectually entertaining. A tall order indeed!

We also agreed that these ideas would have to come, not from the triangulating communications departments of our hoary communal institutions, but from thinkers, activists, scholars, rabbis, influencers, and culture-makers—people who live and breathe the contemporary Jewish experience in all its many forms and who have something important to say.

For generations, the Jewish agenda has been set in a top-down manner. In the Diaspora, institutional leaders and major philanthropists work together to establish our communal priorities, not just on the basis of what is truly needed, but also—even primarily—on the basis of what can be funded. That might have been necessary a generation or two ago, but in today's decentralized, sophisticated, and technologically empowered Jewish world, it is not a good way to engage our best minds in a process that challenges our assumptions and moves us forward as a people.

What we really need—and perhaps have needed for a long time—is a good old-fashioned intellectual *food fight*. A democratized Jewish free-for-all. A spirited brawl between two covers. We therefore set out with the singular goal of gathering and putting on display a collection of new ideas for a new generation of Jews. Our aim is to start not one, not two, but many Jewish arguments. And our hope is that these arguments will percolate and spread, stimulating new initiatives and sparking a sense of fresh possibility at the dawn of a new phase of Jewish life.

Over the course of more than a year, we reached out to potential contributors from every quadrant—from Left to Right, from secular and Reform to Haredi, from Gen Z to our most venerated writers. Our contributors are Israelis and Americans, Europeans and Russian speakers; they are literary, rabbinic, scholarly, and communal figures, journalists and online influencers, and activists. Many, it turned out, were bursting with ideas and eager to be heard.

The essays we received are as eclectic as their authors. Some offer new answers to old but still-important questions: the proper approach to God,

Torah study, and Jewish education; the structure and role of our communal institutions; the importance of the Hebrew language in the future of Diaspora life; the need for a renewed sense of "Jewish pride" in facing the rise of anti-semitism, or giving voice to marginalized Jewish communities. Others raise entirely new themes: the role of new media in teaching ancient texts or calls for the creation of Jewish fantasy literature or a new "Jewish pantheon" to honor the heroes of our people.

Yet despite this variety, some surprising common threads have emerged—enough to be woven together into a collective Jewish fabric that is stronger than we may have previously supposed. Three themes, in particular, stand out.

* * *

First is a belief in the necessity of the conversation itself. Ours is a time of heated mutual exclusion and intensifying polarization—and few feel this as acutely as the Jews. One might even say we invented "cancel culture" centuries ago through the process of *herem* or excommunication, when disputes over doctrine or practice became unbridgeable. Today, everyone seems compelled not just to keep score about various affronts but to keep a running list of "people I will never retweet."

Yet our contributors have set all that aside. Despite their disagreements, they have chosen to appear together in one volume, accepting the underlying premise that such a pan-Jewish conversation is not only possible but urgently needed. For many of them, this is also an act of courage.

Second is the recognition of the State of Israel as a central reference point for Jewish life today. Three-quarters of a century after the founding of the first Jewish state in two millennia, a new form of Jewish identity has emerged in the Land of Israel. Many of our contributors are either Israeli-born or have chosen to make Israel their home. Many others have chosen to focus on a topic related to the Jewish state—either supportively or critically.

For this reason, several offer contributions that call for an "improved" Israel—whether that means overhauling its overtly Jewish (or Ashkenazic) char-acter, its fidelity to modern liberalism, or its relationship with the Diaspora or the land itself. Some see Israel as an embattled homeland that must be protected at all costs; others fear that the new centrality of Israel may have come at the expense of a robust, independent affirmation of Jewish life in the Diaspora.

Yet for all the controversy that the Jewish state engenders, there can be no doubt that this book appears deep into what the political scientist Yossi Shain has called the "Israeli Century"—a time when Jews everywhere have crafted a new identity that is centrally informed by the renewal of Jewish sovereign life in our ancestral homeland.

A third common thread is something we may call a proper sense of Jewish pride. More than seven decades after the Holocaust and Independence, a great many Jews still feel we are missing something, some spiritual quality that is hard to define yet deeply necessary for our survival as a people.

We could have gone on commissioning essays indefinitely. The resulting volume could easily have been twice as long—and we regret that the constraints of time and space required us finally to say, "Enough."

But we are very pleased and proud of the result. Taken as a whole, this singular collection provides a kind of still-life of the state of the Jews in our time, along with a catalogue of the fears, dreams, and plans of a people at a particular moment in history.

**

Indeed, my own belief is that this work constitutes an important contribution to what we may call a "New Torah" for a new generation of Jews.

The word "Torah" or "teaching" has always had a double meaning. There was *the* Torah, representing the five Books of Moses, considered by tradition to be divinely dictated. And then there was simply "Torah," which embraced the entirety of Jewish teaching from pithy proverbs to urgent polemics, from legalistic haggling and interpretation of dreams to medical advice, philosophy, and mystical legends, from prophecy to poetry and prayer.

When the Torah was given on Mount Sinai, we are told, all the Israelites had crowns placed on their heads—symbolizing both the responsibility and the honor of the sovereign individual's pursuit of consequential wisdom.

This has been our mission as a people for thousands of years—and it has always been a creative process, one that proceeded largely through books.

Books define us like no other people on earth. The Bible—a limited collection of texts each written at a certain place and time—trained us in the arts of high-leverage narratives about our past, but also of poetry, wisdom, and law. The Talmud threw tens of thousands of memorized tales, dialogues, legal disputes, medical and business advice, and mystical imaginings into a pulsating food processor that has nurtured the imagination of Jews for millennia. Later still, we expressed ourselves through codes of law, mystical texts, theological and philosophical treatises, and, in the modern era, through novels and screenplays, magazines and newspapers, manifestoes and op-eds. And today it continues, through YouTube and Substack, podcasts and tweets.

All of these are in their own way holy texts. They are holy even if we deny there is such a thing as holiness. They are holy even when their subject matter is utterly secular in nature. They are holy because they are the building blocks of our collective wisdom, our Torah, which is part of our core mission on earth.

Rabbi Yohanan ben Zakkai, the leader of the Jews during the Great Revolt, who salvaged our Torah from the ashes of Roman destruction in the first century C.E., was said to have mastered every form of wisdom, including "constellations and calculations, the sayings of launderers and the sayings of fox-keepers, the conversation of demons and the conversation of palm trees, the conversation of the ministering angels, the great things and the little things" (Bava Batra 134a).

Ben Zakkai was the last political leader of a sovereign Jewish country prior to the Zionist revolution of 1948. "Torah" was, in his time, our wisdom of life, the universe, and everything—and expressed a sense that all of life is inter-connected and bound by the Jewish quest for wisdom and goodness. And it necessarily included the vast multiplicity of opinions, contradictory narratives, and sharp disagreements that any authentic quest requires.

In our own era, when Jewish life once again embraces the entirety of the human experience, our wisdom has expanded to include politics and policy, science, literature and the arts, the sayings of cab drivers and the sayings of tank commanders. Our collective wisdom today is as broad as the disciplines we have mastered (or, in many cases, pioneered) and as deep as our most profound religious, spiritual, or humanistic thinking.

The essays in this collection represent, I would modestly suggest, an important part of this "New Torah"—not to replace the old by any means, but to add another layer for a people that has carried its ancient instincts into our time. For it is not simply sixty-five opinions; it is a demonstration that despite our differences, we remain one people, bound through history and into the future by our timeless quest for wisdom.

***

Every book is necessarily finite, but my hope is that you will not experience this as a finished work. Rather, it is just the beginning of what should be an ongoing conversation, a demonstration that Jewish priorities can be advocated, explored, rebutted, and defended in the broadest possible context—that of the Jewish people as a whole.

Each essay can be read in one sitting. They are organized alphabetically by author's last name, to avoid making invidious choices. They can be read in order, randomly, or even in reverse.

Some will inspire new thoughts, or offer just the right words to express something you have long held on the tip of your tongue. But I encourage every one of us to pay closest attention to those we disagree with. For it is only we, as readers, who can turn this collective exercise into a genuine clash of ideas—and thereby set a course for a stronger, richer, prouder, and more inspiring future for our people.

1

TOWARD A GREEN ZIONISM

Rediscovering Herzl's Environmentalist Vision

YOSEF ISRAEL ABRAMOWITZ

IN 1896, as Theodor Herzl was writing his Zionist manifesto *The Jewish State*, Svante Arrhenius, a scientist in Sweden, was calculating the effects of the doubling of carbon dioxide in the atmosphere by humans burning coal, gas, and oil, which he warned could increase the earth's temperature by a disastrous five to six degrees Celsius.

Yosef Israel Abramowitz is a leader of President Herzog's Climate Forum, was named by CNN as one of the leading six Green Pioneers worldwide, and serves as CEO of Gigawatt Global, an impact investment platform for green energy. He was nominated by twelve African countries for the Nobel Peace Prize for his solar work.

Both Herzl and Arrhenius predicted correctly the course of human events.

While we don't know if Herzl was familiar with Arrhenius's work, Herzl's vision for the future state of the Jewish people was amazingly designed as a corrective to the climate injustice in his day, and he planned for his future state to be carbon-neutral and free of smoke pollution. In other words, back in 1896, Arrhenius issued the first warning against human-created catastrophic climate change, just as Herzl was planting the seeds of his model country that was going to be a renewable light unto the nations and solve the looming climate crisis.

Arrhenius went on to win the Nobel Prize in Chemistry. Herzl created a state-building movement and was buried on the aptly named Mount Herzl in Jerusalem, overlooking Israel's grave climate record.

* * *

Herzl gave us two blueprints of his future state: The first, *The Jewish State* (1896), is a call to action to form a progressive society on the eastern Mediterranean. The second, *Altneuland* (1902), the novel he raced to write as his breath shortened and his heart murmured, recounts the experiences of two passengers on the coal-fired boat *Futuro* who visit the Holy Land twice, twenty years apart, marveling at what the Jewish people were able to accomplish in a generation.

At the heart of Herzl's hope for the future were humanistic values (with a Jewish flavor) and the promise of technology, for which his imagination was astonishingly prescient. As he tired of long train rides in Europe, he looked out the window of his carriage and imagined the future airplane, penning the play, *The Steerable Airship*. Well before radio, Herzl imagined a "newspaper phone" that would ring news and music into people's homes. He had the uncanny ability to take a prototype of an idea—ideological or technological—and to quickly extrapolate to full-scale implementation into the future. And he used *Altneuland* as his platform to help the Jewish public imagine what they could—and mostly did—will into being. But Herzl's vision is much greener than today's reality in Israel.

In Herzl's imagination over 120 years ago, the future state would be a technological wonderland. Electric and telephone lines would exist in every home. Fast electric trains would crisscross the country and even the region; electric boats would skim the Sea of Galilee; electric farming equipment would power the agricultural collectives; and electric cable cars would whirl above city streets to avoid creating traffic jams below. The land would be filled with electric cars ("provided there are enough recharging stations in the area one drives in," he wrote) all managed by cooperatives of drivers—over a *century* before Shai Agassi introduced the same concept via Israel's Better Place venture. And Herzl shared the astounding vision that the future state would be 100 percent carbon-neutral in its power production, replacing the need for burning polluting fossil fuels.

The Zionist movement, including the tree-planting arm of the Jewish National Fund created by Herzl, began as a green movement. And while Zionism today is threatened from within by parochial and extreme voices in the political sphere, from without by Iran and also an international delegitimization movement, the National Security Council in the Prime Minister's Office has recently added a new threat to the viability of Herzl's state: climate change.

Indeed, as Shira Efron of the Institute for National Security Studies at Tel Aviv University writes in a devastating report:

> The Middle East is one of the regions most vulnerable to climate change, including rising temperatures, water and subsequently food shortages, rising sea levels, and increased frequency and intensity of extreme weather events. These changes could aggravate regional instability, lead to mass migration of refugees, and create comfortable conditions for terrorist organizations…climate change also has direct implications for infrastructure, equipment, and defense and weapons systems, as well as the health and level of preparedness of military and security personnel.

Ahad Ha'am famously criticized Herzl's state-fixated Zionism in an essay called "This is Not the Way." While Herzl won the battle within the Zionist movement, Ahad Ha'am's essay is true for Israel's backward climate policies.

About 116 years after Herzl published his fictionalized vision of Israel in *Altneuland,* Elon Musk met with Prime Minister Benjamin Netanyahu. "You know," Musk said, "your entire country could be powered by solar power. The Negev is Israel's energy future. You can deploy solar systems here that will give you more energy than you need—clean energy. Israel is a technological superpower."

Herzl would be disappointed to learn that the Israel of today has deliberately ignored his green energy vision and embraced the polluting and expensive gas monopoly controlled by the barons of our day, planting the seeds of Israel's—and the world's—destruction rather than redemption. Indeed, while Eilat and the Arava are 100 percent powered by the sun during the day and soon also at night, the rest of Israel is powered 90 percent by fossil fuels. This dark monopoly will control and exploit Israel's energy policy for at least another generation, with the state investing more and more tax dollars in gas pipelines and licenses rather than a solar-plus-energy-storage infrastructure. The result is that as the United States and Europe are advancing toward ambitious green goals that will also nurture their future economies with sustainable jobs, Israel is at the bottom of green energy lists in the OECD countries rather than its leader, which Herzl would have wanted.

***

Cruising on the *Futuro* from the poor and underdeveloped Turkish-controlled Palestine through the Red Sea in the pages of *Altneuland,* Mr. Kingscourt says to Friedrich, his Jewish companion:

> With the ideas, knowledge, and facilities that humanity possesses on this 31st day of December, 1902, it could save itself. No philosopher's stone, no dirigible airship is needed. Everything needful for the making of a better world exists already. And do you know, man, who could show the way? You! You Jews! Just because you're so badly off. You've nothing to lose. You could make the experimental land for humanity.

Kingscourt and Friedrich return to Haifa twenty years later and discover a bountiful, well-planned, smog-free, green country:

> In the middle of the square was a fenced-in garden of palm trees. Both sides of the streets running into the square were also bordered with palms, which seemed to be common in this region, the rows of trees served a double purpose. They gave shade by day, and at night shed light from electric lamps which hung from them like enormous glass fruits.

Herzl describes the city in which "automobiles speeded noiselessly by on rubber tires," and he directs Kingscourt in the text to ask, "What's that?" He pointed to a large iron car running along the tops of the palms, whose passengers were looking down into the street. The wheels of the car were not underneath, but on its roof; it moved along a powerful iron rail: "An electric overhead train."

The tour de force of Israel's green energy development, in Herzl's vision, is the Dead Sea Canal, taking advantage of the drop from the Mediterranean down to the Dead Sea. Take note that Albert Einstein received the Nobel Prize in Physics for the photovoltaic effect—the basis of our solar power—only in 1921, so Herzl's green vision didn't include solar power.

> And now they were in front of the power station. While driving down from Jericho, they had not been able to get a full view of the Dead Sea. Now they saw it lying broad and blue in the sun so smaller than the Lake of Geneva. On the northern shore, near where they stood, was a narrow, pointed strip of land extending behind the rocks over which the waters of the Canal came thundering down. Below were, in fact, as far as the eye could reach around the shore, numerous large manufacturing plants. The water power at source had attracted many industries; the Canal had stirred the Dead Sea to life. The iron tubes through which the waters of the Canal beat down upon the turbine wheels reminded Kingscourt of the apparatus at Niagara. There were

some twenty of these mighty iron tubes at the Dead Sea, jutting out from the rocks at equal distances. They were set vertically upon the turbine sheds, resembling fantastic chimneys. The roaring from the tubes and the white foam on the outflowing waters bore witness to a might work.... From here the tamed natural forces were conducted into electric generators, and the current sent along wires throughout all parts of the country. The "Old-New-Land" had been fructified into a garden and a home for the people who had once been poor, weak, hopeless, and homeless.

I remember when Prime Minister Menachem Begin unsuccessfully tried to revive Herzl's Dead Sea Canal. While water remains scarce, Israel is blessed with enough sun to power the whole country day and night—a "Niagara" of sunshine.

* * *

Herzl was obsessed not only with the Jewish Question but the Social Question—the growing inequalities in society. Two years before writing *The Jewish State*, he penned a play called *The New Ghetto*. The main character, Jacob Samuel, an educated, assimilated Jew, organizes a coal miner's strike against the exploitative, stock market-fixing aristocracy, and is killed off in a duel.

The exploitation of coal workers is at the heart of *The New Ghetto*, and the flag that draped Herzl's coffin had two blue stripes and seven Jewish stars—to signify not the days of the week but the humane treatment of workers that could be achieved by a seven-hour workday, which the Jewish state was going to model for the world, along with green energy.

In Herzl's future state, there would be peace with our neighbors and full equality for its Arab citizens. He was moved by the Arab poor on his brief visit to Palestine and held that their lives would be vastly improved by the new technology, including green electricity for all, that the Jews would bring with them.

Fast forward 120 years since the publication of *Altneuland*. My eighteen-year-old daughter, Ashira, and I jump into a taxi in our third attempt to "vandalize" Herzl's grave in Jerusalem. Herzl's bones, much like those of Joseph, arrived in Israel long after his death. He was buried in the State of Israel in 1949, fifty-two years after the First Zionist Congress.

In my bag is the masking tape to paste a Reuters article onto the slab of black granite grave engraved with gold block Hebrew letters. In the taxi, I hear a ping on my "newspaper phone." There is a shouting match in the Knesset. We click on the link of Kan, the national broadcaster, to see and hear members of Knesset—mostly from the opposition—yelling. In the seat of the Speaker's chair is Mansour Abbas, chairman of the Islamic party, Ra'am. A portrait of Herzl hangs above him on the left.

Despite the fact that Herzl imagined a civil political culture, Israel's politics have been intense and often unpleasant in the past several years, with four rounds of inconclusive elections. The political elephant in the room for the past several decades has been if, when, and how Israeli-Arab parties might join a Zionist government and change the political map. The Israeli-Arab sector has been deeply neglected, with vast discrepancies in government policies and spending on education, public transportation, police, infrastructure, and electricity.

"The electric light was certainly not invented so that the drawing room of a few snobs might be illuminated, but rather to enable us to solve some of the problems of humanity by its light," wrote Herzl in *The Jewish State*. "In solving it we are working not only for ourselves, but also for the many other downtrodden and oppressed beings." From his perch in the Knesset above Mansour Abbas, Herzl watches the debate taking place about hooking up unauthorized Arab homes to electricity.

We jump out of the taxi at Mount Herzl, walk past the modest museum, and emerge into the open plaza. On my phone Abbas is still trying to get the Knesset to order but he is calm. The black granite tomb about one hundred yards away is flanked by soldiers and two flagpoles: the World Zionist Organization flag on the right, and the flag of Israel on the left. The soldiers, on a study tour, move on, and so Ashira and I approach and place the phone with the live Knesset debate onto the grave.

* * *

From atop the tomb, Mansour Abbas's voice calls for a roll call on the third and final reading of the electricity bill, to help correct Israel's most blatant climate injustice. Nearly half the chamber walks out to boycott the vote they were about to lose.

Herzl is captivated by the intensity of the debate among Arabs and Jews, all in Hebrew.

Naftali Bennett, then Prime Minister and head of the Yamina Party: "Yea." Benny Begin, son of the former Likud Prime Minister and from the right-wing New Hope Party: "Yea." And nearly everyone else who stayed in the plenary votes in favor, with three abstentions, interestingly from secular Arab parties.

Abbas, from the Speaker's chair, not only declares victory by a vote of 61 to 0 but calls up MK Iman Khatib-Yasin for closing words, which she delivers in Arabic, wearing a hijab.

Herzl appreciates the sweet drama, the attempt to right a social wrong against the Arab citizens, as would have his *New Ghetto* character, Jacob Samuel.

With the historic Knesset vote done, we turn off the phone. Ashira and I sit on the ground in front of the Hebrew letters of Herzl's name and begin our work.

The Jewish Colonial Trust was incorporated by Herzl during the Second Zionist Congress as the under-capitalized bank for the Zionist movement; he would be astounded to learn that the Israel of today has over $215 billion in foreign currency reserves; it also has one of the biggest gaps between rich and poor, with a third of our children living in poverty. The annual budget, which thanks to bringing the Islamic Party into the previous government, finally passed, is a little shy of $150 billion, or about 50 percent greater than Herzl's native Austria.

During the Covid-19 pandemic, Israel needed to raise money to cover the budget deficit caused by the crisis. It went to the markets, offering $5 billion in bonds; it was over-subscribed for $25 billion. Lost amid the pandemic news is a sweet financial footnote that Herzl would have appreciated and Ashira and I, fifteen years after our family's Aliyah from Boston, were there to deliver in person.

One billion dollars of the bond offering was snapped up for a term of one hundred years. *One hundred years.* We tape the article entitled "Israel Sells Rare 'Century Bonds' in Record $5 bln Debt Issue" to Herzl's grave, leave the plaza, and go back to fighting to change Israel's climate-dangerous energy policies and for a more just Israel—a renewable light unto the nations.

* * *

My friend David Matlow, the world's largest private Herzl collector, gave me a pair of blue Herzl socks that I tend to wear on the international stage as I am promoting a comprehensive Israeli solar vision for our country and the world. In one of my recent journeys where I had the privilege of walking in Herzl's footsteps, or at least his socks, I shared a panel at the 2022 United Nations COP27 Climate Conference in Sharm el-Sheikh, Egypt, with the Chairman of the Board of Bank Leumi—the bank once known as the Jewish Colonial Trust. The session focused on new financial models to scale renewable energy to help save the world from the gloomy and accurate climate predictions of 125 years ago from Svante Arrhenius.

Herzl loomed large for me that day on stage at the Israeli pavilion at the UN Climate Conference. What would he have said?

Luckily, I didn't have to wonder, since from the podium, in front of the flag of Israel, came a good, Zionist answer from the chairman of Herzl's bank:

> Ladies and gentlemen, we are gathered here today in light of the global threat of adverse climate changes with long-term and maybe irreversible impact on humanity. There is unequivocal evidence that the earth is warming at an accelerated pace and that the root cause is our own activities.... Israel is making inroads in leading climate tech innovation and investment as well as setting up responsible financing policies by the financial sector. The spirit of the Israeli private sector coupled with the talent from the regulators and incentives from the Innovation Authority, along with Israeli government R&D which lead with $280 million between 2018 and 2020, have created an impressive ecosystem in climate tech innovation.

The chairman then switched from English to Hebrew to close with a quote from an ancient rabbinic work, *Ecclesiastes Rabbah*:

> When the Blessed Holy One created the first human, He took him and led him round all the trees of the Garden of Eden and said to him: "Look at My works, how beautiful and praiseworthy they are! And all that I have created, it was for you that I created it. Pay attention that you do not corrupt and destroy My world: if you corrupt it, there is no one to repair it after you."

The Chairman of Bank Leumi, it should be noted, was an economist by the name of Samer Haj-Yehia, a Muslim Israeli. As he finished his remarks, I could feel Herzl applaud from heaven. We were one step closer to long-delayed climate justice in the Jewish state.

2

CULTIVATING COMMITMENT

A Four-Point Plan for Stronger Personal Ties with Israel

SALLY ABRAMS

OUR GRANDCHILDREN, ages five, seven, and nine, stood atop Masada a week into their first visit to Israel. They gazed across the expansive vista while our guide crouched beside them. I wondered how he would present the story of Masada to children this young.

"Who are the Jewish people?" he began. "That's us. When we stand on Masada we think about our values, what we want to live for." He wove together Jewish peoplehood and our connection to Israel. He then asked them to shout, *Am yisrael chai!*—"The people Israel lives!" The children shouted it one word

---

Sally Abrams is Director of Judaism and Israel Education at the Jewish Community Relations Council of Minnesota and the Dakotas.

at a time, then heard the echo of their own voices returning across the vast desert. In this melding of peoplehood and place, the seeds of connection were planted. In that echo was a profound message: *I am part of our people's story.*

Seeing our grandchildren take their first steps to connect meaningfully with Israel underscores what I have learned in my own improbable and wondrous story: A relationship with Israel provides a wellspring of meaning. It can profoundly shape an expansive Jewish identity. It invites us to be participants in our own people's astonishing saga.

My relationship with Israel is grounded in *ne'emanut.* Often translated as "loyalty," "faithfulness," or perhaps most accurately as "commitment," ne'emanut is a moral good unto itself, independent of other values. I learned this concept from the brilliant scholar Mijal Bitton at a lecture at the Shalom Hartman Institute in Jerusalem. Ne'emanut is not blind loyalty, she explained. It means that even if we disagree with Israel's actions or values, we don't walk away. As in any relationship, when you are in a lifelong relationship with Israel, there will be times when your ne'emanut is tested. Despite Israel's flaws and challenges, ne'emanut enables me to stay in the relationship.

In the fullest expression of this relationship, we encounter Israel in all its dimensions: history, culture, religion, language, politics, and people. Such an encounter takes us beyond the political focus, which cannot substitute for a genuine Israel experience.

***

Not so long ago, the importance and meaning of a relationship with Israel seemed self-evident. That is no longer the case. In the marketplace of meaning, many Jews are searching elsewhere. In setting Jewish priorities, then, what was once a given must now be made explicit.

A 2020 Pew Research Center survey of American Jews showed that 58 percent of adults say they are very or somewhat emotionally attached to Israel. Forty-five percent said that caring about Israel is "essential" to being Jewish, and an additional 37 percent said it is "important, but not essential." Among Jews for whom Israel is important, there will be those searching for ways to deepen their connection. "A strong majority of American Jewish liberals remain intuitively connected to Israel," said the writer Yossi Klein Halevi on Rabbi Ammiel Hirsch's podcast, *In These Times*. "But the challenge is to make that intuition explicit, and to make it intellectually and spiritually coherent. That's hard work. That's the work we must do."

There are concrete steps Jews can take—for example, learning Israel's history, following its news, visiting when possible, studying Hebrew, or cultivating relationships with Israelis. For me, knowing Israel has become inseparable from knowing Israelis. How much deeper is our attachment to a place if we have genuine relationships with the people who live there?

The value of such relationships is reciprocal. Israelis have repeatedly affirmed to me how much they appreciate a connection with Diaspora Jews. One Israeli friend describes it like this: "Once Israelis start listening, they begin to hear things they never knew before. Slowly, this evolves into curiosity about the 'why.' It then evolves into, 'Let's get to know more, this is intriguing,' and then into 'Wow, we have so many similarities even though we are so different,' and finally, 'We are family, when can I feed you?'"

The belief that all Jews are part of am yisrael is the beating heart of our Jewish story. When we connect with each other, we bring that value to life.

* * *

I began seeking a relationship with Israel decades ago, in a very different time. I did not grow up in a Zionist home. My parents deeply identified as Jews, but their primary focus was trying to keep a roof over our heads. They were loving and devoted parents, living under relentless financial pressure.

What I knew of Israel I learned at a weekly Sunday school class, and it aroused my curiosity. I was hungry for something I couldn't name.

Then my friends began attending Herzl Camp in Wisconsin. Along with friendships and fun, this iconic sleepaway camp fosters a deep love of Judaism and Israel. My friends returned home from camp lit from within. Listening to them, I had a dawning awareness of a missing piece, a connection waiting to be made.

I begged my parents to send me to Herzl Camp. A scholarship fund helped me get there for two glorious summers. The seeds of a connection to Israel were planted, and a bond of belonging to the Jewish people was established.

But a trip to Israel was still far off in the future. I did not get there until I was forty-one. In the meantime, when my kids were young, I nurtured my connection to Israel from afar.

I studied the Hebrew language intensively, which proved crucial in my life. Acquiring the language opened a hidden world of Hebrew cultural treasures—literature, music, poetry, and essays. The revival of Hebrew and its transformation into a modern language was the bold act of a determined people. For me, to speak Hebrew with near-fluency—for all my errors and American accent—was to join in the miracle of Jewish national rebirth.

I earned a degree in Hebrew and taught middle and high school classes for fifteen years. I saw the Jewish world break open for some of my students, too.

Hebrew also became the entry point for my connection with Israelis. During the years when I was working hard to learn Hebrew, I wanted someone with whom I could speak the language. By volunteering to house young Israelis sent over by the Jewish Agency to bring a taste of Israel to local Jewish day camps, I found wonderful conversation partners. These young people stayed with us for weeks at a time, forming a warm bond with my family. The experience was enriched by sharing it with friends who also hosted Israelis. It was the beginning of encountering Israel through relationships with Israelis.

At last, in 1998, my husband and I took our family on a long-awaited journey to Israel. Being part of the majority Jewish culture was a new and profoundly meaningful experience. We discovered how it feels when time flows on a Jewish rhythm, when Shabbat's approach is palpable. In exploring Israel, we encountered a place with endless history, stories, diversity, culture, sounds, flavors, and scenic beauty. I chatted in Hebrew with anyone willing to put up with me.

Our weeks in Israel also offered a much-needed dose of reality. Because I did not get to Israel for the first time until midlife, I had a lot of time to build up an imaginary Israel in my mind. Now I could begin the process of getting to know the real place in all its complexity and challenge. I have been back to Israel many times since then, and each visit is a chance to uncover more of Israel's multi-layered identity and strengthen my own.

My lifelong quest for an ever-deepening relationship with Israel has brought a steady stream of wonderful and diverse Israelis into my life: a fellow teacher who became like a sister, fellow bloggers for the *Times of Israel*, colleagues who became friends through our shared work. These Israeli friends have also taken me deep into the cultures of Kurdish, Iranian, and Yemenite Jews, something not so easy to find in the Ashkenazi-centric Midwest.

Each Israeli friend has a fascinating personal story and a confident Israeli-Jewish identity. They are my lens into Israel, refracting Israel's complex reality from their own unique viewpoints. Thanks to these friendships, what happens in Israel has become personal for me.

My relationship with Israel informs my educational work at our Jewish Community Relations Council of Minnesota and the Dakotas. It shapes the way I explain Judaism and Israel to thousands of students, many of whom have never met a Jew. It drives efforts to help our Jewish young people grapple with Israel's many challenges thoughtfully and with empathy for Israelis and Palestinians, open to learning from those whose narrative is different from theirs while standing proudly in their own story.

My relationship with Israel influenced how my husband and I raised our children. Their Jewish identities were shaped by growing up in a home where Israel was an organic part of everyday life through our food, music, conversation, and friendships, and via their own Israel experiences. Our children are all married now and raising Jewish families of their own. Their connection to Israel will shape how their children are raised.

Above all, my relationship with Israel is an essential and irreplaceable element of my identity as a Jew and a human being. I'm a little part of this magnificent story, a story I share with every Jew before me, every Jew alive today, and all those yet to be. I belong to a people and place whom I claim and who claim me, an answer to the hunger that as a child I could not name.

Today I can name it. It's called ne'emanut.

***

Can lessons be drawn from a personal story, one that began in a much different time? Can this concept of ne'emanut be applied today? I believe it can.

We need to think strategically about how to make an Israel relationship accessible and sustainable for every Jew, at each age and stage of life: (1) *Visiting*

21

Israel, of course, is still an unparalleled experience in building a relationship with the country and deepening Jewish identity. (2) *Hebrew language* is the key to Israeli society and culture, so encouraging the study of Hebrew needs to be a Diaspora priority. (3) Helping children form a loving *attachment to Israel* is the foundation, but as they mature, they must learn to grapple with Israel's complex challenges. This needs to be seen as a lifelong quest: sometimes, opportunities missed in youth can be experienced later, with even deeper meaning. Finally, (4) cultivating *relationships with Israelis* is a powerful way to know Israel better and deeply enrich one's sense of belonging to a global Jewish people, a family of families.

In creating meaningful relationships between Diaspora Jews and Israel, let's focus on the strategies that work. Travel to Israel contains outstanding options—organized tours, study abroad programs, Masa Israel Journey, Honeymoon Israel (in which newlyweds, including interfaith couples, connect with Israel at a formative stage of life), and, of course, Birthright. For some, seeing the land of the Bible is what makes the trip so meaningful. For others, it's the history, the scenic beauty, the food, the astonishing diversity of Jews they meet, or the joy in seeing Israel vibrant and flourishing. A visit shifts an imaginary Israel into its full three-dimensional reality. For many, a visit to Israel is a highlight of their Jewish lives.

However, we also need to retain and sustain the Israel experience. Cost and distance limit how often most people can travel to Israel. There are successful strategies to deepen the relationship within the Diaspora. Community events featuring Israeli speakers, scholars, films, and other cultural offerings expose us to current Israeli ideas and trends. Opening our homes to host Israelis who are visiting our communities nurtures connection.

As well, innovative programs like Partnership2Gether (P2G) build relationships through meaningful engagement between Israeli and Diaspora Jews. This program of the Jewish Agency for Israel and the Jewish Federations of North America, in partnership with local Jewish community agencies, pairs Israeli and Diaspora communities, which then generate their own programs to connect people across ages and interests. P2G also creates a rich encounter with Israeli culture. Our Minneapolis-Rehovot partnership just embarked on a new program in which our two communities will virtually view and discuss together Israeli short films, using culture as a springboard to learn more about Israel and each other. The genius of P2G is that it makes meaningful engagement between Israeli and Diaspora Jews accessible to so many.

We must also think beyond our current strategies. Where will our next big ideas in the Israeli-Diaspora relationship come from? Let's harness our enormous creative power to bring forth new ways of deepening our relationship with Israel across broad categories: Israeli music, food, literature, film, television, the arts, religious texts, social issues, and peoplehood. Technology enables a level of engagement that was unimaginable not so long ago.

It will take a steady stream of fresh thinking, but here's one thing I know for sure: Jews are ideas people. We are people who imagine and innovate, who dream and dare. Let's put that to work to deepen the lasting commitment of our people—to Israel and, as a result, to each other.

3

TIKTOK AND THE TALMUD

How to Connect Young People with Our Ancient Wisdom

MIRIAM ANZOVIN

LIKE ATHENA OF GREEK MYTHOLOGY, leaping fully formed out of Zeus's forehead, I emerged suddenly and dramatically from the maelstrom that is TikTok on January 21, 2022. Not literally, of course. In fact, I'd lived for thirty-six years before that day. Yet, in the wider Jewish communal awareness, that date marked my Genesis.

On that day, I released a one-minute-and-twenty-six-seconds-long video on TikTok, the world's fastest-growing social media platform. It was merely

Miriam Anzovin is a Jewish-learning influencer on TikTok. She is the creator of #DafReactions, #ParshaReactions, and other viral content examining the juxtaposition of pop culture, nerd culture, and Jewish culture through a millennial lens.

the latest entry in a series I had created only a month earlier called Daf Reactions. I was (and am) participating in Daf Yomi, the seven and a half year cycle of studying the Babylonian Talmud at the rate of one double-sided folio page per day. At that point, I was two years into the process and, coincidentally, about two years into the pandemic. Like so many of my peers, I had found joy, education, and connection during that depressing, apocalyptic time by seeking refuge in TikTok.

Most importantly, that's where I found content that made me laugh.

Laughter is the most important thing in the whole world to me. There is no greater feeling on this earth than getting someone else to laugh. Whenever I learned the Daf with my study partner, Dan, he would cry laughing at the way I gave over the substance of the text. I used my own voice, my own language, references to pop and nerd culture, and connections to our real lives, with a garnish of extremely dramatic facial expressions. In other words, just the way I normally talked to him about anything I was enthusiastic about. My goal was to make Talmudic learning relatable for him, a person who had never picked up the Talmud before.

To my delight, I discovered that my approach also worked for people with abundant familiarity with the Talmud. When I gave my interpretation of Tractate Shabbat 110 to two rabbis, tears of laughter streamed down their faces. This was encouraging! Maybe I, too, could offer something funny on TikTok to make people smile while sharing my learning journey.

I only expected about fifteen people, tops, ever to see these niche videos— Daf Yomi didn't seem to be a big social media category on TikTok, despite the thousands of learners worldwide participating in the cycle. I imagined that a few secular millennials like myself, also learning and wrestling with the Daf for the first time, would be my audience—that is, people who sought to balance modern sensibilities with a drive and commitment to study Talmud every single day for the better part of a decade and get something meaningful out of it along the way.

I filmed in the style of typical "Reaction" videos that permeate TikTok and YouTube; dramatic camera zooms, emoji stickers, and an *abundance* of hot takes. Sometimes I swore, the punctuation-marks of enthusiastic millennial discourse. In homage to beloved makeup tutorials and influencer aesthetics, I always filmed with perfectly applied, sharply winged eyeliner.

Daf Reactions was also a way for me to fully engage with what I was learning, through the ups and downs of each day, each month, each tractate, each year. A friend told me that they thought the videos would go viral one day. Oh, what a good laugh I had at that idea—Talmud going viral on TikTok? *Gehenom* would have had to freeze over first.

That remained my perspective until that day in January when I studied page nine of Tractate Moed Katan. It proved to be a moment of enlightenment for me in many ways.

***

In that Daf, two rabbinic sages, Rav Chisda and Rav Huna, are having an intense discussion. The question at hand: Could women wear makeup during Chol Hamoed, the intermediate days of the long Jewish festivals of Sukkot and Passover? The Talmud indicates that Rav Chisda's wife, a woman of an age to have children already grown and married themselves, did, indeed, wear makeup on those days. And yet, Rav Huna declared that the practice was intended only for *young* women—not *old* women. He was snidely shading Rav Chisda's wife because of her age! The unmitigated chutzpah! Pure feminist rage flooded through me. How dare he. "My God!" I exclaimed out loud, seething.

My eyes sought Rav Chisda's response.

"My God!" he exclaimed, before launching into an impassioned speech standing up for the right of any woman to wear makeup regardless of age.

When I saw that "My God!" my jaw dropped. The hairs on the back of my neck stood up. Thinking about that moment today, I still get goosebumps. Because, in that nanosecond, I became fully aware of the power and beauty of Daf Yomi, of the Talmud. In my learning up to that point, mainly all I noticed had been the seemingly vast differences between our world and the world of our ancestors as illuminated by the Talmud. But here, there was absolutely no daylight between the opinion, the very words, of Miriam, living outside of Boston in 2022, and Rav Chisda, an Amora, who lived around 300 C.E. in Babylonia.

Time had telescoped. I was suddenly *there*, in the room with them, standing behind Rav Chisda and glaring at Rav Huna. With every line of Rav Chisda's blistering response, I screamed, "Yesssssss! Go off," like the world's most emphatic hype woman. How incredible: If I had never done Daf Yomi, I would never have witnessed this moment and felt that connection with Rav Chisda pull me back through time and space. I would never have understood that while so many things have changed in the vast span of centuries upon centuries, human beings and the universality of the human experience really have not. If he were alive today, I knew that Rav Huna would be guesting on any number of alpha-bro podcasts. You know the type.

I carried that amped excitement with me into filming the video. Sitting at my makeup table, holding a powder brush like a mic, I condemned Rav Huna's statement as sexist and misogynistic. I declared myself to be a Rav Chisda–stan, ride or die. I ended the video by exclaiming about Rav Chisda: "What. A Fucking. Legend."

Within forty-eight hours, the video went "Jewish viral." Daf Reactions, and the image of a blonde woman in a red bow gesturing vociferously while cursing out Rav Huna, was catapulted into the general Jewish popular consciousness. This resulted in great delight and great consternation, depending on whom in the Jewish community you asked. Here was a millennial secular woman, doing Daf Yomi, making a reaction video on the Talmud—of all things—and using slang and *adult language* to convey passionate feelings. Talking about it in a fun, comedic way? Some people immediately understood how what I was doing made the Daf tangible and delighted in discovering a fresh way to breathe life into learning the Talmud. Others, mainly segments of the Orthodox community who claim sole ownership of the Talmud to "protect" its sanctity from "outsiders" and (gasp) women, had a decidedly different take.

Pearls were clutched, fainting couches were fetched, and smelling salts were called for. Sermons and think pieces were feverishly written by aggrieved rabbis who, while hating me, had no qualms about using my name as their clickbait. The immodesty, the *scandal*, the shame, of a woman like me learning Talmud and speaking about it as I do? The bastion of ultra-Orthodoxy in Lakewood, N.J., sent out an SOS flare in an attempt to warn impressionable youth away from the *chilul hashem* of my damaging influence. It was already too late—the excited messages of newly minted fans were already coming from inside the *yeshivot*.

In the intervening months, Daf Reactions grew. The scope of the project expanded as well: Megillah Reactions, Exodus Reactions, and Ruth Reactions came next. Parsha Reactions will follow shortly. Thousands of people have followed me on social media, keeping up with my journey of daily Talmud learning. Many took up learning, or resumed learning, *because of the videos*. ("You make Gemara cool and relevant," a fan messaged me. "You've managed to reinvigorate my learning. I always found the Gemara the best cure for insomnia. You changed that.")

Jewish people whom I have looked up to for years began to follow me and shared my content. Orthodox teen girls in Israel and America began to send me their *own* Daf reactions—not in my style, but in *theirs*. Because they felt their voices and interpretations and reactions to the text had *value*. For each of these I receive, I cry. What I wouldn't have given to have had their courage and confidence when I was Orthodox. When I felt I had no voice or value. Their trust, support, and love for Daf Reactions is the greatest honor of my life.

On Purim, fans from around the world sent me photos and videos of themselves dressed in costume *as me* from the Moed Katan 9 or other videos, often with makeup brush in hand. And even for Jews who do not know my name, chances are that if they have social media, and are invested at all in Jewish learning, for good or ill they have heard of "that blonde woman who does the Daf on TikTok."

***

In these months, I discovered many things about the power and key role of Jewish learning in people's lives, and how literacy in Jewish texts needs to be prioritized as a form of Jewish identity, particularly here in America.

The most common questions I receive are: "Why did you choose to do Daf Yomi if you are secular?" or "How come we haven't heard of you before now?" and, most damning to the wider objectives of increased Jewish literacy: "Why weren't you around when I was in yeshiva/day school/seminary? I would have paid attention!"

Why did I do Daf Yomi? I come from a *ba'al teshuva* family, attended a Lubavitch day school for several years, got my degree in Judaic studies, and spent a long time as a devout God-fearing woman. But, in my early twenties, the cumulative burden of misogyny and personal trauma relating to Judaism left me with a terrifying realization that I no longer believed in a God.

Despite the entirety of my identity being rooted in Jewish observance, I felt this revelation meant I had to completely pull back from all aspects of Jewish life. Otherwise, I believed I would be a disingenuous hypocrite. After all, I truly thought at that time that being Orthodox was the only "real" way to be a Jew.

Seeking to maintain some sort of wistful, peripheral connection to Jewish peoplehood, I devoted my career to working at Jewish nonprofits, which sadly disillusioned me in yet more ways. But one day at work I was lucky enough to hear the late Rabbi Jonathan Sacks speak about the beauty of Daf Yomi. He described it as a book club where you are literally on the same page as thousands of Jews around the world. When the previous Daf cycle was ending, and the new one was on the horizon, I witnessed the vast enthusiasm for Daf Yomi from so many types of Jews. I loved that there was a burgeoning movement of Orthodox women, LGBTQIA+ Jews, and secular Jews, who were taking on Daf Yomi as an act of dedicated Jewish identity.

Around that same time, during Chanukah of 2019, there was a series of truly horrific antisemitic attacks. This solidified my decision to rededicate myself to active participation in something deeply Jewish—something that would be a daily priority in my life for a multiyear commitment, no less. It was, I felt, an added bonus that it would be my seven-and-a-half-year-long "Fuck You" to antisemites. I found beauty in the idea of reconnecting through Jewish learning. I did not need to feel like a hypocrite; I wasn't doing anything that required faith in God—only faith in the Jewish people and a wish to understand where we have been, and where we can go from here.

Regarding the question: "Why didn't we hear about you before now?" the answer is quite simple. Let's be honest: No established Jewish organization would have platformed me. I had to platform myself. All that time I worked in the Jewish community, including at a Federation for five years, nobody saw me as "future Jewish role model" material. Instead, I was told to tone myself down. To stop being funny. I had not attended any prestigious Jewish higher-ed programs. My family wasn't "known" within the Jewish community. I can't play "Jewish Geography." I did not attend a popular Jewish summer camp. I did not go on Birthright. It truly became clear that a person like me was perceived to have little value, because I did not fit the career trajectory of an "important Jewish person."

When I had the opportunity to work on a website owned by the Federation but with (initially) less of a corporate feel, I had an all-too-brief moment where I could create impactful Jewish content. I even hosted a podcast for several years interviewing Jews who were doing innovative things and talking about the overlap of Jewish and nerd culture. I was using my degree, my hard-earned knowledge, and my lived experiences both positive and negative to illuminate Jewishness in all its complexity and glory to any audience I could reach.

Every single one of these projects was eventually shut down by the Federation, because they were not designed to raise money, merely to inspire and educate.

This is a mistake on the Federation's part. The priority should be engaging with young Jews in a way they actually want. Where they actually are already. In a voice they recognize and isn't so boring that it causes narcolepsy.

Access and opportunity to learn Talmud and other Jewish texts is *a birthright for all of us*—as meaningful and powerful a form of Jewish identity as religious observance, or Zionism, or any of the "approved" modes of "being Jewish." This learning is *ours*, regardless of religious or denominational affiliation (or lack thereof), knowledge level, observance level, gender, age, sexual orientation, spiritual belief, or economic status. Affirming this reality needs to be a priority for anyone who claims to care about the future of the Jewish people.

Though I aim to be humorous in my videos, my purpose is serious: to showcase the ways in which Jewish text learning can be a profound and meaningful experience for each of us individually, in our own ways. My commentary is honest: Where I see misogyny, I call it out; where I see wisdom, I help my audience see it, too. And it seems that many Jews have been waiting for something like this.

For Jews who think they cannot learn because they are not religious enough?

Well, here is a person like me—an atheist—taking on this commitment. For those who were discouraged or silenced from voicing their feelings about what they learn in the Talmud? I tell them their personal reactions are valid, normal, and encouraged. The Talmud is recorded discussion and debate. Treating it now as calcified, viewing the sages as semi-saints rather than complex human beings, is an absolute disservice to our ancestors and their real lives and real experiences that are illuminated so vividly in the text. To keep the Talmud locked away, as if behind glass in a museum, safe in yeshivot for primarily only Orthodox men to learn in "appropriate" ways with "approved" opinions, betrays the actual spirit of Talmudic debate and discussion.

Any gatekeeping or barrier to Jewish learning must be removed. We must allow this discourse to expand beyond "safe" parameters of approved language and enforced seriousness. The community cannot engage in pointless hand-wringing over ridiculous fears about intermarriage, reduced synagogue attendance, or any of the obsolete benchmarks of the past that dictate communal fear, when simultaneously they are unwilling to open a door to Jewish identity that so many young Jews would happily choose to walk through.

In creating my videos, I have seen the possibilities of future modalities of Jewish connection: An online community of learners has chosen to join me on my learning adventure, resulting in a "congregation" of sorts based on mutual respect and appreciation where *participating in learning is a marker of a proud Jewish identity.* These people come from across the religious spectrum, from atheists to Hasidim, Ashkenazim, Sephardim, LGBTQIA+ Jews, Zionists, anti-Zionists, and beyond. The Jewish communal institutions need to understand fully that their approach, their hierarchical and rigid corporate structures of power, their biases and assumptions, effectively shove millennial and Gen-Z Jews away from participation in Jewish life.

But I, alongside so many incredible Jewish creators, rabbis, and educators, exist where these demographics already congregate. Because that's where we also spend our time. We are experiencing Jewishness together in authentic and personally meaningful ways.

I am far from the first Jew to have had hot takes on the Talmud. The Jews *in* the Talmud have hot takes on what's in the Talmud. Nor am I the first person to view the sages as flawed but intriguing human beings, nor the first feminist of any Jewish denomination to offer similar critiques. What resonates so strongly with this online community of learners is the influence of my life experiences, the balance of comedy and deeply heartfelt, authentic lessons I include in each video, the multiple identities I embody, and the way I position Jewish learning to be a valid Jewish identity in and of itself.

Well, those things plus the swearing. And, of course, the perfectly applied eyeliner.

4

THE POLITICS OF THE
MIZRAHI MOTHER

A Proven Path to Living with Our Differences

AVISHAY BEN HAIM

ONE OF THE MAJOR CHARACTERISTICS of the modern age has been the rise of absolute ideologies purporting to offer ultimate solutions to the problems facing humanity. These optimistic dreams, however, gave rise to disasters. From the wonderful idea of socialism was born communism which brought brutal wars, totalitarianism, and the deaths of many millions. From the belief

Avishay Ben Haim, Ph.D., is a historian, journalist, and commentator focusing on Jewish and Israeli identity. He is author, most recently, of *Second Israel: The Sweet Gospel, the Bitter Oppression* (Yediot, 2022).

in rationalism and the possibility of complete knowledge was born confusion, relativism, and ultimately post-modern challenges to truth itself. From the exciting technological progress that promised to improve the lives of countless human beings was born the most horrific century in human history, when people used technology to slaughter one another at an unthinkable scale. As one rabbi put it: Humans learned how to control nature before they learned how to control themselves.

These absolute Western ideologies all collapsed. Marxism, fascism, romanticism, communism, socialism, capitalism, liberalism—all these failures had nothing in common other than their conviction that they alone held the keys to solving humanity's ills.

We have seen it in Israel as well. The utopian ideologies that once dominated the public discourse have all collapsed.

The leftist elite abandoned its ideal of Labor Zionism, its wonderful vision of equality and social justice. Even the jewel in its crown—the kibbutz—is but a shadow of its former self. They replaced it with another absolute ideology, that of "peace now." But this fantasy also failed, and almost no one on the Israeli Left today even talks about it.

The same thing happened on the Right, where one almost never hears about the "Greater Land of Israel" with its territorial maximalism. Religious Zionism, too, has lowered the flag of imminent messianic redemption. So, too, have the ultra-Orthodox come to understand that their own absolutist dream of creating a vast, utopian "society of learners," paid for by Israeli taxpayers and donations from abroad, is proving impossible to sustain in the real world.

At the end of the day, we have seen the sun set on all of these Israeli utopian fantasies.

It is no coincidence that these visions were developed and promulgated mainly by Israel's European-immigrant elites, who founded the country but whose conceptual proclivities encouraged them to continue offering impossible, absolute answers.

But these failures have made it possible for a new sun to rise—a different approach, which flows out of the experiences and instincts of the more than half its citizens who did *not* come from Western countries, but who instead came mostly from the Arab and Muslim world.

This is the wisdom of "Second Israel," the Israel of the Mizrahim.

Unlike the European attitude, the Mizrahi approach refrains from absolutes, which always eventually collapse upon their contradictions. Such an approach is especially helpful in addressing a wide range of challenges facing Israel and the Jewish people as a whole—including the apparent clash between secular and religious life, conflicting aspirations of Jews and Arabs in the Middle East, and, perhaps most importantly, the tension between Judaism and Zionism.

***

The main problem with absolute ideologies is that their unbending demands inevitably run aground on the shores of our complicated lived reality. Fundamentalists will never find answers to classic, childish questions surrounding apparent contradictions—between a Jewish and democratic state, between Torah and science, between nationalism and globalism, or between Zionism and Judaism.

The Mizrahi approach is unfazed by such contradictions and even embraces them. This was well expressed by the controversial and ultimately tragic Mizrahi singer Zohar Argov:

> There are unknown things that we won't understand and won't know, but we would do things even though they seem without a rational reason.

In contrast to the arrogant Western approach, Second Israel offers a more modest, less self-confident approach. Instead of ideological certainty, we find an emphasis on humility, loyalty, and respect: Respect for our parents, respect for our nation, and respect for our traditions, even if we don't understand everything. The twentieth-century Jewish philosopher Mordecai Kaplan spoke about the tension between "believing" and "belonging." The Mizrahi philosopher Meir Buzaglo speaks about the tension between *ma'amin* (believing) and *ne'eman* (being loyal). In the Mizrahi approach, belonging and loyalty are more fundamental than abstract beliefs.

This difference, between First and Second Israel, expressed itself not only in questions of ideology and pragmatism in the secular world; it is felt even in rabbinic rulings and the nature of religion itself. European Jews drew sharp lines between the stringencies of Orthodoxy, which often took pride in its refusal to bend to the pressures of the modern world, and the liberal-secular movements that rejected it. Mizrahi Jews, by contrast, lived in a spectrum that ran from highly observant to traditional to secular. And their most influential spiritual guide in the twentieth century, Rabbi Ovadia Yosef, was most famous not for his stringency but rather his leniency. His slogan was an ancient dictum from the Talmud, *koach d'heteira adif*—"permission is more powerful than prohibition."

We are not talking just about our individual selves or the functioning of a religious community, however, but our national identity.

Given the failures of absolute ideologies, it is reasonable to consider the possibility that emotion and sentiment are more compelling, even ideologically, than abstract commitments—and that loyalty to one's nation, tradition, society, and to one's people can thus be more powerful and effective than any ideological beliefs.

The Mizrahi approach thereby offers far more useful tools for managing a complex society like Israel's. We may call it "the politics of the Mizrahi mother" or "the politics of turning a blind eye." The aim is *to preserve peace in the family.* Such an approach de-emphasizes ultimate demands, arguments, and controversies. Instead, it deliberately attempts to blur them. Nowhere is this felt more clearly than in relations between traditional and secular Israelis.

To take just one example: In 2022 there was a major controversy about the presence of *chametz* in Israeli army bases during Passover. The Israel Supreme Court, armed to the teeth with absolutism, demanded that the Israel Defense Forces publicly announce a policy allowing chametz on IDF bases. Instead, the army responded in the tradition of the "politics of the Mizrahi mother": The IDF spokesperson announced that the army would not check soldiers' duffel bags for chametz. The meaning was far from loud and clear; it was, rather, soft and clear: Anyone who wanted chametz could have chametz, but the IDF, committed to the time-honored symbolism of a Jewish army that has always been a pillar of Zionism, would not formally condone it.

The Supreme Court rejected the new arrangement. Why? Because of the policy of absolutes. The country could have easily avoided the debacle, but the court refused to accept that *turning a blind eye is also an option*. And the ability to do so is a crucial tool in handling a complex society with observant and non-observant people who need to live together in peace.

The ruling was troubling for another reason. In effect, it turned a national holiday, which depends on public symbolism far more than individual performance, into a private and personal religious issue, while at the same time undermining the role of the IDF as a core symbol in our Israeli-Jewish identity.

***

Beyond the utility in addressing tensions between observant and non-observant Jews, the Mizrahi approach also offers far more effective strategies for coexistence with the Arab world as a Jewish state in the middle of the Middle East.

Absolute ideologies naturally escalate conflict because of their conviction in the righteousness of their beliefs and their ability to bring ultimate solutions to human problems. As opposed to the endless talk of "solutions" heard across the Western world and in much of Israel as well, if you ask a representative of Second Israel for the solution to the Israeli-Arab conflict, the most likely answer will be that *there is none*, and that's just how it is. That just as there are countries and places where people accept that from time to time there will be earthquakes, tornadoes, hurricanes, or fatal heat waves, so, too, with conflict. They live with the mature understanding that we can't solve every problem.

Because the truth is, we *can't* solve every problem. Only God is almighty, and we should be grateful to live in a miraculous time for the Jewish people, an age of ingathering of exiles and the creation of an independent Jewish state in our ancient homeland. Within these limitations, we must do our best to be moral and decent, and on the other hand to be strong—"genius and generous and cruel," in Ze'ev Jabotinsky's words—with an iron wall to protect the Jewish people, dedicated to keeping the central promise of the Jewish state: never again.

The constant search for instant and utopian solutions to the Israeli-Arab conflict is one of the hallmarks of the gap between First and Second Israel. But there are other things. According to the liberal vision that dominates the Israeli discourse, the way to end the conflict is if both sides just give up their traditions and adopt secular and liberal values. This tendency is similar to Thomas Friedman's absurd and long-discredited "Golden Arches Theory of Conflict Prevention," according to which, as he put it, "No two countries that both have a McDonald's have ever fought a war against each other." The problem is not just that it's false—as the Russian invasion of Ukraine in 2022 proved. The problem is that if your "solution" is predicated on the assumption that people will give up who they are and instead become just like you, it is no solution at all.

In 2020, a number of Arab states, including wealthy and powerful ones like the United Arab Emirates, signed normalization agreements with Israel. These governments achieved genuine peace and coexistence with the Jewish state without "solving" the conflict as a whole, without repudiating their own traditions, and without adopting secular-liberal values. If anything, they proved the exact opposite of what the Western approach had always dictated could be the only possible path to peace: They achieved coexistence not by erasing their foundational political and religious identities but through those identities themselves. The symbolic power of the agreement's name—the "Abraham Accords"—was that instead of denying religious traditions, it leaned into them.

* * *

But perhaps the most important benefit of the Mizrahi approach can be felt in resolving the tension between Judaism and Zionism—a tension that lurks at the heart of some of our most powerful internal disagreements both within Israel and around the Diaspora.

In 1932, the poet Hayim Nahman Bialik wrote the following:

Who will save us from hunger?
Who will feed us bread aplenty?
And who will give us a glass of milk to drink?
To whom do we owe thanks? To whom our blessings?
To our work and our labor.

Bialik's poem was turned into an immensely popular Israeli song, taught to schoolchildren in the state's early years. It represents in many ways the profound transformation in Jewish consciousness brought about by the movement that dominated Israel in its first decades.

Since time immemorial, Jews had given their thanks and blessings to God alone. Labor Zionism, the movement that defined First Israel, taught Jews to thank not God but themselves.

It is important to emphasize that their aim wasn't to harm Judaism but to save the Jewish people. After two millennia of exile, persecution, and humiliation, the most influential Zionist leaders and thinkers were looking for ways to shake the Jews out of the passivity and fatalism they identified with traditional Judaism.

But whether you accept my apologetic historical interpretation or not, today we no longer have need for the radical repudiation of the Jewish faith and tradition. Today we can offer instead a Mizrahi synthesis, the synthesis of Second Israel.

The cradle of European Zionism was *crisis*: the crisis of the appearance of modern antisemitism, the crisis of the failure of the Jewish Enlightenment. The slogan of the Haskalah was: "Be a Jew inside your tent. Be a human being when you go out." It didn't work. It was a false dream. Its failure created a crisis. And from this crisis, Zionism was born.

In the Arab and Muslim countries where Mizrahi Jews lived at the time, no such a dream of Jewish Enlightenment as a path to acceptance ever became dominant—so there never was such a crisis when it failed.

Zionism aimed to create not only a new Jewish state but also a "New Jew." Mainstream Zionist thinkers pushed God and traditional Jewish beliefs from their central position in our history, hearts, and minds. They were well intentioned: They believed that it was imperative to convince Jews to take responsibility for their own survival and prosperity among the nations.

But although the concept of the New Jew was an important piece of the founding of the state, today we no longer need to rebel against our ancestors to survive. In the Mizrahi approach, Jewish tradition is not an obstacle to Zionism but a powerful advantage. If in the West, Zionism was an act of rebellion against the traditions of one's parents, in the East it was an act of *respect* for their traditions, including the ancient belief in the ingathering of exiles.

In 1977, Menachem Begin led the Likud party to power for the first time. It was a revolution for Israel—not just politically but conceptually. The defeat of First Israel, and the rise of Likud largely on the strength of Mizrahi voters, signaled a rejection of the type of Zionism that had ruled until that moment. For the first time, peace was made between the Zionist revolution and Jewish tradition.

Begin taught us to insist on calling ourselves Jews. He insisted on wearing a black kippa and using traditional phrases like "with God's help." This was, however, not a passive, deferential, old-world Judaism. It was still muscular: In his most famous speech in 1981, he lauded the "Jews, brothers, warriors" who fought with him in the underground. But it fully embraced Jewish identity. And it was far more inclusive: You were an integral part of the Zionist movement even if you didn't come from a kibbutz and take part in the radical-secular excesses of Labor Zionism.

Begin also related differently to the Holocaust. Unlike David Ben-Gurion, who insisted that Holocaust Remembrance Day put a focus on the heroes of the Ghetto uprisings because he couldn't stand the narrative of victimhood, Begin emphasized the victims, the weakness, and the horror. If anything, it kindled in him a powerful determination, even anger, born of loyalty and empathy with his people and tradition.

The 1977 election was the point of inflection, when Zionism and Judaism finally came together and found their peace, at least among the majority of Israelis. Since then, Judaism has become part of the strategic strength of the country. If, in the early days of Zionism, the youth movements sang, with Shaul Tchernichovsky, "For in mankind I shall believe," today we can hear the Israeli soldiers before a military operation singing, "We are believers, children of believers."

We no longer need to suffer the alleged contradiction between Judaism and Zionism. We have a new Zionism, a Mizrahi Zionism—again, not in the ethnic sense, but in the conceptual sense. Mizrahi Zionism saw faith as the backbone of Zionism and religious Jews as an asset for Zionism. The leaders of this new Zionism, many of whom came from Ashkenazi families but nonetheless embrace what I am calling Mizrahi Zionism, understood the importance of connecting with the legions of believers, the non-elites, the lower and middle classes, for the sake of the Zionist idea.

In this, they were returning to Zionism's origins, before the rise of Labor. They were drawing upon the same magic that made Theodor Herzl, the founder of Zionism, so successful.

* * *

It is symbolic that both Begin and Herzl chose a similar story, about a little boy from a poor family of believers, to represent the hope of the Zionist idea.

Begin presents a debate between a renowned rationalist philosopher and a little boy from a proud traditional and nationalist family, and he summarizes it thus: "Our little brother, the poor and innocent boy from the Mizrahi family, was right."

Herzl begins his magnificent utopian Zionist fantasy *Alteneuland* ("Old-New Land") with a story about one Dr. Friedrich Löwenberg, who is a stand-in for the author. Levenberg attends an event of the Jewish upper class. When the idea of a Jewish state is mentioned, everyone laughs dismissively. Levenberg takes his leave and then encounters a poor young boy, David Littwak. Like Begin, Herzl chose the character of a young lower-class boy to be the contrast to the Jewish elites and depicts him professing his belief in the Zionist dream, in the Jews' return to the Land of Israel. Levenberg finds himself using the language of the faithful in his response: "May our God be with you." The boy then grows up to become the first president of the Jewish state.

Herzl's lesson, like the Mizrahi message, is that the Jewish faith should play a central role in Zionism. This comes up again at the very end of *Altneuland* where he presents the same historical-philosophical question that appears in Bialik's poem: To whom should the Jewish people be grateful for the establishment of Israel? Herzl presents a conversation among the protagonists of the book. Each has his own answer. One says to the unification of the nation, one says to science, and so on. The last one, with whose answer Herzl chooses to end his book, says simply: "To God."

Why was it so important for Herzl to end his book with this declaration of respect for the Jewish faith? I didn't know until I paid a visit to The Central Zionist Archives in Jerusalem and asked to see the original manuscript of *Altneuland*. After the last word "God," there appeared another line that didn't appear in the published edition. I asked the curator of the Archive to translate the curious line that had been cut. She looked at the century-old text, written by Herzl himself.

After the word "God" appeared the phrase, "And this was the last word."

5

CONFRONT THE NEW COSSACKS

A Jewish Political Survival Guide

DAVID L. BERNSTEIN

THE VERY TERM "COSSACKS" sends shivers down the Jew's spine. We may not know much about these Eastern Slavic people other than their supposed thirst for murdering Jews, but they've nevertheless become a symbol, along with the Nazis, of deadly rampages carried out against vulnerable Jewish communities.

The Cossack riots were pogroms in what today is Ukraine, perpetrated against the Jews during the 1648 uprising led by Bogdan Khmelnitsky against the Polish-Lithuanian Commonwealth. Khmelnitsky is regarded as a hero in Ukrainian lore for standing up against the powers in the region, but for Jews

David L. Bernstein is founder of the Jewish Institute for Liberal Values (JILV.org) and author of *Woke Antisemitism: How a Progressive Ideology Harms Jews* (Wicked Son, 2022).

he was the "Hamil of Evil," the very personification of the sadistic antisemite. Two centuries later, in the wake of Tsar Alexander II's assassination, Jews experienced another horrific spate of pogroms, committed not by actual Cossacks but by equally malevolent figures and frenzied mobs who became indistinct in the Jewish historical imagination. To us, they're all Cossacks.

Such antisemitic attacks were not limited to Europe. My mother, who grew up in Baghdad, was just four months old when about two hundred of her fellow Iraqi Jews were slaughtered while scores of others were beaten and raped in a 1941 pogrom known as the Farhud. She and her family members were sheltered by Muslim neighbors who traded houses with them during the deadliest antisemitic riot in Middle Eastern history.

Jews would not have survived the millennia defying the extirpative forces of history without an uncanny ability to recognize the Cossacks of the day and to take the necessary precautions. As Mark Twain famously commented, "All things are mortal but the Jew; all other forces pass, but he remains. What is the secret of his immortality?" The secret of his immortality, Mr. Clemens, may have been his well-developed sense of danger and, with it, varied survival strategies consisting of, depending on the context, moving to safer areas, currying favor to government authorities, joining forces with more powerful groups, supporting democratic and liberal movements, and building a Jewish state.

Notwithstanding our well-honed survival instincts, the Jew's uncanny ability to recognize the Cossacks has sometimes failed him, particularly when the Cossacks arrive in the form of left-wing ideologues bearing utopian ideals promising universal redemption. These particular Cossacks discharge uniquely cagey mind viruses that tend to overwhelm the Jew's immune system. Under the influence of utopian dogmas, Jews have paid a dear price for lapses in judgment and ideological indulgences. American-Israeli writer Daniel Gordis states "Like moths attracted to the flames that can consume them, Jews have long sought salvation in ideologies that ultimately sought to destroy them. It happened with communism and is being repeated with young Jews' visceral embrace of 'wokeness' that in the name of freedom and equality, snuffs out freedom of thought and equality for Jews." In an October 2017 essay in *Tablet*, the great Yiddish scholar Ruth Wisse cites sources that estimate that nearly half the members of the American Communist Party of the 1930s and 1940s were Jews, unable to see that Josef Stalin and his supporters were among the most brutal Cossacks ever known. Wisse writes:

> This is Soviet Communism we are talking about—that killed an estimated 30 million of its own citizens, including through a government-enforced famine in Ukraine, the details of which even people hardened by Holocaust literature have trouble reading.... This was the totalitarian regime that perfected Orwellian language in a culture of lying that not only camouflaged its evil through innocuous terminology as the Nazis did with terms like resettlement for extermination and cleansing for murder, but justified a culture of spying, expropriation, mass murder, and tyrannical rule in the name of "egalitarianism" and "international peace."

Exactly seventy years ago from the time I'm writing these words occurred "The Night of the Murdered Poets," when Stalin executed thirteen Jewish intellectuals by firing squad in a Moscow prison. Blinded by ideology, a good many Jews nevertheless persisted in their adoration of Soviet Communism, which murdered many more Jews than Bogdan Khmelnitsky could have ever dreamed of.

***

To protect themselves from impending danger, Jews have applied an implicit two-part test in assessing emerging threats from political leaders and movements: (1) Are they favorable to particularistic Jewish interests, such as the security of Jewish communities (and, since its founding, the well-being of the State of Israel)? And (2) Do they advance liberal ideals, such as freedom of thought and speech, in which Jews are most likely to thrive? In other words, Jews assess both threats aimed at them as well as general societal conditions likely to produce those threats.

My mother recounts that in revolutionary Iraq of the 1960s, Jews were drawn to the Iraqi leader Abd al-Karim Qasim, who violently deposed the monarchy in 1958 because the Iraqi-Jewish community perceived him as both warmer to the Jews and a champion of a more liberal version of Iraq, particularly in extending rights to women. Not nearly as transformational as advertised, however, Qasim was overthrown by the Ba'ath party in 1963, and Iraqi Jews once again faced their Cossacks, knowing instantly that the Jewish community was in peril. My mother, among others, immediately planned her exit. Several weeks after her arrival to the United States, the doors of emigration from Iraq closed.

While Jews in America have never faced a campaign of state violence as did Jews in Eastern Europe or the Middle East, neither have they always felt entirely secure. It is for the second of the two criteria Jews apply in assessing the potential danger of a leader or cause—the need to live in a more liberal and tolerant society—that three-quarters of American Jews typically vote for the Democratic party in the U.S. The political scientist Kenneth D. Wald, who has studied Jewish voting patterns for decades, observed in a 2015 interview in the *Washington Post* that American Jews largely embraced the classic liberal model in separating citizenship and religion, which did away with "ethnic particularity as a condition for full membership in the political community." According to Wald, this model "differs radically from their historical experience as, at best, a 'tolerated' minority whose status often changed on the whims of rulers." Democrats largely embraced the separationist model, argues Wald, and Republicans largely rejected it, placing the GOP under suspicion in the eyes of many in the Jewish community of being America's Cossacks. Wald states that when "the Republican party reached out to white Protestant evangelicals, who eventually came to constitute the party's base, Jews reacted negatively because they perceived a threat to the liberal regime."

For many years, conservative critics of American-Jewish left-wing politics have complained that the American Jewish community's identification with the Democratic party is a sign that their danger alert system has failed them; that Democrats, with their association with anti-Israel figures, and not Republicans, should be regarded as the Cossacks. They cite the growing criticism of Israel in the Democratic party and the emergence of progressive ideologues such as "The Squad" in Congress with a penchant for anti-Israel and antisemitic remarks. "It's long past time for Jewish voters to end their longstanding—but unrequited—loyalty to the Democrats, who clearly no longer care about their concerns," argued Andrew Stein and Monica Crowley in the *New York Post* in May 2022.

Until recently, however, the mainstream American Left did not possess a strong core ideology that would likely pose an explicit threat to Jews. To be politically liberal in America was to embrace an ethical obligation to help the needy. American political liberals possessed no theory as to why there are "haves" and "have nots," only that their obligation was to even the playing field. They were decidedly un-ideological. And while Democratic support for Israel was slowly eroding in Congress, the vast majority of Democrats still could be counted on to vote for any AIPAC-backed resolution.

Political progressives, by contrast, until recently only a small minority on the Left, have a well-developed dogma: the "haves" cause the deprivations of the "have nots." And in recent years they've successfully inculcated this ideological strain in mainstream politics and institutional life. Such dogma has significantly raised the stakes for American Jews—not least because they are perceived as being among the "haves." And we see the same progressives applying this oppressor-versus-oppressed narrative to Israel, the majority of whom (according to an August 2022 poll) buy into the settler-colonialist narrative denying the Jewish state's very legitimacy.

Wald recounts that support for Democrats remained steady for several decades but began to weaken in the late 1960s as affirmative action and other forms of identity politics took center stage. Wald notes that American Jews were divided 50/50 on affirmative action and other programs that afforded special entitlements to groups based on race and gender.

Many Jews sensed something dangerous in the identity politics of the time, inimical to their interests. Yet today, as identity politics run roughshod over traditional liberal values, American-Jewish support for the Left has remained unshaken. Many Jewish liberals are in denial of the threat posed by the far Left to the liberal order, which Jews have relied upon for a sense of security and well-being and as a bulwark against the Cossacks on the Right.

***

Today, the conservative critique holds more water: American Jews seem to have developed a blind spot for progressive ideological movements, much as many Jews did for Communism, that undermine liberal values, demonize alternative points of view, and foment hostility against those deemed "privileged." While contemporary "woke" ideology might not lead to the Gulag or mass murder as it did in Soviet Communism or the Chinese Cultural Revolution (the same can be said of the right-wing authoritarian brand of antisemitism in America, which may never lead to rounding up Jews for extermination), it nevertheless presents a real and present danger to the American-Jewish community and shouldn't be taken lightly.

Wokeness fuels antisemitism in several ways. Woke ideology's preoccupation with "privilege"—who has it and who doesn't—has lapsed into accusations of "Jewish privilege." Its adoption of Ibram X. Kendi's "anti-racism" program and his "equity" concept—that any disparity among groups is prima facie evidence of discrimination—easily lends itself to accusations that successful groups, such as Jews and Asians, have achieved success on the backs of other minorities. Its embrace of the oppressor-versus-oppressed binary and the need to "recognize and resist systems of oppression" (often invisible to the naked eye) condition young people to see Jews and Israel as the oppressors. Indeed, while the American Left's identitarian obsession may never produce a Gulag or death camps, it certainly sets off alarm bells among Soviet dissidents such as Natan Sharansky. In his foreword to my book *Woke Antisemitism*, Sharansky argues that:

> With the collapse of the Soviet Union and the triumph of Western, liberal values in the 1990s, I became convinced that this hateful, antisemitic ideology had been defeated once and for all and that there was no place in the liberal order for such radical dogma. We fought against it and defeated it. Unfortunately, now we see it has come back in new forms, often in the name of social justice. In woke ideology, if you substitute the word race for class, you will get almost the exact same Marxist-Leninist dogma in which we were indoctrinated in schools

that became the basis of the hatred against dissidents and anyone who dared question the party line.

Nevertheless, there are good reasons many Jews remain tied at the hip to the Left. Even as the Left has become ideologically charged, the Right has become more perilous and unmoored from its liberal principles. The Cossacks on the Right have guns, argue Jewish political liberals, while those on the Left only have cultural power. And they have a point. For example, Representative Marjorie Taylor Greene, who promotes bizarre conspiracy theories that sometimes involve Jews, can easily be marked a Cossack. Many Jews feel in their *kishkes* that xenophobia found on the political Right spawns antisemitism that can eventually spark violent attacks like those in Squirrel Hill and Poway. In the popular American-Jewish conception, the American Cossack is a gun-toting, Christianity-practicing, pickup-driving, swastika tattoo-sporting white man. I have no idea if Alex Jones, for example, has any ill will (or, for that matter, fondness) for Jews, but his brand of angry, illiberal politics screams dangerous Cossack.

The progressive antisemite is harder to conjure up than the right-wing fanatic, as progressive antisemitism itself is less explicit by nature. Very rarely do we find a raving lunatic on the Left directly calling for the eradication of the Jews. The left-wing Cossack is better disguised and harder to identify. He uses all the right words. The right-wing Cossack speaks openly about Jewish power; the left-wing Cossack about "adjacency" to white power and privilege.

And this less conspicuous assault has fooled too many progressive Jews who desperately wish to remain aligned with the Left, will defend almost any ideological pronouncement, no matter how strange or alienating, and deny the very existence of this variant of ideological antisemitism. For example, Isaac Luria, a prominent Jewish foundation executive, wrote in the journal *Sources* that:

Unfortunately, some Jewish advocates against antisemitism, in the name of defending liberalism, seek to delegitimize anti-racist scholarship like Kendi's by claiming that his racial justice framing

49

is inherently anti-Jewish.... By attacking the ideas that drive movements for racial and economic justice, critics...separate white Jewish interests from the struggles of other minorities for the benefit of authoritarian movements and consolidated power—both in Israel and in the United States.

Indeed, perhaps the biggest threat of wokeness for the Jews is that it renders some unable or unwilling to recognize the well-hidden Cossack in their midst. Inevitably they find themselves offering apologia for antisemites on the Left and twisting themselves into knots defending indefensible and, frankly, silly ideas about America, Israel, and even freedom of speech, which is now viewed by many left-wing ideologues as a shill for white supremacy. They turn in their intellectual autonomy and defer to those with "lived experience," meaning well-curated leftists from minority communities with cultural power, and ignore majorities in those same communities who think differently. Once they sign on the dotted line of deference, they are forced to defend and parrot all manner of *narishkeit*.

In many ways, the ascendency and potential dominance of woke ideology on the mainstream Left present a nightmare scenario for American Jews, one that many still haven't contended with: Neither the Left nor the Right offers a safe harbor against antisemitism or a hospitable political home.

Perhaps it's time that Jews stop fooling themselves. There are Cossacks on both sides of the political spectrum. Our true friends are on neither end. They are the still-too-quiet centrists who thirst for dialogue, rational argument, free expression of ideas, and support for democratic institutions. It's time that we pick up our things and build a new American Center.

6

THE TYRANNY OF "IDENTITY"

Why DIY Judaism Is No Substitute for Tradition

MIJAL BITTON

SOME YEARS AGO, I was invited to a small discussion with a group of leaders of national Jewish organizations. We were asked to reflect on different studies of American Jews and what these can teach practitioners and educators about what it means to serve Jews better. One of the leaders assembled there said that the main thing he learned from the many studies is that to allow people to curate their own thriving, individualized Jewish identities, Jews should go "all

Mijal Bitton, Ph.D., is Scholar in Residence at the Shalom Hartman Institute of North America, the Rosh Kehilla of the Downtown Minyan and a sociologist of American Jews. For further treatment of this subject, see Mijal Bitton, "Liberal Grammar and the Construction of American Jewish Identity," (*The American Sociologist*, 2022).

in" on "DIY Judaism." Young Jews, he went on, just don't want the old traditions or buildings anymore. Educators and rabbis should *customize* Judaism, making it fully applicable to each individual, their choices, and their needs.

His words were met with enthusiastic responses, presumably in the belief that this approach would engage all those Jews who have been marginalized or feel left out by institutional Judaism.

Some might see nothing wrong with this well-meaning enthusiasm for American Jewish leaders shaping an ecosystem designed to facilitate DIY Judaism. After all, to engage the largest number of Jews, doesn't an individualized approach toward Jewish identity make the most sense? Doesn't it in principle embrace the *breadth* of Jewish diversity in all its multitudes?

The logic goes as follows: Old traditions and buildings have boundaries that exclude those who don't conform to their presumptions and demands. But DIY Judaism allows for each person to curate their own Judaism and shape their own Jewish identity, thereby reaching a wider array of Jews. If Jewish engagement helps set our communal standards for success, isn't it obvious that the latter is preferable to the former?

Sitting there, I realized that these leaders were picking up on specific trends that describe large numbers of Jews—those who want an individualized and customizable Judaism that they get to choose and that engages them in their own specific and personalized way. These Jewish leaders then assumed (and maybe even idealized) the curator's approach to Judaism for *all* Jews—even Jews who still embraced traditions and frequented old buildings.

But were these latter Jews—the traditional ones—really engaged in just another version of self-authored DIY Judaism? I want to suggest that thinking so is a mistake—that assuming all Jews engage in DIY Judaism ends up excluding a majority of Jews worldwide who do not experience Judaism as their own individual creation. I even want to suggest that such a Judaism may ill serve even those Jews whose experience it correctly captures but who may still long for tradition in this age of disinheritance. This one-size-fits-all approach to Judaism has serious consequences for the future of the Jewish conversation, Jewish education, and the Jewish people as a whole. It is rooted in what I call the problem of Jewish identity.

* * *

What is "Jewish identity"?

Perhaps there is no other topic over which there is more consensus in our organized American-Jewish community than studying and promoting Jewish identity. We battle over Zionism, antisemitism, DEI, and debate the merits of "continuity." But a largely amorphous conception of Jewish identity has still remained a very much desired object of our collective efforts. Leaders serving all kinds of Jews—Right and Left, establishment and edgy anti-institutionalist, denominational and "just Jewish"—center Jewish identity as *the* project they are engaged in.

While the term "Jewish identity" can mean many different things in different contexts, in recent years it is increasingly used to describe something specific: the product of a sovereign Jewish self. In other words, for many, Jewish identity has become synonymous with subjective and individual ways in which individuals identify as enacting Jewishness. It is this meaning of "Jewish identity" that deserves a critical look.

For large numbers of American Jews, this notion of Jewish identity undoubtedly makes sense, since it reflects their particular experiences. They believe that individuals are free to choose whether and how to actualize their Judaism, and that Jewish identity is wholly dependent on each individual to determine. Jewishness is a matter of individual choice and is subsumed into the larger project of liberated, authentic, and unencumbered "self-realization." There is nothing that Jews *should* believe or do or want—the important thing is that their Jewish identity be entirely a personal choice. And yet the claim that this understanding of Jewish identity includes all Jews ironically excludes those Jews who don't conform to the view of an individualized and completely unconstrained vision of Judaism that it champions.

Although it might come as a surprise to American Jews deeply committed to this specific project of Jewish identity, there are Jews who do not engage in (or who even actively reject) talk of self-realization—whose Judaism is rooted instead in tradition, kinship, and *interdependence*. These Jews do not think of themselves as *choosing* to be Jewish any more than they choose to be members of their own families. They live in contexts and communities that have preconceived notions of what it means to be Jewish—notions at odds with the view of a freely chosen and completely individualized Jewish identity sketched above.

That there is an unacknowledged tension between the goal of universal inclusion and DIY Judaism's vision of Jewish identity became crystalized for me at a panel I participated in some years ago. I was invited with some other scholars to identify trends in American-Jewish life with a focus on Jewish identity.

Midway through our discussion, one of my co-panelists argued that the white-Ashkenazi-majority American-Jewish community needed to be more attentive and inclusive of Jews who embody racial and ethnic diversity. To achieve this noble goal of greater inclusion, she argued that we should approach being Jewish as one of many identities a person might have that intersect and coexist with many other personal identities (sexual, racial, ethnic, and so on). They went on to observe that these identities were intrinsically malleable and could wax and wane over time depending on the individual.

As I listened to this presentation, I felt troubled by the way this form of Jewish identity was offered as the *ideal* description of being Jewish because of its supposed universal inclusivity. This way of approaching Jewish identity simply felt foreign to me. It neither fit the group of Jews I happened to be studying—Syrian Sephardic Jews in New York—nor my own experience growing up in South America and, in my teenage years, living in a Persian-Jewish community on Long Island and studying in a Modern Orthodox Ashkenazi high school. These groups and others simply do not orient themselves to being Jewish as one of many identities they "wear" at will. For them, being Jewish is essential to being who they were, not something optional nor simply part of their identity.

Now, far be it from me to sow division in our already fractured communities by challenging one of the few things around which there's still a broad consensus. Nor do I want to argue that Jewish identity, as the term is currently used, is intrinsically *bad*. What I want to point out instead is that the notion of Jewish identity—which is offered as a neutral description that fits *all* Jews—is, in fact, based on very specific assumptions about what Judaism is and what it means to be Jewish. Without necessarily meaning to, the widespread embrace of this seemingly all-inclusive notion in truth excludes entire communities and populations that don't subscribe to DIY Judaism.

This is not an intellectual game of "gotcha" nor merely a theoretical critique of unacknowledged exclusion. The implications of this near-universal yet unexamined use of "Jewish identity" are tremendous and far-reaching. All of those engaged in Jewish education, Jewish engagement, Jewish philanthropy, and Jewish communal institutions who operate as if all Jews have (or should have) a DIY "Jewish identity" wind up excluding those for whom Jewishness is not an identity, option, or choice.

Most critically, when Jewish identity is presented as the natural and default category through which to understand all Jews, our Jewish educators, rabbis, practitioners, and parents miss out on exploring urgently needed new paradigms through which to engage and educate Jewishly.

***

I can recall once hearing a presentation from a leading Jewish educator who had come up with a pluralistic curriculum for religiously diverse Jewish day schools. This curriculum began by introducing students to the fact that there are multiple and infinite options to "do Jewish" (including *whether to* "do Jewish") and that their Jewish identity would be realized when they chose their own path—one that could continue to change and shift. The rest of the curriculum depicted different theoretical, spiritual, and intellectual approaches toward Judaism for them to explore and consider.

After I listened to him talk, I asked whether this introduction to Judaism alone would disqualify his curriculum as one that was truly pluralistic. After all, it promotes an individualistic Jewish identity that does not (and cannot) capture the wishes of parents and educators who are raising their children with a competing form of Judaism—what we might call "traditional" Judaism.

The conversation soon reached an impasse because this educator could not understand my question. Why, he asked, wouldn't these traditional families be included if he's presenting all pathways as options for them to choose? Couldn't they *choose* the traditional pathway?

And there's the rub. Should traditional Jewish parents—whether they be

Sephardic, Orthodox, just Jewish, or secular Zionists—who are raising their children within Jewish traditions where one does not choose to be Jewish want their children to be told they should *choose* whether and how to be Jewish? I was just such a parent, and, in truth, I would not be happy if my young son went to school and was taught by his teachers that he can and should choose whether and how to relate to his Jewish identity—any more than if he were told he had a choice as to whether he was my son. It's not simply that I object to him being told he is free to choose how to relate to me as his mother. I'd also object to taking a relationship that my son experiences and lives as natural and unconditional and holding it up as something for him to consciously interrogate.

I must admit that my attempt to explain tradition to this educator did not bear fruit. He saw nothing amiss in his curricular offerings and continued to insist that the Jewish identity model at the heart of his work was all-inclusive and fully pluralistic. It simply eluded him that describing something as a choice automatically transforms it and erodes an important dimension of the power of tradition—what the political scientist Benedict Anderson described as "unselfconscious coherence."

After this exchange, I was reminded of a moment of realization I had had long before I became a mother. It was in my early years of doctoral work when I was studying scholarship on Jewish identity and considering seriously what it meant to elevate this vision of the Jewish self. One day my older brother sent my family a video of his daughter which enchanted me. The content was relatively mundane: my toddler niece laughing and belting out a blessing in childish Hebrew before biting into a slice of gooey chocolate cake. But as I watched it over and over again, I came to recognize what was so moving about it: my young niece having been socialized to say words of blessing in Hebrew automatically and thoughtlessly. For her, saying a blessing before biting into a slice of cake was as natural as brushing her teeth before going to bed or saying, "I love you" to her mom. She was *living* Judaism, not choosing to *do* Judaism. The scene seemed to me to capture the antithesis of educating for "Jewish identity."

This kind of traditionalism represents a different path than DIY Judaism and its view of an individualized and curated Jewish identity. The distinction is not about adherence to Jewish practice (after all, Jewish identity allows one to *choose* to rigorously practice Judaism) but about whether the self chooses a Jewish identity or *emerges from a Jewish context.*

A good way to understand the alternative of Jewish "traditionalism" is provided by political theorist Yaacov Yadgar. One of the metaphors that Yadgar uses to explain tradition is that of language. When we grow up and are immersed in a native tongue, it doesn't merely serve as a communication tool. In this context language fashions the very horizon of meaning that makes up our lives and social universe. The languages we know deeply shape what we can experience, understand, and express. We can, of course, decide to learn a new language or limit our use of an older language. But what we don't have a say over is how language shapes us and the very context of our lives.

In other words, the main difference between Jewish tradition and Jewish identity is how we stand in relation to Judaism. As opposed to an individualistic conception of Jewish identity centered on self-realization where the sovereign self curates the Judaism it enacts, Jewish tradition is not chosen at all but rather is the *pre-existing context from which the Jewish self emerges.*

In my research on the New York Syrian-Jewish community, I use a different metaphor to explain tradition—that of family. A family is probably the most basic social configuration in which the current-day conception of identity does not dominate (even in liberal societies that prioritize the individual). Nuclear families are not predicated on voluntary identity choices or a previously agreed-upon ideology. Being part of a family usually just comes with a circular and self-sustaining rationale: We assume that our family matters and that it binds us. Most people overwhelmingly experience being part of a family as something that is unselfconscious, natural, and obligating. It is one of the primary contexts from which our self emerges. We cannot choose to discard our families and the ways they've shaped us at will, and most of us would have moral qualms about rejecting all the duties that families normally place upon us.

In my personal life as a mother, I've oriented myself toward Jewish tradition as the ideal paradigm in which I seek to raise my children—as a deliberate alternative to the model of Jewish identity that is predominant in many sites in the American-Jewish community. I want my children to avoid non-kosher food as naturally as they'd avoid taking a book from the library without checking it out. I want them to note the beginning of Shabbat and stop using their electronics as naturally as they'd stop walking in the street before a red light. Of course, I hope and aim for them to develop a mature understanding within and of this Jewish tradition, but before they are able to engage at that level, I want them raised and educated in a traditional Jewish context—not one where they are told they have many malleable identities (including their Jewish identity), which they should choose and reshape at will.

***

Despite the claims that underlie so much of the discussion in America today about Jewish education and community, "Jewish identity" is *not* universal nor inclusive of all Jews. In fact, when we consider the groups of traditional Jews who both feel and objectively are excluded by such a notion, they include American-Jewish collectives such as Sephardic Jews, Orthodox Jews, immigrant Jews, and others. Moreover, the framework of Judaism as tradition (as opposed to individualized identity) continues to be the lingua franca for most Jews outside of America. Instead of describing a universally applicable vision of Judaism, the American version of "Jewish identity" probably reflects on a global scale the actual experiences of a minority of Jews.

Moreover, my own experiences with liberal American Jews—who many would assume subscribe to Jewish identity—lead me to believe that many of them crave and long for Jewish tradition, including the feeling of a Jewishness *not* chosen but unselfconsciously shaping one's context. As a result, they are often underserved by Jewish institutions precisely because of the institutional embrace of an individualistic model of Jewish identity. But don't take my word for it. Consider, for instance, the growth of Chabad as one of the most important movements shaping Jewish life in America today. Chabad does not offer a space for individual Jewish selves to craft their own version of a DIY Jewish identity. It invites Jews into a preconceived communal life where their selves are shaped within its traditions. Many American Jews are happy to take them up on the invitation.

Where does that leave the problem of Jewish identity? A critical reexamination of Jewish identity would require, first and foremost, a new kind of candor about how it comes with its own system of boundaries and above all its *own version of Judaism*—that is, we need honesty about who and what DIY Jewish identity excludes. This would be a critical first step toward a new exploration and investment in other forms of Judaism grounded in tradition rather than identity—forms that might serve as a wellspring from which to draw new paradigms and methods (and perhaps even a new vision) for being Jewish in the twenty-first century.

7

STAY SEXY

How to Rediscover Jewish Intimacy

CHANA BOTEACH

"YOUR FATHER WROTE A NAUGHTY BOOK!" The children cried in stark British accents across the double-decker school bus. It was 1999, I was in fourth grade, and my dad had just published a book called *Kosher Sex*. Even kids knew it was controversial.

The world had turned to Judaism for some of its biggest ideas, some of which had revolutionized societal beliefs and traditions—monotheism, rest

---

Chana Boteach is CEO of Kosher Sex. Born in Oxford, England and raised in the U.S., Chana splits her time between the U.S. and Israel. After completing her B.A., Chana decided to dedicate herself to taking the wisdom of the erotic secrets of Judaism to a universal audience and bring back the true power of sexual intimacy.

on the weekend, and the Messiah, to name a few. These ideas were radical, enlightening, and disruptive, and were accepted as fundamental to religion. But sex? Who wanted sex advice from a rabbi?

Religion seemed at odds with what happens in the bedroom. To be sure, the great world religions had touched on the topic of sex, but their prescriptions usually hinged around what you can't do, making concessions to sex while keeping it subterranean.

So, people were left in the dark, never really knowing if sex was purely for having children, casual fun, a biological impulse, or shameful lechery. Sex was tolerated as an act separate from the Divine, stemming from the animal part of our nature.

Then came the Sexual Revolution, with its admirable intentions, seeking to bring sex out into the open and lift it from its repression. But now it's evident that neither extreme truly works. Religious suppression of sex on the one side has made a natural act taboo, while secular society on the other has stripped it of any meaning or emotion, leaving people lonely and isolated.

But there is a third way, the Jewish way, where the purpose of sex is not procreation or recreation, but intimacy.

***

In the Book of Genesis, following the creation of the first man comes the mention of the first emotion. It is not greed, jealousy, love, or fear but loneliness. Adam is handcrafted by God, surrounded by other life forms in this Garden of Eden, yet still he feels a void. For all he is and has, there is no one to share it with, no one to experience this perfect world alongside him. God recognizes this profound loneliness, this yearning to connect with another, and says, "It is not good for man to be alone" (Genesis 2:18). He solves Adam's loneliness with the formation of a partner, Eve.

Thousands of years later, man's first emotion still afflicts us.

Contrary to what we often think, sex is not actually everywhere. Married couples are barely having sex at all, and those who are, are having it once a week for around seven minutes at a time, which can hardly contain the passion that's supposed to accompany it. Where it is found, it's usually in the last place it should be: on screens educating teenagers and pre-teens, the intrigue surrounding illicit affairs, or the behavior of predators revealed by the #MeToo movement. Sex has taken a hit, becoming a source of division. We've completely lost sight of what sex is supposed to be in our lives. Where sex can serve best, in a committed relationship, it's nowhere to be found.

Enter Judaism, where sex is regarded in the most beautiful, balanced way. It is an act that employs not just the body, but the mind, soul, and spirit of two people, sewing them together as one. What Judaism understood above all else is that sex is an act of such magnitude that it must be protected and nurtured.

But the rules that we hear of when it comes to sex in Judaism sound archaic, even primitive at times. For this reason, the ancient Jewish teachings have often been painfully misunderstood and misrepresented.

Take the idea of *niddah*, an ancient Jewish custom derived from the Torah. Physical contact is prohibited for around two weeks out of every month while the woman is menstruating. Only once she has dipped in the mikveh can she and her husband be intimate again. While many find it unnatural and counterintuitive to separate from their spouse for half the month, the practice offers a powerful insight about human nature. The beauty of marriage is the oneness and closeness that two people experience together. But often this total access can lead to overexposure and boredom. Judaism, therefore, brings erotic obstacles and elements of forbiddenness within a marriage, after which everything is allowed, in order to renew excitement and attraction. It is separation for the sake of getting closer.

Similarly, married couples are encouraged to be modest even within their marriage and advised not to walk around naked. Again, this seems prudish. But this, too, is intended to optimize sexuality rather than suppress it. We've become accustomed today to the love marriage, a partnership of two "best friends" who share everything and have no boundaries. But in Judaism, a marriage isn't glued together principally by love, but by lust. In order for a couple to continue to lust for each other, there must be continued desire—and it's the obstacles that foster it.

Judaism sees sex as a discipline. It takes the same approach with sex as it does with most human acts. On the animal level, sex is, of course, an impulse, an instinctual act. But though we have the animal within us, we also house the divine. Like anything else in nature, sex is neutral in theory. Once we engage in it, we may imbue it with meaning, and we are affected. Humans crave touch. It is fundamentally overwhelming. Our sex lives are entangled in our mental health, and our bodies get flushed with hormones. But it can also be degraded, often tragically.

In Judaism, our job here on earth is to elevate. To take the ordinary and make it extraordinary—and no act fully realizes this idea the way sex does. In fact, according to Hasidic thought, the lowest things have the highest, holiest sources, but need to be channeled and sanctified. Sex can go in either direction, but whatever way it goes, it will be intense and powerful, for the good and the bad. In the Torah, the word for harlot, *kedesha*, shares the same root word with *kedusha* or holiness. This link between the two seemingly contradictory words is no coincidence. In Judaism, the lower a thing seems in holiness, the higher its source. So, when something bears significant holiness, the potential for its perversion is equally powerful. Sex is a prime example of this phenomenon. This explains our natural fascination with sexual deviance and darkness. Its power is real.

In Judaism, we do not dismiss these urges. We see evidence of the true sanctity of sex through not only its darker manifestations but also its potential for elevation. Our society is well versed in how to devalue certain aspects of sex, but Judaism beckons us to transform it, to return it to its original source.

***

Today, we've come to believe that people can be apathetic about sex, unemotional, and detached, but Judaism recognizes that there is nothing casual about sex. In fact, the first word used to connote intercourse in the Torah is *da'at* or "knowledge": "And Adam knew Eve his wife, and she conceived" (Genesis 4:1).

And that is precisely why Judaism promotes marriage, because that is where sex reaches its highest potential, where people share not only their bodies but their innermost selves at their most truly vulnerable and naked. Judaism comprehends that sex can be more than just a physical interaction.

It can be the fusion of two into one. But this level of intimacy can be reached only with a commitment.

There's an ongoing debate about whether humans are naturally monogamous. Judaism isn't really concerned with that. We are taught that what matters is what you choose—regardless of how you're programmed or designed. So though at times it may not feel natural or easy to be in an exclusive relationship, it is precisely the exclusivity of marriage that facilitates a level of intimacy that other relationships cannot rival. It's a rawness and intensity that can be experienced only within the context of one-on-one. With multiple partners or casual sex, there is a lack of the laser-like focus that monogamy offers. We can truly give all of ourselves only to one person; when we're spread out, it will get diluted.

To be honest, even though I had heard my father's "Kosher Sex" speech enough times to deliver it myself, it was not until I started, at age twenty-eight, a company by the same name that I really started to delve into the sources about sex in Judaism. I became enthralled.

The passages I came across in the Talmud shocked me at first. The way the rabbis engage and discuss topics of sex and intimacy are not only explicit but debated as seriously and as detailed as the laws of Kashrut and Shabbat. Often the stories and examples offered are so wild, I wonder if they're even meant to be taken literally. One of my favorites is about Rav Kahana, a Babylonian sage who lay hiding beneath the bed of his teacher Rav. Unaware that they had company, Rav and his wife began "chatting and laughing," that is, engaging in intercourse. Rav Kahana noted that the passion for his wife was so intense that he likened his teacher to "a man who has never eaten a cooked dish." When his teacher discovered him under his bed and rebuked him for his voyeuristic behavior, he responded: "This is Torah and I must learn." Now that is some next-level sex education (Brachot 62a).

When I was young, there were misconceptions I heard that led me to believe that Judaism was, at best, just rolling with the times, and at worst, totally sexist and out-of-touch. But the ideas and laws I have come across have not only upended those misunderstandings but captivated me. Judaism was not only ahead of its time in its approach, but also *so damned sexy.*

Judaism teaches about having sex in the dark to help transcend the body and experience heightened senses. In Judaism, women are just as sexual a being as a man, if not more—in a deeper, more all-encompassing way. It permits almost any act, position, or novelty that excites a couple about each other; and my personal favorite, that "the Torah mandates the intimacy of flesh during sexual relations," which is precisely the opposite of that widespread, baseless hole-in-the-sheet myth that has followed us for hundreds of years, the origin of which was probably intended to malign Jews as joyless, repressive ascetics.

There isn't enough paper in this book to aptly describe the beauty and relevance of Judaism's approach to sexuality. Rabbinic literature has thoroughly and explicitly discussed the physical, emotional, biological, medical, sensual, and spiritual aspects of sex over an innumerable amount of commentary, teaching us how to approach sex in a way that keeps it holy and hot. In Judaism, sex is not just an act that two people do to each other, but an experience that encompasses and forms them into one. Also, it's still the only place I've ever seen where a man is commanded to give his wife an orgasm.

8

THE NARROW BRIDGE

Embracing the In-Betweens that Make Us Human

NESHAMA CARLEBACH

Between holy and not-yet-holy,
Between light and darkness,
Between Peoples,
Between time,
Blessed is the One in-between…

HAVDALAH has always been my most favorite prayer. As a child I longed for the magic of the braided candle and the sweet song in the darkness, lighting the way from Shabbos to the rest of the week. The week would be different and perhaps less special than Shabbos, but it didn't matter. The celebration of Havdalah carried me.

Neshama Carlebach is an award-winning singer, songwriter, and educator who has performed and taught in cities around the world. She has sold over one million records, making her one of today's bestselling Jewish artists in the world. Neshama is currently writing a memoir and has, through writing and teaching, dedicated the next segment of her life's work toward facilitating healing.

Judaism masterfully acknowledges the space of "in-between" throughout the year, continually connecting time and human processes. The mourner journeys through *shiva*, *shloshim*, and the one-year markings of loss. We count the days of the Omer, marking the steps between Passover's liberation and the revelation on Shavuot. We measure the moon's waxing and waning through the cycle of each month. We treat the ten days between Rosh Hashana and Yom Kippur with reverence, knowing that we cannot truly find forgiveness and create change without taking that time.

Learning how to hold the precariousness of the in-betweens of time can help us navigate the vagaries of the in-betweens of morality and provide important psychological insight. Putting trust in the process of transformation is essential for human growth and is reflected in Jewish wisdom.

Being on-the-way and in-between has filled much of my last decades. The experiences have shaken me, lifted me, allowed me to be reborn again and, ultimately given me a joy I had not previously known. My journey has gifted me this clarity: If we can traverse the confusion and pain of difficult experiences and yet emerge whole, we will likely be even better versions of ourselves.

After the trauma of my divorce in 2012, I experienced a period where I couldn't even listen to music. It just hurt too much. After a self-imposed period of silence, the first melody to return to my heart, the first song I sang to myself, was my father's *Hinei El Yeshuati*, a lyrical setting for verses that introduce the Havdalah ritual. The melody lifted my crying spirit. The words spoke to a deeper longing, promising me that even now, through my sorrow, God would be my shelter. *Velo efchad*—I will not fear.

My father, Rabbi Shlomo Carlebach, died in 1994, just weeks after my twentieth birthday. I took over his concerts thirty days later for many reasons, but mostly because we had bills to pay, and I believed that if I did not work, my family would lose our home. More personally, as my father was the person to whom I was closest, I sang because I felt deeply connected to him through his music and didn't want to let him go. His work became mine so that the world wouldn't forget him and so that I wouldn't have to say goodbye.

When allegations of sexual assault surfaced against him in 1998, I was shocked and devastated. I had not witnessed him behaving that way, and I wasn't able to believe the grief of his accusers. At that point I hadn't yet begun to deal with my own survivor story, having been molested by a family friend when I was nine, or with the grief I had carried and denied for most of my life. So, I said nothing. The story followed me every day, and I never commented.

When the #MeToo movement began in 2017, the allegations re-surfaced. At that point, I saw both my father and the women who accused him through a different lens. It was heartbreaking, but I now heard them. And I believed them. I knew that it was time for me to stand with those who had been violated, even if it meant not standing with my father. Abuse cannot and should not be tolerated in our world, and I felt compelled to use my voice to amplify this message.

During this deeply painful time, I began to call people all over the world searching for clarity, all the while wishing I could confront my father. Then, as the Jewish world became engaged in the #MeToo conversation, not only was my father the target, but his music was banned by many synagogues and organizations around the world.

As a result, whether intentionally or not, I was canceled. My upcoming concerts were called off, and new bookings disappeared. I was told that my name was no longer welcomed at many institutions.

I realized then, for the first time, that if people had been seeing me as an extension of my father, then they had been correct. I hadn't been brave enough to stand alone and define myself in his absence. Until this moment, I had not seen my father fully.

I began to speak publicly and to write about my feelings and realizations. I am writing a memoir and pray that there will be healing in the sharing of these stories. These series of experiences taught me the value of pain and being able to look inside, fall apart, and then stand up again.

* * *

Rabbi Nachman of Breslov calls upon us to acknowledge that life is a narrow bridge but urges not to let fear paralyze us. Even when we are on the narrow bridge, unable to return to where we have come and yet terrified of what could lie ahead, Reb Nachman's words remind us to trust the journey.

Standing in the liminal space between light and darkness, in the tangled span between the holy and the not-yet-holy, is an integral part of the journey. I have inhabited that less-defined expanse for years, a neither-here-nor-there period that gave me the chance to learn how to breathe again and heal. Both sides of the complicated time were defined—and, through it all, Havdalah provided a narrow bridge that would hold me.

Becoming undone along life's winding paths is part of the human experience, and the uncertainty and instability of the in-betweens can be frightening and unsettling. We can be left longing for safety, which can take the form of absolutes, driven by a desire to avoid the in-between and pretend that only black-and-white is real. It is perhaps natural to demonize and idolize, separating ourselves from expectations of perfection and fear of damnation, perhaps because both extremes are far from our more relatable human existences. We can insist we don't resemble the angels and devils we've created. The truth, as always, is more complicated than defensive illusions suggest. Angels and demons are easy. Being human is harder. Accepting nuance and partial truths can be terrifying. Because they offer something other than extremes, bridges can help. Locating them and trusting them is hard.

I've learned, through the many years of struggling with my father's past and his legacy, to experience my own life and Judaism through the lens of the in-between. Of course, it would be easier to see the world in a binary way: something or someone is either all good or all bad. The in-between is too personal, too demanding, too perplexing, too much like looking in the mirror and having to wonder about ourselves. We often do anything we can to protect our inner life from the in-between, choosing illusory order rather than confronting the chaos.

As a survivor of sexual assault myself, a child who has witnessed both the light and darkness of a parent's behavior, one who has been herself canceled, a mother, a Jew, and an activist, I understand the vulnerability born of fear that denies our hearts the chance to navigate complexity. I've lived there. Allowing myself to be still on the narrow bridge and find peace there has been my greatest challenge and triumph.

* * *

What would the Jewish world look like if each of us, and our most intimate tribes, stood for a moment and reflected upon our place on the bridge? What if political activists on such issues as Israel and abortion took stock of their personal "why's" to reflect on their own positions, and then realized that their opponents are not better or worse? What if we accept, even when we can't all pray in the same space with the same intentions, that saying "Amen" to each other's prayers is paramount? What if we prioritized coming together to explore our intersecting and unknowable futures, side by side, letting go of the need to control each other?

Engaging in the topics of inappropriate actions, personal pain, and #MeToo in the Jewish community is not simple. It also opens the door to countless other issues deep within ourselves and our communities, leading us to address cultural trauma in ways we have perhaps avoided for too long. Acknowledging that abusive behavior lives within our community and seeing the ways in which we may have been complicit is terrifying. And looking at the range of behaviors that have been enabled and normalized for generations can be the scariest of all.

So much sorrow lives in the in-between, in the questioning, in account-ability, in the gaslighting, in the silence. But lies and self-deception ultimately distance us from our very Source. It is sadder and more painful to pretend. Seeing ourselves and each other clearly can be painful, but I believe that sur-rendering to and trusting in our own power to overcome these limits is crucial.

It can be tempting to stand still on the narrow bridge, succumbing to the panic in our inner monologues. *How can I keep going? I am unprepared. I am afraid.* The foggy, unknown path ahead can make the future seem scarier than the past. But perhaps the *ikar*, the point of it all, is not to be so afraid that we never try.

Each of us occupies a crucial sliver on our own bridges, with significant distance behind and miles still ahead. May we be blessed to open our hearts and minds to the travelers we meet along the way. May we be blessed to inhabit our lives fully, to embrace and cherish ourselves in our sacred entireties—to even love those in-between parts that may hurt. May we be brave enough to accept the humanness we each embody. May our communities draw on our ancient wisdom of honoring the liminal space while respecting each person's healing journey. May we find the freedom that exists on the narrow bridge.

9

PROUD JEW IN THE NBA

How Keeping Kosher Made Me a Better Basketball Player

OMRI CASSPI

AS THE FIRST ISRAELI PLAYER IN THE NBA, I often drew the attention of Jewish basketball fans across America. I'll never forget one time when we were on the road playing in Boston, and a boy who was probably no more than eight or nine years old approached me after a game. "Omri," he said, "because of you I am proud to say, 'I'm Jewish.'"

I was stunned. Embarrassed, actually. That night, I lost sleep over the boy's words.

Omri Casspi was the first Israeli to play in the NBA, where he played for ten seasons. He is the co-founder and managing partner at Sheva Venture Capital.

I was in my mid-twenties at the time. Until then, I had seen myself simply as a kid from Yavneh who had been exceptionally good at basketball. I was thrilled and grateful to be allowed to play alongside the greatest players in the world. My career so far had been nothing more than an amazing personal adventure. Now, suddenly, I realized I was representing something much bigger than myself. What connected me to this boy?

I decided I'd need to carry myself differently. Not just as a professional representing my team, my league, and my sport. But also as an Israeli and as a Jew.

Over time I reconnected with my Jewish heritage and began to observe some of its rituals. I started putting on tefillin and keeping kosher. I started bringing friends and colleagues on trips to Israel. The impact of this was surprising—not just for myself, but also in how others, especially my teammates and rivals, saw me. It taught me a profound lesson about success, discipline, and the importance of being the best version of yourself in everything you do.

* * *

Yavneh, where I grew up, was a blue-collar town in southern Israel that was home mainly to Jewish families who had immigrated from North Africa in the 1950s. Both my parents were serious about sports. My mother had played basketball in a league; my father, who had a long career in the Israel Defense Forces and the Israel Police, also played tennis as an amateur. The home I grew up in encouraged sports—not just as recreation, but also for building certain elements of character: discipline, teamwork, and determination.

At the same time, it was always clear that sports were not enough on their own. While it built important elements of character, it wasn't enough to turn you into a good person. (I discovered this in the NBA: Even in the world's greatest basketball league, some players are generous, mature, good people—people who made me proud to be associated with them—while others are selfish and self-destructive. In basketball, as in life, one can be great without being good.)

Sports were never seen as an alternative to education. On the contrary, school was my top priority. I was very good at math and English. My parents expected straight-As, and when they thought I wasn't trying hard enough, they'd punish me: "No basketball for a week."

I loved basketball. It helped that I was unusually tall. There aren't many six-foot-one bar mitzvah boys or six-foot-three tenth graders in Yavneh—and I just kept on growing. But I was also good at the game and worked hard at it. My parents kept telling me I had to be the best player I could be.

"He can play for Maccabi Tel Aviv," my high school coach said, referring to Israel's greatest team.

"He should be the best that he can be," my father answered. "He should play for the NBA." No Israeli had ever played for the NBA.

I started playing professionally for Maccabi Tel Aviv at age seventeen—one of the youngest players to turn pro in Israel's history. In 2009, I was drafted by the Sacramento Kings in the NBA in the first round. My parents had been right all along.

But as dedicated as I was to the sport, there were always other things I cared about. Even though we were a secular family, we always saw Judaism as important and positive—the key to being a good person. We loved the Bible. We also loved our country. One of my regrets in life was that I spent my years of military service as an "excellent sportsman," which meant mostly playing basketball, and I did not serve in a combat unit. Call me a Zionist or a patriotic Israeli, I have always been proud of where I come from and who I am.

***

My first few years in the NBA, I was in awe. Living in America, touring the country, making millions at the age of twenty-one, the excitement of having been drafted, and being good enough to keep on playing—these drowned everything out.

But about four years in, when I was playing for the Houston Rockets, I started to feel like I had lost my way. What was unique about me? About my being Jewish? I was in my mid-twenties and still single. Partying late at night, sleeping in late. I felt alone and lost. I had made it to the pinnacle of my sport, but deep down I felt empty and hurting. Like a leaf blowing in the wind.

It was around then that I encountered that boy in Boston, and his words never left my mind. I made him proud to say he was Jewish. But what kind of Jew was I?

I started visiting Chabad houses in different cities. I started eating kosher food. At a certain point I bought my first set of tefillin—and praying with them on became a kind of addiction.

I spent the off-seasons in Israel, where I met Shani Ruderman, the woman I would marry in June 2016, in Tel Aviv. She came to live with me in Sacramento—at this point, I was back with the Kings—where we started to build a family.

I transformed my life. I now had responsibilities as an adult in the real world, not just on the court. And I learned that, unlike in Israel, to be a proud Jew in the Diaspora required effort.

The impact of that transformation was noticed by my teammates. When they asked me why I ordered kosher food on the plane, I said, "Look, there are certain things I do. This is *mine*." And they respected it. Someone like DeMarcus Cousins—he's a tough guy who will never sugarcoat anything, who will tell you to your face *how it is*. He showed deep respect for my Jewish turn, and we became the best of friends.

Another effect of the change I went through was that I started bringing other players to Israel—to show them the country that made me who I was, the land I had never stopped loving. I brought DeMarcus to Israel in 2015, along with other players including Caron Butler, Tyreke Evans, and Iman Shumpert. We landed on a Friday afternoon and didn't sleep the first night. On Saturday morning, we walked from the King David Hotel to the Old City. DeMarcus saw ancient buildings, the holy sites, an entire world that was the background of my childhood. Two hours later, I got a text from DeMarcus: "This," he wrote, "is a life-changing experience for me."

He has since become a great supporter of Israel. The following year, we did it again, this time bringing NBA stars like Amar'e Stoudemire, Shawn Marion, and Rudy Gay, as well as the actor Jeremy Piven.

***

For generations, American Jews told themselves that in order to succeed in America, they had to downgrade their connection to Judaism and their ancient Jewish heritage. That there was something about America that didn't take kindly to Jews who stood out too much.

Maybe it was once true. But my own experience was the exact opposite. My connection to Judaism and my outward pride in Israel gained me respect from teammates and rivals alike. They now saw me as someone true to myself, someone with a backbone, someone who saw a picture bigger than the game.

And it affected my performance, as well. For me, Judaism provided a spiritual anchor, a *foundation*, that allowed me to perform at a higher level than I ever had before. I didn't just become a more fulfilled person. I became a better basketball player, too.

One of the most tragic aspects of playing in the NBA was watching how some young players can't handle getting so much money so early in their lives. It's like an eighteen-year-old winning the lottery. Without mentors and discipline, the money quickly disappears. When I first got to the NBA, three-quarters of the players were broke within five years of retirement.

Fortunately, in recent years a lot has changed. Today, the NBA and the Players Association invest heavily in teaching players not just to keep their money but how to grow it. Big stars like the late Kobe Bryant, LeBron James, Kevin Durant, and Stephen Curry set a powerful example for younger players, investing their earnings and starting venture capital funds. And they have more to offer than their investment. Their experience in the NBA offers significantly added value to young start-up companies just learning the ropes of management, teamwork, discipline, and determination needed to succeed.

And they inspired me, as well. In 2022, a year after retiring from professional basketball, I helped launch a firm called Sheva VC, which helps Israeli startups at the earliest phases.

It turns out that the lesson I learned about how my Jewish pride earned the respect of others isn't limited to the NBA. Today, whenever I attend meetings with other investors or business leaders and I insist on eating in a kosher restaurant, I can tell it makes people respect me more, not less. It's human nature: If you are sure of who you are, if your life is built on a solid foundation, and if you're committed to higher principles beyond the immediate goals in front of you—people will take you more seriously.

So, if I have a message to send out to young Jews everywhere, it's this: Do not be afraid of Jewish pride. Don't ever believe you have to give up who you are to succeed in your profession or to gain the respect of others. If anything, the opposite is true.

And don't be afraid to say it out loud, because you never know who might be inspired by it. That eight-year-old boy I met in Boston a decade ago is now a young adult. Somehow, I inspired him through my success—and he inspired me, in return, to become a proud, responsible Israeli Jew in the world.

10

RESCUE OUR RECIPES

Cultivating Jewish Joy Through Our Culinary Traditions

JAKE COHEN

ONE OF THE BIGGEST CHALLENGES facing the Jewish people right now is the extinction of our recipes. But before we can dive into this crisis, we need to understand Jewish food a little better. Everyone wants a monolith. Something short and sweet and simple to digest when defining Jewish food. However, I've always explained it as the food used to practice Jewish rituals. This is where things get messy. We all read from the same Torah. We all celebrate

---

Jake Cohen is a *New York Times* bestselling cookbook author and a nice Jewish boy from NYC. He wrote his first book, *Jew-ish*, which is about his love of modern Jewish cooking and baking. Jake and his recipes have been featured on Food Network, Food & Wine, *The Wall Street Journal*, Bon Appetit, Food52, and more, as well as *Forbes*, making the 30-Under-30 List in 2022 for Food & Drink.

the same holidays. We all honor the same Shabbat. While there are obviously differences in how Jews practice these rituals across the Diaspora, the most notable variance will always be the food on the table.

These dishes are markers of not only a dedication to our practice of Judaism but also our history. While the classic Jewish food is matzoh, our culinary lexicon has been expanding ever since we fled Egypt. It's a time capsule of Jewish trauma, where poverty, exile, and relocation were the main sources of how we would absorb new ingredients and dishes. But there is no one way to map out what that looks like. Every family will have a unique catalog of recipes documenting their journey.

I have a small green tin recipe box from my great-grandmother, known by the family as Nanny. They were German Jews living in Belgium at the time of the war when my great-grandfather was able to escape a work camp and retrieve Nanny and my grandfather to flee. Their ship to America was turned away at New York, eventually landing in Cuba. They settled in Havana, where my aunt was born and raised, having to flee again before the revolution for New York City. The recipes passed down represent this story. A base of German food with a heavy dash of French influence is met with Ashkenazi recipes shared from their new Jewish community in Havana, as well as a few versions of *arroz con pollo* (my aunt and grandmother still argue to this day about who makes it better).

This is not just an Ashkenazi phenomenon. I have dedicated so much time to preserving the recipes of my husband's Mizrahi family. They were Jews from Basra, Iraq, who fled after the Farhud, settling between Tehran and Ramat Gan, the two places my mother-in-law divided her childhood. As a result, much of their Iraqi cooking (which has a long connection to Indian food due to the role of Iraqi Jews in the spice trade) has Persian influence, and vice versa. Then, when you add in her time living in Turkey with her first husband and learning many of his family's Sephardic dishes, you get another layer to understanding her spreads of Iraqi curry next to Persian *tahdig* next to Turkish eggplant *dolmeh*.

Now, it does need to be said that many of these Jewish foods aren't necessarily Jewish in origin or exclusively eaten by Jews. They include both foods created by the Jewish community, as well as dishes from the communities we lived in, with varying levels of harmony. But that doesn't change the integrity of how we tweaked them to keep kosher or their importance to how these communities celebrated Jewish rituals. You have to understand that above all, these recipes are a representation of our survival. They express our dedication to our faith, balancing tradition and adaptation.

* * *

And that's where we continue to live today, in a constant tug of war between tradition and modernity, but now through the lens of Jewish joy. That is not to say trauma and antisemitism aren't still abundantly present, but we are now in an age of Jewish prosperity that has allowed us to play with our food. I emphatically believe it's time to play with your family recipes.

The most pressing call to action is *writing them down*. More often than not, the matriarchs of the family do not have their recipes documented. When I was learning how to make Iraqi beet *kubbeh* with my husband's aunt, I had to chase her around the kitchen translating the amounts from the glass teacup she used to eyeball every measurement. And in the case of my family, even when there are written recipes, notecards of scribbled cursive often just provide shorthand for the recipe with missing amounts or methods.

You have to get into the kitchen and cook with this generation while you still can. Even if you're just following their commands to recreate their dishes, it is the only way to preserve and pass down that piece of your family's history. These recipes get their flavor from the oral history attached to them, learning the stories and context of how these dishes were a part of our families and the way they celebrated Jewish rituals.

One of my best friends loves to tell this story about how his mother made pot roast for Rosh Hashanah. In her method, she would always cut off the end of the roast before cooking and discard it, a step that was never questioned and just followed by him and his siblings. One day, he was curious as to what the reason for this was and its importance to the recipe. He quickly learned that she did it because her pot wasn't big enough for the full roast. It was an outdated method he had followed because of tradition.

Which brings me to the reminder that we're not in the shtetl anymore. While the preservation of these recipes is crucial from a historical sense, I'm not preaching for stagnation in the way we make them. It's your birthright to continue to adapt these recipes to fit your home, bringing in the flavors and ingredients that have become integral to your family. So, throw fresh herbs and citrus into your *kasha varnishkes*, add Middle Eastern flavors to your babka, or get a bigger pot to fit your roast. Mold these dishes however you need to create a sustainable practice of cooking them, and hopefully not just for the High Holidays but throughout the year.

Just don't get sucked into the belief that there is one best way to make anything. There is beauty to each variation and families who align with one over the other. It's the reason we saw Coca-Cola and Lipton soup mix sneak into brisket braises across America. It's the reason Ashkenazi Jews in Latin America began adding jalapeños and cilantro to their matzoh ball soup. It's the reason we saw a divergence between New York bagels and Montreal bagels. But in America today, we're seeing a major reduction of most foods into one specific idea of what it can look like.

I absolutely despise when a food magazine claims to have the "best recipe" for a Jewish food (especially when developed by a gentile). How can their matzoh balls reign supreme when there is a full spectrum of sinkers to floaters demanded by each family? How can one brisket braise be superior if my family uses tomato and yours does not? Authenticity can only span as far as one family, so find pride in what that means for yours.

Judaism is a practice. Something that requires work and discipline. Our recipes are a part of this practice. And for those of you thinking that you don't know how to cook: That's not an excuse. You don't get into shape overnight. You can't learn a language in a week. You dedicate your energy to the process, and over time you get better. Just remember the cost of not trying is the extinction of these recipes and stories.

If a healthy dose of Jewish guilt is what it takes, then so be it. Now, put down the book, call your Bubbe, and get cooking.

11

TOWARD A UNITED FRONT

Why We Still Need Consensus-Building Institutions

WILLIAM C. DAROFF

AMERICAN JEWS ARE "JOINERS." They often band together to create organizations that serve a seemingly infinite variety of communal goals. This is
reflected in the "alphabet soup" of Jewish organizations in the United States,
which represent the panoply of our community's political opinions, social
concerns, and passions.

One particular group of organizations under increased scrutiny in recent
years are "umbrella organizations," which serve to bring together groups of

---

William C. Daroff is the chief executive officer of the Conference of Presidents of Major American Jewish
Organizations. In that capacity, he is the senior professional guiding the Conference's agenda on behalf of
the fifty-three national member organizations, which represent the wide mosaic of American Jewish life.

organizations to foster their collaboration and give voice to consensus positions of the Jewish community. The impact of such bodies—such as the Conference of Presidents of Major American Jewish Organizations, where I serve as chief executive officer—is often hidden from view, including from those who fund or take part in the activities of their constituent organizations. For this reason, they become the first target of raised eyebrows when subjects like the allocation of philanthropic capital, or the perceived waste of the Jewish "establishment," come up. Who needs an umbrella if it is not raining, right?

And yet, we cannot understate the value of the Jewish consensus-building that these organizations foster, especially in a time of increased fragmentation and polarization over core issues. If anything, we need more of it.

But to understand why this is the case, it is important to take a closer look at why such organizations were created in the first place, and the crucial role they continue to play in advancing the interests of the Jewish people.

***

Of all such organizations, probably none is as encompassing and venerable as the Conference of Presidents, which was founded in the wake of the 1956 Suez Crisis, known to Israelis as the Sinai Campaign. President Dwight Eisenhower's administration had a problem: No representative body voiced the consensus opinions of American Jewry in an age when much of social life was mediated through Protestant, Catholic, and Jewish religious institutions. The United States had just sided with Egypt against Israel, France, and the United Kingdom in the crisis. Yehuda Heilman, the founding chief executive officer of the Conference, began this adventure by bringing a dozen—the number has since grown to fifty-three—American Jewish organizations into the same fold.

As the American Jewish community matured, our community's leadership needed to solve the problem of "two Jews, three opinions" in order to confront the challenges facing our communal interests. Speaking with one voice helped avoid potential misunderstandings. For example, Eisenhower's Secretary of State John Foster Dulles in 1954 queried Israeli Prime Minister David Ben-Gurion about the degree to which American Jews cared about the State of Israel. Ben-Gurion told him that if he doubted the Jews' commitment to Zion, he had only to ask a Jewish child about the story of the Exodus. Starting in 1956, Dulles and his successors would address such queries directly to our organization, a privileged interlocutor for communicating the opinions and concerns of American Jewry.

Today I feel a deep sense of responsibility to reflect the core interests of our community. And I am continually trying to work out how our organization can maintain its relevance, grow its reach, and fulfill the goals for which it was founded.

We have had to remain nimble. The Conference was born in a different time, that of the postwar era, which, in retrospect, looks like a golden age of consensus. The time was characterized by political centrism, broad-based economic prosperity, and norms of deference. As such, the disputes back then seem tame in comparison to our own. Ever since the 1960s, the political center in America has weakened and the extremes gained strength. The same phenomenon presents itself in American Jewish life, both in terms of our politics and of our religious affiliations.

This centrifugal force, which serves to push us all from the center of the spectrum, raises questions about the relevance of inclusive mainstream bodies such as the Conference today. Given the current environment, it is no surprise that some wonder whether it is a fool's errand to share common institutions in an age when agreement on a shared set of priorities is elusive. Instead, they wonder if the component elements of American Judaism should spend more time advancing their own respective institutional goals.

In truth, umbrella organizations such as the Conference play a vital role in our communal life. Because we reject partisan labels, because we have pitched a broad tent, because our organization welcomes actors from across the political and religious spectrum, we serve as a convener of desperately needed, often difficult discussions across the American Jewish community. American Judaism encompasses a chorus of often-discordant voices; a neutral space for discussion and reflection such as ours helps this chorus achieve harmony. Obviously, no shortage of topics exists to generate dissension among American Jews, from discussing Israel's policies and politics to choosing the best strategies to confront the resurgence of antisemitism.

Obviously, we will not agree on everything. But on certain issues, we *must* present a united front despite our differences. Each of us, no matter our movement affiliation or political hue, is threatened by the resurgence of antisemitism in America, which has left in its wake a literal body count in Pittsburgh, Jersey City, Poway, and elsewhere. The Conference amplifies the ability for our community's needs to be heard in Washington, Jerusalem, foreign capitals, and state capitals. It supports efforts that have resulted in hundreds of millions of dollars in funding to secure synagogues and Jewish community buildings. We coordinate efforts resulting in more than half the states adopting the International Holocaust Remembrance Alliance's working definition of antisemitism, which recognizes the overlap between anti-Zionism and antisemitism. We partnered with the Jewish Federations to form the Secure Community Network (SCN), which ensures the safety, security, and resiliency of the Jewish community in North America. Sadly, as the FBI reports that Jews are the most common victims of religious hate crimes, we expect this part of our mission to endure and expand.

With the menace of antisemitism continuing to metastasize, we must continue to counter its spread. We and our partners seek to expand these endeavors, particularly in our outreach to American high school and college students. No student should feel ostracized on campus due to their Jewish or Zionist identity. We must combat the demonization of Jews and Israel in secondary and higher education, which is one of the most prominent fronts in this new antisemitism. The onus is on adults to protect our children; students should not have to view their college campus or their high school classroom as a battlefield.

***

So much of this hatred invokes as a pretext the State of Israel, the incarnation of the millennial dreams of the Jewish people, a country that is thriving despite the rabid hate that it elicits from so many. More than 85 percent of American Jews, according to recent polls, believe that our fortunes are inextricably tied with the safety and success of Israel. We are the tip of the spear of the pro-Israel community, combating the BDS (Boycott,

Divestment, and Sanctions) movement in every arena—locally, nationally, and globally—advocating for the U.S. Congress to fully fund the Iron Dome missile-defense program and other security initiatives for the Jewish state and facilitating face-to-face relationships between American and Israeli officials. For over thirty years, Conference leadership missions to Israel have met with political, governmental, military, and civil society leaders in furtherance of our two countries' bilateral relationship.

The Conference's activities extend to the realm of international diplomacy; we advance Israel's goal of living in peace with its neighbors in the wider Middle East. Our organization, under the leadership of my immediate predecessor and mentor Malcolm Hoenlein, facilitated early conversations that proved crucial to the Abraham Accords, in which Bahrain, the United Arab Emirates, and Morocco normalized relations with the Jewish state.

This longstanding practice dates back several decades. Some Arab and Muslim countries do not yet feel comfortable directly communicating with the government of Israel, so the American Jewish community serves as a means of passing messages and starting dialogue. Meanwhile, on the home front, the Conference is at the forefront of pro-Israel outreach to other religious communities, notably our Christian friends. We are bolstering the American majority for Israel. The results of our work could not be clearer on the ground, as the majority of Americans continue to feel a close kinship with Israel and support a strong U.S.-Israel relationship.

On the global level, we are a vehicle for the humanitarian aspirations of the American Jewish community. I am proud of our recent efforts to help Jews and non-Jews flee from the violence of Russia's war against Ukraine. When the war began, I flew to Poland to see refugees fleeing across the Ukrainian border and to observe the Herculean efforts of the Jewish community to care for those in need—Jews and non-Jews alike. In the early days of the conflict, the Conference convened our member organizations with operations on the ground multiple times each week to coordinate responses.

Through this engagement, we were able to connect American Jewish Joint Distribution Committee (JDC) efforts with Chabad relief efforts to ensure coordination of evacuations. Working together, the JDC, the National

Coalition Supporting Eurasian Jewry, the Jewish Agency for Israel, and the Claims Conference evacuated Holocaust survivors and homebound seniors through ambulance caravans across the border from Ukraine to Poland to Germany. When the United States was slow to open its border to refugees, we worked with HIAS to encourage the Biden administration to resettle refugees.

Our collective efforts, showing the unity of Jewish organizations across the religious and political spectrum, made a difference in opening our nation's doors to those in need. These efforts required great coordination both on logistical and political levels, which is the "sweet spot" for the Conference, as we strive to bring our community together and speak as one voice.

When I was in Poland, seeing how our aid and advice improved the lives of Ukrainian refugees in Krakow and Warsaw, I was reminded of the work of our community in the 1970s and 1980s, when we advocated to free Soviet Jewry, advocating for freedom for Jews behind the Iron Curtain. Such a heroic endeavor does not lie in some irretrievable past but rather informs the work we do today. Eastern and Central Europe rank high on our list of international priorities and, in concert with the Jewish Agency and other partners, we aid those who seek to make Aliyah. I was honored to accompany an Aliyah flight of Ukrainian Jews finding refuge in Israel.

***

Though it may sometimes not seem that way, American Jews really do agree on far more than we disagree. Umbrella organizations such as the Conference represent at least a partial antidote to the needless bickering and vitriol of this moment—in American Jewish life and American life writ large. Each of our members has a unique voice; we aim to hear out everyone to arrive at a consensus. And, more often than not, consensus is found.

There is no doubt that in an ever-changing world, umbrella organizations must adapt. They must resist the ossification and conservatism that naturally creep into legacy institutions. To remain useful and relevant, they must be nimble and proactive.

But I am confident that consensus-building umbrella groups will continue to play an essential role in the coming years and decades, for the need for them only grows as the lives and opinions of Jews become, on the face of it, more fragmented and polarized.

It is only through consensus, and in practice through the organizations that foster and express it, that we can confidently look forward to a brighter century for Diaspora Jews. Only by working together will we co-create, innovate, and communicate with each other, channeling the great diversity and strength of the Diaspora and especially American Jewry. Consensus must not be consigned to the past; it is the cornerstone of successful collective action in the future.

12

THE POWER OF SOFT WORDS

Relationships, Rather than Public Campaigns,
Repair the World

SHLOMO ELKAN

THIRTEEN YEARS AGO, my family and I moved to Oberlin College as emissaries of the Chabad movement. Here, in this intellectual outpost in rural Ohio, we have served the needs of students, faculty, and the broader Jewish community.

We are no strangers to the slogans, placards, and megaphones of the various protests that punctuate campus life, drawing the participation of students,

Rabbi Shlomo Elkan is the rabbi and co-director of Chabad at Oberlin College. Along with his wife, Devorah, and eight children, Shlomo is committed to helping young Jews connect with their rich heritage and history in creative ways. He also serves as a Jewish chaplain in prisons in the state of Ohio.

faculty, and increasingly alumni. During our first week here, students tried to make a "citizen's arrest" of Karl Rove, the former White House Deputy Chief of Staff under President George W. Bush; he had been invited to speak by the College's Republican club.

Generally, these rallies, teach-ins, and petitions are undertaken in good faith with sincere passion, with the goal of making a change on our campus or throughout the world. But time and again, we see such rallies having the opposite effect: bringing about only more hostility and less progress and change.

I think about this often—how public protests can have the exact opposite of their intended effect.

One night not long ago, I was driving to New York City, with two Oberlin students along for the ride. They asked me why I wasn't more outspoken about Jewish causes and, especially, Israel. My answer was simple: "I prefer quiet diplomacy."

The irony wasn't lost on me—that a visibly conspicuous Chabad rabbi, who has been known to stand proudly under a ten-foot menorah or to ride a bike with a sukkah mounted on it and music blaring, would talk about keeping a low profile. But I've come to believe that often more can be accomplished quietly than through noise. I told the students the story of Rabbi Shlomo Riskin, who sought the Lubavitcher Rebbe's public support for a major rally the former was organizing for Soviet Jewry back in the 1970s. Rabbi Riskin felt the Rebbe's blessing would be extremely important, and he knew that the Rebbe was heavily involved in helping Jews suffering under the brutal Soviet regime.

But the Rebbe balked. Making so much noise, he said, could hurt the very people they were trying to help. The Rebbe felt that back-channel pressure or other methods could be applied to persuade the Soviets and help the Jews. The rally took place, and the regime revoked many travel visas in response. Rabbi Riskin did many great things to help his fellow Jews in the Soviet Union, but he never forgot the lesson he learned, and he applied it to his future advocacy.

College students experience a newfound independence. They are often exploring and challenging their identities and questioning how they were raised. In my work with students, a number of common themes emerge.

Perhaps the most prominent is uncertainty: A sense that all of life is on shaky ground, wobbly and unrooted, like sailing a rudderless ship.

This is why it is so important for young Jews—indeed, for all of us—to root ourselves in our ancient traditions. To steep ourselves in the verses of our holy Torah, to wrestle with the words of Rabbi Akiva and the other Talmudic greats, and to follow the path our venerated scholars took into modernity. Our Torah values should inform our modern Western sensibilities and enhance how we engage with the world, rather than our trying to invent novel yet weak connections between modern times and Jewishness.

And when it comes to having a political or cultural impact on the world around us, the highest priority should be to make sure we have our rudder firmly attached to the ship. This cannot be done alone but instead requires seeking out a cadre of teachers, guides, and mentors who can help us stay aligned. This allows us to be honest and authentic to ourselves and the Divine. Once we have this inward and upward component, we can turn our attention outward to others. And this is another reason to choose the quiet path of impact—for it is in deeper values, rather than loud, explicit political ideologies, that more profound changes may take root.

Having such a tradition-based rudder is step one. But there is a second part of it that flows from the first and is no less important.

* * *

The ride from Oberlin to New York is a long one—about seven and a half hours if you don't stop and there's no traffic—so our conversation continued. We spoke about the protests on our campus, and how it seemed that people were always either shouting at no one or locked in vicious arguments. The students in my car looked for alternatives, and we ended up talking at length about how building authentic relationships can be a far more powerful way to change the world.

It is no secret that one of the most fundamental principles of Judaism comes from a single biblical phrase that Rabbi Akiva identified as a "great principle of the Torah": You shall love your neighbor as yourself (Leviticus 19:18). This is also a central pillar of the Chabad movement.

When I was studying for rabbinic ordination, I recall being told that when people come and ask questions, one must make sure always to "answer the person, not just the question." At the time I wasn't sure what that meant, but over many years and the many people who have come to ask questions, I have come to understand it much more deeply.

We need to care about the entire person. A relationship with Judaism and with God isn't just a checklist of mitzvot. When someone asks me about a matter of Jewish law, I need to inquire about them, their mental health, and what are they up to in life. Also, as a community builder and connector, I've found it extremely important to care honestly about the well-being of others, to be ready to cry, to laugh, and to celebrate with them. We have to commit to connecting with others for no other reason than that we all have been created in the image of the Divine, and we share this world.

I once taught a course on campus called Judaism as Activism. Each week, we explored different figures from the Torah and how their lives could inform our own efforts to change the world. The two that generated the most discussion were Korah, who launched a rebellion against Moses in the Book of Numbers; and Aaron, the brother of Moses. The contrast between the two could not be greater: Korah publicly assailed Moses and challenged his right to lead, and ended up bringing only shame and destruction to his people. Aaron, on the other hand, supported Moses as his spokesman and exerted his influence quietly, behind the scenes. Indeed, the Mishna depicts him as a man who "loved peace and strove for peace." Aaron's reward? He became the father of the *kohanim*, the priests who served in the Holy Tabernacle and, later, in the Temple of Jerusalem.

What emerged in the class, however, was that a large part of Korah's failure stemmed from the fact that he stood for little other than the downfall of Moses. When we don't have a true justification for change, the students concluded, we end up only with noise and failure. Aaron, on the other hand, was constantly bringing people together, striving for peace, building relationships, and making change through quiet diplomacy. Those who dedicate themselves to building, rather than just tearing down, are rewarded with success and peace.

In this spirit, Chabad at Oberlin has always been clear in our goals of building the community by connecting students to their own Jewish history and identities. A few years ago, there was a major controversy concerning a professor who had made inflammatory remarks about Jews. I made every effort to avoid the spotlight and instead conducted a number of difficult conversations with administrators and community members—quietly and in private. At the height of the scandal, news outlets from the *New York Times* to the local Jewish newspaper reached out to me for comment. I told them all the same thing: "There is a tremendous amount of good happening in the Jewish community on campus. If you promise to dedicate as much space to the positive as you do to the controversy, only then will I make a public statement."

Needless to say, not a single outlet did so. But though not a single quote of mine appeared in the press, I was fully in the thick of the matter: in the boardroom, in the president's office, and speaking with many students, pushing for what I believed was right. This ultimately forged a relationship of trust and understanding with both the administration and the students, who understood that our only commitment was to strengthening and building the community. This approach has proven itself time and again, whenever we've been asked—whether by students or the college itself—to help with any matter of communal concern, Jewish or otherwise.

***

The Baal Shem Tov, the founder of Chasidic thought, once shared that when two people meet, it should always be for the benefit of a third. Indeed, our connections and bonds should not be for just ourselves. We must think of the community and the good of others. When thinking of the greater community, relationships are elevated above the individuals involved—and in turn, they can have an impact on organizations, power structures, and entire societies.

One of the most profound and difficult elements of spiritual work in Chasidic and Jewish practice is something called *bitul hayesh*. Often translated as "self-nullification," it is taken to mean obliterating one's ego. This is true and good, but I'd propose a more useful way of looking at bitul—in the sense of transparency. Making oneself transparent, much like the glass of a sliding door. Anyone who has accidentally bumped into a glass door will tell you that it is very much there, but it is totally unclouded, allowing for light to shine through.

We can and should exist in a very real way. But our spiritual duty is to become transparent, to allow the light of goodness and Godliness to emanate through us, unmarred by the trappings of self and ego. When we aren't stuck on ourselves, we can listen and connect to others, even to those who see the world incredibly differently from us.

In my time as the Chabad Rabbi in Oberlin, I have sat across the table from people who look, think, and act incredibly differently from me. In every case I have endeavored—often successfully—to find a way to connect through the Divine spark embedded within all of us, to build a bridge rather than dig trenches between us. When we went our separate ways, all of us were humbled and had grown, making small changes that would ultimately become the building blocks of a better world.

Our collective investment in making important changes in society as the Jewish people in ways that might not always be public is essential to our success as a people moving forward. By using the rudder of Torah and tradition to steer us through the choppy waters of the future, by focusing on relationships and quiet change rather than public ideology and protest, we edify our confidence as a people and make ourselves into a driving force that will take on the biggest challenges to our people, including antisemitism, apathy, and lack of literacy.

In this way, we can build the Jewish community's internal connections as well as join with the right friends and allies to make the world a better place. With this in mind, the Jewish people can live in the spirit of our ancient rabbis, who taught us in Pirkei Avot: "Say little and do much" (1:15).

13

SAY YES TO TRIBALISM

The Need for Solidarity in an Atomistic Age

RACHEL FISH

THERE WERE VERY FEW JEWS where I grew up. My family was far from the thriving Jewish communities of the northeastern United States, or the bustling Jewish centers of Chicago, Miami, or Los Angeles. We were not connected to the multitude of communal organizations and agencies that supported Jewish life. I didn't know anything about the "alphabet soup" of the Jewish institutional world. As far as American Jewish life was concerned, we were isolated.

Rachel Fish, Ph.D., is the co-founder of Boundless, a think-action tank partnering with community leaders to revitalize Israel education and take bold collective action to combat Jew-hatred. She has published extensively on Israeli history, Zionist thought, and Middle Eastern studies, and advises on community interventions to reclaim an Israel discourse that is nuanced and complex while remaining accessible to a broad audience.

Instead, our backdrop was the beauty of the Great Smoky Mountains. I was born and raised in a small town in the northeast corner of Tennessee. In this part of the country, we joke that we were raised not just in the Bible Belt, but the Buckle of the Bible Belt. There were multiple churches and crosses dotting the landscape, and I recall, as a little girl learning to read, trying to figure out how to decode the words "Methodist," "Baptist," and "Presbyterian," and asking what they all meant.

The people from my hometown were the salt of the earth: kind, genuine, caring, always holding a door open, and willing to chat with you about anything and everything. Being raised in this environment led me to believe that people naturally care for one another, and that there is always time to help a neighbor in need.

I was also fully aware that my identity as a Jew did not mesh with the majority of my surroundings. It was clear at an early age that my siblings and I were very different from the people around us—our teachers and classmates, my father's colleagues, and the families with whom we spent time. Our Jewishness separated us from the society around us.

But we didn't perceive this separation as a bad thing. It simply was. Our identity was one we embraced, and my parents made sure we valued it. They made sure we knew where we came from, that our history was ours and we needed to know and understand it, and that our identity was both a privilege and a responsibility. This may seem like quite a bit to put on young children, but my parents knew they would have to be intentional in how they raised their children, knowing full well they were doing so in a place that had a tiny Jewish community that required full participation for sustainability and a thriving Jewish future. So, that's what we did.

My parents also served as models, behaving according to what they expected of us, and taught us why their actions mattered. I recall sitting in the hall outside my elementary school classroom while Christian prayers were said at the beginning of the school day. I would wave to my brother, quietly sitting crisscross applesauce across the hall from me, as we waited patiently to return to the classroom. I witnessed my father, who was not a lawyer, go before the school board and explain with precision and calm why this was an affront to the Establishment Clause of the Constitution and treaded upon the separation of church and state. My mother would teach classmates about Jewish holidays so that they would be exposed to traditions and cultures other than Christianity. I remember explaining to peers why I didn't attend every Friday night football game, which is no small thing in the South, and why I didn't eat pepperoni pizza or bacon at the sleepover.

Of course, much of this may seem mundane, but it makes an impression on you as a child. These markers of difference are real and highlight aspects of why you are not like everyone else, which, in my experience, was a positive. I realized at a young age that this difference helped me articulate strongly who I was and why my beliefs were molded the way they were, and gave me the ability to see beyond the small community I lived in.

Understanding at a young age that if my family failed to attend Shabbat services, someone might not be able to say Kaddish—that we had a responsibility to our Jewish community—was a powerful magnet. That sense of belonging pulled me in. We learned that we belonged to a collective, the Jewish people, even if we did not know many Jews or the narratives that connected us through time and space. We attended Jewish summer camp where we experienced "Jewish time" first-hand. The friendships we made with other Jewish kids over the summer emboldened us to engage with the collective Jewish people as a kind of mission.

Of course, there was a degree of naïveté that came with that, but as a child who worked very hard to be Jewish, living Jewishly for those eight weeks offered a sense of breathing space. No explanation, no articulation needed. Just being fully me. A sense of wholeness that came from feeling connected to a people. To a tribe.

***

"If we blow into the narrow end of the shofar, we will be heard far," wrote the acclaimed American Jewish writer Cynthia Ozick. "But if we choose to be Mankind rather than Jewish and blow into the wider part, we will not be heard at all." This is what it means to be rooted in a particular, yet that particular has an impact beyond its own community, to the general and the universal. It is precisely in *knowing* the particular—one's own histories, traditions, cultures, shared narratives—that allows the particular to see itself, to know itself, and to engage with the collective, even with its differences. The collective is not a monolith. It is not uniform. There is power in identifying as part of a collective, in feeling a sense of belonging to a community much bigger than oneself.

This sense of belonging to the collective is innate. It is part of the familial. It is a sense of being part of a tribe.

We know our societies are predicated on all types of tribal affiliations, yet the concept of "tribe" has become a pejorative. Of course, any identity taken to an extreme has the potential to create an exclusionary mindset of "us" versus "them." Yet to deny tribalism becomes increasingly difficult the more we find meaning, create attachments, build narratives, and construct systems for communal cohesion.

This sense of tribalism is not unique to Jews. For all types of people, there are various tribal connections. But in the Jewish collective, particularly in the American experience, identifying as an ethnoreligious tribe is not the dominant way of thinking. And yet, it is precisely this framing that we ought to reclaim for the purpose of shaping our generation and succeeding generations.

* * *

Part of the challenge in encouraging American Jews to embrace tribalism has to do with our history. In the American context, the Jewish community organized itself against the backdrop of a society that prioritized the separation of church and state. The majority of religious groups were Christians who navigated their prior historical experiences by imagining a society that did not privilege one Christian community over another.

As Jews organized themselves in the newly emerging America, they did so along the lines of religious communities. The ethnic component of the ethnoreligious identity of Jews was diminished to integrate more easily into the ethos of the "melting pot." The idea was to embrace an American identity, prioritizing it over other national or peoplehood affiliations. Jews needed to fit themselves and their communal infrastructure within a framework that organized along religious attachment and membership.

In 1790, the newly inaugurated President of the United States, George Washington, exchanged letters with the Jewish community of Newport, Rhode Island, which had built a magnificent synagogue Yeshuat Israel, now known as the Touro Synagogue. Washington wrote that religious liberties were an "inherent natural right," and promised that:

> All possess alike liberty of conscience and immunities of citizenship. It is now no more that toleration is spoken of.... For happily the Government of the United States, which gives to bigotry no sanction, to persecution no assistance, requires only that they who live under its protection should demean themselves as good citizens.

Washington's words made it crystal clear to the Jews of America that they were full citizens in this new sovereign land and were no longer merely "granted" emancipation that could be taken away on a whim. Washington unequivocally recognized the Jews of America as fully American, and their religious identity as strengthening the republic.

For Jews, this level of acceptance was unprecedented. Jews did, of course, experience various levels of inclusion over the centuries, but it was always highly dependent on the context and the individuals who controlled the larger societal infrastructure. Part of the promise of equality in America, however, was that it was based on *religious* equality.

And so, through the nineteenth century, Jews emphasized their religious rather than ethnic identity. Jews were understood, and to an increasing degree understood themselves, to be a confessional group, a religious community, similar to other religious communities, with the same protections and rights as the dominant Christian majority.

Although Jews were gaining acceptance in America, the price of this acceptance seemed to be a need to dissociate themselves from the larger Jewish collective. "We consider ourselves no longer a nation but a religious community," the Reform Movement wrote into the Pittsburg Platform of 1885, which would establish the basic tenets of Reform Judaism for more than half a century, "and therefore expect neither a return to Palestine, nor a sacrificial worship under the sons of Aaron, nor the restoration of any of the laws concerning the Jewish state."

This was no small matter. It was nothing less than an attempt to disentangle the religious beliefs and practices of Judaism from Jewish peoplehood. American Jews, led by the Reform movement, strove to avoid the perception of loyalty to a people beyond the nation's borders. This modernist universalism expressed itself in religious practice no less than in tribalism: the rejection of Shabbat laws and dietary restrictions based upon halacha, and the outright disregard for traditional dress and priestly concepts of purity, compounded with the distancing of the American Jews from the collective Jewish "ethnos." The Pittsburgh Platform's flagrant disconnection from the ancient concept of *am yisrael*, the People of Israel, was a clear and powerful symbol, one that stood for more than half a century, until it was replaced by the Columbus Platform of 1937.

By the late 1930s, however, two fundamental things had changed. First, the Nazis had come to power in Germany, and fascism was spreading throughout much of Europe, imperiling the center of the global Jewish population. By this point, denying the connection to Jews around the world was seen by many Jews as reprehensible.

Second, the demography of American Jewry had changed. If in 1885, the Reform movement represented the outlook of the majority of German-Jewish immigrants who had formed the core of the American Jewish community for decades, by the 1930s millions of Jews had come to America from Eastern Europe, speaking Yiddish and carrying with them a powerful sense of Jewish tribalism even as they abandoned the religious practices of the Old Country.

American Jews now felt a shared sense of collective identity—regardless of the differences nationally, linguistically, ethnically, culturally, and in terms of religious practice—that was strong enough and real enough to overturn the framework of the Pittsburgh Platform.

Yet despite this, there was something about the uniqueness of the American "melting pot" that continued to suggest that one's particular allegiances would need to be displaced for universalism to thrive and survive. The influences of the German-Jewish ideology continued—and continue to this day—to affect the instincts of many American Jews, who still feel uncomfortable with overt affirmations of "the tribe."

There are some obvious sectors of the Jewish community that did not embrace this, of course. The Orthodox community remained particularistic and tribalistic, at times even shunning modernity to do so. Similarly, those who identify strongly with Zionism feel a powerful connection to am yisrael.

At times, however, much of American Zionism has been constructed upon a framework of crisis rather than the positive narratives of peoplehood. This means that when various crises emerge for the Jews, like when Israel faces threats of terrorism and war, or perhaps when Jews in another foreign country face resurgent antisemitism, American Jews pull together in solidarity with our brethren abroad.

But what happens to successive generations of American Jews who do not feel the same obligations as their parents and grandparents to their fellow Jews abroad, or who do not want their peoplehood to be predicated upon a sense of crisis? What proactive narrative has been constructed around am yisrael to ensure it remains a core value of Jewishness? Has enough been done in our Jewish education to ensure literacy within our community to engage with our different Jewish identities—ethnically, culturally, and religiously?

* * *

In our own time, "tribalism" carries a negative connotation for many Americans, including most American Jews. To many, it suggests a narrow chauvinism. But if we understand tribalism as the connection of a people sharing a single historical arc despite different lived realities, combined with a core set of ethical and moral aspirations, then we can begin to understand the merits of the idea of the tribe.

Ours is an age of hyper-individualism. Yet there is, as a result, a deep desire to connect and belong to something bigger than oneself. This search for belonging and community pervades our society as we see greater feelings of loneliness and isolation, dividing people into niche echo chambers where they don't engage with the nuance and complexity of our world.

And yet, we Jews are part of a vast collective, full of identities, differences that abound on every possible front—ideologically, politically, spiritually, culturally—and we should embrace the cacophony of our tribe—a tribe predicated on a sense of being deeply rooted in our Jewish roots, with all the messiness this entails, while feeling a sense of responsibility and urgency for the world beyond our own. A mission that we take ownership and agency while responding and attending to the needs of the *ger*, the stranger.

The essayist and critic Leon Wieseltier, in a commencement speech to Hebrew College in 2005, put it this way:

> There is no choice between particularism and universalism. Nobody comes from nowhere and nobody goes nowhere. There has never existed a perfectly particular individual or a perfectly universal individual. Absent the reality of the universal, we could not speak to people unlike ourselves, and they could not speak to us.... And when we understand each other, it is also because of the reality of the particular. For it is the concreteness of our lives that makes it possible for us to imagine the concreteness of other lives. If we ourselves did not suffer, we would not know how others suffer; but we suffer in our specificity. Our sympathy for others, is not a feeling for the general, it is a feeling for a different particular. So the particular, too, is a universal condition.

When we achieve a dynamic relationship between the particular and the universal, when that balance is most intense and difficult to reconcile—that is when we achieve a type of equilibrium. That is when our particular elements, our tribal needs, are most aligned with our responsibilities to the universal—the tribe of humanity. And this ought to be our North Star.

How, in practice, may we begin to reclaim a sense of Jewish tribal identity and engage with our ethnic particularism? We must imagine opportunities in areas like parenting and early childhood education to start these conversations early, often, and with deep substance. Spiritual, mental, and physical well-being requires feelings of belonging and connection to the community. The ethnoreligious tribal identity of Jewishness is an antidote to so many of the challenges the current generation is facing—feelings of isolation, lack of belonging, and the search for a life of meaning and value rooted in something larger than oneself. Reclaiming and centering our peoplehood is part of the answer to so many of these challenges.

After my children were born, we had a tradition of singing to them at bedtime. As their heads lay on their pillows, we always sang at least two songs: Hatikvah and Shema. Our aim was to give our children a clear understanding that they are part of a people, a nation, and a religious group. Together these elements combine to infuse their identity with a sense of peoplehood that is rooted in the particular, yet extends beyond it to a larger human project that is worthy of their energy and passion: to build a more humane world from within the Jewish values they have inherited. So may the sound of the shofar, from its narrow end, send the clear clarion call, through its larger end, to be heard and acted upon.

14

MOVE TO ISRAEL

A Third Way for the Anxious Diaspora Jew

BLAKE FLAYTON

IN 1964, Hannah Arendt sat down for an interview with *Zur Person*, a German television news series that ran for several decades. When asked why, even though she did not at the time consider herself a Zionist, she joined a Zionist youth group in Europe once Hitler came to power, she answered:

> If one is attacked as a Jew, one must defend oneself as a Jew. Not as a German or world citizen or as an upholder of human rights, but as a Jew. But what could I specifically do as a Jew? It was my clear

Blake Flayton is a recent graduate of George Washington University writing as a weekly columnist for the *Jewish Journal*. He made Aliyah to Tel Aviv in September of 2022.

intention to work for an organization. For the first time, to work with the Zionists. There was no alternative. It would have been pointless to work with the assimilated, I never associated myself with such people.

She then exhaled the smoke of one of the many cigarettes she lit during the segment.

Arendt may not have known it then, and perhaps she would have strongly objected to it, but her explanation as to "Why Zionism?" is the same one that compels thousands of Jews from Europe and around the world to move to Israel still today.

Like Arendt, these Jews find themselves caught in the middle of a historic rise in antisemitism, squeezed between two poles: religious observance of Judaism and secular assimilation. On one side is a Judaism deeply committed to the principles of the Torah and Talmud, flourishing spiritually but lacking the liberal and cosmopolitan values that many Jews strive to fulfill. On the other side is assimilation and detachment from Judaism both as a faith and as a nationality, committed not to fellow Jews but to healing the world. When faced with animosity from the non-Jewish world, we search for a solution, an avenue to express our identities and fight back against its attackers in a fulfilling way. Arendt simply acknowledged the fact that Zionism offered, and was designed to offer, a way out.

When David Ben-Gurion, Golda Meir, Chaim Weizmann, Ze'ev Jabotinsky, Ahad Ha'am, and many, many more, felt similarly "caught in the middle," they turned to Zionism as well. They were all raised in observant homes but pined for the enlightened intellectualism of the non-Jewish world. To their dismay, this world was just as antisemitic as were the roving gangs of Kishinev, and the Jews facing this antisemitism in Prague or Paris were devoid of both the rich shtetl-born spirituality they grew up with and also nationalist impulses that create a sense of unity. They knew, as Theodor Herzl came to know, that the Jewish future in Europe was bleak. In turning their gaze to Palestine, they found a third way, a place for young, scrappy Jews to cultivate a deeply Jewish world without sacrificing their egalitarian universalism.

Israel still serves in this role today. It frees the Jew from choosing between attending synagogue every Saturday and severing their connection with Jewish peoplehood.

***

This is the logic that compelled me to make Aliyah in the autumn of 2022 at the age of twenty-two. I realized that the Diaspora no longer offered the rich Jewishness I wanted to live out. In watching young men in kippahs and young women in modest clothes traverse the Great Lawn of Central Park on Saturday afternoons, I felt a painful desire to feel as connected to my people as they were, but through my own unique expression of Judaism.

That connection is growing impossible to find. More often than not, it seems, the only way to express a proud Jewish identity in the Diaspora is through religion.

It is not lost on me that I'll be immigrating from one Promised Land to another. This city, this Manhattan neighborhood from which I now write, was once my family's *Goldene Medina*, offering them the promise of economic stability and religious tolerance. Just a block north of my apartment is Katz's Deli, a block south is Russ and Daughters Deli, and a block west is Yonah Schimmel's *knishery*. Around me are streets named for legendary rabbis, and circling my apartment are a thousand shuttered synagogues. The stone Magen Davids towering above fire escapes remind the busy commuters and drunken students that through these alleys once walked one-tenth of the world's Jews, and all the customs and culture that sprang from them. That is, if they even bother to look up.

I've written before about how haunted the Lower East Side feels. There are certainly not as many Jews as there once were (though there is still a community), yet there is Jewishness everywhere, or rather, there are Jewish decorations everywhere. But without Jews to breathe life into them, the homages feel like exhibits in a museum rather than staples of a community—a graveyard of what once was.

It is not at all the case that the Jewish spirit of the Lower East merely evaporated into thin air. Rather, it moved to Crown Heights, to Monsey, and to pockets of the Upper West Side, where one can still expect to find a Jewish experience booming with life and culture. The Jewishness of downtown Manhattan hasn't been completely depleted, either. Rather, it has been replaced. In its stead is a Jewishness that subverts text-based faith to left-wing ideology. An increasingly popular method of supporting one's own identity for the young Jews of America is citing their own work in social justice causes; their universal approach to global issues.

This isn't new for the Jews of the Lower East Side, many of whom during the turn of the twentieth century spearheaded the labor rights movement and defined themselves holistically as Jewish socialists. But an important distinction should be made between the self-flagellating, apologetic nature of today's Jewish liberals and the wide acknowledgment back then that the Jews were indeed their own people who carried something particularly Jewish to bequeath to the world, whether it be Yiddish theater, Jewish newspapers, or Jewish trade unions.

Today, an astounding number of Jews cannot name three Yiddish authors, let alone three concentration camps they were murdered in. A dismal array of Jewish newspapers dwindles in American cities. And "Jewish activism" from the left has morphed into chastising the Jewish people and the Jewish state, justifying attacks against the observant population, and defending antisemites in power simply because they share one's political denomination.

The shift in public opinion among this population against the State of Israel is par for the course. If Tikkun Olam now guides your definition of Judaism, the facets of your own sovereign state, especially one with a horrendous reputation in progressive circles for defending itself, seem superfluous at best and downright evil at worst. You grow increasingly queasy at the thought of holding any power because power is acquiring an increasingly bad reputation. Left-wing doctrine has also successfully convinced you that you are simply among the white majority in America, and if you are truly no different from the white majority, why should you need a land of our own? You will then use your Jewishness as a justification for delegitimizing Israel, since your Judaism is one defined by a twenty-first-century understanding of progressivism.

It appears that the decline of secular Jewish culture and the decline of support for Israel are one and the same, and plummeting simultaneously. This phenomenon isn't new. During a recent discussion on antisemitism on college campuses, Natan Sharansky, the renowned Soviet refusenik and human rights activist, noted: "If you have a Jewish person with no connection to faith and no connection to Israel, their grandchildren will not be Jewish, will not feel Jewish." Sharansky's words draw heavily on his days in the Soviet Union, a regime that served as a textbook example of how Judaism, deprived of both religion and nationalism, can be squeezed into near oblivion. If Josef Stalin died before he had the chance to kill Russia's Jews en masse, Stalinism lived on through the slow erasure of Jewish identity. It triumphed in the abolition of Hebrew and Zionism, in completely universalizing the Jewish experience, in replacing the Magen David with a hammer and sickle. Sharansky and his fellow Jewish dissidents risked their lives in trying to make it to Israel, making the correct judgment that any Jewish future in Russia would be perpetually stunted and shunned so long as the Jews were simply just like any other Russians. And especially if fellow Jews become convinced that this was a good idea. As Sharansky is said to have put it many years ago, "When Jews sacrifice identity in exchange for universal freedom, they wind up with neither."

**

Then there is Israel. In Israel, I have found that I can eat on Yom Kippur, text on Shabbat, and walk hand in hand with my partner of the same sex and still feel profoundly Jewish. Even when I am cursing the lack of public transportation from Haifa to Tel Aviv on Saturdays and retweeting Israeli politicians who are looking to chip away at Haredi influence in the Knesset, I still feel profoundly Jewish.

This is because after so much reading and writing about the Jewish people over the last several years, in Israel I feel as though I'm surrounded by my subjects, my case studies, my fellow travelers exploring the ins and outs of our identities, rather than foreigners. I am among people who are living the wildest dreams of our ancestors, who are continuing to write the story of the Jewish people whether they have considered it or not. One may bemoan the secular culture in a city like Tel Aviv, ambivalent to the religious principles of Judaism. But one would be wrong. Tel Aviv now stands as the "third way," the epicenter of the Haskalah, the liberal Zionist movement, and the Jewish secular movement, which has done its fair share in ensuring our survival as a people. Its plays are in Hebrew. Its newspapers automatically concern the Jewish people. Its politics pull not just a country, but the Jewish story in its entirety. I feel a part of this world, and I feel that if it no longer exists in New York, so be it.

My Aliyah comes with less analytical reasons as well. I desperately want to improve my Hebrew. I figure the best vantage point to write about Israel is from Israel, and I believe in the need to meet plenty of Israelis from all walks of life. The move won't come without its sentiments, either.

Walking back from a coffee shop this morning, I noticed for the first time a small park directly across from where I live, dubbed I. L. Peretz Square for the renowned Jewish playwright. I was filled with instant glee upon remembering the significance of my current stomping grounds. At the turn of the century, Peretz was able to create masterpieces of the Jewish canon such as *Bakante bilder*, *Khasidish*, and *Folkstimlekhe geshikhte*. It then dawned on me, however, that the reason Peretz is still emblazoned in the minds of the Jewish people of today, and also of the Lower East Side, is because of his stern conviction that the Jewish people were particular. He trusted and championed our uniqueness. Scholar Sol Liptzin quoted Peretz as saying: "Every people is seen by him to be a chosen people, chosen by its peculiar history, geography and ethnic composition." Peretz is also noted to have thought of Jewish literature as "grounded in Jewish traditions and Jewish history," and as "the expression of Jewish ideals." Yet he was still able to hold these beliefs even while publishing manuscripts on science, technology, and economics—showing his commitment to the academic subjects of the West while committed to Jewishness simultaneously.

I looked around at the neighborhood after reading his plaque and wondered how many Jews living here can say the same.

* * *

"I wasn't addressing my personal problems as a Jew," continues Hannah Arendt in explaining her decision to join the Zionists. "Belonging to Judaism had become my own problem. A political problem. I wanted to do practical work, only Jewish work." Arendt sees her initial turn toward Zionism to be political, knowing she had to honor Jewish particularism in order to "address her personal problems."

Indeed, if you are a Jew who feels there is a void in your soul, whether you feel unsatisfied in Jewish political expression, Jewish art, Jewish socialization, or Jewish culture in general—move to Israel. That's what it was built for. Israel is here to serve as a third way for the anxious Diaspora Jew, who so desperately wants to contribute to the tapestry of Jewish life in the most fulfilling way possible.

I will miss, genuinely and earnestly, walking on the same ground that my grandparents once walked. I will miss reveling in the mythology of Ellis Island and the Statue of Liberty and the tenement houses I so cherish. I will miss Tompkins Square Park, knowing that both sides of my family once owned homes within a 200-foot radius of this green refuge. But the Jewish people have not carried a suitcase throughout the millennia just to escape oppression. Our liturgy points to Zion for redemption first. It is my sincerest hope that fellow Jews, who seek to redeem themselves, who seek the third way between observance and assimilation, will, too, join me in the Promised Land and never look back.

15

OUR BIBLICAL BIRTHRIGHT

Reclaiming the Land-of-Israel Narrative

YISHAI FLEISHER

MY FRIEND, Arthur, recently texted me a picture he took from a major wine store in his hometown of Phoenix, Arizona. It was of a Psagot Winery display. "There was a time," he wrote, "when I would have to order a case of Israeli wine from KosherWine.com, but now I can go into the local Total Wine store and there is a huge variety of great Israeli wines. This is one of the blessings of Israel becoming stronger and having a further reach that is reverberating out into the world and touching us out here in Arizona."

Rabbi Yishai Fleisher is the International Spokesperson for the Jewish community of Hebron, home of the Biblical Tomb of the Patriarchs and Matriarchs. He is a broadcaster on the Land of Israel Network and has been featured on CNN, Al Jazeera, Fox, *Vice*, BBC, and more. He holds a J.D. from Cardozo Law School.

What Arthur referred to as "blessings" can also be understood as "soft power": the non-military influence a country has around the world. Israeli products, now in local stores, do not merely represent the success of small businesses in exporting and selling their products abroad. Rather, they are an exercise in the power of a story: the story of Israel as a normal and legitimate nation-state.

You may ask why Israel really needs a narrative of legitimacy and normalization. Well, it probably wouldn't need it if there weren't a sustained campaign to delegitimize the Jewish state on global campuses, in the media, and in international institutions. Calls to boycott, divest, and sanction Israel aim to tarnish Israel's name and scare future supporters and friends away from a "pariah," thereby causing Israel to be isolated and weakened in the long run.

In response, Israel sends out a myriad of soft-power messages. Indeed, if Israel had to be good at counter-terror in the twentieth century, it must be good at counter-narrative in the twenty-first.

Soft power in the digital age demands an updated narrative. The heady days of Paul Newman in *Exodus* or Cecil B. DeMille's *The Ten Commandments* are gone, and the evocative memories of the Holocaust and the Six-Day War have faded. Today, Israel's new soft-power arsenal includes the hit TV series *Fauda*, which dramatizes Israel's military prowess, and *Shtisel*, which provides an endearing entry to Israeli ultra-Orthodox society. Both of these are powerful tools to normalize and anchor the Jewish state in the minds of millions. Israel's technical and innovative prowess is also familiar to some.

But the Psagot Winery display in the Phoenix wine shop featured more than just bottles of delicious wine. It also showed a map of the Land of Israel with the wine regions highlighted: Judea and Samaria, known to some as the "West Bank," proudly accentuated along with the Galilee and the Golan Heights, as well as the coastal plain just north of Gaza.

This innocent-looking map of Israel's many wine regions, including the biblical heartland where Psagot wine comes from, actually sends a powerful message: This is the ancient territory of Judea, this is where the Jews made wine 3,000 and 2,000 years ago, this is where the Bible happened—and this is where it is happening again today.

And by drinking this wine, you can be part of national liberation and much-awaited decolonialization, part of biblical miracles and God's promise, part of historic justice, or simply part of drinking great wine from a cool country called Israel. This wine is not scary or morally dubious, and if a friend catches you drinking Israeli wine you will not be scandalized, de-platformed, or canceled—because it's likely she has a bottle at home, as well.

The wine is top-notch, the map is historically accurate, Israel is flourishing on its land, and all is good and right. Right?

* * *

The haters, of course, have their own maps. On October 27, 2021, Palestinian leader Mahmoud Abbas visited Tunisia where he inaugurated a new Palestinian Authority (PA) embassy. There, on a huge mural, the map of "Palestine" was displayed—encompassing almost the exact borders of the State of Israel. In response, the scholar Daniel Pipes tweeted: "Tunisia's President #KaisSaied joined with PA's #MahmoudAbbas to inaugurate the new 'State of Palestine' embassy in Tunis. Note them standing in front of a magnificent map that symbolically eliminates the Jewish state of Israel."

So, what is this alternative map of "Palestine"? For the last 2,000 years, Jews have faced many forms of "replacement theology"—the idea that God has ordained one group or another to be the "new Israelites" instead of the Jews. This time we face a *replacement narrative* that gives an alternative name to the land and a *replacement map* that appears to give legitimacy to the anti-Israel claims. This narrative and this map are being pumped out by millions of dollars' worth of social media campaigns, keyboard warriors, and campus lecturers. Even Arab children in Hebron try to sell tourists a keychain of a map of "Palestine"—totally erasing Israel. And it's not just a map and a narrative war that are at work erasing Israel. It's also on the ground in the biblical heartland, where a massive land grab is taking place. The result of the Olso Accords has been to allow the PA to take over what the agreements refer to as areas A and B—the limited areas that were agreed to be not entirely under Israeli control. The hot battlefront, as of this writing, is in Area C where the agreements grant full Israeli rule. In eastern Jerusalem, in the environs of Bethlehem, the land-grab is enormous, and this is also happening inside Israel's internationally recognized borders as well, in the Negev and the Galilee.

To keep the Jews from galvanizing and pushing back, violence is always close at hand, not only in Judea and Samaria but also in mixed Arab-Jewish cities. This was all too visible in Operation Guardian of the Walls, in May 2021, when ten synagogues were torched by jihadist mobs in what had been considered "peaceful" mixed Arab-Jewish cities.

Indeed, the war for the land is coupled with a war of symbols. The flag of Palestine seeks to replace Israel on the land and in the global consciousness.

* * *

Sadly, some Jews in Israel and around the world have blinded themselves to the coming threat: A choked, ghettoized Israel, too small for its population, under threat of jihadist rocket fire from areas that surround Jerusalem and control the high ground. And internationally, a Taliban-like jihadist Palestine boasting more legitimacy than the ancient tribe of Israel that was reborn in ancestral Judea—whose image is defaced.

Without much of a fight, Israel is giving up on the heartland of Judea. Having been disembodied for thousands of years, many Jews are still ghetto-minded. That is, they think like non-land owners and non-sovereigns. They believe that land doesn't matter—a position that is totally anathema in the rest of the Middle East. The pro-Palestine activists sense this weakness and are exploiting it.

By giving up Judea and Samaria, Israel is shooting its own most compelling narrative in the foot. Israel's natural story is that of an ancient nation that comes from a land called Judea—*Yehud Medinta*, the Jewish State, as it was known in Persia 2,500 years ago. Being ancient and indigenous, having had two commonwealths here, both with capitals in Jerusalem, gives Israel a superior legal, historic, and cultural claim as well as a great global narrative. But when Israel forgoes its biblical brand, it forgoes its own ancient identity and basic winning story. Giving up on Judea means giving up on the Bible—the most popular story in world history, and instead allowing "Palestine" to be presented as the indigenous brand.

Instead of these self-inflicted blunders, Israel and its supporters must not abandon the heart of the Zionist project, which is the Land of Israel itself—both physically and symbolically. Israel's territorial integrity must be maintained, while the idea that another people has an absolute claim to self-determination on Jewish tribal land must be extinguished. There should be no illegal land grabs, no enemy flags, and no jihadist indoctrination in Jewish territory. The non-Jews living on this land should know and respect that the Jewish state is sovereign in the Land of Israel. Israel should hold on to its land as a priority and a fundamental asset.

***

Despite all this, there have been some points of light. One of the great successes of our time is the Abraham Accords, the historic agreement between Israel and, as of this writing, four regional Arab countries. One often-overlooked aspect of the Abraham Accords is the name itself. The term implicitly indicates that the agreement is between descendants of the children of the biblical Abraham—Arabs and Jews alike. For Israel, this is a crucial identification in its quest for normalization in the Middle East.

One of the main avenues of attack coming out of the pro-Palestinian narrative has been the buzzword "occupation," which used to refer to the military rule in parts of Judea and Samaria but now has become the default label for the Jewish state *in its entirety* on campuses, at international organizations, and in left-leaning media. The condemning language "Israeli occupation" says all that the enemies of Israel want to say: that Israel is a white colonialist interloper in the Middle East, a European holdover, a foreigner grabbing Arab lands, and an abuser of the human rights of the true indigenous people. Given pressure and time, the reasoning goes, occupations are bound to end.

The occupation narrative machine has many levers. For example, using UNESCO, the United Nations body in charge of recognizing world heritage sites, the anti-Israel crowd has asserted that foundational Jewish sites like Jerusalem, Bethlehem, and Hebron are actually Palestinian cities and Palestinian historic sites under "occupation." Any campus protest against Israel will feature the word "occupation," and most *New York Times* articles will throw in an editorialized jab like "Israeli-occupied East Jerusalem."

But what is the counterword to "occupation"? How do you convey Israel's deep history in the land and the Jewish people's indigeneity to the Middle East? How do you invoke the flavor of ancient history without sounding like a Bible-thumping extremist? What word can bridge the Arab-Jewish divide?

The answer is "Abraham."

When U.S. Vice President Mike Pence visited Israel in January 2018, he made a televised speech at the Knesset:

> Nearly 4,000 years ago, a man left his home in Ur of the Chaldeans to travel here, to Israel. He ruled no empire, he wore no crown, he commanded no armies, he performed no miracles, delivered no prophecies, yet to him was promised "descendants as numerous as the stars in the sky." Today, Jews, Christians, and Muslims—more than half the population of the Earth, and nearly all the people of the Middle East—claim Abraham as their forefather in faith.

Pence's admiring words for the children of Abraham foreshadowed a time when traditional but progress-hungry Arabs would embrace and ally with the biblically-inspired and forward-thinking Jewish state under the banner of their mutual ancestor, Abraham.

The UAE also appears to have embraced Abraham as a uniting force in the region. A massive religious complex known as "The Abrahamic Family House" is already under construction in Abu Dhabi, featuring, in the words of a Dubai newspaper, "three main buildings—a mosque, a church, and a synagogue that will encourage peaceful co-existence and acceptance of the three Abrahamic faiths Christianity, Islam, and Judaism in the UAE's capital city."

No wonder anti-normalization forces like the Palestinian Authority are apoplectic. Their life mission has been to delegitimize Israel through inculcating the terms "colonialization" and "occupation." Now it is Israel's turn to capitalize on the Abraham Accords narrative by reemphasizing the fact that Israelis are an ancient indigenous people, and by creating a touristic brand around Abraham and the biblical sites in the Holy Land. Israel must not squander the branding opportunity of the Abraham Accords. The first step, of course, is to strengthen Jewish presence in the places associated with Abraham, most of which are located in Judea and Samaria.

* * *

Like the name Abraham, the Bible as a whole is the bedrock of Jewish attachment to the Land of Israel, and Israel's secular founders knew it. They understood that biblical consciousness—even if detached from its theological aspect—was needed to make a historical claim on the land. The Hebrew Bible was alive for them, as was the promise and practicality of the return to Zion. The stories of the Bible gave both Jews and pro-Israel Christian Restorationists, like Arthur Balfour, the fervor to join the fight for Jewish liberation.

Israel as the land and the people of the Bible has tremendous soft-power resonance. But today the Bible is not in its zenith. American universities that used to study the Bible in the original Hebrew now barely crack open the Holy Book—and when they do, it is to criticize rather than to connect. Much of Europe has gone post-Bible and post-God. The secular wing of the Israeli educational system has sucked the life out of the Hebrew Bible while Israeli universities are home to the last academic vestiges of Biblical Criticism, which serve only to erode respect for the Holy Book.

When biblically-minded people hear the word "Hebron," they immediately think of Abraham's famous land-purchase negotiation for a burial plot for his beloved wife Sarah, which became the resting place for the majority of Israel's First Family. They recall King David ruled in Hebron for seven years before moving his capital to Jerusalem. And they know that a mammoth Herodian monument to the biblical patriarchs and matriarchs still stands in Hebron today.

But a non-biblically minded person, without those associations, will more likely connect the city with violence, intolerance, and danger. And that is just fine with the jihadist narrative machine, which seeks to eradicate the biblical story, with its identification of Jews as the people with an ancient, possessory connection to the Holy Land. They have targeted every avenue of Israel's legitimacy and have teamed up with the Progressive and European set which has replaced classical religion with "human rights," in which the abused Palestinians are the indigenous people of Palestine, while Israel is nothing but white colonialists occupying the land of dark-skinned people.

Israel, for its part, has done very little to strengthen the association of Israel as the land of the Bible. Curiously, when you land at Ben Gurion Airport, you do not meet any signs that tell you that you have arrived in the Holy Land. Only the folks catering to Christian tourism, especially Arabs in the Old City of Jerusalem, seem to have caught on to the real reason most visitors have actually arrived.

**

Instead, Israel needs to embrace its biblical narrative and lean in to the Abrahamic brand. One such effort, inspired by America's Route 66, is the Israel Biblical Highway.

There are many beautiful and historic roads in the world, but only one traverses the heart of the most powerful and influential story in human history. Sweeping from north to south, the ancient biblical highway, today Israel's Route 60, journeys through seven storied and holy cities in the Land of Israel.

The road begins in the Samarian city of Shechem (Nablus)—the first place that Abraham and then later Jacob arrived in the Land of Israel, and where Joseph is buried. The Biblical Highway then traverses south to Shiloh, where the Tabernacle stood for 369 years. Next, it arrives at Beit El (Bethel) where Jacob experienced a vision of a ladder connecting Heaven and Earth. Yet further south, the Biblical Highway meets the heart of the world—Jerusalem, Israel's capital, where King David reigned and where two Jewish Temples stood.

From Jerusalem, the journey continues south through the terrain of Judea and reaches Bethlehem, where the Matriarch Rachel is buried and where the Davidic dynasty began. The road then arrives at Hebron, where Abraham made his first purchase of land and where the founders of the Jewish people are buried. The highway finally ends in Be'er Sheva (Beersheba), capital of the Negev desert, where Abraham and Isaac dug their wells and taught wayfarers about the One God.

To serve travelers seeking to be part of this celebrated story, plans for the restoration of the Biblical Highway include visitor centers, rest stops, educational scenic overlooks, and a dedicated app to guide travelers through the ancient sites and stories and provide access to the modern amenities on the highway. Throughout the road, there are lots of attractions, including wonderful communities, Jewish and Arab, world-renowned wineries, restaurants, heritage sites, and hospitality.

It should be easy for every Israeli student to recall the classic stories that took place along the highway, and every historically-minded global tourist should be able to see the places where the legendary stories that are the foundation of their faith actually occurred.

While the Jewish people and lovers of Israel can continue to celebrate the amazing gift of the rebirth of the Jewish state, the fight is far from over. Now is the time to reassess the path ahead. Firstly, and always, Israel needs to be in control of the situation. Strength garners respect and sends the signal that Israel is here to stay. Underneath and beyond that hard power, Israel needs a strong soft-power brand to win back hearts and minds. Pushing the ethos and the unifying name of the Abraham Accords is a fantastic way to connect with regional allies and convey Israel as ancient and relevant in the Middle East. Indeed, even renaming the Middle East "the Abrahamic Region" would be to Israel's advantage—and would just be true. A strong Israel, with a strong narrative, will be a breath of fresh air to a region looking for a new passion and purpose to replace the jihadism that has retarded peace and progress for all of Abraham's children. The future is a strong Israel surrounded by strong Arab states working for the betterment of all the peoples of this region. But to accomplish this, Israel must throw off the counter-narrative of Palestinianism which seeks to undermine and replace Israel in toto. There is no compromise with this replacement brand. A strong Israeli story will work organically with a strong presence on the ground and will ensure Israel's success moving forward.

16

TEACH THE IDEA OF

THE JEWISH PEOPLE

Protect Young Jews from the Intellectual
Assault on Their Identity

DAVID GEDZELMAN

THE NOTION that the Jews constitute a people with common purpose, history, and destiny has inspired generations. The idea of the Jewish people
is contoured and complex, articulated through a broad range of sources—
narrative, legal, poetic, and liturgical—over thousands of years.

The Jewish people is also a composite concept: neither wholly a tribal
matter, connected to the circumstances of one's birth, nor only a matter of

---

Rabbi David Gedzelman is President and CEO of the Steinhardt Foundation for Jewish Life.

faith, creed, or observance. It is dialectical in nature, comprising seemingly contradictory categories and definitions. One is born Jewish, but one can also choose to be Jewish. It includes a comprehensive religious system, with culture and language, but it is about one's family and origin as well.

Jews have understood their connections to each other across geography and history as that of a single covenantal people for millennia, certainly predating modernity and reaching back to antiquity, with foundations in the biblical era. There is no Jewish religion without the Jewish people; and, I would argue, the Jewish people loses its mission and purpose without the Jewish wisdom tradition that is meant to be lived out in our communal life.

Although many American Jews may not have adequate language to articulate the complex conceptual framework that underlies the idea of the Jewish people, to anyone familiar with the long history of Jewish texts, ideas, and traditions, little is as self-evident as the simple fact that the Jews have been a people, sharing a sense of common collective destiny, for a very long time.

So, it may come as a surprise that the very concept of the Jewish people is under attack today in American academia, including in the mainstream of contemporary Jewish Studies.

Jewish peoplehood has been characterized by a growing number of scholars as a thoroughly modern construct, an invention born of the ideas of modern nationalism, with no real connection to any sense of groupness, national identity in exile, or covenantal connection among the Jews who lived before the modern era. Worse yet, the inclination to want to be connected to those of similar Jewish origin or commitment is condemned by these scholars as being necessarily racist in nature.

But while this new trend in academia has taken hold, Jewish educational contexts for school-age children have been bereft of curricula or programming aimed at helping students understand the rich concept of Jewish peoplehood, explore textual bases for what the Jewish people is, or engage with the unique amalgam of the universal and the particular that is the fundamental Jewish proposition.

Put this together with the most recent trends in the academic field of Jewish education, which privilege the emotive and experiential over the learning of substance, concepts, and facts, and it turns out that we have reached a unique moment in Jewish communal history, a "perfect storm" that leaves our young people wholly unprepared to understand for themselves, and to explain to others, why it may be worthwhile to see themselves as part of the Jewish people at all. No one is giving them the tools to find value in the idea of the Jewish people, and they may soon find themselves in a college context that is outrightly hostile to the very idea of the Jewish people, however they might explain it.

Put simply: A central pillar of the next generation's Jewish identity is under direct assault, and we are giving them almost nothing with which to defend themselves.

* * *

In the spring and summer of 2022, I conducted a series of interviews with Jewish educational leaders and practitioners to discover to what extent Jewish peoplehood is being taught in our community's educational settings. I spoke with heads of national Jewish educational institutions, faculty at schools of Jewish education, leaders of innovative educational initiatives as well as practitioners in the field. *Not one* could identify a comprehensive curriculum, program, or initiative designed to engage students in North America about the idea of the Jewish people, its textual sources, development over history, and what it can mean today. An exception that proves this rule is a course about the Jewish people offered by Young Judaea's Israel-based Year Course—but this only brings the question into sharper relief: Why is this kind of conceptual exploration substantively absent from Jewish education *in* North America?

Part of the problem, it seems, is structural. "Since the infrastructure of North American Jewry is built on the synagogue," David Bryfman, CEO of the Jewish Education Project, told me, "most Jewish educational platforms don't teach about the Jewish people, but rather they teach about ritual, prayer, and religion. Similarly, day schools are religiously structured, not civilization-based." Some of the people I spoke with suggested that while there may be no formal curricula focused on the Jewish people idea, there are nonetheless educational contexts, formal and informal, that work to give students and participants a "sense" and "feeling" of belonging to the Jewish people. The idea of the Jewish people in our educational contexts is implicit, I was told, but not explicit.

Yet there is a deeper problem. At precisely the time when Jewish youth most need the tools to be able to understand and explain what Jewish people-hood is, Jewish education as a whole has shifted away from what theorists call "cognitive" learning (i.e., concepts, facts, history, and what we traditionally call "knowledge"), toward more emotion- and experience-based learning. Indeed, what is today considered the cutting edge in Jewish education denigrates the goal of possessing knowledge altogether, arguing that there is a binary choice to be made between education that empowers learners as "producers of their own knowledge and experience" and education that sets the possession of knowledge as its goal—without entertaining the possibility of doing both.

In two recent essays, Jon Levisohn, associate professor of Jewish educational thought at Brandeis University, makes this binary argument. Writing in a 2019 essay called "A New Paradigm of Jewish Literacy," Levisohn critiques what he calls a "set of cognitivist assumptions," such as valuing knowing the sources behind the laws of Kashrut and Shabbat, in favor of modeling and teaching practice in an experiential way:

> But if we are willing to challenge those cognitivist assumptions, then we may envision a kind of literacy that does not involve being able to name and explain, but instead, involves being able to proceed within a particular cultural space—enacting the relevant practices and doing them well.

That seems a false choice. Even John Dewey, the founder of progressive education in the United States, understood that cognitive content, not just experience, should be presented in the educational context—just not in a way that fails to take the questions and experiences of learners into account. As the educational philosopher Israel Scheffler wrote, "The growth of cognition is thus, in fact, inseparable from the education of the emotions." We need both.

It is certainly important for young Jews to have positive affective experiences and to feel a sense of Jewish belonging, but shouldn't we be also working to combine those feelings with *knowledge* about what the Jewish people actually is? Shouldn't young Jews, before they are told by their professors and fellow students that the Jewish people is a racist modern construct, have some opportunity to explore this central concept—its texts, its ancient origins, its unique history—in a more sympathetic environment? As one professor of Jewish education I spoke to admitted, "teaching kids to feel a sense of Jewish belonging is necessary, but not sufficient."

***

This assault on cognitive content in the Jewish educational world is especially dangerous at a time when fundamental changes have taken place in academia with regard to the idea of the Jewish people.

Today, Jewish students entering college suddenly find themselves in a world where an academic elite, armed with a critical approach to nationalism, peoplehood, and group identity, has formulated a new orthodoxy according to which the Jewish people is a modern construct that was invented to further the political aims of Zionism, rather than the other way around. Nor has this orthodoxy limited itself to specific disciplines like Middle Eastern studies or political science but has penetrated into Jewish studies itself.

For example, Noam Pianko, who leads Jewish Studies at the University of Washington and was until recently the president of the Association for Jewish Studies, draws upon the work of Benedict Anderson, Eric Hobsbawm, John Lie, and Shlomo Sand to suggest that the very idea of the Jewish people is an altogether modern construct with little continuity with premodern Jews.

Clearly, Jews have for millennia consistently used terms like *am yisrael* (the People of Israel) or *bnei yisrael* (the Children of Israel) to describe the Jewish people. This should be obvious to anyone familiar with Jewish texts. It would be absurd to suggest that their use of "Israel" rather than "Jewish" somehow means that a sense of Jewish peoplehood was absent from how Jews saw themselves.

Yet this is precisely what Pianko argues in his 2015 book *Jewish Peoplehood: An American Innovation*. Because the specific term "the Jewish people" may have emerged in the modern era, as opposed to "the Jews" or "Israel," Pianko claims there was no overarching self-conscious sense of Jewish civilizational collectivity beforehand. To make this claim, he must ignore how terms like "His people Israel" and "Your people Israel" are used throughout traditional Jewish liturgy. The Siddur—the central text of Jewish prayer, whose compilation spans more than a thousand years from the ancient rabbis through the medieval period—leaves no doubt about a clear, explicit sense of Jewish peoplehood. Yes, the term "Jewish peoplehood" may have been coined in the twentieth century, and championed by Mordecai Kaplan, but it describes an evolving reality that far predates it.

Yet despite his questionable logic, Pianko is far from alone. One of his influences, John Lie, a professor at the University of California at Berkeley, makes a similarly misleading argument in his 2004 book *Modern Peoplehood*. Referring to the Hebrew Bible, he writes, "The very term Israel connotes a mixed community of faith rather than an ethno-national group." In fact, in Lie's view, Jewishness before the modern era was wholly a matter of faith. Furthermore, because Jews were splintered during the first century C.E., he argues, modern assertions of a continuous chain of collective identity going back to antiquity are anachronistic—an argument crafted, it seems, solely to detach Jews from their ancient history.

These scholars are quick to draw far-reaching conclusions. In their view, a commitment to Jewish peoplehood necessarily posits an allegiance to an exclusively lineage-focused racialism that eschews openness and understanding. The ease with which they start comparing a commitment to Jewish peoplehood with Nazism is disturbing. Here's Pianko describing Israel's Law of Return, which grants automatic citizenship to Jewish immigrants:

> In the establishment of the Law of Return, which, it must be noted parallels Nazi racial logic in granting any person with one Jewish grandparent automatic citizenship in the State of Israel, Jews have enacted and formalized the very blood basis of membership used by antisemites. And even in situations where a direct relationship to racial thinking is not as obvious, the language of modern Jewish peoplehood is inflected with what are essentially quasi-racial concepts, in its focus on a shared essence inherited through descent, blood, and birth.

What Pianko leaves out is that Nazi racial logic saw a one-quarter Jewish lineage as being enough to contaminate one's non-Jewish origins, while the Law of Return actually does the opposite, seeing as much as three-quarters of a person's non-Jewish lineage as in no way compromising one's inclusion in the life of the Jewish people. In other words, the Law of Return is an appropriation that turns the insidious racism of the Nazi legal categorization of Jews completely on its head, overthrowing racial exclusion with Zionist inclusion. Bad-faith scholarship, of course, cares little for such nuances.

**

Equating Jewish peoplehood, as expressed in the Law of Return, with Nazi racialism is not just bad scholarship; it's also bad history, for it ignores the glaring fact that Jewish notions of status have never given lineage or birth exclusive power of determination.

Pianko's argument ignores the simple fact of *conversion*: not only current rising trends of conversion and inclusion in North American Jewry—which alone should be enough to shatter his racialist claims—but also any basic understanding of what I call the "covenantal openness" displayed throughout our traditional sources and texts.

Because this covenantal openness is fundamental to both understanding Jewish peoplehood and to refuting the claims of these scholars, it is worth looking at in some detail.

One can find in the Hebrew Bible, as well as in rabbinic texts, a continuous line depicting the Jewish people, or "Israel," as a dialectical hybrid of birth and choice, blood and faith. From its beginning, Israel is not a single tribe but a cluster of tribes. Birth is important, but it is not everything.

At the moment of the Exodus from Egypt, the biblical text exhorts us to remember the Exodus in the future by re-enacting the eating of the Paschal Offering, whose blood secured the redemption of Israel (Exodus 12:37–50). That same passage then makes it clear that if there are "strangers" living with us, not born of the Covenant, who also want to eat the Paschal Offering and remember the Exodus, they should be encouraged to do so as long as the males among them are willing to show profound commitment by undergoing circumcision.

Joining the Covenant of Israel is, in other words, extended to those not born as Israelites—not as an afterthought, but at the foundational moment of Jewish peoplehood, the Exodus from Egypt.

Lineage, therefore, is not solely determinative. If one desires to join this people, one can do so, but in a ritual of blood demonstrating that one can will away one's biological destiny and assume another. Among the ancients, this is exceptional.

Covenantal openness is demonstrated in a pointed way in the Book of Ruth, as well. Ruth is born of a supposedly hated people, the Moabites, but she becomes a member of Israel when she declares, "Your people shall be my people, and your God shall be my God" (Ruth 1:16). So decisive is this affirmation of covenantal openness that the book ends with the genealogy of her descendants—in which we discover, in a moment of stunning literary drama, that she is the great-grandmother of King David, who represents the future of the People of Israel.

In the rabbinic tradition, covenantal openness is highlighted, for example, by the Talmudic story in Tractate Shabbat concerning a series of non-Jews who approach two leading rabbis, Hillel and Shammai, to be converted to Judaism (31a). In each case, the non-Jew offers impossible conditions for his conversion. Shammai harshly rejects each applicant. Hillel gently takes each of them in and subsequently shows them why their conditions do not make sense. Hillel's position, it should be noted, is presented as the prevailing voice—and later, it was the school of Hillel that almost always was seen as overriding the opinions of the school of Shammai.

This is not to suggest that converts have always been accepted with the same degree of openness or warmth as that prescribed by Hillel. Three hundred years after Hillel, it became illegal in the Roman Empire for Jews to convert others to Judaism, and Jews internalized this. Hence the rabbinic notion that we turn away the convert three times. But conversion in Judaism has always been a reality, and the descendants of converts are fully integrated into the Jewish people. In our time, exactly when "Jewish peoplehood" is a supposedly new and racialist construct, joining the Jewish people through conversion is on the rise—a fact that Pianko and Lie conveniently ignore because it would eviscerate their thesis.

It is no accident that the biblical narrative begins, in the Book of Genesis, with the story of a family. The Jewish people *is* an extended family, and it is meant to have an open adoption policy. In practice, it is a multiracial family, challenging Western conceptions of race and lineage. In our foundational texts, in other words, being born into this extended family is of co-equal importance with choosing to be a member of this family.

Yes, it would be easier to define being Jewish either as a closed line of familial descent or, alternatively, as a system of values and wisdom divorced completely from the notion of birth and family. The idea of the Jewish people cannot be neatly fit into either-or categories of nation, religion, biology, or culture. The universalism of our tradition does not contradict or negate its particularism—and vice versa.

The modernist scholars of nationalism would have us believe that any Jewish national concept we might discern in our ancient texts must be the product of reading them through a nineteenth-century European nationalist lens. But the opposite is the case. The Jewish people's capacity to maintain a sense of global connectedness among communities worldwide throughout centuries of exile actually *brought* the possibility of the national idea to the attention of those European thinkers who sought to affirm ethnic and national identity against the empires of Europe that had oppressed them, as the important scholar Anthony Smith has shown. Indeed, the Jews were the original demonstrators of what the modernist scholars of nationalism call "mass nations." Our peoplehood always included all classes and subgroups.

***

Some of the educators I spoke with suggested that in the congregational part-time education sector, often called Hebrew School, teachers are hesitant to teach about the Jewish people for fear that it could distance the many children who have a non-Jewish parent. But if teaching about the idea of the Jewish people involves demonstrating the covenantal openness that can be found in traditional sources, there should be a warm and enthusiastic way to include children whose families include non-Jewish parents without leaving out the fundamental reality of the Jewish people. That is as true for sixth graders as it is for young adults.

It is past time for the Jewish community in North America to develop curricula and train teachers to present the idea of the Jewish people as a central pillar of who we are. Programs that give participants a sense of belonging to the Jewish people should pair the experiential environment with explorations of the vast, rich content embedded in our textual tradition. Birthright Israel, for example, could offer a series of learning experiences—both textual and experiential—about Jewish peoplehood and Zionism, both during and after the trip. Educators in Jewish camps and day schools should make the implicit explicit, offering curricula that give students and campers the tools to articulate with facts, texts, and ideas their own sense of belonging to the Jewish people.

The scholarly assault against Jewish peoplehood cannot be divorced, of course, from the constant characterization of Zionism as a form of European white colonialism rather than the national liberation movement of the Jewish people that it is. If there is no Jewish people, then, of course, there can be no Zionism. If the Jews don't exist in any essential historical way, then of course they have no right to self-realization and self-determination.

We need a comprehensive effort to teach our children about the idea of the Jewish people, its origins in the Bible, its evolution over millennia, and its realization in the Zionist revolution. We need to help our young people understand that anti-Zionism is essentially the *negation of the Jewish people* and that the negation of the idea of the Jewish people is nothing less than a cancellation of Jewish identity—a form of ideological genocide, erasing a people intellectually.

We owe our young people an education that gives them the knowledge they need to articulate, affirm, and celebrate their connections to the transcendent, beautiful reality that is the Jewish people.

17

REINVENT JEWISH GIVING

The Case for "Return on Investment" Philanthropy

MARK GERSON

IN 2012, I had a terrific summer intern named Lucas Zelnick. My early attempts to keep him working for me were thwarted by his insistence that he should go to college. My later attempts were thwarted by his decision to be a comedian.

Lucas's comic material is based on his having grown up a wealthy Jewish kid on New York's Upper East Side. In one of his routines, he reflected on his experience of the bar mitzvah circuit:

Mark Gerson is the co-founder of Gerson Lehrman Group (GLG) and the co-founder and Chairman of United Hatzalah of Israel, the world's first and only national system of crowd-sourced volunteer first response. He is author of *The Telling: How Judaism's Essential Book Reveals the Meaning of Life* (St. Martin's, 2021) and teaches the Bible each week to primarily Evangelical leaders. He and his wife, Rabbi Erica Gerson, live with their four children in New York City.

> Your parents' friends would give you a lot of money and you had to pick a charity to give a lot of money away to.... Every charity these kids picked operated at the intersection of an out-of-reach humanitarian crisis and then what specifically they were into.... It would be like: Josh Feltzer donated *fifty thousand dollars* to stop post-Apartheid racism in South Africa through *guitar lessons?* Why does every kid in Honduras have a skateboard? The Goldfarb Bar Mitzvah was last Wednesday, and Benjamin *loves* skating...

Everyone familiar with Lucas's subject will acknowledge that this is funny—vindicating, I suppose, his decision to turn down my job offer and pursue a career in comedy. But why is it funny?

A comparison might be helpful. Raising money for charitable causes is not the only familiar use of bar mitzvah gifts. Many young men and women receive cash instead of or in addition to the charitable contributions. They typically invest the cash in a diversified array of stocks, bonds, and funds—not, in other words, in anything that would provide a comedian with any material.

Why is there such a difference between how young Josh and Benjamin would give rather than invest money? If this were a question about hypothetical thirteen-year-olds, it would not be worth asking. But it's not. Children that age, particularly on matters concerning significant amounts of money, are guided by their parents and influenced by society—both in the moment and by what they have learned up to that point.

***

The fact that giving has become literally comical is—for us Jews—sadly ironic. There are only two times in the Torah when God tells us that we can make a deal with him—and both concern the same subject. What could be so important to God? We find out in Deuteronomy and the Book of Malachi, when God tells us that we will be blessed (which means that our material needs will be assured) if we give generously and enthusiastically to the poor.

And Deuteronomy was not even the first time when God instructed us on the importance of giving well. In Exodus, the Jews—anxious about Moses's apparent delay in returning from Mount Sinai—resolve to collect their gold and fashion a leader in the form of a calf. The Golden Calf is considered the ultimate sin committed by the Jews as they wandered through the Sinai desert after the exodus from Egypt.

Traditionally most commentators have seen the Golden Calf as a sin of idolatry, impatience, and a lack of faith. The story is about all of those things. But in the Jerusalem Talmud, Rabbi Abba bar Acha identified another problem—one pertaining to a defect in the "character of this people."

The defect? He said: "They're solicited for the Golden Calf and they give. They're solicited for the Sanctuary and they give."

The character flaw was that their giving, like that of Lucas's Benjamin Goldfarb and Josh Feltzer, was not thoughtfully allocated. But if the Golden Calf story teaches the importance of not giving badly, then what, exactly, is giving well?

This should be easy to figure out—because everyone agrees with what constitutes deploying money well. It is a simple calculation. The numerator is the desired outcome. The denominator is capital deployed. The result is the return on investment (ROI). The greater the ROI, the better.

Everyone who deploys capital does this calculation all the time, either intentionally or intuitively. An investor calculates how much money his deployment of capital is likely to generate, on an expected basis, at a point in the future that he chooses. Consumers base their decisions on how much utility (fun, functionality, satisfaction, learning, and so on) they expect to receive for the dollars they spend. Sports team owners want to sign players who will contribute to the most victories for the dollars they are paid. Political candidates consider which techniques to use (advertising, canvassing, polling, and so on) on the basis of what will produce the most votes per dollar spent. Gift givers care about what present the recipient will value the most within the price range.

Yet, there is one significant exception to the rule that ROI guides capital deployment. This is, ironically, the most important use of capital—*tzedaka* or charity, the spending that can directly save lives, ameliorate suffering, and create opportunity. No one would, in his capacity as an investor, put money into a company because lots of others are doing so, because he is moved by the customer testimonials, or because his grandfather invested in the company. In fact, most people who have made significant amounts of money to donate have done so in the opposite way—by marshaling scarce resources to create an opportunity they discovered that was overlooked or dismissed by others.

But lots of givers—even self-made wealthy people, who by definition have accumulated wealth by being so good at ROI—often abandon the ROI mentality and give for the aforementioned reasons, among others. The result is good comedy material for Lucas—but a bad allocation of the most important kind of capital.

* * *

Some philanthropists recognize that they do not use ROI in their allocation decision, but say that it can't be used—or can't be used often. Is this so?

I am the co-founder and chairman of United Hatzalah of Israel—the crowd-sourced system of volunteer first responders that Eli Beer and his colleagues pioneered. United Hatzalah has approximately 7,000 volunteer EMTs and paramedics throughout Israel and responds to about 1,900 calls each day. This enables victims of pre-hospital trauma (heart attacks, strokes, accidents, drowning, choking) to be treated within the precious minutes that may separate life from death.

Our annual budget is approximately $56 million. In 2021, a study of approximately 5.9 million emergency calls from 1,200 jurisdictions appearing in the journal *Prehospital Emergency Care* determined that 6.9 percent of 911 calls qualify as potentially life-saving interventions (PLSI). Assuming a similar number in Israel, we can guess that United Hatzalah responds to around 131 PLSI calls a day, or 47,815 a year. If we assess everything other than PLSI calls at zero dollars, a philanthropic donor can cause a trained, equipped volunteer to be at the side of a victim in a PLSI situation for $1,171.

Of course, most non-PLSI calls should not be valued at zero dollars. Many emergency calls that are not PLSI are also serious—and rapid response is valuable. These include mothers giving birth suddenly, elderly people who have fallen and need to be stabilized before they can move, people with severe abdominal pain, and new parents deeply concerned about an apparent issue with their children.

Other non-PLSI value includes the many non-medical benefits that United Hatzalah provides—from humanitarian services (such as regular quasi-medical visits to lonely Holocaust survivors), international relief (from Ukraine to Puerto Rico) to the bonds that are created among all sectors of society—Jews and Arabs, secular and religious—as a result of volunteers from all backgrounds working together to save people in need.

Such non-PLSI calls, too, have to be valued at some amount—as everything valuable is worth something. This is not hard to do. There is a widely accepted concept in public health of disability-adjusted life years (DALYs), which values providing a year of healthy life at one and everything else at a different fraction of one, depending on the severity of the condition. This can be easily applied to United Hatzalah.

Let's say the *average* value of a non-PLSI call is approximately 15 percent of that of a PLSI call—and includes the social value generated when people of all segments of society build relationships by working together to do something all agree is sacred that is embedded in every call. At 15 percent, United Hatzalah, therefore, responds to the equivalent of 265 additional PLSI calls a day, beyond the 131 actual PLSI calls. In other words: United Hatzalah treats the equivalent of 396 PLSI calls a day—or 144,540 each year. With a budget of $56 million, that means that a donor is paying just $422 for a potentially life-saving intervention or its equivalent.

When I have discussed the ROI concept, some people have pointed out that it works especially well with United Hatzalah—as the numerator (PLSI) is easy to calculate and put over the denominator of money donated. This statement is generally offered in the context of saying that another organization (typically the one supported by the person making the statement) does very valuable work that just can't be measured.

The remarkably high ROI that United Hatzalah provides is what makes it uniquely great. But its ability to calculate ROI is not what makes it unique. Every organization, whether or not they calculate it, has an ROI that can be ascertained by its management and donors.

Let's take an example of a category where people have told me that ROI can't be used: advocacy. This includes organizations devoted to fighting antisemitism, supporting Israel, increasing tolerance, or ending bigotry. Such organizations deploy a variety of techniques—including educational programming, engaging leaders, conferences, online advertising, trips, issue advocacy, and more.

How would ROI work? It's simple. The denominator for these groups is, as always, the annual budget. The numerator is the number of people who will be influenced multiplied by the depth of commitment. The depth of commitment is an important consideration, as there is a difference between someone whose support for Israel becomes a rooting interest and someone whose support becomes a life mission. There can be approximations and projections in the commitment assessment, just as there are in all kinds of business situations. It is fine, so long as the approximations and projections are rigorously construed and consistently tested.

One such organization is Eagles' Wings. Eagles' Wings identifies young Evangelical pastors with significant churches, large social media followings, and other indicators of leadership and influence. Before engaging with Eagles' Wings, many of these pastors have never met Jews—and relate to Israel as a theoretical place they read about in Bible studies.

Eagles' Wings operates on the premise that the most reliable way to cultivate a love of Israel and the Jewish people is through immersive experience and community. Accordingly, they bring groups of thirty pastors from around the world on a twelve-day trip to Israel. In Israel, pastors go to the City of David, the Western Wall, United Hatzalah headquarters, Tel Aviv, Christian sites in the north and in Jerusalem, Bethlehem, and Masada, as well as a Shabbat dinner at the home of an Israeli.

Following the trip, the pastors participate in the Eagles' Wings community of like-minded pastors who have also made the trip. They take trips for their own church communities to Israel, host Celebrate Israel nights, forge partnerships with local Jewish communities, and speak widely from the pulpit and in the media about Israel and other Jewish concerns and issues.

The ROI is easy to approximate. The denominator is $5,000—the cost of taking a pastor to Israel. The numerator are the tens (and sometimes hundreds) of thousands of people who will be introduced to Israel through the leadership of these pastors. Adding the administrative costs (which are offset by the revenue Eagles' Wings receives for running church trips), the ROI on a person brought to love Israel, Jews, and Judaism through an Eagles' Wings pastor is clear. It costs between approximately seven cents and ninety cents per person influenced—with the variation determined by the following of the pastor.

* * *

Does all of this mean, however, that one's Jewish philanthropic commitments should be determined *solely* by calculating the ROI? No, and the reason is provided in Deuteronomy (15:10), where Moses says that we can make that deal with God, which requires that we give "without a grudging heart"—that is, with enthusiasm.

Why, so long as the right amount of money arrives at an appropriate destination, does the biblical author care that it be given enthusiastically? Because when we are enthusiastic about something, we are likely to do more of it—and, like all emotions, enthusiasm is contagious. But how does such enthusiasm fit together with the rigorous, calculating methodology of ROI? There are two ways.

First: Everyone is excited by, and most are inclined to socialize, a good ROI. This is the case ranging from a stock that trades at an unreasonably low multiple to a sale at the local ice cream parlor. The enthusiasm that we have for ROI for less important uses of capital should surely be extended to donating—where, properly deployed, even a relatively small amount of money can save lives, ameliorate suffering, or create opportunity.

For instance, I am the co-founder and Chairman of African Mission Healthcare, which partners with Christian missionary doctors and hospitals in Africa to provide clinical care, build infrastructure, and do training. One of our major initiatives is our SAFE (Surgical Access for Everyone) program. A donor to the SAFE program can *know* that a contribution of $350 will enable a woman to receive a Caesarian section (where the alternative is death or inconceivable degradation), and a contribution of $880 will enable a child born with a congenital deformity to walk. An investment of just a few hundred dollars can save or transform a life; that is an amazing deal, and cause for the excitement of Deuteronomy 15:10.

Second: Jewish philanthropy has so many different areas where one can achieve a spectacular ROI—making it easy to compound the enthusiasm of achieving ROI by doing so in an area where one is drawn. A seeking and serious Jewish giver will, over time, become exposed to examples from many of these categories and more. It is easy, for reasons that are explicable and mysterious, for a prospective donor to find his passion.

The category to which one is called may not be the category that offers the highest ROI (such as saving a young life). But that's okay. We are commanded in Exodus to be a "kingdom of priests and a holy nation," and a well-functioning kingdom requires excellence in many areas. A Jewish giver can easily fall in love with one or more specific categories—and then use a rigorously constructed ROI methodology to best allocate time and money *within* it.

Once a donor becomes enthusiastic about a category, he can—with rigor, discernment, discipline, and diligence—find an organization that delivers spectacular ROI within it. For instance, there is saving lives (United Hatzalah), strengthening Jewish commitment (Manhattan Jewish Experience and Birthright Israel), building the love for Israel among Christians (Eagles' Wings), Jewish religious education and leadership (Ohr Torah Stone), supporting Jews with special needs (Friendship House), partnering with Christians to support Jews in need (International Fellowship of Christians and Jews), and many more.

***

If the benefits of ROI giving seem so obvious, why do many donors not act accordingly? There are always alternatives to one way of doing something—and here there are at least four. The first is that of Lucas's hypothetical bar mitzvah boys. Donors contribute in accordance with what they like more than what recipients need. Josh likes guitar, Benjamin likes skateboarding—and the adults in their environment may like music, art, memories of glory days, or status.

The second, and often related, alternative to ROI is charity as a *consumption good*. The donation to the synagogue one attends, the private school where one's child studies, the park where one takes a daily walk, the place one is stimulated by lectures, or the museum where one enjoys art might qualify for a charitable tax deduction. These are all important places that need money to function. And it is certainly admirable to voluntarily contribute to a public good that one privately enjoys. But there won't be philanthropic ROI, because these gifts are not really philanthropy. They are shared consumption goods with tax-deductible status.

The third is that of a donor who relies on brand names. These are the famous organizations, many of which have been around since before the founding of Israel. Brands work the same in tzedaka as they do in the economy.

In the best case, they provide a signaling function that connotes reliability, consistency, quality, and therefore, buyability—setting a return floor on the investment. However, we know from the discipline of the commercial market just how fragile brands are—and how, to maintain their value, they need continually to earn the trust, loyalty, and affection of customers.

Every company in the Fortune 500 had an outstanding brand at the time of its listing. Yet, only 10 percent of the companies in the 1955 Fortune 500 list are still there now. Thus, the donor to a charity with a known brand will have to decide whether he is donating to the equivalent of Pepsi and Pfizer—or of Blackberry and Blockbuster.

The final category is what we may call negative ROI. The organization is in fact doing more harm than good. A donor might want to go on a "service trip" to a foreign country to clean or paint at a hospital—when the doctors on the ground would all say that these trips take a lot of time to plan and accommodate, they have plenty of painters and cleaners locally, and they could really use the cash he spent on the trip to buy medical equipment or to train a nurse anesthetist. A donor might contribute clothing to the poor in a foreign country, and inadvertently degrade the country's otherwise high-employment and tax-generative textile industry. A donor might contribute to his alma mater with a DEI apparatus that encourages students to get offended, see themselves as victims, perceive classmates as oppressors and promote intersectionality—with inevitable antisemitic ramifications. A donor might give to a "Jewish" organization with a benign-sounding name that slanders Israel in public forums.

All four alternatives to ROI giving (and the real thing) have one thing in common. They likely will be wrapped in the same language, and illustrated with stories, of how the donor's "generosity" is transformative, extraordinary, and life-changing for so many people. It may be true. However, the donor should regard this with the same skepticism that he would regard any marketing, and rigorously investigate the ROI in that and other organizations before making a commitment.

Of course, the opportunity to consider the deployment of charitable dollars with the same ROI mindset that we do with investment dollars extends beyond Jewish giving. For instance, there are 45,000 veterans' charities in the United States—and any ROI mindset (or economic logic) would lead to consolidation. I was discussing with a Jewish philanthropist how businesses merge all the time (creating an enhanced ROI for their shareholders) while non-profits rarely do. He said that he was talking with a gentile friend of his, who is one of the country's leading transactional attorneys. The attorney said to him that his toughest "deal" was negotiating the merger of two non-profits—which ultimately, and for no good reason, failed.

But as Jews, we are given the awesome gift of the Torah—and its fundamental teaching about the importance and opportunity of giving well. We can be the "light unto the nations" that the Prophet Isaiah dreamed of for us when it comes to giving. We just need to start by cutting right to the source of truth—the numerator and the denominator that determine ROI—and enjoy the enthusiasm that the Bible rightly tells us accompanies good giving.

18

WE ARE ALL REFUGEES

Jewish Lessons for a World on the Move

ROYA HAKAKIAN

THERE IS A LOT IN COMMON between a birth and a forced departure from one's homeland. Both are journeys from a familiar place of comfort to a cold, blinding abyss into which the newborn and the newly-expelled pour pain and tears. This unchosen space—terrifying, disorienting—betrays all the senses. The ear cannot make out what it hears, if it hears at all. The eye, if it sees, cannot decipher the meaning of what it sees. And no scent, touch, or taste measures up to those of the past.

Roya Hakakian is the author of a selected volume of poetry in Persian, *For the Sake of Water*, and three books of nonfiction in English, including the acclaimed *Journey from the Land of No: A Girlhood Caught in Revolutionary Iran* (Crown, 2005) and, most recently, *A Beginner's Guide to America: For the Immigrant and the Curious* (Knopf, 2021).

It is lucky that we forget our births. But the same cannot be said of our departures. Of those who experience them, some try to forget while others can do nothing but relive them. When they reach a new land, much of what these immigrants eventually become will depend on how they choose to look upon this past. So, too, much of how they choose to redefine themselves, or whether they endure as a people, will also depend on how they reconcile with the memory of that departure. It is a trial of leviathan magnitude through which Jews have gone time and time again, not unscathed but intact.

This experience, which has been quintessentially a Jewish experience, will become far more common in the next few decades. Climate change is expected to uproot nearly one-third of the world's population. The pending crisis—and especially how to cope with its fallout—will offer the opportunity to history's primordial refugees to guide future refugees on how to cross into a new land while remaining rooted in the values of their past. In this way, the two communities can engage in a new context and in a shared place—that is, in landlessness.

* * *

I know of the abyss. I entered it in 1984, and by 1985, it had disgorged me in America. The passage, originating in Iran, led to a year-long stay in several cities in Europe, an interlude that bore no resemblance to the Europe of tourism ads. We lived stacked together, a dozen or so women, in a tiny two-bedroom flat. The only reprieve I found from that chaos was at the standing section of the Vienna Opera House on weeknights, for ten shillings a performance. My ultimate destination, the Hasidic enclave of Brooklyn's Borough Park, was also far short of any immigrant's dream of America.

My disillusionment was compounded by the quintessential fury and melancholy of most teens, though mine were somewhat more warranted than most. My brothers, who had resettled in the area along with several other Iranian Jewish families, could hardly comfort me as they were still reeling from their own displacement. Rather than adapting to America, they seemed to be dissolving themselves in it. They had adopted the religious practices of the local community, which required far more devotion and rigor than the Judaism they had previously exercised. Perhaps the discipline of orthodoxy filled some of the void that exile had left behind. Or perhaps they were trying to resolve their now-ambivalent feelings about Iran and Iranianness by fervently embracing their Jewish identities. Whatever the reason, it imbued them with enough self-righteousness to allow themselves to instruct *me*—the girl who had just fled the mandatory hijab laws—to not wear pants or sleeveless dresses, to which I unhesitatingly said, "So why did we leave Iran at all?"

"Forget Iran!" I heard at every turn. But as unsettled and disoriented as I was, I knew that I could not do two things: I could not be the Jew they wished me to be, nor could I forget Iran. Soon I moved away to live on my own as a self-inflicted outcast. And since my critics, who thought me an inadequate Jew, had somehow convinced me that they were the custodians of Judaism, I felt like an outcast from Judaism, too.

* * *

Certain scenes—an exceptional dogwood in the neighbor's yard, a street musician at the entrance of the supermarket—occur and reoccur, yet we pass them by, looking but not seeing. Wisdom, too, can be within our reach but go untouched. Some twenty years after that jarring American beginning, the publication of my first book in English—a memoir of coming of age in revolutionary Iran—took me on a tour that also included countless synagogues and Jewish community centers throughout the United States. On many occasions, I would have to sit through Shabbat services prior to my talk, listening to the scripture I had not heard in many years. Then one day, hearing the words I had heard so many times before, I felt a stir within: *zecher litziyat mitzrayim*— "Remember the exodus from Egypt."

Nothing about any prayer had ever touched me in the past. It had simply been synagogue noise to me before. But now that I was in its presence after so long, I was hearing it afresh. Those three words, in particular, seemed to be addressing me. Again and again, they appeared with a stubborn insistence that was reminiscent of my own. They were repeated with a certain compulsion, at times irrelevant to whatever other lines that had come before or after. *Remember your departure!* Departure overshadowed the other words now to make the origin of the departure, Egypt, nearly irrelevant. This command to remember rang far more as an invitation into the abyss. And I thought that perhaps by having narrated the tale of my own exodus, I had, in fact, followed that command. Through writing, the printed form of remembering, I had obeyed. And the act had returned me to the community I had left and placed me among those who had kept their covenant to remember. So devoted had they been—the stubborn members of the most ancient book club—to this divine task that they read the same book over and over again for centuries. Even the course of their worship was choreographed around the Book, the record of their past. During every service, the congregants rose to their feet when the Book came into view. They reverently passed the Book to that day's honoree whose privilege it was to carry it, press it to his chest tightly as if it were a living thing made of flesh and blood. The honoree circled the sanctuary, while others reached to kiss the Book. Someone lifted the Book, like boastful champions holding up a prize, and turned in every direction, then marched a proud march to an ornate arc, dressed the bejeweled Book in elegant fabric and shelved it for the coming week.

There I was, not *the* writer, but *a* writer among book-worshiping people. I had written of my exodus, as those ancient writers had written of that original. I had remembered my departure from my Egypt. Therefore, I was a Jew.

***

It is counterintuitive, and yet, remembering is, in fact, a way out of the abyss. It acknowledges the loss, which is the first step to making peace with the past. Remembering leads out of the abyss because it grants one the chance to "return," albeit only in the mind, to the moment when one had been denied the right to stay.

There is only one way to be exiled from a country, but a hundred ways to return and replant oneself in it—through literature, art, and music, as so many displaced Jewish artists, writers, and intellectuals have done throughout history. So, too, one can return through recounting and recording the individual tales of one's departures.

To pen one's exodus story is to shape history according to one's will. The pain of exile is always compounded by the fact that those who drove one out become the tellers of the history of the events that led to that departure. We, who have fled authoritarian regimes, know well how history, like every other aspect of life and culture, comes under assault by the tyrants who must deface, reform, and rehabilitate all things to suit the needs of their own narrative. For the authoritarian, the only form of historiography is a twisted form of a Greek narrative. It is always the account of a bleak time under a formidable evil, which a hero—the Leader—battled against and conquered. The authoritarian is incapable of telling the stories of the non-heroic, ordinary people—of those whom he could not tolerate, and thus, were forced to flee—of the exiles. On the other hand, Jews, the ancient escapees, have had to be the historiographers of ordinary and powerless people, or else large swaths of their history would have vanished.

If fleeing has a conceptual antithesis, it is writing. Writing is the undoing of a hasty escape: It is to tether oneself in the record, to an account, so that one can be known, seen, and heard. It is to upend everything that the authoritarian leader wishes to do. It empowers the very people whom he had to keep insignificant in order to rule them. It is to give voice to those whom he expelled and entered an unknown land over which they have no mastery. It is in writing that one lays claim to the past, the first step to belonging.

In telling the story of the past, we tell of what we saw. But in how we tell it, we tell the story of who we are. To remember—accurately, truthfully, is to post a "You Are Here" sign inside the labyrinthine edifice that exile is. If lost, one can always return to one's origin to find a way forward. To remember is not all about the past. It is, more importantly, a way to create a blueprint for future generations.

The Bible is, among other things, a catalogue of the many divine miracles that God performed to save His chosen people from lethal dangers. But surviving is not enough to carry a nation for more than 3,000 years. It has been through the act of remembering that Jews have performed the other essential, albeit mortal, miracle that has made it possible to endure, and thrive. At our New Years, when there is every reason to look to the future, drink, and be merry, we turn solemn to reflect upon the bygone year. We review our conduct and resolve to do better. To not be afraid to look back is to stare into loss and failure. A grim exercise, yet how else can one redeem oneself?

The greatest experience of loss in Jewish history occurred in 70 C.E. After the fall of the Second Temple, the Jewish tradition had every reason to disappear. But rather than turn away from it, the people stared into the ruin to find a way out of it. In thinking about how to rebuild, the notion of a divine experience so overshadowed the rest that the place of that experience became irrelevant. Thus, a new way of worship came into being. When we could no longer go to the High Priest or offer sacrifices, we educated ourselves, addressed God on our own, and let prayer be our sacrifice. We adjusted all of our practices and tradition to the new reality of our homelessness. We understood that we must claim the abyss to get through the abyss.

As we scattered around the world, we had to reconcile with the notion that each one of our communities would make a history separate from the rest. Our lives separated, our experiences diverged, and, inevitably, our narratives multiplied. Yet, despite all the variations, we remained one people. We chose to be bonded not in the sameness of our stories. Insisting on uniformity would have been impossible under the circumstances. It would have also been against the spirit of a tradition that has always fostered debate and viewed opposing opinions not as a threat but an opportunity for reflection and growth. Ultimately, it is not in the sameness of our stories that we have remained one people, but in the experience of shared brokenness, of our common ruptures.

In one of the many Jewish community centers where I was a guest speaker, the child of a Holocaust survivor once commented, after my talk, that my family, Jews of Iran, had, in fact, been driven out of our homeland just as the Jews of Europe had been driven out of Europe during World War II. It pained me to object to her, knowing that it was the affection she felt for me and for what she had heard that she was mistaking for kinship. But I did object. I said that we had left not because Iran turned on its Jews as Europe did during the war. We left because Iran turned on itself. Jews were not the chief targets in post-revolutionary Iran. Indeed, secular Muslim Iranians faced a far greater threat than Jews ever did. Iran ceased to be home to most of its citizens, except for observing Shiite Muslims. Everyone who could leave, did. Religious minorities, including the Jews, who, according to the new post-revolutionary constitution, were no longer equal citizens, had an easier time applying for asylum. I told her, no, the cause of our departures was not the same, nor do we need to streamline our narratives to feel connected. Our ancient tradition would not have endured as long as it has if it could not afford the variety of the narratives of all its separate communities. We do not need to edit our histories or tweak our narratives to fit an overarching script. We remain a people, in part, because no matter the causes, we all have and continue to cross borders.

The secret of our survival as one people will become more staggering as future generations cross borders into new lands in search of habitable lands. The future refugees of the world will wonder how they can retain their identities in the face of the loss of their homelands. That is when our values and commitments will become scrutinized, and possibly embraced.

It is we who can show that their rupture from their homelands does not need to destroy them as a people; rather, it may be an opportunity to reconfigure their traditions to adapt to the new circumstances. When the world struggles with displacement, we have the opportunity to guide the bereft to rise from the ruins and to build a more reliable home in the mind. We will then become the chosen people once more, chosen to help another generation through their abyss and see them through their painful births.

19

HOW TO FIX "TIKKUN OLAM"

Why Judaism Can't Be Reduced to Universalist Activism

AMMIEL HIRSCH

THE PHRASE "TIKKUN OLAM," or repairing the world, first appears in the Mishna as a halachic device to protect weaker parties from unduly harsh outcomes. For example, Rabbi Gamaliel instituted a change in how divorce decrees were written, thereby preserving a divorced woman's ability to remarry, *mipnai tikkun olam*—for the sake of repairing the world (Gittin 34b).

In our times, "Tikkun Olam" has assumed much larger dimensions. What began as a legal concept to protect vulnerable individual Jews has come to mean

Rabbi Ammiel Hirsch is the senior rabbi at Stephen Wise Free Synagogue, a Reform congregation on New York's Upper West Side, and author of *The Lilac Tree: A Rabbi's Reflections on Love, Courage, and History* (Wicked Son, 2023).

the collective Jewish responsibility to repair a broken world. Today, "Tikkun Olam" describes the Jewish obligation to improve society, with particular emphasis on the disadvantaged. It is most often employed by liberal Jewish movements to describe our involvement not only in individual cases of hardship but primarily in the effort to craft just policies affecting society-at-large.

The Aleinu prayer, recited daily, offers a contemporary theological framework:

> It is our duty to praise the Master of all… *l'taken olam b'malchut Shaddai*, to repair the world under the sovereignty of God.

Our present-day understanding of "Tikkun Olam" captures the essence of collective Jewish morality: the sanctity of life, the dignity of every human being, protecting the weak, social responsibility, peace, freedom, justice, righteousness, compassion, and mercy. Judaism is an activist faith, a philosophy of discontent with what is, in comparison to what should and could be. We are partners with God in the unfinished work of Creation and thus required to act on behalf of others:

> Whoever is able to protest the wrongful conduct of members of his household and does not, is punished for the wrongs of the members of his household. If he is in a position to protest the wrongful conduct of the people of his town and does not, he is punished for the wrongs of the people of his town. If he is in a position to protest the wrongful conduct of the whole world and does not, he is punished for the wrongs of the world. (Shabbat 54b)

Jews are obligated to care about, advocate for, and protect all people, not only Jews, because we are in fellowship with all human beings. "I have grasped you by the hand… and appointed you a covenant people, a light of nations, opening eyes deprived of light" (Isaiah 42:6–7). Thus, God compelled a reluctant Jonah to go to the non-Jewish city of Nineveh and preach the message of repentance and social repair. The urgency of universal justice compels Abraham to challenge

God's intention to destroy the non-Jewish cities of Sodom and Gomorrah: "I have selected Abraham to do what is just and right" (Genesis 18:19).

To the extent that "Tikkun Olam" describes our collective Jewish efforts to do what is just and right, it presents Jews and Judaism in the best possible light. Who can be opposed to Jews seeking justice for all humanity? We should be proud of our prominence in social causes. The term has become so familiar that it is regularly used by non-Jews to describe collective responsibility, especially from those who are well-off toward those who are not.

However, "Tikkun Olam", like every other value, is not absolute and does not exist in a vacuum. It must be weighed against other Jewish values. The universalism of "Tikkun Olam" must be balanced with the particularism of *klal yisrael*—Jewish peoplehood. *Ahavat habriyot*—love of humankind—must be balanced with *ahavat yisrael*—love for the Jewish people. It is not one or the other. It is both. The uniqueness of Judaism and the source of its moral power are in our commitment to the Jewish family and all the families of the earth at one and the same time. The Aleinu prayer speaks not only of "Tikkun Olam" but also of Jewish distinctiveness: "Who has not made us like other nations, and did not place us as the [other] families of the earth."

Jews who shelter behind walls of self-absorption, who want only to be left alone, who care nothing for the problems of the world, truncate and distort Judaism no less than do Jews who care only about universal matters, expressing no concerns for the needs of our own people. Since I am a Reform rabbi and a liberal, I will leave it to others to analyze all of the many inadequacies of other Jewish movements, and will focus on the challenges within liberal Judaism, constituting the vast majority of American Jews.

***

American Jewish liberals have a history of discounting and rejecting Jewish peoplehood. The Reform movement was born in full, enthusiastic, and even messianic embrace of the Enlightenment. "We recognize in the modern era of universal culture…" the movement declared in its 1885 Pittsburgh Platform, "the approaching realization of Israel's great Messianic hope for the establishment of the kingdom of truth, justice, and peace among all men…." From the perspective of nineteenth-century Jewish liberals, universal values supplanted national identity. "We consider ourselves no longer a nation," the declaration continued, "but a religious community."

Twelve years later, when Theodor Herzl launched the Zionist movement in Basel, Switzerland, he placed Jewish peoplehood at the center of Judaism. "We are a people—one people," he wrote in his 1896 manifesto *The Jewish State*.

The American Reform movement, however, rejected Zionism—not primarily on the grounds of practicality or feasibility—but because it was "un-Jewish." Reading Zionism into the teaching of the Hebrew prophets constituted "poison instilled in sugar-coated pills," said the then-president of Hebrew Union College, Kaufmann Kohler. "It undermines the very foundation of Reform Judaism...it is un-Jewish." The mission of Reform Judaism, said Kohler, was to "transform the national Jew into a religious Jew." He was echoing the words of Rabbi Abraham Geiger, the founding father of the Reform movement in Germany. "The People of Israel no longer lives," said Geiger. "It has been transformed into a community of faith."

"America is our Zion," the Reform congregational arm, the Union of American Hebrew Congregations, similarly resolved in 1898. "Here in the home of religious liberty, we have aided in founding this new Zion.... The mission of Judaism is spiritual, not political. Its aim is...to spread the truths of religion and humanity throughout the world."

Within fifty years, liberal Judaism reversed itself because our faith in the Enlightenment's promise to solve the Jewish problem had been obviously and catastrophically wrong. The twentieth century was saturated with the poison of Jew-hatred and soaked with the blood of Jews. Germany, the Enlightenment's poster child, in many ways the most advanced civilization in the history of the world, destroyed European Jewry.

The 1920 Reform prayer book included this:

By Thy grace, O God, it has also been given to us to see in dispersion over the earth...a sign of blessed privilege. Scattered among the nations of the world, Israel is to bear witness to Thy power and Thy truth. Not backward do we turn our eyes, O Lord, but forward to the promised and certain future.

Twenty years later, this promised and certain future went up in the black smoke of incinerated Jews. None of the nations of the earth that the Jews were "privileged" to be scattered among opened their doors to significant numbers of Jewish refugees. The anti-peoplehood gospel of nineteenth- and early twentieth-century Jewish liberals was bankrupt. Their faith in the "approaching realization of the great Messianic" era of "truth, justice, and peace among all men," was a calamity—such a fine statement on what human beings could be like, if only they weren't human.

They were also wrong about Judaism. They—not the Zionists—had been expressing un-Jewish views.

At no time in Jewish history was separation from the Land of Israel considered permanent. We never abandoned the dream of return, and never considered dispersion a blessing. At no time did the Hebrew prophets forsake Jewish peoplehood in pursuance of universal values. To the contrary, universal aspirations emerged from, and were a result of, Jewish particularism, a function of Jewish peoplehood, not its negation. To contend that the Hebrew prophets only cared about repairing the world, and not about the well-being of the Jewish people, is to misunderstand and disfigure the entire prophetic tradition. All of the Hebrew prophets were of the Jewish people, by the Jewish people, and for the Jewish people.

"Tikkun Olam" ripped from the moorings of Jewish peoplehood is not Jewish universalism; it is just universalism. Hosea was not Hegel. Micah was not Mill. Jeremiah was not John Locke. At no time did the rabbis sever the Torah from Israel, or God from the people. As Rabbi Abraham Joshua Heschel put it in *God in Search of Man*: "For us Jews there can be no fellowship with God without the fellowship with the people Israel. Abandoning Israel, we desert God."

Judaism absent Jewish peoplehood is not Judaism; it is something else. Whenever Jews abandoned their ideological—or practical—commitment to *am yisrael*, they eventually drifted away. This was precisely the accusation leveled by Reform Zionist Rabbi Abba Hillel Silver toward his anti-Zionist colleagues in the pre-war years. By continuing to insist that the Jews are "no longer a nation, but a religious community," Silver contended that Reform rabbis were reconstituting "Paul's insistence upon a religious creed entirely divorced from nation and land." In a scathing critique, he noted that this declaration of Reform rabbis "was the first of its kind ever made by an assembly of Jewish religious leaders," implying that had the Reform movement continued down this path, we, too, like the early Christians, would have eventually drifted away from Jewish civilization.

***

This anti-peoplehood spirit still lives in liberal Judaism. It retreated for three generations because of the immense traumas inflicted on our people in the twentieth century. But two generations of American Jews have now grown up with no personal connection to past Jewish catastrophes and perceive no existential threats against our people. Unlike the American Jews who lived through the Holocaust, Israel's founding, the Six-Day War, and the Yom Kippur War, and the struggle to free Soviet Jewry, many younger progressive Jews who were not even born the last time Israel fought a full-scale war consider Israel the neighborhood bully oppressing an indigenous minority, not a beleaguered remnant of persecuted Jews facing down daily threats of extermination. They look at the Jewish world, and they see what their nineteenth-century ideological forebears saw: Jews protected and prospering. The uptick in antisemitism in the United States hardly dents their confidence. They feel safe and secure, eager to join fellow progressives in rectifying the wrongs of the world.

Thus, while the majority of American Jews, including liberals, are still strongly supportive of Israel and identify with the collective aspirations of the Jewish people, some younger progressive Jews are returning to their nineteenth-century ideological roots: acute sensitivity to universal justice, a mistrust of power and the use of force, and a defiant impatience to break with the past.

But there are newer, more radical ideological overlays to twenty-first-century Jewish progressivism. The hard Left now believes that universal values have not only supplanted national identity but that Jewish national identity itself is morally defective. To them, Jewish peoplehood means whiteness, privilege, injustice, chauvinism, and racism—part of the oppressive power structure that subjugates and exploits racial minorities and indigenous peoples. Moreover, unlike nineteenth-century Reform Jews who were American nationalists—they loved this country so passionately that for them it was the "New Zion"—many young progressive Jews today are conflicted not only about America's politics, but its founding principles.

It is unfortunate that the Reform movement does not commission professional surveys to investigate the beliefs and practices of our rabbinical students, rabbis, and lay members of Reform synagogues. Non-Jewish organizations like the Pew Research Center, and some Jewish organizations such as the American Jewish Committee, commission periodic surveys of American Jews. But since we do not investigate ourselves, we can rely only on circumstantial and experiential evidence, along with whatever information we can glean from the surveys of other organizations.

All these point to a worrying and dangerous trend that, if not blunted, will wreak havoc on American Judaism. Those inside the movement who interact with Reform rabbis, seminary students, and Jewish professionals in other progressive Jewish organizations recognize the dimensions of our problems.

The intensity of our commitment to klal yisrael is weakening, replaced by a relentless single-minded focus on "Tikkun Olam." We are so preoccupied with the mission and rhetoric of Jewish universalism that our commitment to Jewish peoplehood can barely be heard beyond a whisper. When we do still engage in the business of the Jewish people, our tone is often so critical or angry as to drown out any sentiments of ahavat yisrael contained within. The problem is not that we speak the language of Jewish universalism, but that it seems to be all we speak about. The problem is not that we care about the conditions of the Palestinians, but that we seem to care little about the safety of Israeli Jews.

Our movement has joined coalitions with other social justice organizations whose leadership is anti-Zionist and even antisemitic.

We are ordaining non-Zionist and even anti-Zionist rabbis. I have spoken with rabbinical students who tell me that to voice positive sentiments about Israel is to invite angry opprobrium from the student body, with little support from the faculty. These are not mere differences of opinion on Israeli policies, but a discomfort with, and at times, a wholesale rejection of, the very idea of a Jewish state. The issue for anti-Zionist progressives is not only Israeli behavior but its very existence. Reform rabbis' social networks are filled with angry and intolerant voices condemning and intimidating those who express pro-Israel opinions. But it is not only Israel; there is a general turning away from liberal principles. Paralleling the growing influence of the American hard Left, Reform rabbis report a growing intolerance of diverse opinions within the movement—an oppressive expectation to conform that stifles debate and free speech, the beating heart of liberalism.

Jewish peoplehood speaks the language, not only of peace, but of Jewish solidarity, responsibility, identity, and mutuality. Many Reform rabbis do not even bother to preach about Israel or Jewish solidarity anymore. It is too controversial and costly. They quote Micah's inspirational vision of "beating swords into plowshares and spears into pruning hooks" (Micah 4:3), but not his final words: "You will keep faith with Jacob, loyalty to Abraham, as You promised on oath to our fathers in days gone by" (Micah 7:20). They quote the soaring words of Amos: "Let justice roll down like water and righteousness as a mighty stream" (Amos 5:24), but not the centerpiece of his worldview: "I will restore My people Israel. They shall rebuild ruined cities and inhabit them, they shall plant their vineyards and drink their wine…. I will plant them upon their own soil, nevermore to be uprooted from the soil I have given them" (Amos 9:14–15).

The spirit of this new progressivism was expressed by Jewish author Michael Chabon in his keynote address at the 2018 commencement ceremonies of the Hebrew Union College—Jewish Institute of Religion (HUC–JIR) Los Angeles campus. To enthusiastic applause from students—the future leaders of American Jewry—and no effective response from the national HUC–JIR leadership, Chabon characterized Judaism as a "philosophy of separating people, like every other religion." "Judaism is one giant interlocking system of division," he said. "We are not those people over there."

To students who were accepted to HUC–JIR under a policy that if they are living with a partner, that partner must be Jewish, Chabon said:

> An endogamous marriage is a ghetto of two…. I want [my children] to marry into the tribe that prizes learning, inquiry, skepticism, openness to new ideas. I want my children to marry into the tribe that enshrines equality before the law and freedom of conscience and

human rights.... There will be plenty of potential partners for my children to choose—a fair number [of whom] are even likely to be Jews.

My guess is that sometime within the next generation or two, the fever will subside. Future generations will regard our era much like we regard the era of the anti-Zionist, anti-peoplehood Reform Jews of the nineteenth to mid-twentieth centuries. They embarked on a half-century odyssey to discover foreign lands, but pressure from within, and the calamities endured by our people from without, brought them home. It took fifty years, but eventually the Reform movement reunited with, and remarried, the Jewish people.

It will not take that long this time around. Unlike the nineteenth century, there is a Jewish state that is the center of world Jewry and growing more influential by the year. Israel will flourish with or without progressive American Jews. It is progressive American Jews who need Israel. The Jewish people will prevail with or without anti-peoplehood Jews. It is anti-peoplehood Jews who need the Jewish people, as our own movement discovered last century.

The future of Judaism in the twenty-first century is Jewish peoplehood, and all those who abandon Jewish peoplehood will be as leaves falling from the tree. For in the end, what are the prospects of the continuity of the people, if the people are not committed to their own distinctive continuity, and does not even agree philosophically that it is a legitimate objective and a social good? Is it possible to sustain the Jewish people without being committed to the Jewish people? Can Judaism exist without Jews?

While fifty years from now there may be fewer American Jews, most of those who remain will likely be fully committed, philosophically and practically, to the Jewish people and the Jewish state. Otherwise, their Jewishness would not have withstood those fifty years. In twenty-first-century America, where assimilatory pressures are as strong as they have ever been, those who are not committed to Jewish survival will not survive as Jews.

The will to Jewish distinctiveness ensures Jewish distinctiveness. The will to continue leads to continuity. There is a ferocity to Jewish survival instincts, an indomitable sense of Jewish destiny, as old as Judaism, itself.

This spirit will remain among the remaining Jews.

20

PRAISE THE LIVING JEWS

An Alternative to Holocaust Education

DARA HORN

IN 2021, after spending twenty years studying and teaching Hebrew and Yiddish literature and publishing five novels that were all deeply embedded in Jewish life and history, I published my first nonfiction book, which was called *People Love Dead Jews: Reports from a Haunted Present*. If you're reading this essay, I probably don't have to explain to you what it was about, because if you're an English-speaking Diaspora Jew, you already know exactly what that title means.

The book, in short, was about how people in non-Jewish societies tell stories about dead Jews that make them feel better about themselves, and

---

Dara Horn is the award-winning author of five novels and the essay collection *People Love Dead Jews: Reports from a Haunted Present* (W.W. Norton, 2021) and a scholar of Hebrew and Yiddish literature.

how living Jews are required, in both subtle and blatant ways, to erase themselves to gain public respect.

The book begins with the illustrative true story of a young Jewish man working at the Anne Frank House in Amsterdam in 2018, who was asked by his employers to hide his yarmulke under a baseball cap. This was the same museum where, a year earlier, the international audio guide display had listed Hebrew, alone among its audioguide offerings, without a national flag. It was apparently on-brand for the Anne Frank House to send Jews into hiding. You see, the museum wanted to teach its millions of mainly non-Jewish visitors about the Jews' humanity—the humanity of the nice dead Jews, that is, not the living ones doing gross things like living in Israel or practicing Judaism. In the book, I explored this dynamic in dozens of situations around the world, ranging from the benign maintenance of "Jewish heritage sites" to the rather more malign lethal attacks on American Jews in recent years, along with the media apologetics that accompanied them. As I put it, people love dead Jews. Living Jews, not so much.

Since the book came out, countless readers have asked me to provide a "solution" to this problem. Considering that antisemitism in its various forms has been going on, in a conservative estimate, for twenty centuries, this is a rather big ask. No, dear readers, I have not solved this problem for you. However, over the year I have spent traveling around the country and speaking with readers of every background about this dismal subject, I do now have what may be a very useful suggestion, and one that I would recommend as a priority for the American Jewish community: education about the actual content of Jewish culture, for non-Jews.

I've been thinking seriously about this idea since embarking on a research project, commissioned by a general-interest magazine, about American Holocaust education. The story of how American Holocaust education grew and flourished is a fascinating one that can be told in numerous ways, but the short version is that this communal priority originated in the 1970s, separately and almost simultaneously, with Holocaust survivors and with a group of mostly non-Jewish educators, when various cultural circumstances (ranging from well-publicized American Nazi Party shenanigans and a surge of Holocaust denial to a shift among educators looking for more "affective" learning models) made the topic compelling to a wide audience. Over several decades, people both inside and outside the Jewish community successfully pushed for Holocaust education for a broad public, which took the form of museums, state educational mandates, and organizations that continue to develop and refine school curricula for teachers to use in classrooms, along with extensive training resources and professional development opportunities for educators. At this point, any American public or private school teacher can easily attend a free or low-cost high-quality professional workshop or webinar on how to teach the Holocaust, complete with ready-made lesson plans, on almost any day of the year.

Whether or not this proliferation of resources is "good for the Jews" is a very open question that I have explored elsewhere. But I am raising the subject here because no matter what one may think of American Holocaust education, it is a model of success in getting a non-Jewish public on board with an educational commitment regarding Jewish history.

It is fair to criticize the outsized role Holocaust education has often played over the past four decades within the Jewish community, especially given that, according to reliable national surveys, many American Jews at this point consider "remembering the Holocaust" to be a core aspect of their identity, rather than any actual content of Jewish culture or tradition. But it is disingenuous to point this out without noting that Jews whose only attachment to Judaism comes from "remembering the Holocaust" are typically not people with much, or any, Jewish education at all. It is hardly surprising that their knowledge of Jewish culture consists of the sole thing that non-Jews are taught about Jews, because their Jewish education is the same as that of their non-Jewish peers. Merely lamenting this reality would mean overlooking the possibilities it presents. The fact that non-Jews are now expected or even required to learn about the Holocaust in school demonstrates that it is possible to change the public conversation about Jewish history and identity and to change the baseline about what people outside the organized Jewish community, both Jews and non-Jews, are expected to know.

My suggestion here is to use Holocaust education's paradigm of success by insisting that these same educators also teach people who Jews are.

***

In public events for my book at colleges and universities, students of every background often ask me questions that betray a foundational ignorance about Jewish identity. Are Jews "white"? Aren't Jews supposed to be "religious"? Can someone be "anti-Zionist" without being "antisemitic"? What is "Zionism" anyway? Is fill-in-the-blank-incident "antisemitic"? Occasionally these questions are posed in a hostile way, but I've been surprised to find that usually, they aren't.

I've encountered vastly more ignorance than malice. Many of these non-Jewish students are actually asking about how they can be, in today's parlance, "good allies." But it is difficult to be an ally of any kind when you don't know anything about whom you are allying with—by which I mean, when you literally don't know anything at all about what it means for someone to be Jewish. Often these questions are asked by Jewish students as well. None of these people know what being Jewish means, for one simple reason: No one has ever told them.

At these events, I have found that I need to answer these very basic questions by pointing out that the questions themselves are fundamentally flawed. It is unenlightening, for instance, to apply categories of "race" or "religion" or "ethnicity" or "nationality" to a group of people who pre-date all of those categories. It is also unenlightening to discuss "Zionism" or "antisemitism" with people who are fundamentally unfamiliar with either idea, associating the former only with internet slurs and the latter only with either mass violence (anything short of genocide can apparently be dismissed as a "lone wolf"), or a middle-school-level explanation of "prejudice." ("Don't hate people because they're 'different,' because really they're just like everyone else!"—a lovely sentiment, I suppose, if Jews hadn't spent the last 3,000 years not being like everyone else.)

These questions that I've encountered, even when they are well-intentioned, are a symptom of something that non-Jewish societies have always attempted to do with Jews, which is to put Jews into a box that the non-Jewish society finds familiar, whether that box is "race" or "religion" or "ethnicity" or "nationality" or whatever else makes sense as a category in that society. The problem is that after 3,000 years, Jews invariably pre-date the box. Fortunately, this is not a hard problem to solve if one is willing to put in the effort.

Millions of people across America have now been educated about Nazi ideology, a multifaceted morass that can only be understood after educators introduce many overlapping layers of information, including the impact of propaganda, mob psychology, economic free fall, national shame, scapegoating, conspiracy theories, pseudoscience, and the fragility of democratic institutions. This sort of education has required an enormous amount of time and resources. It would actually be much easier to educate those same people about the impact of monotheism, covenant, commandment, land, conquest, exile, and creative reinvention and institution-building after a catastrophe—that is, to tell the story of how a foundational counterculture ran its way through the history of the West by rooting itself in deep literacy, communal institutions, integrity in the face of outside pressure, and a commitment to a concept of law that transcends individual rulers.

This overview wouldn't need to take up any more time in class or in a museum than Holocaust education does. Its value is obvious on its own terms because despite the small percentage of Jews in the world, Jews are hardly bit players in Western history and culture; Jewish culture is foundational to Western civilization. And like Holocaust education, an education on the absolute basics of Jewish life would surely result in many "universal lessons" that are "applicable to today." How do people preserve a culture in a changing world, and how do they decide when and how to adapt it? What kind of discourse is required for a diverse society that actually allows differences to flourish? What does literacy consist of, beyond decoding words? How do people build institutions—indeed, what *are* institutions, and how are they different from buildings or monuments or communities? What features might make them both robust and flexible enough to endure over generations, and what efforts might be required to sustain them? How does one create a legal system that doesn't rely on rulers or demagogues? What possibilities for renewal persist after catastrophic events?

This is an opportunity to change the course of Jewish life in America by defusing some of the unspoken antisemitism that often fills the vacuum of ignorance. It is also an opportunity to give Jews outside of organized Jewish communities access to basic information about what it means to be Jewish. But what I find most compelling about this possibility is the opportunity to change the course of life in America in general by introducing clarity to a topic about which millions of people are intensely curious, and by sharing our strengths with our neighbors in a way that people of any background can understand.

* * *

Logistically, Holocaust education is one place to begin this process, if only because the structures for it are already in place—and because Holocaust educators themselves are deeply aware of this deficit in their teaching, and they are eager to correct it. In this approach, lessons about the Holocaust taught in schools or presented in museums would be changed and amplified to begin with basic information about Jewish identity, culture, and life. This is already happening, though in a limited way, across the newer Holocaust education resources I have investigated. Many such curricula now include a new emphasis on pre-war Jewish life, and newer museum exhibitions sometimes include introductory material that begins as far back as the Hebrew Bible. There is also a push among Holocaust educators to include pre-war material tied more deeply to the actual content of Jewish life—showcasing religious or Yiddish-speaking Jewish life, for instance, or explaining the rhythms of the Jewish year, rather than simply exhibiting victims who are "just like everyone else."

Teaching this material as part of Holocaust education, however, would only be a starting point. To do this in a meaningful way, it would be necessary to introduce this material separately from a Holocaust context. A few appropriate places to do so would be in courses covering ancient civilizations, human geography, world history, and world cultures, as well as in American history—in the same way that groups like the Quakers and Puritans and various Native American nations are introduced and described to students. This isn't a particularly big lift, to be honest. All I'm suggesting is that students should encounter Jews in their social studies textbooks somewhere outside of a mass grave.

The deep reluctance of the Jewish community to teach this material to a broader public can be traced back to insecurity among American Jews, some of which is quite warranted. More than a little of that insecurity is due to a profound illiteracy among American Jews, which is a result of an earlier generation's successful assimilation, alongside the deeply internalized anti-semitism that motivated that assimilation.

Somehow, people managed to overcome these profound and usually unspoken fears to teach the public about the Holocaust. It's unfortunately true that the Holocaust story conformed to non-Jewish society's pre-existing ideas about Jews as people who ought to be powerless, which undoubtedly contributed to this subject's unconscious appeal. However, I have found that when I have challenged this attitude among non-Jews, people are surprisingly receptive to moving past it. It's far past time to overcome our insecurities and teach the wider world about the broader story of the Jewish past and present.

* * *

Some readers may ask: But is now really the time to propose this idea, in our wildly polarized America? The answer is yes, *because* of our wildly polarized America.

Various circumstances led to the public buy-in on American Holocaust education in the 1970s and 1980s, some of which were directly contradictory. For instance, the need to confront Holocaust denial required a focus on what educators call "cognitive learning," or straight-up information. But the "affective learning" movement that piqued many educators' interests in the subject of the Holocaust was all about shifting the educational focus away from information-dumping in favor of tapping into students' emotional lives. This obvious contradiction in motives did not hinder the introduction of Holocaust education; if anything, it provided educators with even more motivations for introducing this material, making it all the more urgent.

Circumstances in today's polarized American cultural climate are similarly ripe for a new introduction of Jewish cultural information to the public, for similarly contradictory reasons.

In politically progressive settings, the push for reevaluating history and social studies education to make it more inclusive of minority experiences provides an obvious opening for teaching about Jewish culture, for educators hoping to demonstrate their commitment to "diversity." In politically conservative settings, the push against these progressive ideas and in favor of more traditional approaches provides an equally obvious opening for teaching about Jewish culture, for educators hoping to demonstrate their commitment to "traditional values."

American Jews on either side of the partisan divide will object, with ample justification, that educators on the other side have been poisoned by their side's brand of antisemitism and will therefore be inhospitable to the possibility of including Jewish culture in their educational agendas. I would have thought this, too, if I were basing my judgments on what the internet was telling me, rather than on meeting people around the country and talking through this subject with them. I will at this point remind readers of what I have encountered in my extensive travels around the country speaking with people about the role of Jews in a non-Jewish society, not only with the college students I mentioned earlier, but also with educators at every level, including teachers, museum professionals, curriculum writers, and people who train teachers: There is far more ignorance out there than malice.

The people on the ground in these settings, despite the overhyped stupidity amplified by the algorithms in your pocket, are largely operating in good faith and are very eager to do the right thing by their students and by the broader public they are educating—the "right thing" being to open people's minds to new ideas. People who choose to work in the highly challenging, poorly compensated, and profoundly underappreciated field of education are doing so because they are deeply committed to the idea that it is possible for people to change. We should be, too.

Education is always motivated by idealism. Some of that idealism will inevitably fail. But the only way to guarantee its failure is to never try. As I've learned in the past year, people really do love dead Jews. I think it's worth the risk of introducing them to living ones.

21

THE KEY TO CONTINUITY

How to Forge New Links Across Generations

LAURA JANNER-KLAUSNER & ALLY GOLDBERG

WE JEWS ARE LIKE A FAMILY, where children react very differently to the same parents depending on their birth order and whatever the family may have gone through when they were young.

Ours is the family of Jewish generations. Our debate here, about Jewish families and Jewish generations, is happening between the two of us: Laura, a British-Israeli sixty-year-old rabbi, and Ally, a British writer in her twenties.

Rabbi Laura Janner-Klausner is the former senior rabbi to Reform Judaism in Britain and the rabbi of Bromley Reform Synagogue. She is an executive coach working particularly with male CEOs.
Ally Goldberg is a freelance writer and passionate advocate for the Jewish community whose work has been in many Jewish publications including *Kveller*, *Times of Israel*, and *The Jewish Chronicle*.

The two of us agree that there is a palpable rift between the Baby Boomers (born 1946–1964) and their successors, Generation X and Millennials (born approximately 1965–1996). They have both seen how the media is constantly telling us about the tension between these two groups—whether using the phrase "boomer humor" to describe something deeply unfunny, or "Millennial" becoming synonymous with an obsession with smartphones and avocado toast.

Jewish intergenerational debates now often focus on the meaning of the Holocaust, of Zionism and post-Zionism, of interfaith or inter-heritage marriage, of the use and abuse of language and whether any boundaries are helpful at all.

Let's start with the "oldest child." Is it true that Jewish Boomers are like firstborns, realistic and duty-bound, overly responsible and often bossy? As the first generation after the Holocaust, they were in some way tasked, if not explicitly then at least psychologically and emotionally, with rebuilding the Jewish world. Many felt duty-bound to "marry in," to have Jewish children and to teach them in the same way they were taught by their parents.

The second child might be seen as suffering from "middle child syndrome." Maybe they tend to be rebellious and anti-authoritarian. This is Generation X, the age group characterized by being left alone much more than the previous generations. They are known as the latchkey generation, because of how often they had to let themselves into an empty home. Like the middle child, they might be perceived as cynical and lazy, when this behavior might stem from disillusionment. In their dissatisfaction, they reject the duties and traditions that their predecessors embraced and seek to forge new paths, which appear to those older than them to be simply a cry for attention and a childish desire to be different. This manifested in a number of ways in Judaism—first with a wave of feminist reform. The 1970s saw the first female rabbi, and the 1990s witnessed the birth of the Jewish Orthodox Feminist Alliance. This period was also the beginning of acceptance for LGBTQ+ Jews.

Some might see the youngest child as self-centered and spoiled. This is often the perception that Boomers and Gen Xers have of Millennials. For this reason, Millennials have earned the nickname "Generation Me." Having grown up in a time characterized by higher rates of education, easier access to technology, and a generally more liberal view of their duties, many believe that Millennials have it easy. They are seen as childish and impractical, but it can also be said, in their defense, that they simply hold different priorities than previous generations did. Millennials are much less interested in financial success and tend to focus their energy on societal change. They talk openly about mental health, which is something that the Boomers were never taught about and did not discuss. These conversations are often seen as reflecting self-absorption and obsession with their own problems, but Millennials have a level of self-awareness that, arguably, has never been held by any generation before them.

So how do these different generations of Jews, whose perceptions and life experiences are so very different, talk together? We (Laura, who is on the cusp between Boomer and Gen X, and Ally, who is on the cusp between Millennial and Gen Z) have been talking about these differences for a few years. It turns out that many of them result from our understanding of Judaism and what it means to us.

* * *

Ally's Judaism is about questions. Brought up in a Liberal household, she was taught to question everything, from the contents of each *parasha* of the Torah all the way to even her belief in religion. She questioned the concepts that were held dear to the people around her, one of the main ones being the idea of "marrying in." She once asked her mother what had made her want to marry a Jewish man, to which her mother responded: "I feel that if I ended up with a non-Jew, I would be finishing the job that Hitler started."

She discovered that this is a view shared by many Jewish people. Emil Fackenheim, the Canadian Jewish philosopher, said that after the Holocaust there were 614 commandments, instead of 613. The additional commandment was to not give Hitler a posthumous victory by assimilating and marrying out. Ally was confused by this because, while her mother and grandparents had not married out, they had definitely assimilated. Like most Ashkenazi Jewish families in the Diaspora, they didn't speak Yiddish, they Anglicized their surname, and in some senses, one could say that they minimized much of their Jewishness in order to fit in.

Ally and many other young Jews wonder: Where is the line? Is it purely about marrying out, or is assimilating and rejecting outward signs of Judaism— even as someone who has married another Jew—just as bad?

It is increasingly common, at least in the United Kingdom, for young Jews to revert their Westernized surnames back to what they used to be, to ask to be called by their Hebrew first names, and altogether to reclaim the elements of Judaism that were washed away by mass assimilation. We all may want to preserve Judaism, but the different generations have different ways of going about it. While the Boomers, still reeling from the pain of the Holocaust, were much more concerned with having ethnically Jewish children, many Millennials see the loud, proud representation of Jewish culture as being an equally important part of the path to preservation.

Ally will always share her Judaism with her partner, whether they are Jewish or not, because she loves Jewish culture. So perhaps, even more so than questions, that's what her Judaism is: love.

* * *

Laura's Judaism is about duty, responsibility, and doing the right thing. Mitzvah. She strongly believes that we have a duty as a citizen, as a Jew, to do certain things. But love? Loving being Jewish, yes, loving Israel, very much. But other love, emotional love was secondary. "It doesn't matter what you feel. Tough luck if you don't feel love." The idea of honoring and respecting one's parents, for example. It says that in two different ways in the Ten Commandments, but it does not say love. Our interpretation of honoring our parents is making sure they have clothes, making sure they have food, making sure you don't contradict them in public. It's very practical. And Judaism as a whole feels practical. If you believe in God, great. If you don't, you're still Jewish, and therefore in some ways it doesn't matter what you feel about it. What matters is your behavior.

Laura was introduced to her husband by her aunt—the same person who introduced her parents. One of the reasons that both couples were introduced was because people looked at the externals. "He's left wing, I'm left wing. He's Jewish, I'm Jewish." The two of them were externally similar, and the understanding in much of the Jewish community is that if two people are a good fit, then from that, love will grow. In that case, love is secondary to duty.

Laura believes that while it's a beautiful thing that so many young people are looking at Judaism through a lens of love and joy, she is sad that there is a decreasing emphasis on duty and responsibility.

* * *

Conversations among the generations are deeply important. So many people in the older generations feel ostracized or alienated from the younger Jewish communities. They may feel pushed aside, as though the Millennial desire for Judaism's evolution is a personal attack, a way of telling them that their views are outdated and unwanted. They want to fight to preserve the community and to ensure its survival, and the way they know how to do that is by pushing the Judaism that they were raised with, the kind that they know and love. The younger generations, for their part, often feel like the Boomers are clinging onto a version of Judaism that is no longer fit for its purpose. They believe that for the community to survive, we must adapt to an ever-changing world. The answer lies somewhere in the middle: preserving our past yet evolving to preserve our future. Ultimately, we both found that we want the same things for the Jewish community. We want it to thrive and grow.

Despite the media's insistence that intergenerational tensions have never been worse, we struggle to believe that. We think back to old Jewish stories like that of the Fiddler on the Roof, where the elders clung to "tradition!" and the youths challenged them at every turn. This is the way intergenerational conversation has always been, and one day the current Generation Z may grow up and be horrified by how their children live their lives.

In the meantime, we must learn to see each other beyond the micro-conversations that occupy our minds, and look at the macro, to look at what Judaism really is: a people that love learning, food, silliness, joy, and music. All of us can fit in the big, lovely picture that is Judaism, which is far broader than just synagogue or religion. It is an ancient civilization, kept alive through willpower and perseverance and a desire to survive.

22

NEEDED: MORE JEWS

Why We Should Actively Promote Conversion

TAL KEINAN

THE JEWISH STORY includes two episodes of fundamental redefinition of the enterprise of Judaism. The first is the Exodus from Egypt, when the Jews received their foundational document and became a nation. The second is the Roman expulsion from the Land of Israel in the first and second centuries C.E., when the Jewish nation was forced to abandon a traditional sovereign life. Judaism underwent a radical transformation, adopting a

Tal Keinan is the author of *God Is in the Crowd: Twenty-First-Century Judaism* (Random House, 2018). Born and raised in the United States, he immigrated to Israel where he served for eighteen years as a fighter pilot in the Israel Air Force. Keinan lives in New York and works in airport infrastructure development.

complex virtual governance structure that would, almost miraculously, keep it coherent as a people through 1,800 years of worldwide dispersion, all without central leadership.

Judaism may be facing its third episode of redefinition, corresponding, like the first two, with a geographic dislocation. For two millennia, Diaspora (or "exile") was the most useful description of Judaism's physical footprint. This is no longer the case. The Jews have concentrated in two geographies, Israel and North America. Both jurisdictions are decidedly philosemitic in the context of Jewish history, and the barriers to assimilation are historically low. These two forces—geographic concentration and societal welcome—threaten the entire Jewish enterprise with dissolution, in that Jews today are Jews by choice, and they are not choosing Judaism in numbers that will sustain the Jewish enterprise as we know it.

For the first time in generations, we must ask ourselves: *Should there be Jews?* And if we answer in the affirmative, what exactly are we willing to do to survive and thrive as a people?

Conversion for marriage in North America, a trend usually associated with the threat of Jewish dissolution, may actually be one of the most potent tools in the Jewish survivalist toolkit. At the end of a book talk in a New York suburb, a woman approached me with the following observation: "I have five grandchildren and all of them are Jewish. As the statistics you cite in *God Is in the Crowd* suggest, this puts me in a minority among Jews of my generation. My husband is a convert to Judaism. Had I married a man who was born Jewish, I believe the outcome would have been different." I have heard variations of this story in subsequent book talks across the United States. In addition to the preservation of numbers in a period of Jewish population decline, the act of conversion, even for the sake of marriage, may help preserve two of the qualitative forces that hold Judaism together in this age of choice: Jewish knowledge and Jewish commitment.

Even in the most perfunctory of conversions, the converting spouse is exposed to a body of Jewish knowledge that the average born Jew is not guaranteed to encounter. The spouse who is born Jewish benefits indirectly from this exposure to Jewish knowledge. Dedication to a course of study and the public celebration of the convert's new identification with the Jewish people represent a commitment to Judaism, both by the converting spouse and by the spouse who requested the conversion—a consequential request, implicitly demanding serious commitment from the requesting party.

Of course, the idea of using conversion as a strategy to promote Jewish continuity is controversial. Most serious objections are motivated by concern for the integrity of Judaism, a concern I share. But the actual meaning of the term "integrity of Judaism" is not at all obvious, and requires some unpacking. It may be broken into three components: ethnic integrity, spiritual integrity, and functional integrity, each of which should be addressed differently.

***

The notion of *ethnic integrity*, supported by the practice of Jewish identification by matrilineal descent, with very limited paths to Judaism through conversion, has been in practice for about 2,000 years and is ripe for challenge.

We should begin by challenging the very concept of ethnic Jewish purity. The fact that most Jews of Lithuanian (for example) descent are light-skinned and fair-haired, and that most Jews of Yemenite or Ethiopian (for example) descent are dark-skinned and dark-haired, should suffice to dispel illusions of Jewish ethnic homogeneity. That divergence in appearance is not the result of evolution. Our ancestors mixed with their neighbors. Identification by matrilineal descent is not divinely prescribed. The paths to Judaism in the Bible included nearly everything *but* matrilineal descent.

Matrilineal descent as the test for Jewishness is a post-Second Temple convention, and there is nothing that makes it unchallengeable. It is worth asking what principle is protected by rigid reliance on matrilineal descent by some in positions of Jewish leadership, notably the Israeli Chief Rabbinate, as the ultimate arbiter of Jewishness.

A genetic research study published in 2018 found that nearly 25 percent of the entire Latin American population carries Jewish ancestry. That is about 200 million people. Surely, thousands of these people carry unbroken matrilineal Jewish lines. Assuming they have no knowledge of or commitment to Judaism, should they be considered more Jewish than a knowledgeable and committed Jew who happens to have converted or, for that matter, the committed and knowledgeable child of a Jewish father and a non-Jewish mother?

It has been implied, perhaps jokingly, that the real test of Judaism in the twenty-first century is not whether your grandmother was Jewish, but whether your grandchildren will be Jewish. In practical terms, if we aim to perpetuate Judaism in a coherent form, the number of self-identified and practicing Jews is of far greater importance than the number of people who descended from a Jewish maternal grandmother.

* * *

Spiritual integrity: Some would argue that there is a "Jewish soul'" that would be compromised by the admission of insincere converts. I agree that sincerity should be a criterion for broad-based recognition of a conversion, but how is sincerity measured? More importantly, what is the cost of misjudging a convert's sincerity?

During the Diaspora period, when Jews lacked global leadership, a community rabbi in Poland might officiate over the conversion of a local gentile. That conversion might be reviewed by some of the rabbi's local or regional colleagues but would not be subject to the scrutiny of most of world Jewry. A rabbi in Morocco, for example, would not have opined on the conversion. He would not have heard of the conversion. He would probably not have even been aware of the Polish community in question.

Within several generations, the original conversion will have either succeeded or failed on its own, without the intervention of Jewish leadership. Success would be defined by the convert's descendants considering themselves simply Jewish, and by their community considering them simply Jewish. After some number of generations, the descendants would become unaware of their ancestor's status as a convert. Failure would be defined by the convert's Jewish line ending through assimilation, just as many matrilineal Jewish lines end.

So, the question of spiritual integrity works itself out organically, over the generations. There is little evidence that converts have had a corrupting influence on Judaism as a whole. In fact, from the beginning, the Jewish story is replete with examples of converts and their descendants who made outsize contributions to Judaism's vitality and continuity, from Ruth to Rabbi Akiva, to some of the great Tosafists of the Middle Ages.

***

Functional integrity. Unlike Christianity or Islam, Judaism is concerned with function, or behavior, much more than with faith. If a person fails to embrace Jesus as his savior, it is difficult to consider that person a Christian, regardless of how he is born or behaves. Although the words "religion" and "faith" are often used interchangeably, Judaism cannot be considered a religion in the same way the other monotheistic movements are. As Arnold Eisen, chancellor of the Jewish Theological Seminary, once joked, the Jews believe in one God—at most.

Although there is a Jewish religion, with a rich and complex theology, Judaism is more than a religion. It has been described as a people, a nation, a tribe, and even a family. How does this family function? What does it mean to function Jewishly on an individual level? As far as the Israeli Chief Rabbinate is concerned, it means adopting the prescriptions and prohibitions of the Orthodox Jewish religion—keeping kosher, observing Shabbat, and so on.

Most Jews recognize that there are other, nonreligious ways of functioning Jewishly. Dedicating years of one's life, perhaps risking one's life, for the physical defense of the nation-state of the Jews may be one of these. Promoting Jewish life through charity and volunteer work is another. Jewish study is a third. Each of these behaviors promotes the survival of Judaism and the welfare of the Jewish people in different but essential ways. It is difficult to rank their utility in an order that would be accepted by most Jews. One could not convince most Jews, for example, that Israel's survival could be ensured solely through religious observance. Relatively few born Jews engage in all of the behaviors above. Many engage in none.

Although Judaism loses its coherence if the definition of "Jewish behavior" is left entirely to the individual Jew, there is utility, and indeed real integrity, in accepting a broadened definition of Jewish function and practice, which includes nonreligious behaviors that promote the sustainment and enrichment of Judaism.

* * *

I am not arguing for relaxed standards for conversion and recognition of Jewishness. I am arguing for broader, more thoughtful standards that prioritize the vitality and survival of Judaism by emphasizing knowledge of Judaism and commitment to the Jewish people. I am arguing for a universal standard of Jewishness that maintains our coherence as one people. That standard need not be accepted as "Jewish enough" by any individual Jewish leader, just as the Polish rabbi's conversion was not necessarily accepted by the Moroccan rabbi.

For the first time in 2,000 years, we have a global imprimatur of Jewishness in the form of eligibility for Israeli citizenship under the Law of Return. Whether that right is exercised or not, it can serve as a universal bar. I am arguing for a Law of Return fashioned not after the Nuremburg Laws, which served Israel's core function at the time as a physical refuge for world Jewry, but from a global Jewish consensus around the essential components of Jewishness, which serves what may be Israel's core function in an age of Judaism by choice. In *God Is in the Crowd*, I propose mechanisms for establishing that global Jewish consensus and for creating a seat for world Jewry at the legislative table at which this bar would be set. Of course, mine are not the only mechanisms that have been proposed.

But before engaging with mechanics, we must first ask the fundamental question of this age of Judaism by choice: *Should there be Jews?* It is incumbent on those who answer affirmatively to recognize our demographic trajectory and to challenge thoughtfully those Jewish practices that can be amended to serve Judaism's top priority—survival.

23

THE MOUNTAIN OF SPICES

Recovering the Erotic Core of Judaism

BENJAMIN KERSTEIN

THE QUESTION OF JEWISH SEXUALITY has obsessed both Jews and their adversaries for thousands of years, yet it is surprising how rarely it is talked about today. Jews, of course, have been writing about sex for millennia, yet we rarely speak of an explicitly *Jewish* sexuality even among ourselves.

This is especially tragic because the Jews have a very distinct sexuality, one that has influenced our culture, thought, religion, and lived experience for centuries. It encompasses some of the most profound ideas in Judaism: the

Benjamin Kerstein is a Tel Aviv-based writer who publishes at benjaminkerstein.substack.com and benjaminkerstein.com. His memoir *Jews of Privilege: The Story of My Secret Civil War* is forthcoming by Wicked Son.

sacred and the profane, purity and impurity, love and creation—including of the world itself—deep analysis and detailed application of the law, mysticism and magic, liberation and transgression.

The Jewish people's struggle with the mystery of sex is an ancient one. It began in the pre-Christian era and likely emerged out of the relationship between Judaism and paganism. While pagan societies had their own detailed mores and regulations related to sexuality, they were, for the most part, fairly liberal on questions of sex.

Judaism was far more puritanical than its pagan counterparts. Even before the rabbinical tradition emerged, the Written Torah proscribed adultery, fornication, homosexuality, and other variations on nonheterosexual or non-reproductive intercourse. The essential principle on which these regulations were based was, for the most part, the dichotomy of purity and impurity.

Ancient Judaism was not, however, a "sex-negative" religion. The very first commandment was to "be fruitful and multiply," which was, of course, a commandment to have sex. But ancient Judaism's positive views of sex went well beyond the mechanics of reproduction. Indeed, one of the greatest literary works to emerge from the Jewish tradition is a remarkably explicit celebration of the erotic, and its place as a sacred text was insisted upon by some of the greatest ancient religious leaders—if not without some controversy.

The Song of Songs, ostensibly though almost certainly not written by King Solomon, may be the most beautiful of all the books of the Bible, and certainly the most esthetically pleasing from a literary point of view. It is a dialogue between two lovers, and along with them a strange chorus that seems at times to be the city of Jerusalem itself, and is unabashedly about sex.

Indeed, there is not a hint of any "platonic" form of love in the poem. The passion between the two lovers, and the city's passion for them, is one of furious desire, and this desire is unmistakably physical. The voice of the beloved is heard, the scent of the beloved is intoxicating, the sight of the beloved is exalted, and the touch and taste of the beloved's flesh are sought with orgasmic intensity.

This passionate sensuality is captured throughout the poem's evocative and beautifully detailed imagery: "My beloved to me is a bag of myrrh, lodged between my breasts" (1:13); "his fruit is sweet to my mouth" (2:3), "his left hand was under my head, his right arm embraced me" (2:6); "your breasts are like two fawns, twins of a gazelle, browsing among the lilies" (4:5); "a garden locked is my own, my bride, a fountain locked, a sealed-up spring" (4:12).

To a certain extent, this eroticism has been lost in translation. The explicitness of the Song of Song's sexuality has been obscured by centuries of puritanical translators, and can only be grasped fully in its original Hebrew. There is, for example, the poem's shockingly explicit fifth chapter, which in the original is enough to send one rushing for a cold shower. In the somewhat expurgated version, the opening of 5:4–5 reads, "My beloved thrust his hand into the latch, and my heart was stirred for him."

This is double entendre enough even in translation, but in the original the evocation of digital penetration is impossible to miss: *Dodi shalah yado min-hahor ume'ai hamu alav*. The word commonly translated as "latch" is in fact the Hebrew word *hor*, which in modern Hebrew means only "hole," and in one biblical concordance I consulted is translated as "hollow, depressed ground between hills," which is as poetic and exact a description of the *labia majora* as can be found in literature. The word translated as "heart"—*me'ai*—is an even more explicit expurgation, as the term in fact refers to the internal organs as a whole, the entirety of the interior body. In the same censorious manner, the word translated as "stirred," in fact, also means "filled," a decidedly unplatonic metaphor, given the context.

The next line becomes even more explicit, and just as puritanically translated: "I rose to let in my beloved, my hands dripped myrrh, my fingers, flowing myrrh, upon the handles of the bolt." In the original, however, the term "let in" is in fact *liftoach*, or "to open," implying the expansion of the vagina and spreading of the legs in preparation for penetration. The phallic implications of the term "bolt" should be obvious, and the secretions implied by "flowing myrrh" equally so. The entire passage, then, despite all efforts of the translators, is more or less clearly a description—and a beautiful one—of the commencement of intercourse.

It should be noted, however, that perhaps the *most* beautiful aspect of the Song of Songs is that it is not a work of pure lust. The particularly Christian dichotomy of love and lust is foreign to it. In the poem, sex and love are the same thing. The book is a call both for sex and the one person with whom one desires to have it, as expressed in the final line, "Hurry, my beloved, swift as a gazelle or a young stag, to the mountain of spices" (8:14).

It should not be surprising that the Song of Songs became an object of controversy among the sages. Yet, in a remarkable passage from the Mishna, it is clear that it also came to be seen as something like the essence of the Torah.

> All the Holy Scriptures defile the hands.... Rabbi Judah says: the Song of Songs defiles the hands, but there is a dispute about Kohelet. Rabbi Yose says: Kohelet does not defile the hands, but there is a dispute about the Song of Songs.... Rabbi Akiba said: Far be it! No man in Israel argued that the Song of Songs does not defile the hands. For the whole world is not as worthy as the day on which the Song of Songs was given to Israel; for all the writings are holy but the Song of Songs is the holy of holies. (Yadayim 3:5)

The implications of the passage, in historical context, are quite remarkable, because it underlines the most extraordinary aspect of the Song of Songs, which makes it unique not only in Judaism but in Abrahamic religion in general: *It is the only piece of sacred pornography to survive the monotheist revolution.* Sacred pornography was commonplace in ancient polytheism, and verboten after its downfall at the hands of Roman Christianity. All except for this one survivor, which, as Rabbi Akiba says, constitutes the holy of holies, the heart of Judaism's most sacred text. This means that sex, the erotic, also lies at the heart of Judaism.

* * *

This is not to say, however, that the centrality of the Song of Songs turned rabbinic Judaism into a "sex-positive" religion. Indeed, the traditional Jewish attitude toward sex was—and is—one of profound ambivalence. The rabbis, by and large, expressed this, as was their wont, through detailed regulation.

The rabbinic laws in regard to sex are, needless to say, myriad and complex, and appear throughout the Talmud and later halachic literature. The Talmud has, for example, a strong hostility toward masturbation. Yet at the same time, it states that, within marriage, almost any sexual activity is permitted. Nor does the Talmud neglect the question of physical intimacy. It does not simply endorse but requires nudity during intercourse to enhance intimacy—quite contrary to the "hole in the sheet" myths about Orthodox Jews.

This tendency toward ambivalent regulation is expressed perhaps most fully in one of the greatest halachic works—Maimonides's monumental Mishneh Torah.

Given that he was a doctor, it should not be surprising that Maimonides is extremely explicit and detailed on matters of the body, and nowhere is this more evident than in his writing on sex. The chapter Issurei Biah ("Forbidden Intercourse"), which tackles the issue at length, contains, by Maimonides's own admission: "37 mitzvot: one positive commandment and 36 negative commandments," a formidable set of regulations by any definition.

In many ways, Maimonides's work exemplifies the sexual ambivalence present throughout the rabbinic tradition, to such a degree that it is simply impossible to define it as sex-negative or sex-positive. In the chapter on Shabbat, for example, Maimonides writes, "Marital relations are from the pleasure of Shabbat." In Issurei Biah, moreover, he advocates a kind of absolute sexual freedom within marriage, saying, "A man's wife is permitted to him. Therefore, a man may do whatever he desires with his wife."

It should be noted, however, that in the Mishneh Torah, Maimonides is giving his own interpretation of what the sages recommended in matters of sex. When it came time to give his own opinion, as he does in *The Guide for the Perplexed*, he takes an essentially sex-negative position, saying, "The law about forbidden sexual intercourse seeks in all its parts to inculcate the lesson that we ought to limit sexual intercourse altogether, hold it in contempt, and only desire it very rarely."

While this mostly sex-negative attitude may have prevailed in the realm of the halacha, however, the sex-positive attitudes of certain traditions and especially the legacy of the Song of Songs became immensely powerful and influential in the mystical tradition. In the Kabbalah, eroticism is ubiquitous and, in many ways, essential. It is related not simply to human relations, but to the creation of the world itself in what was called the *ma'aseh bereishit*.

This mystical eroticism gave pride of place to the Song of Songs, which took on a wholly spiritual interpretation *without* sacrificing its essential eroticism. It concentrated, above all, on the Shechina, seen as the female "indwelling" of the unknowable God.

The great secular scholar of the Kabbalah, Gershom Scholem, described this view in his masterwork *Major Trends in Jewish Mysticism:* "The mystery of sex, as it appears to the Kabbalist, has a terribly deep significance. This mystery of human existence is for him nothing but a symbol of the love between the divine 'I' and the divine 'You,' the Holy One, Blessed be He, and His Shechina." As Scholem asserts, the Kabbalah "was tempted to discover the mystery of sex within God himself."

It seems clear, then, that while the rabbis sought to regulate and sometimes repress sexuality, they essentially failed. The drive, as it always does, reasserted itself, and the repressed returned. Halachic tradition sought to consign sexuality to the marital bedroom, while the mystical tradition saw it as the metaphysical essence of Creation—the world entire.

* * *

Given the immense history of the Diaspora, the non-Jewish world's view of Jewish sexuality has been an important and often extremely negative phenomenon. The Jews' own struggle to deal with it, and sometimes counter it, was long and often bitter.

Throughout the Middle Ages, for example, Jewish men were cast as the opposite and other to non-Jewish sexuality. Where non-Jewish men were masculine and strong, it was believed, Jewish men were perceived as fundamentally feminine and even vaguely hermaphroditic.

When modern antisemitism emerged, and especially in the propaganda of the Nazi movement, a different and much uglier view of Jewish male sexuality was adopted. It was personified in *Der Stürmer*-style caricatures of Jewish men as lecherous, slathering, fat, sweaty perverts. In this context, Jewish male sexuality was above all seen as disgusting.

The attitude toward Jewish women, by contrast, was far more ambivalent. From the late Middle Ages onward, Jewish women were often identified as something like the personification of the beautiful, exotic woman of the East. The "Jewess" was a powerful seductress who sought to tempt the non-Jewish man into erotic malfeasance, but who also must be conquered for the West and ultimately converted to a chaste Christianity. One sees this, for example, in the character of Jessica in Shakespeare's *Merchant of Venice* or the actress-adventurer personified by fictional characters like Arthur Conan Doyle's Irene Adler and real-life figures like Sarah Bernhardt.

In the post-Holocaust era, negative stereotypes of Jewish sexuality both persisted and, in some ways, were even more widely disseminated, albeit in more benign forms. In today's media, non-Jewish cultural products—and quite a few Jewish ones, such as the films of Woody Allen—tend to portray the Jewish man as unattractive, weak, neurotic, and vaguely perverse feminized males who are nonetheless highly sexed to a disturbing extent. Perhaps the most popular recent version is the hapless Howard Wolowitz on the sitcom *The Big Bang Theory.*

The stereotype of female Jewish sexuality, by contrast, has changed considerably. In contrast to the seductive, desirable persona of old, Jewish women now tend to be portrayed in a *more* derogatory manner than in the past. The stereotypes include the materialist, demanding, and sexually manipulative Jewish American Princess; the ugly but happily promiscuous slut; and the whiny, petulant, and shallow harridan.

More than anything else, however, Jewish sexuality tends to be portrayed as *comical.* The sexualized Jew—male or female—is essentially a buffoon, a blunderer who cannot navigate the sexual mores of the non-Jewish world, and whose every effort at pleasure or eroticism is played for cheap laughs and tends to get them. The idea of a *serious* eroticism, of a specifically Jewish exploration of the mystery of sex, is seen as so ludicrous that it simply cannot be taken seriously by non-Jewish media.

These stereotypes, however, have been challenged and in many ways overcome by Zionism and the emergence of modern Israel. Zionism's famous search for a "New Jew" has led to the creation of the persona of the *sabra*—the native Israeli man or woman. This persona is almost the polar opposite of the non-Jewish stereotypes of yore.

For Jewish men, it is quintessentially expressed by the image of the IDF soldier: unabashedly masculine, confident, conquering, sensitive, and usually quite handsome. For Jewish women, it still contains elements of the exotic, but also an assertiveness, dynamism, beauty, and vaguely androgynous sexuality that contains elements of the warrior—due to female army service—and the dominatrix fantasies that enrapture more of the world's male population than would ever admit it.

Outside of Israel, the most potent expression of a serious Jewish sexuality has been, strangely enough, in commercial pornography, especially in America. The list of Jewish participants in the porn industry—including some of its most iconic performers—is a long one: Raylene (real name Stacey Bernstein), Joanna Angel (raised Orthodox, and Jewish to the point of exhibitionism), James Deen (beloved by women the world over until he was felled by sexual misconduct allegations), Nina Hartley (a living legend among those in the know), Naomi Russell (daughter of a rabbi), Ron Jeremy (another legend felled by misconduct allegations), Herschel Savage (yet another legend), and Jenna Jameson (the biggest porn star of all time and now an outspoken convert).

Perhaps out of fear of the inevitable *shanda*, this heavy Jewish presence in porn is rarely talked about by the Jewish community itself, and there is no doubt that, given that it combines sex and money—the two most potent forces in late-capitalist society—porn is in many ways a dangerous and often ugly business. But at the same time, this shadow expression of Jewish sexuality is an important one, because the "porn star" is, above all, a serious object of desire. People want to watch, to *gaze* upon them. Given that mainstream American culture still, by and large, portrays Jewish sexuality through derogatory comedy, it is in some ways only in pornography that a different Jewish sexuality is expressed: A "new American Jew" who can fuck without fear of mockery and being mocked, and in doing so force the non-Jew to confront his own contemptuous fantasies of the Jew as a sexual being.

***

For centuries, the Jews have been forced to contend with their sexuality in two ways—interior and exterior. Within the lived experience of the Jewish people themselves, the attitude was not so much sex positive or sex negative, but rather *sex fascinated*. Sex was seen as a mystery that cannot be solved. Its ultimate nature, like that of God himself, was believed to be unknowable. Thus, Jewish sexuality became one of *exploration*, in which every possible manifestation of the erotic was discussed, analyzed, regulated, experienced, reified, and, at the hands of the Kabbalists, declared to be the essence of the divine.

This sexuality, however, has been and still is under constant challenge from the non-Jewish world, a world that has arrogated to itself—without asking us—the right to define Jewish sexuality as it wishes, usually to our detriment, whether through demonization or contemptuous mockery. In this regard, our task is to assert our right to this sexuality of exploration without apology, shame, or fear of the shanda.

For ourselves, we have before us the simple task of continuing our exploration, our journey into the labyrinth that is sex and sexuality, whether it is the mystic physical romance of the Song of Songs, the assertive sexuality that Zionism has created, or the shameless indulgence in the pleasures of the flesh represented by pornography.

The assertion of a particular sexuality has often been a liberating force for oppressed peoples, a way of reconnecting with their abused bodies and an expression of a deep love for a previously repressed self. Jewish sexuality, then, is and can be a source of strength, one that embraces the deep mystery that the Jewish people have always found in sex. A mystery that stands between the disembodied call of the beloved and the desire to meet, once again in the flesh, upon the mountain of spices.

24

THE JEWISH SPIRITUAL QUEST

Finding God in the Twenty-First Century

YOSSI KLEIN HALEVI

JUDAISM IS A BRIDGE between two aspects of the Divine: *hamavdil,* the Creator Who "divides," distinguishing between the holy and the mundane, Israel and the nations, Shabbat and the six days of the week; and *echad,* the "One" who is beyond distinctions, resolving all contradictions within Its being.

Those two aspects are reflected in two paths of Jewish devotion. The conventional path of hamavdil seeks to sanctify our world of fragmentation, while the mystical path of echad longs to experience the Divine unity within the multiplicity of creation. The paradox of the Jewish mystic is to be grounded in the rituals and devotions of hamavdil, even as one actively seeks to experience echad.

Yossi Klein Halevi is a senior fellow at the Shalom Hartman Institute in Jerusalem. His most recent book is the *New York Times* bestseller *Letters to My Palestinian Neighbor* (Harper, 2019).

Hamavdil is the world as it is; echad is the world as it one day will be. But until the messianic revelation of the unity of existence, Jews resist the pull of premature universalism, whether religious or secular. "Not yet," the Jews insist, even as they maintain the vision of restored wholeness, *tikkun olam b'malchut Shadai,* the reparation of a broken world through God's manifestation on earth. Meanwhile, Judaism maintains its complex dance, sanctifying distinctions, the slow accumulation of the good. Hamavdil is the means; echad is the goal.

But some cannot wait until messianic times to experience echad. Throughout Jewish history, individuals and groups of mystics have arisen who sought God's all-pervading presence, the interconnectedness hidden in our world of separation. From the ancient prophets through the Kabbalists and early Hasidim, mystics have infused Judaism with a reminder of God's tangible presence, and that the final stage of a religious life is transcending the consciousness of hamavdil. Not just monotheism as a principle of faith but as a lived experience.

The longing for a world of oneness while maintaining Jewish distinctiveness in an unredeemed world is an ongoing tension at the heart of Judaism. Abraham Isaac HaCohen Kook, the first Ashkenazi chief rabbi of the land of Israel and one of the great mystics of the modern era, lived on the fault line between hamavdil and echad. Rabbi Kook expressed his attempt to resolve that struggle in an essay, "A Fourfold Song," which celebrates a human being's four commitments or "songs," from the Whitman-like song of oneself to devotion to one's people, service to humanity, and finally, a cosmic embrace of the entirety of life, encompassing all songs. "And then there is one who rises with all these songs in one ensemble, and they all join their voices…. The song of the self, the song of the people, the song of humanity, the song of the world all merge in him at all times, in every hour. And this full comprehensiveness rises to become the song of holiness, the song of God, the song of Israel, in its full strength and beauty."

Rabbi Kook's intent is to honor the spiritual integrity of each of those songs, though he is obviously referring to himself as the "one who rises with all these songs in one ensemble." In asserting that the "song of Israel" is identical to the all-encompassing song of existence, Rabbi Kook identifies the universal spirit as the essence of Jewish particularism, a Kookian dialectic that seeks to resolve his own conflicted soul.

Rabbi Kook tried and failed to create a spiritual movement in his image. He even envisioned his yeshiva in Jerusalem, Mercaz HaRav, as a center for the renewal of prophesy. Instead, his disciples, many of whom went on to found the Gush Emunim settlement movement, tended to emphasize his nationalist loyalties while neglecting his universal message. In the Kookian movement, hamavdil absorbed and effectively neutralized echad.

* * *

The fate of Rabbi Kook's spiritual universalism tells us much about the state of the God encounter within contemporary Judaism. We live in an era of extraordinary Jewish diversity. One can express Jewish commitment through Torah study, Zionism, feminism, social action, and community building. But the quest for an unmediated encounter with the Divine has been largely forgotten, confined to a few Hasidic groups that still recall their founders' hunger for God.

There is good reason for the waning of the God quest within the Jewish people. A life of striving for an intimate encounter with the Divine requires deep faith in God's existence and accessibility. The last two centuries haven't been kind to Jewish belief. The rise of secular ideologies, mass emigration and assimilation, the Holocaust, and the forcible erasure of Jewish memory in the Soviet Union, have all undermined the vitality of faith.

Since the 1960s, many thousands of Jewish seekers have turned to the East, unable to find a spiritually stimulating home within Judaism. In a perhaps apocryphal but revealing story, a guru told a rabbi: Your people is very spiritual; my ashram is full of Jews! Though rabbis and community leaders have long bemoaned the mass exit of many of our most spiritually talented seekers (some of whom have gone on to become world leaders in the spiritual quest), little serious thought has been applied to creating alternatives able to offer Jewish versions of the one-pointed quest for the Divine presence found in the best of the Indian ashrams. It is not enough to tinker with existing Jewish forms, like making Friday night services more "spiritual." A moral life and the observance of mitzvot are prerequisites for a Jewish spiritual life; but the search for the living God requires more.

***

What is required is a new form of Jewish institution, a kind of Jewish ashram, where ritual practice and religious study have only one purpose: furthering the quest for God. Given the cataclysmic upheavals in Jewish life over the last two centuries, Judaism is long overdue for new expressions of the mystical quest. Those upheavals, it turns out, foreshadowed the fate of humanity as a whole. As the world of the twenty-first century becomes ever more terrifying and dangerous, increasing numbers of people, including, of course, many Jews, are turning for meaning and guidance to spiritual paths. We desperately need institutions that can address the need of serious seekers, drawing on the Jewish contemplative tradition while sensitive to contemporary sensibilities.

For the last forty years, I have been part of a small circle in Jerusalem devoted to renewing the practice of Jewish contemplative meditation. Unlike some currently popular forms of meditation like mindfulness, contemplative meditation is explicitly God-centered. As in other mystical traditions, the Jewish path of contemplative meditation focuses on religious imagery and active longing for an encounter with God, placing the Divine encounter at the center of the meditation work.

The practice I share with my friends is rooted in traditional Jewish concepts and techniques, culled especially from Kabbalah and Hasidism. At the same time, we gratefully draw inspiration from other mystical traditions that bring the seeker closer to God. We are blessed to live in a time when the interfaith encounter has opened up the hidden spiritual resources of multiple traditions, allowing us to learn from the mystical experiences of other faiths. To experience oneness requires simultaneous rootedness and expansiveness, the rigor of adhering to a specific tradition, and the flexibility to absorb the wisdom of humanity.

In the last few years, our Jerusalem circle has begun bringing this work outward. Daat Elyon: The Center for Spiritual Training is a Jerusalem-based group headed by Rabbi Yoel Glick and devoted to Jewish meditation and mystical study. During the Covid-19 years, the use of technology has widened the reach of Daat Elyon, drawing seekers from around the Jewish world. Daat Elyon is building a strong online presence, offering courses in mystical study and meditation.

Daat Elyon's goal is to foster inner growth and transformation. All spiritual work begins with relentless self-examination, a confrontation with the personality flaws and negative habits and thought patterns that obstruct the God encounter. At the same time, students are introduced to the wisdom literature of Jewish and general mysticism. Prayer is extended from formal times to a constant practice throughout the day—what mystics call nurturing the habit of God's Presence.

The heart of the work is meditation. It is through silence and sustained concentration that the individual mind forms a link into the mind of God. Jewish meditation is no mere adaptation of popular meditation practices but a venerable tradition in its own right extending back into ancient times. In his groundbreaking work, *Meditation and the Bible*, the late Rabbi Aryeh Kaplan, who helped re-introduce classical Jewish meditation to contemporary Jews, makes a compelling case based on textual reading that the prophets were trained in meditation techniques. His other classic work, *Meditation and Kabbalah*, introduces the English-language reader to a wide variety of Jewish esoteric contemplative approaches.

The next step in the development of Daat Elyon is the creation of a full-time center in Israel that would sponsor retreats and offer options for a prolonged stay, training seekers and forming small groups of meditators. These future spiritual leaders will be role models for Jewish communities around the world.

For Jewish mystics, the purpose of the Divine encounter isn't only personal experience but the ability to become a vessel for the spiritual invigoration of Judaism and the Jewish people. The fruits of intensive spiritual work are an expansion of heart and mind: increased capacity for service to others, enhanced intuition, and a growing sense of God's tangible presence in one's daily life and struggles.

Every religion requires adherents willing to transform their lives into a spiritual laboratory, testing the possibility of the God encounter. The work, inward and painstaking, goes largely unseen. But judging by historical precedent, when a spiritually committed group ripens, the potential of that work to help renew Judaism and the Jewish people can be transformational.

25

ARGUE LIKE A JEW

Rediscovering the Rabbinic Art of Disagreement

WILLIAM KOLBRENER

JEWS HAVE MADE ARGUMENTS, joked about arguments, and even argued about arguments for two millennia. The worst part of Jewish assimilation: we have started to argue like the *goyim*.

University progressives and right-wing Republicans love their codependent dance while leaving the rest of us on the sidelines. Twins, but not identical twins, their fundamentalist DNA is the same. As opposites, they attract, competing with one another in self-righteous indignation. Moreover, they need each other, justifying their existence through their mutual hate. Today,

---

William Kolbrener is professor of English Literature at Bar Ilan University and director of academic development for ISGAP; his *Literature and the Sacred: A Future for the Humanities* is forthcoming.

Jews have adopted this argumentative dynamic, becoming the worst kind of idealists, adhering to singular ideologies, never allowing for ambiguity, ambivalence, or doubt.

We have forgotten that disagreement is the Jewish way of conversation.

Arguing like the goyim tears us apart. We are so invested in the argument that we forget what we are arguing about, our shared history, our lived experience, the books we both read *and* live: the Jewish Library of Life. This library includes not only the volumes of the Talmud and Jewish Law, Midrash and Kabbalah, Mussar and Hasidut, and, of course, the Bible, but also those volumes of Jewish philosophy and Hebrew poetry, the Yiddish theater, *klezmer*, the history of shtetls in Poland, cholent recipes, and Israeli dancing. Jewish life starts with multifarious encounters with this world, in all of its messy uncertainty. Arguing like the goyim means losing out on the Jewish Library, on our shared experience of books, art, and ritual. The noise of polemic drowns out the poetry of life and pulls us out of the texture of our shared existence into argumentative extremes. William Shakespeare, who had his feet on the ground, understood that "those in extremities are the most abominable creatures."

The rabbis say that hell and argument were created together on the second day, the day of division. The dualism of the second day of creation, not just upper and lower waters, good and evil, but the *division itself* brings conflict into the world. In the bizarre arithmetic of Maharal of Prague, the two of division is greater than three. Two wander off in separate directions, distinct lines, never meeting. The introduction of the third as an object of shared attention, love, and devotion—history, God, tradition—brings the two together in a triangle. The wandering lines of narcissism come together; *disagreement*, not as an end, but as a way of life becomes possible.

The all-or-nothing way of looking at the world also takes away the understanding, through *not* knowing, the humility, wonder, and awe, the experience of the melancholy, and even the tragic. We have been made to believe that only a few can claim the privilege of trauma, and so recognize life's fundamental imperfection only in politics, now the measure of the soul. When every argument is irreconcilable, the soul internalizes the fighting mentality. We can't tolerate ourselves, let alone others. We live for the argument.

Argument and dispute are translated by the same word in Hebrew, *makhloket*. They resemble one another closely but are not the same. *Argument* is winner-take-all. But Jewish *dispute*, going back to the sages of the Mishna and the Talmud, always ends with a "to be continued." Opposing views do not expire; you never know when they will come in handy. Although, for example, we follow the opinions of Beit Hillel, Beit Shammai's decisions will apply in the world to come. The God of the Rabbis says, "these and these are the words of the living God." When an argument is in good faith, all perspectives, all voices have standing. They just see a complex world in different ways. Rejected views are preserved, learned, and understood. When two people argue, it will always be about *them*. But when there's something in-between, shared and loved, devotion to the beloved becomes more intense than devotion to the self. This is the great gift to the Jews; we have something we love to argue about.

But everyone likes the prospect of a fight. Even rabbis accustomed to dispute sometimes let their zeal get the best of them, seeking conquest. After all, arguing is a pastime, a permissible form of combat, not for the battlefield, but for the living room, the office, the classroom. No longer gendered, it's not just testosterone-based. The glory of winning, of shaming the opponent, is not just for Homeric heroes like Achilles. If we could, some of us would drag our defeated opponents in an argument naked through the dirt. Arguments become the way we bolster our self-importance, turning conflicts over lunch into struggles of world-historical importance. No one cares about the truth; it's just the argument that matters.

***

The Talmud tells a cautionary tale about a rabbi who goes too far, who gives up everything for the sake of an argument. Rabbi Nekusah encounters a group of feisty heretics who badger him, looking for a fight. They get him going, he is both angry and self-righteous. He engages. Although he wins decisively, *no contest*, in the end, he is the big loser.

The debate between Rabbi Nekusah and the heretics turns into a Martin Scorsese movie of ruthless and gratuitous violence. The heretics bait the rabbi with questions, and he cannot resist the fight. His blood boils; he gets pulled in; and they end up agreeing to a fight to the death: "Whoever wins bashes the other's brains out with a hammer." Nekusah triumphs; he inflicts the punishment. The heretics are left bleeding, their brains crushed, defeated, dead. There is an equivalent of an extra bullet in their faces just to make sure.

In the aftermath of the confrontation, the rabbi's *talmidim* are jubilant like over-enthusiastic football fans, reveling in the defeat of the heretics. They also caption the victory, claiming Nekusah's victory as divine providence: "*You* had God on your side; and you won: hurrah!" Then the action hero becomes introspective; he sobers up from this adrenaline rush. Nekusah quiets his students and rebukes them: "Stop cheering and start praying." In the silence that follows, the rabbi sees their confusion and explains. "Pray for *me*," he says. "My mind once shone with diamonds and sapphires and is now turned into burnt-out coal." The precious stones showed the rabbi's former brilliance, the spent coal leaving him now a burnt-out case. The polemic not only exhausts him, it *ruins* him. Diamonds as precious stones epitomize refinement; the coal, grossly material remains inert, burnt, without life.

For whatever Nekusah rebukes his students, he is guilty of himself. And he knows it. Power gave him illusions of grandeur. He understands his claim "I am bringing about God's will" shows the hubris of the self-convinced redeemer. Nekusah is the Hebraic Oedipus, understanding that God, even in victory, is not necessarily on his side. His former bravado, the need to be right at all costs for total victory, he comes to understand, comes from a lack of self-worth, a suspicion that he may be wrong. The audience of students is not an accidental feature of the story. In the end, Nekusah tells his impressionable students not to follow his path. He realizes he has squandered his life on a meaningless argument.

Nekusah, and the editors of the Midrash, want readers to grow out of their cartoonish view of God, to transcend the child's perspective of a God who never defies expectations, and whose conception of good and evil corresponds exactly with our own. The God who defies expectations cannot be claimed as a cheerleader. Fundamentalists on every side, on the progressive Left as much as on the Right—everyone has their version of the sacred—claim God "on their side." They are united in suppressing doubt, ambiguity, and uncertainty, anything that might taint the purity of the mission.

That is why the rabbis present the stand-off with the heretics as a battle. Nekusah says to his students: When you weaponize your arguments—even "just" with hammers—there is collateral damage. The pounding takes its toll. As it turns out, this is Nekusah's only show, his one and only appearance in the Talmud. After the fateful "all-or-nothing," even as a winner, he is forever banished from life-giving disputes, those of the living God, because he could not resist the urge to win. He became so involved in the argument with the heretics that he loses the Jewish ability to disagree. When the Mishna says, "Be ready to answer the heretic," Maimonides explains, have the answer ready, but *avoid argument*, even more so, he says, with another Jew. Be ready to discuss and dispute that for which you share a mutual love, but in the absence of that, argument will lead to irreconcilable differences and hatred. The middle ground, between the warring extremes, gets lost.

Nekusah's message against soul-destroying polemic should resonate today. Doubt on the Right has long vanished, doubt on the Left is more of a stance than an activity. So devoted are both sides to their causes that they feel the need to coerce others, for *their own good*. There are all sorts of arguments for what turns out, in the end, to be fighting to the death. Jewish dispute, however, is different; it may end in acrimony but not cancellation. Beit Shammai does not walk away from the table because things don't go their way. Life goes on. They even marry off their daughters to the sons of Beit Hillel. Jewish argument is like Jewish humor: it both wounds and heals at the same time. It hurts, but it also allows moving on. But today the dynamic of grievance culture on both Left and Right leaves everyone nurturing the wounds of the past, such that we forget what binds us: our commitment to a Jewish future.

If there were ever a need for a *shmita*—a "sabbatical year" for argument— now would be the time. But the fruits will not come immediately. Without cultivating lost books and practices, the soil remains inhospitable to everything but the weeds that strangle the rest of us. Right-wing conservatives and ultra-Orthodox do not have a monopoly on Jewish tradition nor do woke progressives have a monopoly on skepticism. We must claim both, as we educate our students out of their extremism. We must re-envision Jewish education as a practice opposed to ideology (what is iconoclasm if not the simultaneous adherence to skepticism and belief?). Condescending to the least common denominator is not education, but indoctrination.

As leaders and instructors, we must have the courage to engage in a non-polemical form of teaching, trusting skeptical young people to find their voices instead of giving them one of the ready-made ones supplied by fundamentalists. So much of the discussion of the last century has been centered on "Who is a Jew?" that it distracts from the more urgent question: How to bring Jews into the Jewish Library, as readers of volumes of the past, and writers of new volumes for the future.

We must remember the responsibility to the dream we are in the midst of fulfilling and revive Jewish conversation. We must remember our blessed moment before it's too late. The blessing—to live freely and openly as a Jew, to live in a Jewish state, to know in the rest of the world—though, of course, it won't happen again!—that there's a refuge if things really go south. We cannot detract from our common mission—Jewish flourishing and survival.

After the destruction of the Temple in Jerusalem, the rabbis created the original and ever-expanding Jewish Library, a sacred and ever-growing space for discussion and dispute. With dispute, with saying "We don't know everything," rabbinic Judaism turns the "coming after" of destruction into an "in-between." They transform catastrophe into a transition. The perfection of Jewish life represented in the Temple now lies in the past and in an unknown distant future.

In the meantime, we live in a present of imperfection and diversity. Today, we must reclaim the rabbinic tradition where dispute does not end a conversation but continues it. We cannot afford but to leave all-or-nothing arguments to the goyim. We must learn again to turn our arguments into disputes, to argue again, like Jews.

26

SEPARATION OF CHALLAH

An Ancient Ritual Opens the Door to Our Mothers' Wisdom

LIHI LAPID

MY SISTER-IN-LAW texted me innocently: "Should I bring challah Friday night?"

That same evening, I attended a "Separating Challah" (or "Dough Offering") ceremony—an event that has, in the last few years, become highly popular in Israel among secular and moderately traditional women. Of course, the separation of challah has always been one of the rituals that took place in the privacy of traditional Jewish homes. In the last few years, however, it has left the family kitchen, the domain of grandmothers and mothers, and has been

Lihi Lapid is a journalist, commentator, and speaker on contemporary women's issues. She has written three bestselling novels including, most recently, *On Her Own: A Novel* (HarperCollins, 2023).

transformed into a beating (and rising) heart of women's public gatherings.

Throughout history, in almost every traditional Jewish community, women were banned from the public sphere. It was understood that their place was in the home—and especially the kitchen. This was the realm of women, because public life was closed to them.

Throughout most of history, women and girls weren't taught to read or write; formal wisdom and knowledge were the preserve of men. A few women would insist on learning, but only when the door of Enlightenment burst open were Jewish girls allowed to join the world of formal study.

The change that took place in the status of women over the last century, in other words, is something new. The way we live today is different from almost any time in the past. And still, even today, many women in many societies live without freedom, without the ability to express themselves. They are shunned from the public sphere. Some by choice, others by overwhelming social pressure.

It's important to remember that our grandmothers, and their mothers and grandmothers before them, generation after generation of Jewish women—despite everything we've been told—really did want to have their voice heard. They didn't want to remain silent. But they had almost no opportunity. And so, they tried to find their voice within that world and its cloistering limitations.

Before they learned to read and write, women had only one way to pass on their wisdom: orally.

Jewish women would meet up in the women's section of the synagogue, listening from behind the *mehitza* to speeches suffused with male wisdom, but also passing to each other their own female wisdom. But the core of that wisdom—about life in the home, family, relationships, parenting, what to expect in childbirth, or how to handle a sick child or a problematic mother-in-law—was conveyed in the home, and above all in the kitchen.

And so, the ritual of separating challah was born.

***

The ritual goes like this: Any time dough of more than a certain amount of flour (about 3.5 lbs.) is prepared, one must set aside about an ounce of dough. That portion is then burned while a prayer is recited. It is from this that the term "challah" is derived—only bread that has undergone this ritual prior to baking may be served.

Already in ancient times, the moment of separating challah was considered a *sha'at ratzon*, a moment of divine benevolence, when the Heavens open to our prayers—similar to the moments after a brit, when the *sandak* or godfather is blessed with a special moment of divine benevolence.

This ritual became the focal point of the gathering of women, a women's-only moment of community. Women could speak freely, together. This was their public sphere. A public sphere inside the home. In the kitchen.

It was here that women found their voice—together and apart from the men. It was the only way they could talk to other women, sharing and passing their immense knowledge. Knowledge about life, relationships, family and children, overcoming challenges, and handling the mother-in-law.

It was this ritual that allowed them to pass their life wisdom from mother to daughter to granddaughter. Rivers of knowledge, written nowhere, cited from memory, flowing from older women to younger women. While kneading the dough, alongside the blessings and prayers, they added wisdom of their own.

Some of the women, those with strong opinions, the wise ones, who had studied informally, became unofficial leaders among women. Leaders to whom other women turned for wisdom.

Over the years, women tried to make themselves heard, and men tried to silence them. Some were suspected of witchcraft, others were banished from the community, but Jewish women fought for their voice.

* * *

The challah-separating ceremony, which is gaining popularity in Israel today, has aroused disdain and criticism among some quarters. I tried to understand why, so I turned to Ofra Finkelstein Bouskila, a friend from Migdal Ha'emek, who had experienced that disdain. "Separating challah is not just a mitzvah," she says, "but a very spiritual ritual. I'm not observant, but I was raised with religion around me, and one of the few rituals I observe is separating challah. It's part of the human mosaic that symbolizes the melting pot of Israeli society.

Maybe the criticism comes from the fact that it's a ritual of 'ordinary people'?"

The first time I attended such a ceremony was at the apartment of a friend, a neighbor whose daughter was set to get married a few days later. I had never heard of the ceremony, and I arrived curious, eager to learn about a women's ritual I'd never known. Sometime afterward, I was invited by another friend, Juliana from Netanya, to another challah-separating ceremony. The difference between the two was significant because of the different personalities of the women who hosted. In both cases, however, I saw women gathering together, rejoicing, hearing about a tradition that has almost disappeared, a chance to preserve the wisdom of women that for thousands of years percolated in a place that was just for them, for these women, to give voice to their unique character.

Like anything else that becomes fashionable, so, too, do these challah-separating ceremonies sometimes feel overly commercial. Sometimes they feel like they're proselytizing for Orthodoxy, or fundraising for a charity, and they lose some of their original distinctiveness.

Many women have come out against the ceremonies, saying that we shouldn't want to go back into the kitchen, that it entrenches the kind of docile femininity that has no place in our world.

I believe, however, that those of us who live far outside the kitchen have nothing to fear—nobody's going to put us back there. Quite the contrary: We should help other women who still need support in realizing their dreams, and extend a hand. And there are many such women. Women locked in their homes. Women who face a real threat of physical or economic violence.

We need to remember, and respect, what the women of previous generations did for us. We need to preserve the wisdom they fought so hard to pass down. Not to let men erase it or silence us.

We no longer need to bake our own challah to find the opportunity to talk. Today we have many ways to lead, to speak, and to make our voice heard far from the kitchen. But today in Israel there are still political parties without any women representing them—*because* they're women. And women accept this silencing. They even cast their votes in favor of the same male Haredi establishment that systematically silences them. They have every right to, of course, but it's sad nevertheless.

We—as Jews and as human beings—need to help every girl or woman who has been silenced.

So, I texted back to my sister-in-law that yes, I'd be delighted if she brought challah on Friday night. My sister-in-law has a Ph.D. in psychology. She bought the challah at a wonderful bakery in her neighborhood. An amazing thing indeed.

The separation of challah is a warm and wonderful tradition. Challah serves as a strong access point to Jewish identity, whether secular or observant.

Every Jew must be able to choose for himself or herself which rituals to practice. We should make sure we connect the Jewish world together and prevent any further division, or "separation."

27

EMBRACE THE CHAOS

Affirming the Edgy, Creative, Crazy Side of Being Jewish

NOLAN H. LEBOVITZ

IN JUNE OF 2022, my wife and kids and I left our home in Los Angeles and headed to Israel for a family vacation. On the way, we stopped in New York for a few days. We visited the Tenement Museum, took a tour of the Eldridge Street synagogue, saw a Yankee game, attended a Broadway show, and then we all headed to the airport for a ten-hour flight to Israel on El Al.

We arrived at JFK a little early, and my wife took the kids to buy some snacks for the long flight. I decided to stretch my legs and walk up and back down the long hall of Terminal 4. As I came back to our gate, I heard the familiar airport-announcement chime over the loudspeaker.

Rabbi Nolan H. Lebovitz is the senior rabbi at Valley Beth Shalom in Encino, California. He has written and directed two documentary films, *Roadmap Genesis* (2015) and *Roadmap Jerusalem* (2018).

Ding, ding, ding… and then, "Aloha everyone."

I turned to my left, and directly across from our gate was that of an American Airlines flight to Honolulu. At the microphone was a most pleasant-looking young woman wearing a flowery lei.

"Aloha, we're about to depart on our journey to Hawaii, the island of Oahu."

I looked at the New York crowd at that gate and I could taste the recipe of excitement and relaxation. They were headed to Hawaii. Some were already dressed in Hawaiian shirts and flip-flops. All of their shoulders had loosened.

The woman with the lei continued, "Please form a single file line and we'll begin our boarding process soon. Mahalo!"

There on my left, I watched New Yorkers float with a sense of calm and serenity to form a single-file line and patiently wait to board this jetliner to their island paradise.

Then, I heard the chimes again over the loudspeaker. *Ding, ding, ding…* A deep, gravelly voice began, "Eeehh…."

Even in the inaudible vocality, I could feel Israel getting closer. "*Gvirotai v'rabotai,* welcome to El Al…."

Without waiting for the end of the announcement, Jewish families of all kinds—New York Haredim, Los Angeles Ashkenazim, New Jersey Syrians, Israeli Mizrahim, some with three children, some with ten, all took five or six steps forward toward the gate and began to crowd the security officers as if we'd never even heard of a line before.

I glanced back at the tranquil boarding of the flight to Hawaii, and then I gazed upon the chaos of my people. Hawaii or Israel? Granted, I already had a ticket, but seeing these two groups, with which did I really want to spend the next ten hours?

Here, before us all, was the choice between two very different kinds of journeys. On the left was a choice of calm and comfort and relaxation, a journey to paradise; and on the right was a life that is active and challenging and familial and chaotic. In looking at those two scenes, I realized that we all stand at that fork in the road often, forced to choose between different kinds of journeys, different kinds of lives. At that moment it hit me that part of my job as a rabbi today is advocating for Jews to choose the journey on the right.

***

I really do love Hawaii. As a matter of fact, outside of Israel, if you asked my kids where I'd choose to be, I have no doubt they'd say the Aulani Disney Resort in Hawaii. After reading a draft of this essay, my wife made me promise that we would visit Hawaii again. This isn't a disparaging talk about Hawaii or Cancun or any of the other places we go on vacation. Please, don't email me and justify your next vacation to Club Med. I get it.

We face a more profound dilemma than where we vacation. The choice before us all is whether we reach for comfort and relaxation, or whether we reach for meaning. Why do we take our families to Israel? To craft our identity. To reconnect with purpose. To rediscover meaning. A journey to Israel is as much a journey inward as a journey abroad.

If meaning is the end goal we desire, then an acceptance of chaos is the cost to get there. Judaism encourages us, actually demands of us, a degree of vulnerability to chaos to feed our spiritual growth, for wisdom, for purpose.

The Torah seems to go out of its way to explain to us that the entire process of Creation unfolded out of a sense of chaos:

> When God began to create the heaven and earth—the earth was an unformed void (*tohu vavohu*)—a chaotic mess—with darkness over the surface of the deep, and the spirit of God swept over the water (Genesis 1:1–2).

Chaos and messiness have always manifested as the precursor to creation and progress and meaning. It's a step that most of us don't enjoy. In the *Guide for the Perplexed*, Maimonides commented that our sages believed that tohu vavohu meant mourning and crying. Our sages clearly cast a negative light on chaos.

We don't like feeling uninformed, unaware, or unsure. We enjoy feeling like experts, aware, and in control.

We control every aspect of our lives and steer our experience toward comfort. We control the way we listen to music, consume entertainment, and receive our news so that we're not presented with an unknown or challenged by an adversarial opinion. We have engineered our lives to feel comfortable at every moment. How many remote controls do you have in your living room? Some of us even have a universal remote that does everything but control the universe.

If it's true that we prefer comfort and control as human beings, then it's true for Jews as well, except even more so. We value education and accomplishment so much that whenever I address my congregation, I know I'm speaking to doctors of every field, attorneys of every kind of specialization, educators dedicated to various abilities, and financial experts of every strategy. We are a people whose expertise extends to everything.

On Rosh Hashanah, we recite the liturgy, *hayom harat olam*—today the world was born, or perhaps more precisely, today the world was pregnant with possibility. In a synagogue, we come together at the beginning of the Jewish year to acknowledge that life is fragile. We confront profound truths, and some of them make us uncomfortable. We contemplate God and prayer, family and fertility, individuality and community. On Yom Kippur, we face absolute fragility in contemplating life and death. It's challenging and uncomfortable, and absolutely necessary.

Synagogues around the world all claim to be welcoming and want to make you comfortable. But comfort is actually not what brings us to shul. We go because we're looking for meaning.

It's in the synagogue that we chant our people's language, even though most American Jews don't understand Hebrew. It's in the synagogue that we speak of God more in a single High Holiday service than most of us do during the rest of the year. It's in the synagogue where we are reminded that time moves faster than we'd like, and we know it because we look around the sanctuary and see all of those who are no longer physically present. None of that is comfortable. All of it is meaningful.

In 2010, Brené Brown delivered a TEDx talk called "The Power of Vulnerability." Brown is a scholar who studies courage, vulnerability, shame, and empathy. She's the author of five number-one *New York Times* bestsellers. Her lecture has been viewed online by more than 58 million people. Brown explained that her research studied people who didn't feel worthy of love or belonging versus people who did feel worthy of relationship. She found that everyone who felt worthy of connection possessed two shared qualities: courage and vulnerability. As she explained:

> They believed that what made them vulnerable made them beautiful. They didn't talk about vulnerability being comfortable, nor did they really talk about it being excruciating.... They just talked about it being necessary. They talked about the willingness to say "I love you" first, the willingness to do something where there are no guarantees, the willingness to breathe through waiting for the doctor to call after your mammogram. They're willing to invest in a relationship that may or may not work out. They thought this was fundamental.

Living comfortably is not our only goal in life. We all aspire to live a life of meaning. We acquire meaning through relationships, learning, and personal growth. To achieve relationships and personal growth, vulnerability is a necessary component. To face vulnerability, we need courage. To face life's challenges, we need courage. What does Jewish courage look like in the face of vulnerability?

In the biblical Book of Kings, society proves overwhelming for the prophet Elijah, and he runs away from the Northern Kingdom of Israel down through the Negev wilderness, to a mountain called Horev, otherwise known as Sinai. He enters a cave, the most secluded place imaginable. And it's there that Elijah utters the words, "*I am alone.*" And God answers him with the single word, *tzeh*—"Come out" (I Kings 19:10–11).

God tells Elijah: Come out and face the world. Come out and stand vulnerable. And it's there that Elijah faces a mighty wind, and then he faces an earthquake, and then finally a fire. And after the fire, Elijah famously hears the "still, small voice"—the soft, delicate voice of divinity, of courage, of conviction, of purpose.

This is the reason why we believe that Elijah visits a child at a circumcision, or why he visits us on Passover before a renewed sense of freedom, or why we sing of Elijah at Havdallah before we encounter the challenges of each new week. We need to be reminded of that voice to go out into the world with courage, conviction, and purpose.

This is the voice of inspiration that spoke to Jacob when he laid down his head to sleep on the rock. It was the voice of destiny that spoke to Moses from the burning bush. All Jews have stood vulnerable at one time or another, and this is the voice that speaks to us all.

* * *

After several years of pandemic and political strife, we are all emerging out of degrees of chaos. Especially now, in this restart, in this renewal, it is imperative for the Jewish community to come together and recognize that sometimes we do not have all the answers. We must accept the chaos together, and our vulnerability before it.

In 1980, Rabbi Harold Schulweis, who served at the same pulpit in Los Angeles that today I have the honor of serving, delivered a Yom Kippur sermon titled "Accepting Our Vulnerability." Rabbi Schulweis declared that "Rosh Hashanah is not Yom Kippur…. Rosh Hashanah is the celebration of strength. Yom Kippur is the commemoration of weakness. Rosh Hashanah is the celebration of independence. Yom Kippur is the commemoration of dependence. If we split them, then we have a half-truth. And there is nothing more deceitful than a half-truth."

Since Rabbi Schulweis spoke those words forty-three years ago, the world has changed, but fundamentally, we have remained the same. Constantly now, the world presents us with half-truths. Therefore, what we need now more than ever is not only to acknowledge our vulnerability but to practice our courage. In this case, courage is not stubbornness. Courage means an openness to vulnerability and a willingness to change the way we live. We have to have courage to bring others close. We have to have courage to learn new ways forward.

If we ever hope to bridge our fractured society, it's by approaching our brothers and sisters across the aisle, not with certainty, but with courageous openness. If we ever hope to heal family strife, it's not going to be through stubborn will and a need for control, but with courageous compassion and a vulnerability to chaos. If we ever hope to create a relationship with God, it's not going to begin through ego, but through humility.

A miracle occurs on Rosh Hashanah, and it's not the creation of the world.

Jews from every corner, every walk of life, every stream of ritual observance, come together to hear the shofar blast. The miracle is that for the briefest of moments, Jews stand silent and listen. The blast of a ram's horn brings awe and deference to a people that doesn't stand in a line. It forces us, once a year, to divest ourselves of our certainties, to confront our vulnerability, and to look directly at the tohu vavohu that rages below.

Our worship has changed, our location has changed, our language has changed, our dress has changed, but the blast of the shofar is the same sound that we heard at Mount Sinai during God's Revelation. It's the exact same sound that we heard the year before that, and that our grandparents heard, and their grandparents before them. The shofar represents the sound of the eternal.

Never once have I ever regretted plunging into the challenge of an El Al fight. That chaos that we bring on one another, that's all of the generations of tumult and vulnerability of our people trapped into a giant metal cylinder flying at 35,000 feet. When I land in Tel Aviv and take my first steps in the small section of the Mediterranean Sea that belongs to our people, Israel teaches me how to walk with courage and pride in a place that is soaked in vulnerability.

To stand at the gate and turn right is to admit that I belong with all of them. Through the chaos, the bickering, and the kvetching, we all stand vulnerable together. Let's celebrate that. We are a large dysfunctional, complicated, ancient family that has, over time, mastered the art of creation out of chaos. Let's decide to turn right into chaos more often. Let's resolve to summon our collective courage. Let's endeavor to join our spiritual journey forward the only way we know how—together.

28

AGAINST PRESTIGE ADDICTION

Stop Seeking Validation from Those Who Hate Us

LIEL LEIBOVITZ

ONE OF MY FAVORITE HASIDIC stories goes something like this: Once upon a time, a little shtetl somewhere in the Pale of Settlement was rocked by very big news. A celebrated Rebbe would soon ride into town, ask a difficult Talmudic question, and reward whoever could answer it with a purse of gold coins and his beautiful daughter's hand in marriage. Naturally, then, the news made the townsfolk excited, and when the wise, old master finally appeared, they all lined up to receive him and cheer. The Rebbe thanked them curtly, asked his very complicated question, and then announced that he would be leaving town in exactly three days.

Liel Leibovitz is editor at large for *Tablet* Magazine and the co-host of its popular podcast, *Unorthodox*.

The next morning, he was swarmed with hundreds of young men wishing to take a stab at the answer. These weren't the best and the brightest, merely guys who figured they had nothing to lose. The Rebbe heard them all patiently and thanked them all for coming. They were all wrong.

Day two was a bit better. This time, only dozens of dudes showed up, and you could tell just by looking at them that they were the smarter sort. Each carried four or five leather-bound volumes underarm, and each came with reams of notes. None, alas, could crack the Rebbe's riddle.

And so, on day three, the Rebbe awoke to find only ten gents seeking an audience. These were truly the cream of the crop, and it was evident that they'd spent the previous two days studying furiously. Each presented meticulously researched and beautifully argued theories, and the Rebbe thanked each warmly with a handshake and a shot of schnapps. But the question remained unresolved.

The next morning, the Rebbe mounted his horse and began riding away. This time, there were no cheering throngs, crushed as the town was that none of its boys were up to the task. But just as the Rebbe had reached the edge of the forest, he heard a voice begging him to stop. He turned around and saw a young man running toward him. It wasn't one of the students who'd visited him previously; in fact, the young man didn't look like much of a student at all.

"Did you come to try and answer my question?" the Rebbe asked.

"No," said the young man. "I came here because I wanted to know the answer."

Tears welled up in the Rebbe's eyes. He hopped off his horse and gave the young man a long, tight hug.

"You," the Rebbe said. "You are the answer."

What about us modern Jews? Are we the answer, too? Do we care about our ideas and our traditions enough to chase them to the edge of the forest, or are we just here hoping for a fat purse, a good match, and a life of comfort and praise from the powers that be?

Poke at this question, however gently, and the answer you'll get will not thrill you. Put bluntly, Jews—Americans, to be sure, but increasingly, Israelis too—are suffering from a debilitating public health crisis: a collective and deadly addiction to validation, especially from those who hate us most.

***

Consider, for example, the mysterious case of the American campus.

Saunter onto any well-manicured quad these days, and you are likely to see, betwixt beer pong and batty pronouns, some subtle reminder that Jews aren't welcome here. Maybe it will come in the form of faux eviction letters, like the sort Jewish students in NYU awoke one morning from uneasy dreams to find tucked under their dorm-room doors. Maybe it will be your friendly college activist, dressed as a surprisingly Germanic-looking Israeli soldier, stopping you en route to Starbucks and asking you if your yarmulke means you condone the brutal murder of Palestinian babies. Or maybe it'll be something more well-mannered than that, like Berkeley's student groups declaring that they will no longer allow any speaker who supports the idea that the Jews have the right to a state of their own in their indigenous, historical homeland.

These, alas, aren't fictions. They're ripped from recent headlines. And yet, as Jewish parents and students continue to bemoan the growing vitriol inflicted on them by our self-appointed intellectual and moral betters, virtually none are willing to simply walk away from the abuse.

You can tell them that university education has grown criminally expensive, jumping from 23 percent of median annual earnings in 2001 to a vertigo-inducing 38 percent a decade later and rising. You can tell them that university education has grown irreparably stupid, with one recent federal survey finding that only one-quarter of college grads were deemed proficient at "using printed and written information to function in society, to achieve one's goals and to develop one's knowledge and potential." You can tell them that a college degree no longer guarantees a leg up, especially not in a digital economy whose most important skillsets could be just as easily learned on YouTube or a brief coding class and whose most transformative billionaires (see under: Thiel, Peter) are now actively offering qualified young people a small fortune if they forgo college and go into business instead. Apple, Google, IBM, the Bank of America: None require a B.A. anymore.

Why go, then? Why rush to associate with failing institutions no longer remotely serious about the goals and the virtues that had made them world-famous, especially when the quality is dwindling, and the returns diminished?

Because for most Jews, a degree from Harvard is the ultimate affirmation, a sign that they—or their children, or both—have made it here in America.

The same is true everywhere you look. We moan about the culture's tailspin into an ideologically induced fever, yet it never occurs to us to stop gobbling up the swill its commissars cram down our throats. We groan about corporate America's plastic piety, forcing each brand of adult diapers or gluten-free cookies to take public stands about anything from abortions to the war in Ukraine, yet we would never think of just not buying. All we do is bingewatch and impulse shop. All we want is for the cool kids to like us. And so, like high school's biggest losers, we play along and take it on the chin and argue meekly—if at all—when attacked and hope, really hope, that the coveted invite to the party is imminently forthcoming.

It isn't, just like it didn't come in Cordoba or Belarus or anywhere else at any other time in history. Jews are outsiders, which is the source of our moral courage and, paradoxically, the engine of our survival. We can have a good century or three somewhere, enrich the soil with blood, sweat, and careers, but, eventually, we always return to the same realization: We persist because we adhere to a different set of ideas, ancient and brilliant and true. When we do, we thrive even as the colossi around us—Salve, Rome! Khairete, Greece! Merhaba, Ottoman Empire!—stumble and fall. Stand out and you will be all right. Fit in and you, too, will collapse.

* * *

To avoid this unpleasantness, then, four pressing orders of business are now upon anyone wishing to avoid becoming yet another of Jewish history's grim statistics.

First, free your mind. Remind yourself of that timeless quip by Benjamin Disraeli who, when accosted by a hater, replied, with cool hauteur, that when his attacker's ancestors were brute savages on an unknown island, his own forefathers served as priests in King Solomon's Temple. The Great Good is not elsewhere; it's right here, in the same practices and beliefs that have propelled so many of us to greatness for so long under such trying and divergent circumstances.

Which, naturally, leads us to dictate number two: There's nothing sadder than a dumb Jew. You don't have to let that beard or that skirt grow long and go all-in on Orthodoxy, though it's fine if you do. But you do have to spend at least as much time familiarizing yourself with what your tradition actually says as you do on, say, browsing Zillow for that perfectly affordable split-level ranch house in a good school district. Read some scripture. Study some history. Brush up on that Hebrew. Find your own fascinations, whatever they may be, and indulge them. Do it for a little bit, and you'll find that you don't care as much what the Very Smart People, on TV and on campus, and at your dinner party, think.

But we live in the real world, and thoughts and feelings alone, bless them, aren't enough. Actions matter, too, so—commandment number three—start by surrounding yourself with people who like you for who you really are, not for some thwarted version of who they'd like you to be. These new friends may not be at your old country club, or your old alma mater, or your old political party, but they're out there, and they believe the same things you believe, and they're just as lonely and freaked out as you are. So, reach out to them and before you know it, you may find yourself involved in some pretty hopeful stuff.

Like what? This is where the fourth principle sinks in: Be a Zionist. More than a hundred years ago, Zionism bestowed upon us the spirit of Jewish liberation, and liberated Jews don't stick around and let their enemies define or control them. If someone tells you they don't like you, walk away and do your own thing. Big Ice Cream wants to boycott your people? Make your own ice cream and make it more delicious. Big College wants to divest? Start a better one. Waste not one precious minute under the sad impression that you are under any obligation to debate with your detractors. Don't believe for even a blink of an eye that if only you present the right argument in the right way, the haters will open their eyes and embrace you warmly. It's never going to happen, a fact that seems to elude even some otherwise hardened Israelis. Instead of futzing about with *hasbara*—a fool's errand if there ever was one—they should tell their carping foes precisely where they should stick it and then spend every available second and shekel building something new and exciting. It's this generative spirit that has always kept us rolling along, this ability to know when to divest from decaying and demeaning institutions and build new, lively, and essential ones.

And so, build on, brothers and sisters, with pride and with joy. Don't wait for the cavalry to come. I have bad news: It's not coming. I have good news, too: You're now the cavalry, and you have everything you need to save yourselves, and, quite possibly, your country. But nothing worth doing ever happened by waiting for another's permission or praise. Remember, then, just this: No matter how complicated the question, the answer is always us.

29

TO DIE AS A JEW

Living Well in the Face of Mortality

MELANIE LEVAV

WHEN HE WAS FIVE YEARS OLD, our youngest child began learning how to write the letters of the alphabet. Each day, he came home from kindergarten, proud to show us his newest accomplishment. "Big A, little a, what begins with the letter A?" he asked, repeating the words of his beloved teacher, as he showed us his carefully constructed letters and the picture he had drawn of something that began with the letter of the day.

Rabbi Melanie Levav is a board-certified chaplain, licensed social worker, certified end-of-life doula, and second-career rabbi passionate about helping people to live well in the face of mortality, inspired by Jewish wisdom.

On the fourth day, the day of "Big D, little d," he came home with a drawing of a stick figure flat on its back.

"What's this?" we asked.

"*Dead,*" he replied, rather innocently. "*Dead* begins with the letter D."

Of course, *dead* begins with the letter D. His Zayde, for whom he is named, died before he was born. And his Bubbe died when he was just two years old, too young to have permanent memories of her kissing him from head to toe each time we brought him to visit her. And just a few months before starting kindergarten, he'd gone to help say goodbye to our dear friend Nancy as she was dying of breast cancer. "*Dead* begins with the letter D" was a normal response for a child growing up with stories about dead people.

Bubbe and Zayde—my in-laws—were both Holocaust survivors. Their legacies loom large in our family. We talk often about their families of origin, the family members we never met. We visit their graves and read the lists of their siblings and parents killed at Auschwitz—names they requested to be engraved on the back of their own gravestones, to have a physical remembrance of their names. We use Bubbe's challah cover and Zayde's challah knife on Shabbat and holidays. We wear jewelry that Zayde, a watchmaker by trade, made with his hands in his jewelry store, and we eat food made from Bubbe's delicious recipes. Bubbe and Zayde, while now long dead, are very much part of our lives.

So, it wasn't too surprising that our child came home with a drawing to remind us how we've normalized conversations about death in our family. "*Dead* begins with the letter D" also made sense developmentally, as children begin to understand the concept of permanence at around the age of four. Death is permanent. We'd never see our friend Nancy again, we'd never see Bubbe again, and our youngest child would never get to meet his Zayde. But in speaking about them regularly, in telling stories about them—even after their deaths—their lives are very much part of our own.

"I am grateful to you, O Living God, for returning my soul to me...." Every morning, the Jewish liturgy offers us a prescription to remind us of our mortality. *I am grateful*—the first words uttered upon waking—serve as a reminder that waking up is never guaranteed. We offer words of gratitude for the return of our soul to our body, as traditional Jewish belief teaches that our souls separate from our body at the time of death, and the rabbis of the Talmud say that "sleep is one-sixtieth of death" (Berachot 57b).

As we go to sleep at night, we recite the *shema*—our Jewish declaration of faith—"Listen up, Israel, God—our God—God is one." This is the same shema recited as part of the end-of-life prayers at the bedside (the *vidui* or confession), and it is the same shema we are instructed to say when our life is in danger. Bookending our days with meditations on death isn't exactly how we explain this liturgical routine to our children. As adults, however, we come to recognize its meaning.

Or do we? After seeing too many families go through an acute crisis as a result of our inability or unwillingness to talk about dying, I pivoted my career to focus on improving end-of-life care and conversations in Jewish communities.

It doesn't seem like most people think about their own mortality daily, whether or not they recite the traditional Jewish liturgy. It's easier to avoid thinking about death. It's easier not to talk about dying. After all, doesn't the Torah instruct us to "Choose life"?

* * *

Too many families end up in crisis around the end of a loved one's life because they don't talk about or plan for death. We're afraid to talk about hard things. We fear that talking about death might bring it closer, might make it contagious, might even awaken the Angel of Death. Jewish wisdom, however, has much to offer when it comes to confronting death.

"Repent one day before you die," says Rabbi Eliezer in the Talmud.

"But does a person know when they will die?" his students ask.

"All the more so you should repent, lest you die tomorrow," he responds (Shabbat 153a).

Being mindful of our mortality might just help us live. The awareness that tomorrow is never guaranteed helps us direct our actions more positively. Talking about death while we are well can add meaning to our lives by helping us recognize what matters most.

A number of years ago, I attended a spiritual care conference in Israel, where the great Talmudist, the late Rabbi Adin Steinsaltz, was a featured speaker. There he spoke about how educators can most easily teach their students about things they or others experience—but when it comes to death and dying, this we cannot teach from experience.

Rabbis in the Talmud often wondered what it felt like to die. As their teachers neared death, their students asked that the rabbis appear to them in a dream after they'd died. Such was the case of Rava, whose teacher Rav Nahman lay dying:

Rava said: "Master, appear to me [in a dream after your death]."

And so, he appeared to him. Rava said to Rav Nahman: "Master, did you experience pain in dying?"

Rav Nahman replied: "Like the removal of hair from milk" (Moed Katan 28a).

Dying, we learn, can be a very gentle process, free from pain. But Rav Nahman then adds a twist: If God were to call him back to the land of the living, he concludes, he would not want to return, because it would mean a return to the *fear* of death, and that fear is too great.

Stories like these emphasize the value of confronting our mortality, of normalizing the fear of dying. Making Jewish wisdom about death and dying accessible to new generations is essential in helping them live well in the face of mortality, guided by Jewish values and practice.

Over the last few generations, it's become more common for people to die in hospitals and long-term care facilities, removing the physical act of dying from our homes. When my in-laws were growing up in Eastern Europe before World War II, witnessing death wasn't so rare; family members usually died at home. Death was seen and heard more often than most of us experience today.

The work of the sacred burial society, those Jewish community members who take on the holy tasks of preparing the body for burial, was traditionally done anonymously. But it need no longer be so secretive. Holding respect for the dead as the highest honor, reminding ourselves of the certainty of death, can encourage us to think about how we wish to live. Talking about death and dying opens up conversations about life. Talking about how we want to be cared for in our final days, about what Jewish rituals we would like performed upon our death, can raise essential questions about Jewish life and living.

Many of us know at least something about the Jewish rituals after death. But as for the period *before* death, when a loved one is reaching the end of his or her life, many of us have precious little to go on. Yet the ancient Jewish sources actually provide plenty of guidance: From the daily liturgy's offering of a death meditation upon waking and again at bedtime, to Talmudic stories and rules meant to imbue a constant awareness of our mortality, Jewish wisdom teaches us to integrate the awareness of death, of our finite nature, into our daily routines—giving our lives new levels of meaning.

***

From the moment of death onward, we have Jewish rituals designed to elevate respect for life, from the role of the *shomer* in sitting with the body, providing sacred accompaniment as the soul begins its journey of separation, to the ritual washing of the body done by members of the *hevra kadisha*, the sacred burial society, to the wrapping of the body in shrouds, and ultimately, returning the body to the earth through burial.

And beyond burial, we have an elaborate series of rituals to guide us through grief and mourning, from *kaddish* and *shiva* to *yahrzeit* and *yizkor*. Jewish rituals around grief and mourning are better known than those performed just before and after death, but that does not necessarily make them more accessible. Sitting shiva requires a community to support the mourner during the acute stage of grief. Reciting kaddish traditionally involves praying in a quorum of at least ten adults. These rituals are designed for the community, elevating the idea that the mourner is not alone. The idea that the mourner is not alone is also highlighted in the words we say upon exiting a shiva house: "May God comfort you among the mourners of Zion and Jerusalem."

But what about so many Jews, in the United States and elsewhere, who do not live in an active Jewish community? We will need to reimagine Jewish rituals around death and mourning as an opportunity to reengage in Jewish life and living, using the experience of the death of a loved one as the spark.

"Life's ultimate meaning," wrote Rabbi Abraham Joshua Heschel, "remains obscure unless it is reflected upon in the face of death." Talking about and reflecting on death can help us live lives of greater meaning and connection. Following the Talmudic rabbis' lead in imagining what our own death might be like, we, too, can gain perspective on what matters most in life. Contemplating our mortality can help unlock meaning in every living moment. Talking about death will make life better.

30

WHY EXILE MATTERS

How to Rebuild Diaspora Culture Without
Using Israel as a Crutch

SHAUL MAGID

IN MAY 1942, there was a momentous meeting of American Zionist leaders
with David Ben-Gurion and Chaim Weizmann at the Biltmore Hotel in
Manhattan. American Zionists, led by Jewish philanthropist and communal
leader Jacob Blaustein and rabbis Steven Wise and Abba Hillel Silver were
present. The topic of discussion was the state of American Zionism.

Shaul Magid is professor of Jewish Studies at Dartmouth College, Kogod senior research fellow at the
Shalom Hartman Institute of North America, and senior fellow at the Center for the Study of World
Religions at Harvard University.

Ben-Gurion and Weizmann wanted to convince American Zionists to focus their efforts on one goal: Jewish statehood, or what Ben-Gurion called *mamlachtiyut*. Blaustein, Wise, and company considered the proposal and agreed on one condition: that Jews in America would not be considered living in exile *(galut)* but rather in the Diaspora *(gola)*. These American Zionists did not want to be considered as living in some deficient state of Jewish existence, but rather a more neutral state of dispersion. And they wanted Ben-Gurion and Weizmann to acknowledge that.

With the shift from galut to gola, exile significantly diminished as an operative category, at least as far as American Jews were concerned. But what is lost when Jews abandon the concept of exile, or claim that it has ended with the establishment of a Jewish state? As it happens, a great deal. The attempt to erase exile may, in fact, contribute to some of the gravest problems facing today's Jewish global life and the Jewish national project.

"Virtually all Zionist theories and activists have agreed in one way or another," wrote Arnold Eisen in 2014, "*galut* (exile) and *gola*...must be opposed, condemned, denied legitimacy." From Zionism's earliest architects to most of its contemporary advocates, it has remained common to assume that Zionism's success is dependent on the idea that Jewish life in the Diaspora is precarious or dangerous—in effect, an inferior state in which to live.

Eisen's viewpoint is shared by many others. For example, in 1984, Israeli philosopher Eliezer Schweid wrote that the "rejection of Jewish life in the Diaspora—*shlilat hagola*—is a central assumption in all currents of Zionist ideology.... In its most extreme formulation, the idea of *shlilat hagola* implies that the condition of exile will ultimately destroy the Jewish people, first of all in the moral and spiritual sense, and afterward in the physical sense as well, whether by discrimination and persecution, or by assimilation."

But despite the agreement reached at the Biltmore Hotel, according to which exile would effectively end with the establishment of a Jewish state, the larger negative valence of exile has persisted. In 2006, Israeli writer A.B. Yehoshua said, "If you don't live in Israel, your Jewish identity has no meaning at all.... Judaism outside Israel has no future." In a completely different register, but expressing similar sentiments, Zvi Yehuda Kook wrote, in 1967, "Every

Jew living in Israel…is observing the Torah, and every Jew living outside the Land of Israel, religious or not, violates the law and this violation is a sin."

What if today, so many decades after exile was to have effectively ended, history has reached a point where, instead of negating or even derogating exile, we should be articulating and advocating its virtues? What if we, Diaspora and Israeli Jews alike, still *need* exile?

To explain what I mean, it is worth first looking at four different examples of exile-affirmation, each represented by a prominent twentieth-century Jewish figure. Each comes from a radically different perspective, but taken together, they offer ample reasons why the Jewish people as a whole might consider changing course and embracing the virtues of exile.

***

As Hasidic courts recovered from their decimation in Europe after the war, Menachem Mendel Schneerson of Lubavitch and Yoel Teitelbaum of Satmar rose as two Hasidic leaders to become true visionaries of postwar American Hasidism.

Their visions differed greatly. Lubavitch carried a broad intellectual mystical tradition, while Satmar focused more on traditional Talmud study and developed a mentality of separation and piety. Chabad—the Lubavitch organization—focused on outreach to alienated Jews, Satmar on protecting themselves from foreign influence.

Seemingly opposites, regarding the necessity of exile, they are quite similar.

Both Schneerson and Teitelbaum were wed to the notion that Jews still lived under a divine "decree of exile" that may be reaching its end, but that end had not yet arrived. Schneerson goes a bit further, using the term *hatkhalta dige'ula* (the beginning of redemption) or *l'alter lage'ula* (the immediacy of redemption). Yet even with that highly charged language, Schneerson did not tell his followers to immigrate to the land of Israel en masse. In fact, he prevented many of his Hasidim from immigrating to Israel, sending them instead to far-flung diasporic locales to finish the work of exile.

In that sense, both were anti-Zionists, even as Schneerson was less overtly so (in contrast to his two predecessors, who were vehemently anti-Zionist).

Schneerson and Teitelbaum, I contend, were both anti-Zionist because they both rejected, in principle and practice, the maxim of "Negation of the Diaspora."

Teitelbaum's recognition that part of what Zionism seeks to achieve is emptying the Diaspora of Jews, of ending the exile, presents a theological challenge distinct from the existence of the state itself. He thus asks: What is the role Jews in the Diaspora play in cultivating the culmination of exile? Here Teitelbaum deploys rabbinic and later kabbalistic understandings of the *necessity of exile* as a theological precept that must be maintained. He knew quite well that Zionism was not solely about the establishment of a state but also ending the exile, which he believed was tantamount to undermining the redemptive process—and thereby undermining Judaism itself. Thus, for Teitelbaum, Zionism was anti-messianic:

> Being exiled in every land is necessary in order for there to be Torah and devotion to God in all the lands to purify the air of the world in preparation for the indwelling of the *Shekhina*…. But this all requires preparing the air of the entire world to be fit to receive the sanctity of the land of Israel. Thus, righteous ones must be spread throughout the world to prepare the air. Due to the sins of our generation our strength has been weakened such that there is no way to accomplish this except by residing in all places.

Establishing a secular state in the land of Israel is one thing. Negating the Diaspora is another. While the former may be prohibitive on halachic grounds, the latter is prohibitive on theological grounds, truly "forcing the end."

Schneerson, by contrast, is not known as an anti-Zionist, and many of his followers have become part of right-wing Zionist movements. But a careful study of his writings, particularly about America, shows him to be a deeply committed theological Diasporist—and, in my view, not a Zionist at all, even though he was pro-Israel. By this, I mean that he believed that the Messiah cannot arrive until the work in the Diaspora is done. "Negation of the Diaspora" could only represent for him an anti-messianic approach.

Schneerson once spoke about "the exile to America" as a very great descent that could culminate in an "incomparable ascent." And in a striking passage in *Kfar Chabad Magazine* in 1951, Schneerson wrote,

> It is a mistake if we conceive of the worldwide dispersion of the Jewish people in exile as a catastrophe.... As the Jewish sun set in one land, it has already begun to rise in another.... Now that the great powers in Eastern Europe have been destroyed by Fascism and Communism, America has become the focus and fountainhead of Jewish survival.... American Jewry must recognize this sacred historical mission which Divine Providence has entrusted to it at this critical moment of our struggle for survival.

What we see in Schneerson and Teitelbaum, and the immense movements each led, are two Hasidic examples of how exile is viewed positively and necessary, not only existentially, but also theologically and even politically.

* * *

Yet while the fundamental affirmations of exile were being developed and applied in the two most powerful Hasidic movements in the United States, a parallel process was taking place in the depths of secular Jewish literary culture in America. Its principal focus was on the Yiddish language and the culture embodied by it.

Does exile have a language? If exile is more than homelessness, displacement, or deterritorialization; if exile is a state of mind, a state of being, in what language is it expressed? What language best embodies the experience of Jewish exile? This question is addressed by Isaac Bashevis Singer, the celebrated Yiddish writer born in Poland who later immigrated to New York City where his stories and fiction were widely read in many languages. Singer's essay "Yiddish, the Language of Exile" was originally written in Yiddish and was found in his archives under the title *"Der goles yid un yidish"* (The Exilic Jew and Yiddish). It was not published in its original until 2011, but an English version appeared in 1976—a time when a great many older American Jews still spoke Yiddish.

While exile was often viewed from inside the tradition as a form of punishment or at best an "error," Singer came to recognize that exile should better be seen as "a link in religious evolution." In his view, Jews and Judaism are what they are, in all their beauty, *because* of exile. "In my later years it became clear to me that only in exile did Jews grow up spiritually." If Jews had had power and land, they would never have achieved the spiritual heights they achieved:

> Jewishness would never have reached its religious heights had Jews remained in their land. Endless wars and ever-repeating occupations by stronger neighbors would eventually have transformed the Jews into an Arab tribe.... Only because Jews enjoyed a minimum of worldliness could they achieve a maximum of piety. The exiled Jews were aware of this, and they never aspired to be restored to their former state.

Here Singer can thread the needle of his Zionism without the negation of exile. For him, exile is a religious category and only relates to a religious state of being. Because Singer rejected assimilation, he became a Zionist, but he always believed Zionism had to remain a purely secular idea. Israel, he wrote, "would not be the Jewish state they have prayed for in the long night of exile."

While Modern Hebrew, as the secularization of *lashon hakodesh* or the "Holy Tongue," might have become the language that sought to transcend exile, the true language of Jewishness *(yiddishkeit)*, and thus the true language of exile, was Yiddish.

Yiddish is important for Singer because in it is expressed a sense of Jewishness, a longing, an embodiment of the Jewish soul that produced the greatness of Judaism. Hebrew may speak to the revival of a people, but Yiddish expressed their longing, their hope, their moral compass, and their dreams. Other Jewish diasporic communities had their own languages and dialects that Singer readily acknowledges. But for him, there is something about Yiddish that expresses precisely what the new Hebraists wanted to erase: exile. Not as an error or punishment but as an other-worldliness that produced a sense of identity that was beyond religion. Yiddishkeit, Jewishness, an "esoteric" expression of the exilic experience.

***

Exile was not just an important category for thinkers in the Diaspora, how-ever. Even some Zionist thinkers understood its necessity even *within* the sovereignty of a nation-state.

In his posthumous book *Briti Shalom: Right, Left, War, and Peace*, Rabbi Shimon Gershon Rosenberg, known as Rav Shagar, discusses exile *within* sov-ereignty as a necessary rejection of the Negation of the Diaspora. In Shagar's essay "We Have Not Won in Amona," he writes about the Israeli govern-ment's decision to dismantle the illegal settlement of Amona and the settlers' ostensible victory in violently preventing the army from evacuating them from its grounds. The scenes of settlers and the army fighting one another in the evacuation of Amona in February 2006, a year after the evacuation from Gaza, were a shock to many Israelis. Shagar, in particular, felt that the forced evacuation of Jews from Gaza in 2005 and events such as the confrontation in Amona marked a turning point in religious Zionism. It showed the weakness of the movement's vision and the need for a revision of its program.

In the essay, Shagar reflects on the nature of exile as an operative category within the orbit of state sovereignty:

> We should [continue to] build [the territory] of Judah. However, as a community (*kehilla*) and not as a state (*medina*).... There is a notion of exile which is the recognition of a dream that has not yet materialized and yet there is a lack of will to abandon it. This is different from an exile that is about alienation and strangeness. The alienation is drawn from the lack of completeness, combined with the realization that the dream cannot be manifest here and now... This will not cause a rupture in the covenant but rather will protect the notion of "not yet."

He continues in a more explicit manner:

> It is forbidden for us the negate the exile. The ethos of "Negation of the Exile" or the substitution of belief in God with the belief in the

IDF, this in my view is what turns the state into an entity of violence and power. Rather, we must fold exile into the state itself…the establishment of the state is not a rejection of exile but rather…redirects exile into the state itself and thereby elevates it to its next phase, the phase of the political, to a state of justice and compassion.

Shagar views the positive and constructive notion of exile as a humbling force that enabled Jews to develop a deep, empathetic, and ethical posture toward the world and toward themselves. He recognized like few other religious Zionists the hazards of sovereignty as that which could erase both a relationship to the divine and a sense of humanism toward the "other." This, Shagar suggests, is the underside of sovereignty.

What exile contributes is a sense of humility, what Shagar calls the "not yet." The occupational hazard of sovereignty and power is what the rabbinic sages call "forcing the end," on Shagar's reading, translating "not yet" into "now." For Shagar, sovereignty can be, should be, a new phase of exile, a way to create a state with the ethos of exile, a "state of justice and compassion," not "violence and power." Exile for Shagar is not a geographic place but an existential state, one that has positive and constructive, even essential traits that need to be integrated into sovereignty and not banished from it.

What is perhaps most noteworthy about Shagar is that while he was a prominent rabbinic thinker in the religious-Zionist tradition of the elder Rabbi Kook, his argument at heart is a secular one—more similar in some ways to Singer's than to those of the Hasidic leaders. Teitelbaum and Schneerson both required taking a theological position about the nature of messianic redemption. Singer was writing in a world, unlike our own, in which Yiddish was still a plausible vehicle for the embodiment of the Jewish spirit divorced from theology. As against these, only Shagar's argument continues to offer a plausible articulation today that may resonate in both the secular and religious Jewish vocabularies.

It is an argument that may be summarized as a call for the preservation and affirmation of those elements of exile that gave the Jews their unique spiritual and moral character—not just in the Diaspora, but perhaps most importantly in the modern State of Israel.

* * *

Where does that leave us? As the historian Israel Yuval has argued, the notion of a "decree of exile" is a rabbinic myth. It was a hermeneutical move to enable the covenant to survive the trauma of deterritorialization. But this myth became deeply embedded in a binary of exile and redemption, the unhappy state of alienation and the ecstatic promise of liberation through sovereignty.

This binary distorts the Jewish nature of the "Jewish state" by creating an Israeli culture that rejects *in toto* thousands of years of Jewish cultural development; while also effectively forcing Diaspora Jews to choose between the rejection of Israel and acceptance of their inferior status.

But is this binary really necessary or even healthy for Jewish life in the twenty-first century? I would argue that it is not—and that much can be gained by embracing the virtues of exile.

In his 2022 book *The No-State Solution: A Jewish Manifesto*, Daniel Boyarin makes a case *against* "exile" and *for* what he calls "Diaspora nationalism," a state of no-state, a nationalism of multiple particularities engaged in the cultivation of collective life in conjunction with the collective lives of others in the Diaspora.

There is much worth thinking about in Boyarin's proposal. But where we disagree is that he deems exile an "unhappy state," essentially buying into the rabbinic myth of exile that needs to be overcome. I suggest exile as a necessary state, a healthy state, with Singer, a state that cultivates longing and engagement with the world, a state of perpetual "not yet" that generates a productive "hereness" where Jews can embody a mission that reaches beyond any notion of divine election and enables the cultivation of Torah for the world, and not as a shield to protect Jews *from* the world.

Of course, the rabbis do present a minority view of exile as "necessary," but that is largely buried under the longing for some redemptive return to sovereignty and power. Zionism has taken the fantasy of erasing exile as its *raison d'etre*, even written into its national anthem. But what has transpired is not the true erasure of exile and a return to sovereignty and responsible hegemony, but rather the acquisition of sovereignty combined with the mentality of victimhood which has produced what Shagar calls a state of "violence and power."

I am instead suggesting that the Jewish people, including those who identify as Zionists, reconceive their project as an *exilic state*—a state, if one must
exist because states *do* exist, that embodies Shagar's "not yet" or, as Singer
proposes, a state that is *not* the state that Jews have longed for. As much as
many have prayed for the culmination of exile, the irony may be that it is
precisely exile that we need to save us from our worst selves.

Zionism undermines itself, in my view, when it seeks to end exile. Instead,
it should seek to embrace it. But such a revision would require courageous
minds and believing hearts.

31

THE VIRTUE OF INCLUSIVITY

We All Have Something to Contribute to the Mosaic

MANISHTANA

SCENE: Crown Heights, 1992—the Crown Heights riots having erupted just a mere summer earlier—and there I am: an African American Chabad Orthodox ten-year-old (nearly eleven!) standing in a kosher pizza parlor. The ubiquitous stares are front and center, despite my family being one of the three main Chabad-affiliated Black families in Crown Heights, having weathered the storm of the riots alongside our paler coreligionists and our non-Jewish skin-folk.

One particular Chabad patron seems furiously curious at my presence. He stalks over to me, clearly with the air of someone about to interrogate with

---

MaNishtana is the pen name of Rabbi Shais Rishon, an Orthodox African-American-Jewish writer, speaker, rabbi, and author of *Thoughts from a Unicorn: 100% Black. 100% Jewish. 0% Safe.* (2012).

the battery of inquiries I've gotten wearily accustomed to at this point, even as a ten-year-old:

"Are you Jewish? [Yes.] When did you convert? [I'm not a convert.] Are your parents converts? [My dad, yes. My mother, no. Her family has been Black and Jewish since they got here in the 1780s.] Did…"

Y'know. The usual.

But he doesn't ask that.

Instead, he points accusingly at my T-shirt, barking, "Who got you that shirt?"

I look down at my shirt—illustrations of Black men in various occupations, framed with the words "The Hardest Job in America Is Being a Black Man"—and answer, "My father."

"Well," the older man, at least in his forties, hisses with fire in his eyes. "Before he says that, he should try being a *White* man."

And then, suddenly, there is a gob of adult spittle on my pristine sky-blue T-shirt.

Fast forward two decades, and there I am: Still not yet the rabbi I am today, but now a writer and speaker on racial and religious identities and how the intersections tend to manifest and clash in the American landscape. I'm at a Shabbaton in the country. (I'm from Brooklyn. Anywhere with more than seven trees outside of New York is "the country.") The crowd is a politically left-leaning, amiable even if heavy on the "woo" bunch. The blessing for the wine is about to be said for *Kiddush*. This is when I realize that there is no kosher wine anywhere. Apologetically I ask if there is any available, which ends up delaying the proceedings by, from my perception, no more than five or ten minutes. But judging from the—admittedly few—irritated side-eyes darted in my direction—it might as well have been forty years.

Now, I anticipate two very distinct reactions from two very distinct groups to the above anecdotes.

***

To the first, the reaction of liberal Jews will almost certainly be to say that "their" community (meaning, a non-Orthodox one) is "more welcoming," painting traditional communities as backwards not only on issues of religion in a modern world, such as gender equality, social justice, and gay rights but also in race relations. Yet there is a blatant refusal to acknowledge—and almost pathologically so—that the issue of race in Judaism on the Orthodox–non-Orthodox axis is no different than how racism in America manifests in the North as opposed to in the South.

The antagonistic conservative-traditional "Are you Jewish?" is the same as the nonchalant progressive-liberal "So…what's *your* story?" because they're both expressing an identical suspicion: "I don't think you belong here, so explain to me why you are in this space. How are you Jewish?"

(By the way, I'm fine, thanks. How are *you*, Jewish?)

And as for the second anecdote, the traditional-Orthodox retort will likely skew along the lines of feeling validated at how "non-religious" the Left is, bequeathing Judaica to their communities rather than Judaism behind a hollow secularized "Tikkun Olam" (repairing of the world). As if politics that place a premium on inclusivity, equality, and social justice are inherently anathema to "Torah-true" observance.

Of course, both reactions are merely symptoms of the virus of the larger denominational Jewish paradigm, with its stark battle lines declaring, "*We're* the good Jews, *they're* the bad Jews."

Actually, let's take a closer look at the messy American Jewish world: Every successive denomination—from Reform to Orthodox to Conservative to Reconstructionist to Humanist—has defined itself in negatives, moving in one direction in response to one or many other denominations moving in a different direction. And each denomination, rather than looking solely to the Torah or the Talmud—some more or less than others—has taken Judaism into its own hands, injected subjective social norms, and self-defined what makes a "good Jew."

Ideological clashes between socially-conscious Jews—who pursue charity and philanthropy and social justice while eschewing the ritual observances and demands of the religion—and the more traditional, observant, ritualistic Jews—who value insularity over positive interaction with the non-Jewish and differently observant Jewish world—are thus framed in the context of who is the "better" Jew.

Meanwhile, neither side takes a moment to consider that, arguably, *both* sides are doing Judaism wrong, especially if they are not acknowledging the right that the other side is practicing.

To be fair, the argument can be made that the existence of denominations provides a Jewish space to exist in for people who don't completely agree or identify with some of traditional Judaism's dogma, whereas before, in a pre-denominational world, it was either be Jewishly observant or leave the Jewish world completely.

While this may be ostensibly true, the flip side is that it also removes the drive for accountability, leaving Judaism potentially to be inherited by the worst of us, merely because they are "dedicated" to what has been arbitrarily determined to be a "true" Jewish value.

In the centuries before the break, a Jew was forced to be present and improve the Judaism they inhabited. When a Jew did something reprehensible, it fell upon other Jews to show that one person's actions did not represent "Judaism." Nowadays, the briefest glimpse of the social media landscape reveals that all we are currently concerned with is proving that one person's actions doesn't represent "our" Judaism, particularly when they're of a different denomination. Or we can just leave that denomination and go somewhere else entirely.

"This is why I'm not Orthodox."

"That's why I don't agree with Conservative."

"I left the Reform movement because of this."

We've created a trail of excuses that lead all the way until one reaches, "This is why I don't identify as Jewish." And with these aforementioned denominations, we're moving closer and closer to Judaism-"inspired" religions, and further away from Judaism itself. As it stands, the Orthodox and non-Orthodox denominations essentially worship different Gods.

One God says: "Hey, remember all that stuff about keeping Shabbat and eating kosher? LOL. No biggie, just be good to people."

The other God says: "MOAR PRAYER! Also, can you raise some rents for no reason? Your tenants aren't Jewish, so it's negligible if you take more money out of their pockets to give *tzedaka* (charity) to some worthy Jewish causes."

Those are not the same God. And *neither* of those are the God that says: "Hey, it's great that you're awesome to your fellow humans, but it's almost sundown so don't forget about all the responsibilities you have to Me, the Being who put all of you here in the first place. Also don't be crappy to people because honestly, you're not doing Me any favors saying how devoted you are to Me when you're being crappy to My other creations."

* * *

The thirteenth-century Rabbi Hezekiah ben Manoah (also known as the Chizkuni) quotes the midrash Pesikta D'Rav Kahana, in which Rabbi Akiva explains that the Ten Commandments were listed on two separate tablets for a reason. The first tablet, with the first five laws including Shabbat, idolatry, and the like, represents *bein adam lamakom,* those commandments concerning the relationship between Man and God. The second tablet, with the last five decrying theft, adultery, and lying, represents *bein adam l'chavero,* the commandments of the relationship between Man and Man. But when the Enlightenment occurred in the early nineteenth century, it was more than just a break away from the traditional Jews it would later label as being "Orthodox." Each "side" of the break ideologically took only one tablet and began declaring that it was more "whole" for it, rather than realizing that they were both equally broken.

What we—as American Jews, and as citizens of global Jewry—need to understand and actually ingest, is that we all have something to learn from each other. We all have something to contribute to the mosaic of Judaism. Some of us more than others, some of us less. But no one has the full piece or the full picture. More traditionally observant Jews might learn more about how to interact with the non-Jewish, or even secular Jewish world, and put the concept of *derech eretz* (social decency) into actual practical use. Non-traditionally observant Jews could glean the deeper aspects of Judaism—the ones that many Jews flock to Buddhism or yoga to find—but are right in our backyard. And all of us could learn that injecting our ethnicity and experience into our Jewish practices is not an anathema to anything except the contrived Jewish monolith that is invoked to pound square pegs into circular holes when we're confronted by a Jewish too "exotic," too "religious," or too "liberal" for our tastes.

If all the world's a stage, then Judaism is an amazing and eclectic cast, each one of us with our own unique story, with no two tales alike. Yet that's a difficult message to get across, particularly with American Judaism's pathological cognitive dissonance where Jews will acknowledge that there were twelve distinct yet equal tribes, yet simultaneously see different Jewish ethnicities or observance styles as different spots on a totem pole.

We need to get back to remembering that God, like any good doctor, said, "Take these *two* tablets, and call Me in the morning."

Maybe we should start taking that advice. Powerful things happen when we do.

32

AN END TO ASHKENORMATIVITY

Let's Put Bagels-and-Lox Jewishness Behind Us

HEN MAZZIG

MY IRAQI GRANDMOTHER has been a source of incredible wisdom throughout my life. Whenever I find myself in trouble or losing my way, she always tells me to go back to the beginning—or in Arabic, *al-bidaya*.

The Jewish community would benefit immensely from my grandmother's advice.

In recent years, Jews have been mired in endless, unproductive arguments about a wide array of topics, from where the Jewish people fit into the mainstream racial hierarchy in America to whether one person or another

---

Hen Mazzig is the founder of the Tel Aviv Institute and author of *The Wrong Kind of Jew: A Mizrahi Manifesto* (Wicked Son, 2022).

is "authentically Jewish." Are Jews "White," or "White passing"? Can the term "Jews of Color" include *all* Jews who have no recent European heritage, including Mizrahim? Such questions are obviously legitimate, but our obsessive discourse has made it hard to remember where we started. We, too, need to go back to *al-bidaya.*

So where did the Jewish story begin?

We could start by going back to 1500 B.C.E., with a history of the earliest Jews and their neighbors on the coast of the Mediterranean Sea, the Nile River, and Mesopotamia.

Or we could begin with the Jews who built the ancient Israelite kingdoms in the very land where I am writing these words, a meeting place of the ancient seats of civilization—the deserts of Arabia, the Fertile Crescent of Babylonia and Assyria, the Mediterranean islands, the great cities of Egypt, and the highlands of Asia Minor.

I could even start centuries later, in the time of the Second Temple, when Jews—all of whom were likely brown Middle-Eastern people—dedicated their lives to worshiping our God in Jerusalem.

While this Jewish history is well documented in scripture, literature, and archaeology, it seems that many of us have forgotten our roots. We have come to embrace a kind of Christian-inflected communal identity, seeing ourselves as mainly a religion or faith-based community. But to be Jewish is much more than any particular custom or practice or doctrine.

Above all else, we Jews are a people. This distinction is critical because many of those who engage in antisemitism justify their hatred of Jews under the pretext that we are "just a religion." In so doing, they deny our connection to one another as a people, as well as our connection to the land of our ancestors.

Though Jews are originally Middle Eastern, we experienced one of the longest diasporas of any people. As a result, our identity has been diluted by the practices and thoughts of the peoples and nations where we have lived. This also explains why so many of us have little connection to what being Jewish is really about. We abandoned our original, indigenous identity in exchange for acceptance and assimilation.

One specific group of Jews, however, remains the strongest living reminder of where we came from.

When people ask me what I am passionate about, Judaism is likely what I mention first. Ask me where I'm from and I'll first say Israel, knowing full well that the true answer is far more complicated.

My father was born in Tunisia, my mother was born in Iraq. Hearing this, people often ask me, "So you're Arab?"

"No," I answer. "I'm a Jew." More specifically, I am a Mizrahi Jew.

Few people—Jewish or non-Jewish—know who we are. Within the broader Jewish cultural framework, Mizrahim are outliers. Our culture shatters stereotypes and unspoken rules about what being "Jewish" means. Our story derails popular narratives many want to propagate about Jews, antisemitism, and most controversially, Israel. It upends expectations about Jews and race, the Middle East and religion, politics and oppression.

In other words, Mizrahim are, across the Diaspora and around the world, the wrong kind of Jews.

Mizrahi Jews are living, breathing evidence of the indigenous Jewish connection to the region that today is known as the "Arab world." It wasn't always Arab, of course. Until a few centuries ago, before the conquering empires arrived, taking our land and stripping us of our identity, indigenous peoples lived there in relative harmony, with the Jews among them. Jews, accordingly, are, of course, not White, or at least not in the way our current conversations about race define it. Those who try to place us neatly into Western racial categories not only propagate a historical falsehood but rob us of our history as indigenous people.

To be Jewish is to be a part of an ancient agricultural nation connected with a specific land. Mahrina Shije, an entrepreneur and expert in global development who is both Native American and Jewish, once described it perfectly:

[Jews] have had a spiritual and stewardship relationship with the land of Israel since the beginning of our collective memory. Land relationships and stewardship are a critical foundation for any tribe's indigeneity.

There are many ways to prove this connection. Around the world, dating back thousands of years, Jews pray while facing the land of Israel. Our major festivals—Sukkot, Passover, and Shavuot—commemorate the ancient Israelite pilgrimage to the Temple in Jerusalem, and all have thematic connections to the annual phases of farming the land. Our broad system of commandments, known as the halacha, contains dozens of mitzvot that can be observed *only* in our ancient land—including a commandment to refrain from farming it, letting the land rest once every seven years.

Nor does our similarity to other indigenous peoples end with our "stewardship relationship with the land." On Shabbat, we invite spirits to our homes to bless us, which we call the Angels of Peace. We also maintain our connection with our ancestors every Passover by retelling the story of the Exodus as if "we ourselves left Egypt," and by pouring a cup of wine for our elder, Elijah the Prophet.

The same cannot be said for Christianity or Islam, which expanded through the world through conquest, colonization, and forced mass conversion.

Today, Judaism is widely understood as a religion, and in some ways, that's technically correct. More than that, though, Judaism is an indigenous practice that we have mistaken for religion.

This is a difficult concept to grasp given how ideas about "religion" have been ingrained in all of us. But in my experience, young Jews understand this idea better than most. We live in a time when so many lack a true sense of identity, knowing who they really are. Everyone wants to be *unique* in some way, which is understandable. And while every single human has something that makes them special, we must contend with the fact that the Jews are a genuinely unique and diverse people with a beautiful story. We should look inwards as a community, embrace our story, and rejoice in the diversity of our people and the story of our origin.

**

As a Mizrahi Jew, I don't fit well into what is known as "Jewish culture." I enjoy bagels, but I don't consider them *my* cuisine. I have no opinions about whether Katz's Deli is better than Langer's. I'm not even sure which animal pastrami comes from. For me, Shabbat comfort food includes okra, pink beets, pumpkin, hard-boiled eggs, hummus, and pita bread. My grandma doesn't make chicken soup during the holidays or even when I'm sick. Instead, she whips up a batch of stew whose name most of my Ashkenazi friends can't even pronounce.

None of my family members look or sound like Larry David, Sarah Silverman, or Bernie Sanders. Frankly, they look more like the Arabs who owned the chicken restaurant that Larry David called "an antisemitic shithole" on an episode of *Curb Your Enthusiasm,* or the cartoon Pharaoh in *Prince of Egypt* who famously declared, "Enough! I will hear no more of this Hebrew nonsense."

What might also come as a surprise to most readers is that my grandparents *did* experience the Holocaust. It just looked different from what most of us see in movies or learn about in school. The streets of Nazi-sympathetic Iraq and Nazi-occupied Tunisia, where they lived, weren't lined with swastikas. No one scrawled *"Jude"* on their homes or businesses. And none of my grandparents spent time in Auschwitz or Dachau or Buchenwald.

The death camps they would have been sent to—but thankfully avoided—had names that are less widely known. Their neighbors were shot and raped in antisemitic riots, which most Diaspora Jews have never been told about.

So, not only do I not fit a Jewish stereotype, I'm not a part of the culture that most Diaspora Jews define as Jewish. That brand of Jewish just isn't mine.

Of course, I still experience prejudice. But that comes from both Jews and non-Jews alike. While neo-Nazis regularly threaten my life because I'm a Jew, many Jews take issue with me for being a gay Mizrahi. Believe it or not, I've been told on more occasions than I can count that I am not "really Jewish." That I am, in other words, the wrong kind of Jew.

And still, I keep calling out antisemitism, whatever the ideological or political camp it comes from. Of course, it's not hard to call out antisemitism when it comes from the far Right, when White nationalists march through streets shouting, "Jews will not replace us."

Although I've proven my liberal credentials time after time, I'm also not afraid to shine a light on how progressive movements exclude Jews. I also have the audacity to be an Israeli who believes that Israel is not the perfect utopia they told you about in Hebrew school. A country doesn't have to be perfect to be beautiful, though.

I'm not afraid to hold your favorite role models and celebrities accountable when they express bigoted views against Jews or Israel. But with time, I've grown more measured. While many Jews are quick to cancel someone for their bad or misinformed opinions, I try to educate people and build common ground. Rather than rush to punish, I look for ways to find redemption for those whom half of Twitter would burn at the stake.

Within the Jewish space, I'm frequently off message. I just can't share my story of beating back hatred against Jews and the centuries of subservience my ancestors survived without *also* mentioning that Mizrahi Jews still face inequalities today. Though I'm not the kind of Jew who likes to air our dirty laundry in public, I'm also not the kind of Jew who would hang my own people out to dry.

I'm not a silent Jew either, and I don't give cover to antisemites. Bigots cannot buy my silence, even at the price of acceptance. I don't choose politics over truth, and will not protect my friends over my people. I will not kneel before *any* movement that refuses to offer Jews a seat at the table.

When I feel rejected by Jewish society, I don't scour for acceptance from adversaries. I am not viewed by antisemites as a "good Jew," for I know that according to antisemites, there's no such thing as a "good Jew." When I encounter Jews who push a hateful ideology against our own people, I choose to be bad over being useful.

I'm bad at meeting expectations of what Jewish should look like, sound like, or think like. I'm bad at looking the other way at bigotry, whether it comes from within our community or from people who claim to stand up for marginalized groups but harbor hatred, ignorance, and apathy toward Jews.

I'm also "divisive." At least, that's what I'm told.

I'm not the only one. Jews like me exist. Our experiences differ from those of the mainstream, and we deserve respect. Whenever I'm given an opening, I bring up my family's history, even when it's uncomfortable or absent from a textbook.

Worst of all, I continue to be Jewish—and a loud Jew at that. No matter how much I fail to live up to others' expectations, I will never stop owning my

Jewish heritage. My refusal to be quiet about it begins every day with my Star of David around my neck, never tucked away or hidden from view.

I am the wrong kind of Jew, and I feel good about it. I love every minute of being Jewish on this earth, and the legacy of every Jew before me—including but not limited to Mizrahim.

When I ask questions, they're complicated ones. When I am questioned, I give even sharper answers.

I will not assimilate. I refuse to give up my own essence in all its complexity, even if doing so would appease those who can't understand it or resent it.

***

It takes the sun's light eight and one-third minutes to reach the earth. So, while we are living in this moment, everything around us is elucidated by the past.

By telling the full story of the Jewish people, by accepting the countless rays of light our history sends us, we can all see more clearly.

And that story cannot be told without the story of Mizrahi Jews. And not just about our history, cuisine, and culture. It has to go deep into the real contradictions of our lives. It must grapple with the invisibility that taints our experience, and explore concrete ways we can achieve full equality and dignity.

I am not the only person capable of telling the Mizrahi story. I am, however, the only one who can tell *my* Mizrahi story. My tale crosses countries, continents, boundaries, and controversies. Mizrahim don't need a history book. We don't need a memoir. We need a manifesto.

I will not present the Mizrahi experience like a textbook or an assortment of artifacts under plexiglass at a museum. We must take the Mizrahi story out of its case, touch it, and even leave a few fingerprints. I don't want people to just read about being Mizrahi—I want them to experience it too. To really understand one's story, you have to feel it. It's the only way you and I can see our whole selves and the infinite possibilities before us.

But for that, we have to start by going beyond what "Jewish" means to the people around us, those who may love or hate us, those who form the accepted narratives about the "right" kind of Jews. We need to go back to *al-bidaya*—or in Hebrew, *b'reishit*. We must go back to the Beginning.

33

AN AGGADIC JEW

Liberate the Power of Jewish Storytelling

RUBY NAMDAR

I'M OFTEN ASKED: "What kind of Jew are you?" Usually, the question is followed by a menu of options: "Religious or secular?" "Reform or Conservative?" and so on. And sometimes, in especially interesting cases, I'm also asked if I'm a "halachic Jew."

These are the moments I particularly relish. I get a kick out of the surprised smile on their face, the curious wide eyes, when I offer my answer. "No," I tell them. "I'm an *aggadic* Jew."

Ruby Namdar is an Israeli-American author born and raised in Jerusalem to a family of Iranian-Jewish heritage. His latest novel *The Ruined House* (HarperCollins, 2017) won the Sapir Prize, Israel's most prestigious literary award. He lives in New York City with his wife and two daughters.

As for the next question—"What does *that* mean?"—I answer in a typically Jewish fashion: "Let me tell you a story."

More than forty years have passed since my first Talmud class, and I can still remember vividly how grotesque and absurd it was. I was a student in an ultra-secular middle school in Jerusalem. Even the name of the class was bizarre: *Toshba*. The unfamiliar, indecipherable term, which turned out to be an acronym for *torah sheb'al peh* or the "Oral Law," all but proclaimed the pedagogical catastrophe I was about to endure.

The bell rang its jarring electric chime, and a short, bland-looking man drifted into the classroom. Round and balding, he had watery, bulging eyes and a small moustache laying claim to his upper lip. He was dressed like a caricature of an Old-World Jew: shapeless blazer, nominally white shirt yellowed from what looked like decades of ironing, black pants with frayed cuffs. This archaic apparition of a man had worn-out black leather shoes and a black kippa that looked like it had been cut from the same piece of fabric as his pants. It, too, had frayed edges.

The teacher's soft voice and foreign accent contrasted sharply with the rowdy, sweaty, youthful disposition of the class, the school, and Israeli society as a whole.

The text that he chose to teach us, or was chosen for us by the supervisors of the Toshba curriculum, was also about as distant as possible from the concerns of these secular schoolkids—a choice could only be described as a chronicle of failure foretold. Without any warning, this little man thrust us into the thick (pun intended) of an unfathomably uninspiring halachic question regarding the thickness of a barrier erected by unnamed neighbors in a courtyard between their homes, which, by the time the matter had come to our attention, had been lying in ruins for many centuries in ancient towns with unpronounceable names and whose locations had been lost to the mists of time.

"In the case of the neighbors who wanted to build a barrier in the courtyard," announced the Talmudic Tractate Baba Batra in a decisive tone, "they should build the wall down the middle. In places where it was the custom to build *gavil gazit kepisin levinin* they build all in accordance with the custom of the land. *Gavil* one gives three *tefachim* and the other gives three *tefachim*.

Gazit one gives a *tefach* and a half and the other gives a *tefach* and a half. With *kepisin* one gives two *tefachim* and the other gives two *tefachim*. With *levinin* one gives a *tefach* and a half and the other gives a *tefach* and a half."

We looked, stunned, at the little man with the black kippa, who explained in an infuriatingly patient voice all the assumptions, of both engineering and law, behind this bewildering passage.

The climax of the class arrived when the Hebrew text of the Mishna ended, and the Talmud switched over to full-blown Aramaic. *"Mai mechitza?"* one of the ancient Babylonian disputants asked rhetorically, before delivering an immediate winning retort: *"Guda!"* The final impenetrable word echoed pointlessly across the classroom.

After a few seconds of silence, my friend, Danny, a venerable wise-ass, whispered in my ear: *"Gudagudagudaguda!"* He cracked himself up over the comical, prehistoric ring of the word as it rolled off his tongue like a boulder tumbling down a mountainside.

I have no idea how we survived our Talmud class for the rest of the school year. It has been completely wiped from my memory. But I cannot forget the barrier that grew ever higher between us and the world of the Talmud with every twist and turn of the halachic discussion about walls, fences, building materials, and yard sizes—a discussion so irrelevant to our lives that it seemed to have been designed for the sole purpose of making sure nobody ever looked past it to see what else might be lurking in this strange, alien world.

* * *

Fortunately for me, the story does not end there, as perhaps it was supposed to end, and as it indeed ended for most people of my generation. Ironically, it was a different part of the Talmud—the part that had been relegated to the margins by many generations of uncompromising, humorless yeshiva methodology—that would capture my heart and magically rope me in. The same body of work whose halachic discussions had left me on the outside looking in would eventually open its gates of *aggada*—the creative, unfettered collection of stories, parables, and fables that were inexplicably interlaced among the legalistic, analytical discussions of the law. It lit up the dialogue, each time anew, with its wild imagination, impressive intellectual freedom, and blissful lack of inhibitions.

Like every serious addiction in my life, my taste for the exotic, intoxicating flavor of the aggada took time to acquire.

I didn't grow up with a tradition of Torah study, and certainly not of Talmudic scholarship. I never studied in a yeshiva, and it's highly doubtful that in the land of my forefathers, the city of Mashhad in northeastern Iran, there could be found even a single set of the Talmud. By contrast, the broadly expressive, sun-drenched words of the Bible had made a deep impression on me through the superb Tanach classes our ultra-secular Israeli schools knew how to teach. Even the poetry of the Siddur and other liturgy, which I encountered through our not-too-frequent visits to the synagogue, had from a young age pulled me into its magical beauty and mystery.

The Talmud, on the other hand, was a locked garden. For some reason, it always struck me as an old, dilapidated thing, twisting and convoluted, sealed with the mark of Otherness and alienation. Even the minimalism of the aggadic story, with its predilection for the extreme and the absurd, initially struck me as a bit perverse—not appealing in the least. It took me some time, driven by an inexplicable determination to keep going back and trying again, to develop a taste for its peculiar art of storytelling. I came to see it as a wild game of intellectual hide-and-seek, where text and reader are competing to dig up the subtext buried between the lines.

Another thing I understood, which took me some time before I could say it out loud, was that the aggada isn't just not-preachy and not-self-righteous; it is genuinely subversive. No Talmudic sage or rabbinic superhero is cut even an inch of slack for the slightest moral lapse. Unlike the self-righteous pietists today for whom rabbis are infallibly holy and pure, the aggada goes out of its way, again and again, to show us the true human condition, which is never pure or morally perfect.

The pleasure I took from the aggadic mindset only increased the more deeply I understood this last point. It reached its peak when I encountered the darkest, boldest of Talmudic stories—such as the erotic-theological odyssey of Rabbi Elazar ben Dordia, the obsessive whoremonger who was determined not to leave a single prostitute on earth unvisited. The determination of this serial sex addict was not meant to be read only as a cautionary tale, but also as an inspirational story of conquest and repentance.

This was the first time I understood what the clever system of concealing the Talmud's true nature had tried to hide from me: *The Talmud in general, and the aggada in particular, is an extremely unorthodox text.* The famous passing of wind unleashed in a moment of heated passion by the aggada's most famous whore, for whom Ben Dordia had crossed seven rivers weighed down by a purse full of gold coins; the fart that had cleared the sinner-rabbi's moral haze and sent him on a heroic, beautiful journey of repentance—that very same fart also awoke me from my own dogmatic slumber, born of the ignorance and prejudice imprinted from my youth. It opened my eyes to the subversive, bold, and infinitely refreshing nature of the Talmudic story and allowed me to appreciate its timelessness and relevance to our own contemporary human struggles.

Like a culinary connoisseur who moves on from popular drinks and foods to their more refined and purist versions, I, too, moved on, over the years, from modern Hebrew editions of the tales of the sages to their unmediated Talmudic origins. Aramaic, that mysterious ghost-language of my youth, became clearer and more compelling with every reading. The Talmudic craft of storytelling, too, the concise narrative that invites colorful, creative explication, started tugging more and more at my heart.

I look back today to that long-forgotten Toshba class about the thickness of a courtyard wall, and I think of how the Talmud once seemed to me so foreign, burdensome, and pointless, but has now become for me an object of intense intimacy—and I'm amazed at the journey I've taken.

***

I do not mean for any of this to come across as an attack on the world of halacha. Many Jews find in its study and practice a great source of meaning and inspiration. But for every "halachic Jew," there are so many others for whom the demanding, analytical, practical universe of religious law is off-putting, and certainly not a realistic source of Jewish identity.

This is not new. As opposed to what is widely believed, the halacha was never the common denominator of Jewish identity. It never played the decisive, unifying role that rabbis and halachic educators claim it did. Jews lived and practiced in innumerable ways, according to a variety of ancient and new practices, some of which are known to us, but most have been lost to time. The halachic discourse has always been restricted to a small group of scholars, an intellectual elite talking mostly among themselves, a kind of meta-culture that hovered above the endless tussle of Jewish daily life in all its colors, flavors, and scents.

That same elite, over many generations, pushed the aggada to the sidelines, treating it like a kind of illustration meant to attract laymen too thick-skulled and crass to appreciate the nuances of the cerebral halachic argument.

Fortunately, the Talmud's authors were much smarter than those who claimed ownership of it in the generations that followed. From the Talmud's perspective, the aggada was no less important than the halacha. There is no indication in the Talmud that the aggada was a minor character in the Talmudic drama, a kind of decoration for the halachic text or folk entertainment for the ignorant.

The opposite is the case: The most important, inspiring moments in the Talmud, those in which the same rabbis who spent days and nights arguing about the law are suddenly made to stand historical, moral, and theological judgment—those are the moments of aggada, not halacha. Sometimes I wonder if the truth is even further from what is claimed: Maybe the cold, cerebral halacha is actually the substructure on which the sages built their most important discourse—that of the aggada. Some might want to stone me for making such a subversive claim, but I'm willing to stand behind it, at least as a possibility worth considering.

* * *

In modern times, when "identity" is something fluid and intensely personal, rather than being dictated from above, the aggada has become even more important. Today, the *story* is the central tool for any discussion of identity—both the individual story, as derived through the various forms of psychotherapy; and the collective story, as told by historians, sociologists, journalists, politicians, and ideologues who weave the fabric of meaning that unites us as a civilization.

Along these lines, the Jewish story—as is reflected in the narratives of the Bible, the aggada and midrash, as well as modern Jewish literature, which to me is a direct continuation of these ancient narratives—is the most important tool for identity available to us as modern Jews.

We live in a time when our search for meaning comes well before any search for norms dictated from without. The ancient Jewish texts, which tell our eternal story, are a gold mine of meaning which, despite their age, remain surprisingly relevant. The freedom of thought, boundless imagination, and disarming intellectual honesty of our sages offer an amazing source for inspiration and a wonderful model for us to imagine a Jewish future built on the same values, images, and compelling stories that were the bedrock of our ancestors' Jewish identity.

The "aggadic Jew" may have never fully disappeared, but it is nonetheless vitally important to declare, loud and proud, his return to the center stage of Jewish identity in our time.

34

UN-HIJACK HUMAN RIGHTS

How a Movement Founded by Jews Can Be Restored

HILLEL C. NEUER

THE YEAR 2023 marked the seventy-fifth anniversary of two seminal events in modern history: the United Nations' adoption of the Universal Declaration of Human Rights, and the creation of the first Jewish state in two millennia.

In 1948, it seemed natural that supporters of Israel such as Eleanor Roosevelt and René Cassin were also leading figures at the United Nations in crafting its human rights declaration and ushering in the international human rights movement.

Hillel C. Neuer is the executive director of United Nations Watch, an independent nongovernmental human rights organization based in Geneva, Switzerland.

Today, however, in the most influential human rights circles, it is the opposite: Jews who do not publicly disown their attachment to Israel, as well as non-Jews known for supporting the Jewish state, are pariahs.

Jews need to understand the seismic transformation that has taken place within the human rights movement. In the last half-century, it has turned against Israel and its supporters, channeling a new form of antisemitism. The time has come to undertake an effective strategy to fight back.

Such a strategy, however, is at hand. A few indomitable organizations still hold out against the tide. Given enough transformational help, a new human rights movement can emerge, one that is loyal to the principles that first animated the movement three-quarters of a century ago.

But to understand how this is possible, we need a closer look at how "human rights" became so central to the global conversation in the wake of World War II—and how it was subsequently commandeered by the radical forces that control the discourse to this day.

* * *

Few people today are aware of just how much of the global human rights movement that emerged in in the second half of the twentieth century can be traced to the work of heroic Jewish lawyer-activists who were proud of their heritage.

René Cassin was a French legal scholar and judge who served as a founding member of the UN Commission on Human Rights, co-drafted the Universal Declaration of Human Rights, and was awarded the Nobel Peace Prize in 1968. He was also a public defender of Israel's rights. On the eve of the Six-Day War, Cassin published articles in *Le Monde* and elsewhere arguing that Gamal Abdel Nasser was the aggressor under the law, while Israel had the right to defend its "legitimate right to exist." In 1968, when a UN human rights summit targeted Israel, Cassin, head of the French delegation, walked out in protest.

Cassin's work was influenced by Hersch Zvi Lauterpacht, the towering international law authority of the twentieth century, who published his International Bill of the Rights of Man in 1945, which was credited for inspiring the Universal Declaration of Human Rights as well as the European Convention on Human Rights. He conceived the idea of including in the charter of the Nuremberg Tribunal the legal concept of crimes against humanity, which was used to convict Nazi war criminals. Lauterpacht was also a lifelong Zionist activist who taught himself fluent Hebrew, founded the World Union of Jewish Students, married a Sabra woman from Jerusalem, and, at the request of her niece's husband, Abba Eban, contributed in 1948 to the drafting of Israel's Declaration of Independence.

A contemporary of Lauterpacht was Raphael Lemkin, the Polish lawyer who initiated the UN Genocide Convention and coined the term. In Warsaw, before the war, Lemkin advocated for Jewish minority rights in Poland, published articles and poems in Hebrew, taught law at a Zionist rabbinical seminary, wrote a Yiddish column in the leading Zionist daily newspaper, and was secretary-general of a Zionist organization.

Across the ocean, one of the leading figures of the U.S. civil rights movement was Morris Abram, a Jewish lawyer from Georgia who won landmark cases for the equal rights of African Americans, and who helped draft the UN convention against racial discrimination. Abram was also president of the American Jewish Committee and a leading advocate for the right of Jews to emigrate from the Soviet Union. In 1993, after serving as U.S. ambassador to the UN in Geneva, he created UN Watch, an independent organization to hold the world body to its Charter principles—which I have had the privilege of directing for nearly two decades.

For these Jewish trailblazers of international human rights, their commitment to both universal principles and Zionism was regarded as complementary. After 1967, however, attitudes in the world of human rights would dramatically change.

* * *

Very soon after the founding of Israel, some in the West already began to depict the Jewish state in demonic terms. In the 1950s, the renowned historian Arnold Toynbee, who had earlier described the Jews as a "fossilized" and "extinct" society, literally wrote that Zionism was "demonic." He pioneered the idea that the movement for a Jewish homeland was a form of Nazism. In his monumental *A Study of History*, Toynbee accused the Zionists of being "disciples of the Nazis" who chose "to imitate some of the evil deeds that the Nazis had committed against the Jews." In January 1961, as reported in the *New York Times*, Toynbee told students at Montreal's Hillel House that "Jewish treatment of Arabs in 1947 was as morally indefensible as the slaughter by the Nazis of 6,000,000 Jews." In his books, he wrote that Israel's crimes were even worse than those of the Nazis.

Toynbee's libels didn't stick at first. At that time in the Western world, Israel's struggle against Arab armies was seen as David fighting Goliath.

In June 1967, however, everything changed. Soon after the Six-Day War, some Western European leaders, eager to appease the oil-rich Arab world and perhaps to alleviate Holocaust guilt, began to characterize Israel as an aggressor. Charles de Gaulle, France's president, and hero of the French resistance to the Nazis, spoke at length at a November 1967 news conference about the "apprehensions" many felt at an empowered Jewish nation-state. "Some even feared," he said, "that the Jews, hitherto dispersed…would, once they were reunited in the sites of their former greatness," acquire an "ardent and conquering ambition."

Meanwhile, the analogy of Zionists as Nazis was propagated throughout the Soviet Union and disseminated by its global disinformation apparatus throughout the Third World. Drawing upon classic antisemitic themes and popular antisemitic sentiments across both the Soviet bloc and the Arab world, Israel became the singular evil lurking behind every form of Western malfeasance. Eventually, in the West, the Communist meme became a mantra of the New Left. Toynbee's narrative of Israel as a Nazi-style aggressor began to stick.

A new mutation of antisemitism had emerged. The Jewish state was not acting in self-defense but was rather a colonialist, imperialist, and racist aggressor. By 1975, the United Nations General Assembly, the same body that had once voted for a Jewish state, declared Zionism to be a form of racism. In the United States, university campuses, liberal churches, the labor movement, and others on the Left gradually turned against Israel.

The shift in the culture influenced the human rights movement. There were some activists like Bob Bernstein, the head of Random House, who published dissidents such as Andrei Sakharov, Natan Sharansky, and Václav

Havel, and who formed Helsinki Watch to monitor basic freedoms behind the Iron Curtain.

But a more dominant camp emerged from the Vietnam antiwar movement, and it targeted anti-Communist regimes allied to the U.S. in the Cold War. This camp was deeply influenced by the Left's 1960s ideology of anti-colonialism, in which the traditional Marxist paradigm of class struggle was replaced with a Manichaean view of a world divided between the West and the rest.

***

Perhaps no one person has embodied this radical ideology more than international law professor Richard Falk, a prolific author who taught at Princeton University and served for years on the advisory board of Amnesty International's U.S. branch, on a Human Rights Watch board, and as an official of the UN Human Rights Council (UNHRC).

Falk admired violent radicals who attacked Americans. In 1973, he defended Karleton Armstrong, who pleaded guilty to bombing the University of Wisconsin Army Mathematics Research Center, which killed a researcher and injured three others. Falk appealed for full amnesty for those who used violence to oppose the "illegal, immoral, and criminal" war in Vietnam.

In 1979, days after Ayatollah Khomeini seized power, Falk reassured the world, in a *New York Times* op-ed entitled "Trusting Khomeini," that "the depiction of him as fanatical, reactionary, and the bearer of crude prejudices seems certainly and happily false." Khomeini's entourage, insisted Falk, had "a notable record of concern for human rights." In 2004, Falk wrote the foreword to *The New Pearl Harbor*, a conspiracy tract about the September 11, 2001 terrorist attacks authored by his disciple David Ray Griffin, which Falk praised as "authoritative."

In 2007, Falk published an article accusing Israel of planning "a Palestinian Holocaust," which he said was "especially painful" for him "as an American Jew." Falk has previously described his family background as "assimilationist Jewish with a virtual denial of even the ethnic side of Jewishness." When useful, however, he invoked his status as an ashamed Jew.

The next year, at the request of the Palestine Liberation Organization (PLO), Falk was appointed by the UNHRC to a six-year term as Special Rapporteur on Palestine, tasked with investigating "Israel's violations of the principles and bases of international law."

Falk went on to champion Hamas, justifying their use of violence and hailing their "spirit of resistance." He insisted that Hamas aimed for "long-term peaceful co-existence."

Over time, like others in the world of human rights, Falk became obsessed with Israel. In a 2011 blog post outlining the twenty-first-century agenda for the Left, Falk ranked "support for the Palestinian Solidarity Movement, including its BDS campaign" at the top.

* * *

Falk was not alone. Kenneth Roth, who recently retired after three decades as director of the powerful organization Human Rights Watch (HRW), relentlessly depicts Israel with Nazi-like terms, accusing the Jewish state of "crimes against humanity." Over the past two decades, whenever Israel's cities and towns were targeted by Hamas and Hezbollah with thousands of missiles, HRW rushed to publish reports condemning Israel. These were then regurgitated by Arab-sponsored UN commissions of inquiry and sent on to the International Criminal Court as grounds to indict Israeli leaders and officers.

Like Falk, Roth was born Jewish. He has little, if any, attachment to the Jewish people or faith, identifies primarily as a member of the Left, and rarely speaks about his Judaism except to invoke it as a shield when condemning Israel.

Under Roth's leadership, HRW hired anti-Israel activists such as Sarah Leah Whitson, Joe Stork, Omar Shakir, and Sari Bashi. The result, according to a 2010 article in *The New Republic*, was that the organization published more reports on Israel than on brutal dictatorships in the region such as Iran, Syria, Saudi Arabia, and Libya. The objections of HRW's founders—notably Bob Bernstein, its founding chair emeritus, who in a bombshell *New York Times* op-ed in 2009 accused the organization of having "lost critical perspective" in its obsession with Israel—fell on deaf ears.

In 2010, George Soros announced a $100 million grant to HRW. Roth now had carte blanche, and his anti-Israel animus only intensified. Year after year, Roth and HRW pilloried the Jewish state.

In April 2021, this culminated in HRW's publication of a massive, 224-page report accusing Israel of "apartheid" and "persecution," which amount to "crimes against humanity" that are "among the most odious crimes in international law." The report involved three years of work by more than thirty people, including Roth.

Not coincidentally, a year later, in February 2022, Amnesty International published its own 280-page report, entitled "Israel's Apartheid against Palestinians: Cruel System of Domination and Crime against Humanity."

Kristyan Benedict, a senior Amnesty campaigner who has been accused of making antisemitic remarks and of threatening to "smack" a pro-Israel activist, tweeted gleefully about all the Amnesty T-shirts and other merchandise to support their "End Israeli Apartheid" global campaign, along with "loads more resources"—including an Amnesty online course about Israeli apartheid, an "End Israel's Apartheid" social media toolkit, flyers, stickers and posters, and a blueprint on how to lobby MPs to support their campaign.

When Amnesty official Philip Luther came to Israel to present the report, he was asked by the *Times of Israel*'s Lazar Berman why the organization has yet to apply the same apartheid investigation to China's treatment of the Uighurs, Turkey's treatment of the Kurds, and other countries such as Iran, Iraq, and Syria. "There were discussions about where [else] we might start to do it," explained Luther. "But we haven't started."

Let there be no doubt: When the world's largest human rights organizations orchestrate global campaigns to portray Israel falsely as a racist state that commits crimes against humanity, indeed as the *most important* human rights villain in the world, they have been poisoned with the hatred of antisemitism.

* * *

So, what is to be done?

Jews will always be engaged in universal human rights. Intervening to fight injustice is part of Judaism. The biblical Abraham became the first human rights lawyer in recorded history when he intervened to challenge God's plan to destroy the wicked cities of Sodom and Gomorrah, pleading: "Would You also destroy the righteous with the wicked? Shall not the Judge of all the earth do justly?"

Although we are obligated to call out the lies and distortions coming out of what were once respectable human-rights bodies, this cannot be the exclusive focus for those who truly care about human rights. The challenge today, rather, is to find alternatives—international human rights organizations that continue to fight the good fight in the spirit of the movement's founders and have not been hijacked by anti-Western ideology and antisemitism masked as human rights and anti-racism—and to invest in their expansion. To rebuild the human rights movement, in the spirit of Lauterpacht, Lemkin, Cassin, Abrams, and Bernstein—but through alternative institutions.

To be clear, such worthy groups exist today. One is the Human Rights Foundation (HRF) based in New York. Thor Halvorssen, its founder and CEO, was born in Venezuela. His family members suffered under the regimes of Hugo Chavez and Nicolas Maduro, and he has a visceral resistance to authoritarianism. HRF is best known for its annual Oslo Freedom Forum, an elegant conference featuring dissidents from China, Cuba, Russia, and other tyrannies. The event brings together activists, journalists, artists, and philanthropists. Garry Kasparov, the Russian world chess champion and dissident, serves as chair of HRF and is an active presence at the Freedom Forum.

A like-minded organization is the Raoul Wallenberg Centre for Human Rights, founded and chaired by Irwin Cotler, Canada's former justice minister and one of the world's preeminent international human rights lawyers. My former teacher at McGill Law School, Cotler has for decades acted as counsel for political prisoners around the world. Cotler is also one of the most articulate voices fighting anti-Israeli bigotry and serves as Canada's special envoy to combat antisemitism. With his gravitas, the Montreal-based center enjoys access to high-profile figures, which it has used to advocate effectively on behalf of political prisoners in Russia, Iran, Venezuela, and elsewhere.

Finally, there is UN Watch in Geneva, the only human rights group dedicated to fighting anti-Israel bias and antisemitism at the United Nations, where it holds accreditation as a non-governmental organization. UN Watch monitors the world body by the yardstick of its Charter and promotes funda-mental freedoms for all.

A key participant in the debates of the UN Human Rights Council, UN Watch's speeches have been viewed online by millions. When the Islamic Republic of Iran was elected to the UN Commission on the Status of Women, UN Watch led a successful campaign to expel the regime. Less well known is UN Watch's work to defend courageous dissidents, such as by bringing them to testify at the United Nations to call out their oppressor regimes, many of whom, ironically, sit on the UNHRC. UN Watch leads a coalition of twenty-five small human rights groups, which together organize the annual Geneva Summit for Human Rights and Democracy. The gathering provides a global platform for dissidents from regimes such as Belarus, China, Cuba, Iran, Russia, Venezuela, and Zimbabwe.

Taken together, organizations like HRF, the Raoul Wallenberg Center, and UN Watch form the core of what could emerge as an alternative global human-rights movement, one dedicated to the principles of freedom, rights, and human dignity that first animated the movement—and a much-needed alternative to the anti-Western and anti-Israel agenda dictated by HRW and Amnesty.

Such an outcome, however, will require a massive investment. Today, HRW has 600 employees, a $100 million budget, and $238 million in assets. Amnesty International, a sprawling global organization with millions of mem-bers, has 2,500 staff in seventy countries, and in 2021 spent $374 million.

By contrast, HRF, the Raoul Wallenberg Center, and UN Watch *com-bined* have a staff of sixty, and an annual budget of about $14 million.

What the world of human rights desperately needs is a massive counter-ini-tiative—effectively a rebirth. Far-sighted philanthropists who care passionately for both human rights and Israel need to come forward with an ambitious and innovative funding plan, to help existing and new human rights organizations change the narrative—to move away from falsely demonizing Israel and the West, and to focus instead on helping millions of victims in desperate need of the world's attention to fight tyranny and abuse. The potential to scale up the impact is significant, by producing exponentially more social media campaigns, reports, legal briefs, op-eds, press releases, conferences, videos, podcasts, and meetings with decision-makers. The effect would be to change the narrative—to fix what is wrong in the culture of human rights.

In the twentieth century, Jewish visionaries gave the world universal human rights. It is time for a new generation to save their legacy—to turn human rights away from its present obsession with Israel and the Jews, and toward saving humanity from the rampant abuses of evil regimes around the world.

35

DEEP ROOTS MAKE STRONG BRANCHES

Build Our Future by Investing in Our Common Heritage

IRINA NEVZLIN

FOR YEARS NOW it has seemed that the Jewish people, both in Israel and around the world, is living perpetually on the brink of a crisis. Israelis worry about terrorism, constitutional reform, the economy, the Iranian nuclear threat, the treatment of minorities, public transportation, healthcare, and

Irina Nevzlin is an Israeli entrepreneur and chair of the board of directors at the Tel-Aviv-based ANU: the Museum of the Jewish People, which is the largest Jewish museum in the world. She is also President of the Nadav Foundation, Founder and Chair of IMPROVATE, and the author of *The Impact of Identity: The Power of Knowing Who You Are* (2019).

religion-and-state issues. Diaspora Jews worry about antisemitism from Left and Right, relations with Israel, assimilation, the cost of Jewish education, and, of course, the politics of their own countries.

Is all this fear, at once polarizing and paralyzing, simply a product of the volatile public climate around us—or are there deeper, internal Jewish issues at play?

We all want Israel to be stable and prosperous, and we want the Jewish people to thrive. So, how did we get to the point where so many of us feel locked into an adrenaline-infused, us-versus-them struggle against other Jews?

Yes, the world has gone through upheavals, of which the global pandemic and the war in Ukraine are only two prominent examples. But Jews have faced upheavals of their own. The tectonic shifts we are seeing, both in Israel and throughout the Diaspora, are shaking up our communities. We are seeing layers upon layers rising, falling—like a young piece of land being formed.

The first step toward finding our bearings in the chaos is to focus on what unites us. And what unites us, more than anything else, is our common heritage.

Jews have spent thousands of years building an identity based on common ethnic roots and traditions of text, practice, lore, and values. We didn't have a country, an anthem, a flag, or an army of our own. But we had our heritage—including an ancient dream of returning to our homeland.

Today, nearly half the Jewish people call themselves Israeli. Having our own country is a vision fulfilled, but it's also a bit of a shock, creating two fundamentally different conditions for the formation of our identity: Israel and Diaspora. Having our own country means living as part of a majority for the first time in millennia. It is a whole new form of Jewish identity. Meanwhile, the other half of our people remain a minority in their respective countries, as in times past.

Over the centuries, we honed our skills as survivors, newcomers, and out-siders in many different political and cultural contexts. We were all minorities, so we were all in the same boat. We knew we had no choice but to be open-minded and adaptable to change.

But the change of becoming a majority in our own land was unprec-edented and sudden, especially coming on the heels of the greatest horror and devastation in our people's history. Seven and a half decades later, we are still trying to understand it, still trying to figure out who we are, how to relate to the other half of world Jewry, the half that continues to live as a tiny minority in every land. We will eventually untangle how to live as one people. But the process is scary, hard, and slow.

We have been, and will always continue to be, part of something utterly unique in human history. Israel is a young country, and given the complicated region we live in, we could have long ago found ourselves in a country that was not a democracy. There still is, and will always be, work to be done to ensure our future as a democratic state.

The Jewish people is like an extended family, and Israel is like the family's home, where tensions run high and the range of emotions is extreme. When confronted with change or unrest, we see what is happening as through a magnifying glass. We experience everything as louder, deeper, and more intense than what we see taking place in other countries. But this is also part of our identity. Our borders comprise the most sophisticated hi-tech alongside the most ancient ruins. We have deserts that bloom and produce some of the world's best wines. Employees argue fiercely with their bosses—and it's not seen as a bad thing. In fact, one of the national pastimes is arguing loudly about politics. This is part of who we are as individuals, as a people, as a nation.

For me, this is testimony to just how much everyone cares for each other and for the country. People help one another in the street, pray for the recovery of terror victims, and send money to support families in need. It's okay to disagree, provided you are ready to listen—and as long as you do it as a family would. But only by being rooted can we be open-minded enough to disagree and still accept, respect, and love each other.

* * *

The future of our people depends on how we respond to the upheavals and learn to make changes—together. But how do we remain together as a single people, always remembering we are one? By being rooted. The one thing that defines us and will never change is our common roots. Our ancestors, the heritage that was passed down to us—these are enduring. They are what we share as Jews. The map of the Jewish people is not only about Left or Right, secular or observant, Israel or Diaspora. These are but branches on a single tree, whose roots go deep underground.

Being simultaneously rooted and open-minded does not necessarily create conflict within the individual—the way it often does in the political sphere, where rooted is associated with "Right" and openness with "Left." On the contrary, both rootedness and open-mindedness flow directly from a strong connection to our Jewish heritage. Everyone can make this connection in whatever way works best for them: through textual study, prayer, language, food, family history, music, or art. I am not an observant Jew, but I feel strongly connected to my roots, my ancestors, and the pillars of my tradition.

These roots are something we are born with and something that will never change. The connection is not always obvious, but it is always there, waiting to be discovered and strengthened.

I realized this during my first visit to Israel as a young teen after the fall of the Iron Curtain. Before I left home, my mother sat me down to talk about traveling abroad. She tried to prepare me for the fact that everything would be unfamiliar: strange smells, peculiar food, foreign sounds, and odd behavior. I had no idea what to expect.

My grandmother and I stayed with a family in the city of Rehovot, near the center of the country. I was amazed to see vendors selling food on street corners; and the smell wafting from the pizza shop was like heaven on earth. But despite the foreignness of it all, I felt strangely comfortable and completely at home—so different from the out-of-step feelings that had infused my life growing up in Moscow. It seemed so odd that the first time I really felt at home was in Israel, with a strange family, in a place I had never been. I had made my first connection.

* * *

Connecting to our roots should begin at an early age. If we want to nurture a generation of vibrant, confident, and open-minded people, our schools should focus on building a strong identity through our common heritage. This goes beyond studying Jewish or Israeli history. It means being introduced to Jewish traditions and core texts. Most of all, it involves teaching them to ask questions. Without asking questions, it's hard to find answers.

In Israel, we have been talking about educational reform for years. As time goes by, our youth become increasingly disoriented in a world focused on a vague notion of universalism.

Surviving in a tumultuous and changing environment, however, demands that we imbue in our children a deeply ingrained sense of who we were as people, where we are now, and where we're going. It's only natural to compare ourselves to other countries that have been around for centuries. But in order to thrive together over the next seventy-five years and beyond, we need to accept that we have changed dramatically, and continue to change, as a people.

With half of us a majority and the other half minorities, Jews in Israel and the Diaspora have to build a stronger common identity, both as individuals and as a people, based on our roots. Let us educate our children so they may be confident that no matter what happens, they have a solid foundation on which to build the future—together as one people.

36

EXPAND THE ABRAHAM ACCORDS

Cracking the Code of Coexistence

HOUDA NONOO

IT IS A QUESTION AS OLD AS TIME: What is needed for lasting peace in the Middle East?

Politicians and business leaders have pontificated about it for decades, yet the code was finally cracked in 2020 when Bahrain, Israel, the United Arab Emirates, and the United States signed the Abraham Accords. As I sat there on the White House lawn on September 15, 2020, the excitement was palpable as we turned the page on Middle East peace and started a new chapter.

Houda Nonoo served as Bahrain's ambassador to the United States from 2008 to 2013. She is the first Jewish person to be appointed as ambassador from an Arab country.

I was honored to receive the call two days earlier, when I was invited to be part of the delegation of Bahrain's Foreign Minister, H.E. Dr. Abdullatif bin Rashid Al Zayani, for that auspicious day. There were so many things going through my mind as we watched the signing ceremony right before us.

During my five years serving as Bahrain's ambassador in Washington, I made many new friends who, when they learned I was Jewish, often asked if I had been to Israel. I always said, "Not yet." In my heart, I hoped and prayed for the opportunity, but I was determined to wait for the moment when circumstances would allow such a visit. As a loyal and committed citizen of Bahrain, I naturally respected the reality of the situation. I could only dream. And hope. And wait. And dream some more. As I sat on the White House lawn, I remember thinking how the time had finally come, and I would now be able to visit family and friends in Israel.

Another thought that went through my mind was what got us to this point.

The truth is that what got us to this point was the fact that our region recognizes that *coexistence* is what ultimately propels the Middle East forward, irrespective of these Accords.

* * *

Bahrain, an island long known for its tolerance, coexistence, and freedom of religion, has always welcomed people from different faiths and backgrounds to its shores. Modern Jewish life in Bahrain began in the 1880s, when Jews from Iraq were looking for better economic and living prospects and decided to leave for India. On the way, the boat stopped in Bahrain, and they liked what they saw and decided to stay.

Since then, Jewish life in the Kingdom has flourished. Many of our families were traders and started their own textile, electronics, and money exchange businesses. Others worked for oil companies, banks, and schools. We have always been part of the fabric of Bahraini society. In 1934, Abraham Pinchas Nonoo, my paternal grandfather, was elected to the municipal council—he was the first of many Bahraini Jews to serve in government positions. His grandson, Abraham, was appointed to the Shura Council, which is the Upper House of Parliament, in 2001. I was appointed to it in 2006, as was my cousin Nancy Khedouri in 2010; she continues to hold the position today.

Our Bahraini Jewish families have always lived alongside Bahraini Muslim families. Our grandparents shared stories of their neighbors helping to heat their food on Shabbat. Generations later, we naturally continue to celebrate important events together, including attending each other's weddings, participating in their iftar meals, and their visiting our recently renovated synagogue. Under His Majesty King Hamad bin Isa Al Khalifa's leadership, Bahrain has been committed to spreading a culture of peace, dialogue, and coexistence. These values are inculcated within us as young children, and they guide how we live as adults.

Growing up in Bahrain, everyone knew we were Jewish. I went to a Catholic School and was taught by nuns. My friends were of different religions and backgrounds, and we grew up respecting each other's differences. I never felt the need to hide my religion. We celebrated together our major holidays like Ramadan, Hanukkah, Diwali, and Christmas.

This kind of mutual respect was inculcated within us as children, so naturally when I went to Washington, it was important to me that Bahrain host the first interfaith iftar, inviting different faith communities to join us. It is something I carried back with me when I returned to Bahrain and invited my Muslim and Christian friends to join us for the Jewish festivals and for my son's wedding, the first Jewish wedding to take place in Bahrain in fifty-two years.

Our community is flourishing. We are blessed to live in an Arab country that provides equal opportunities to us, as it does to citizens and residents of all religious backgrounds. Over the years, many have asked me what it was like to be appointed as the first Jewish ambassador from an Arab country. The truth is that non-Bahrainis are more surprised by my appointment than Bahrainis are, because His Majesty has always supported equal rights and opportunities for people of all faiths. It did not strike me as odd that someone from the Jewish faith would be appointed to this position.

As a member of Bahrain's Jewish community, I often speak about the Kingdom's commitment to coexistence from the perspective of the Jewish community, but just as Bahrain is home to the oldest operational synagogue in the GCC countries, it is also home to the oldest church in the region, which is in Manama.

Last year, the largest Catholic church in the region opened its doors in Bahrain. The cavernous Cathedral of Our Lady of Arabia seats 2,300 people. As Bahrainis, we are incredibly proud of our county's commitment to all faith-based communities, including Jews, Christians, Muslims, Bahá'í, and Hindus, as well as the importance we place on making sure that each community has a beautiful place to pray and celebrate their festivals together. Bahrain's Hindu Temple is over 200 years old. In November 2022, we welcomed Pope Francis to Bahrain for the first time. It was his second time visiting the Gulf, following his visit to Abu Dhabi in 2019. The Pope's visit to the United Arab Emirates kicked off a Year of Tolerance for the country, which was supported by several initiatives. A book was published to mark the special occasion, and it included chapters on all the faith-based communities living in the Emirates.

Over the past fifteen years, the GCC countries have established their own interfaith centers. The first to open its doors was Saudi Arabia's King Abdullah bin Abdulaziz International Centre for Interreligious and Intercultural Dialogue (KAICIID) whose vision is to promote and employ interreligious dialogue to support conflict prevention and resolution, sustainable peace, and social cohesion, and to promote mutual respect and understanding among different religious and cultural groups. I have had the privilege of working closely with KAICIID since joining their advisory board in 2019.

Over a decade ago, His Majesty King Hamad bin Isa Al Khalifa said, "Ignorance is the enemy of peace." That is the mission behind Bahrain's King Hamad Global Centre for Peaceful Coexistence. In Qatar, the Doha International Center for Interfaith Dialogue (DICID) is dedicated to interfaith dialogue and intercultural cooperation. In Oman, the Al Amana Centre is an ecumenical and interfaith organization built upon the legacy of Christians working with their Muslim hosts and neighbors from different faiths represented in Oman. The United Arab Emirates is set to open the Abrahamic Family House in 2023, which is an interfaith complex on Saadiyat Island in Abu Dhabi. It will house a mosque, church, and the country's first synagogue. The other GCC countries have also created platforms to spread interfaith and coexistence.

Simultaneous to this happening, more expatriates from the West and the East have and continue to move to the Middle East. They bring with them their cultures, traditions, and religions. More and more of our children are choosing to go to university in the West, and, in doing so, they meet people from other backgrounds and cultures and so naturally the GCC has put a larger focus and emphasis on coexistence. We recognize the opportunities it brings in diplomacy, business, and arts and culture.

If you follow the trend lines you will see that before any of the GCC countries established peace with Israel, they first focused on coexistence and reaching out to the global Jewish community. Bahrain has been doing this for decades, and the UAE has been doing it for some time as well. For those asking for hints as to who is next, my response would be to follow which countries are already putting time and effort into their coexistence and interreligious programming, and who is reaching out to the global Christian and Jewish communities. That's the first step, and there are already others doing that. It is not a question of "if" for some of them, but "when."

As a citizen of this region, I am filled with excitement to see the construction of a new Middle East, one based on coexistence and prosperity. Coexistence is the foundation that allows our region to move forward. It is the way we raise our children, and it is a core value we hope they will carry throughout life.

37

MAKE FUN OF EVERYTHING

Why Humor Is the Key to Jewish Pride

CLAUDIA OSHRY

FOR AS LONG AS I CAN REMEMBER, being a proud Jew has been the best thing about me. Sure, I'm good-looking, hilarious, smart, talented, gorgeous, unique, kind, and did I mention, beautiful? But above all that, I've always been a Jew first. A proud one at that. It wasn't ever a question for me. I grew up in a house, in a community where the principles of the Torah were engrained into who we were as people. We lit Shabbos candles, went to shul, and learned Hebrew in school. The Israeli Day Parade was the social event of the season, for crying out loud!

Claudia Oshry is a comedian, podcast host, and *New York Times* bestselling author. She is the creator of the popular Instagram account @GirlWithNoJob, amassing more than 3 million followers.

Pretty much everyone I knew was Jewish. And if they weren't Jewish, they had a deep admiration and respect for Judaism. Zionism wasn't perceived as a bad thing. It wasn't a four-letter word like it is now. It was an admirable quality, one that people respected and wanted to support. That acceptance was something I never even noticed. It was a privilege I deeply took for granted. Yes, I knew we were the Chosen People, but back then I didn't feel "chosen" or even particularly special at all, because everyone around me matched my enthusiasm and love for Judaism. I figured it would always be that way, and I know that ten-year-old me would be crushed to learn about how things changed as quickly as they did.

I was never a particularly motivated or serious student as a kid. School mostly felt like an inconvenience to me, something I did between watching *Gossip Girl* and the *Real Housewives*. Once, in the eighth grade, we were continuing our education of the Holocaust when we opened our textbooks and began the chapter on Rabbi Ephraim Oshry, the prolific Orthodox rabbi who not only survived the Kovno Ghetto and Nazi concentration camps but also went on to publish his writings about what he saw and how he leaned on his Jewish faith throughout. Despite the horrors he lived through during World War II, Rabbi Oshry studied Torah, *survived*, and spent the rest of his life teaching the world about how he lived through the mass genocide of his people with his faith completely intact.

Instantly, I felt everyone in the classroom's eyes on me, a feeling I wasn't familiar with but wasn't necessarily troubled by either. Ms. Sokolow, my teacher at the time who wasn't particularly dazzled by me, asked me: "Claudia, is there any relation?" I stood up straight, held my head high, and my eyes glistened as I proudly told my peers that, yes, Rabbi Oshry was a close relative of mine and that his family now lived in New York, where they ran a yeshiva in his honor. I cannot remember a moment in my life when I was prouder of who I was and where I came from. My classmates were in awe, as was Ms. Sokolow, who was not a woman you could easily impress.

When we were young, being a good Jew felt easy because it *was* easy. It was all done for us. Our parents set the tone, and we simply followed. But at a certain point, it is on us to continue that tradition and set the tone for our own lives. It goes without saying that there are disadvantages to growing up in a bubble as I did. Whether it's the lack of diversity, real-world experience, or a skewed perception of reality—the list goes on and on. That bubble doesn't allow you to grow into a fully formed person who can truly exist in this great, big world. It feels protective until you grow up and realize it was also restrictive.

But is it bad for me to romanticize that protectiveness? The safety of it all? Of knowing nobody was ever looking down on me or simply disliking me for no reason other than the fact that I wore a Star of David necklace? Is it wrong of me to say that in some ways I miss that comfort?

The comfort of telling someone you'll be traveling to Israel without getting the not-so-subtle side-eye. The comfort of knowing that you can bring up your faith without the possibility of the person on the other end of the conversation disliking you. The comfort of sharing your love of Judaism and Israel online without death threats and Hitler jokes. That last one may sound trivial or rare, but as someone who pretty much lives on the internet, I can tell you that not only is it not infrequent, but it has become standard practice.

After sharing bits and pieces of my life online through Instagram and my blog, I found myself graduating from college with a unique opportunity. I could take the safe path and interview for jobs in tech or media, get a 401k and live a happy and stable life. Or, I could run with the momentum I had created thus far and see if I could swing it as a full-time content creator on social media. This was 2016, when "influencer" was barely a word, let alone a career path. Never being one to play it safe, I went with the latter. My family was, of course, thrilled. Seven years later, I now host one of the top comedy podcasts in the country, I am on my second national sold-out comedy tour, and I am a *New York Times* bestselling author (not to brag or anything).

But being funny isn't just something I chose to be. It's who I am. It is central to who I am as a proud Jew. Jews are wired to be funny. It speaks to how we see the world, how we deal with hardship, how we share our joy. Comedy is one of our biggest gifts to the world.

When I began growing my platform online, it was never really a question of whether I'd share my Judaism. I was building a brand around me, and "me" meant Jewish. Sharing my faith wasn't some big decision. I didn't sit around a table with a team of advisors outlining the pros and cons. It was something I didn't even think about sharing, because that's not how I was raised. What's wrong with the fact that I'm proud of where I come from? *Who would dislike that?* I thought. Well, as it turns out, a lot of people.

* * *

Knowing what I know now, entering my career with that sort of sentiment was naïve. It didn't feel like it back then, but I had made a choice in being vocal about my love of Israel and Judaism. I didn't see it that way at the time, because I was raised to believe it wasn't a choice but rather a given. In an earth-shattering way, I came to learn that it isn't the most popular stance to take.

It was a jarring moment for me to enter the public space and find that so many of my Jewish counterparts didn't share my pride. It was especially disheartening (and shocking) to see that within the comedy community. That pride was once a constant in my life and it seemed to disappear into thin air the instant I became recognizable. I found myself completely alone when searching for a community of proud Jews. It is no secret that the entertainment industry is full of Jews, but it's one thing to be a Jew and a whole other thing to be a *proud* one.

As a certified pop culture nut, I can tell you without question that I know everything there is to know about celebrities. I live, eat, sleep, and breathe pop culture. Nobody on this earth knows more about it than I do. I host a daily podcast breaking down the minutiae of what's going on in Hollywood—who's breaking up, who's making up—and even I find myself newly discovering celebrities who have Jewish backgrounds. It is something they *never* touch on. So even me, the world's biggest pop culture fanatic, who also happens to be obsessively Jewish, didn't know about their faith. How weird is that? It's almost as if they're not...proud?

The general sentiment of the American Jewish community is that it often feels like the world doesn't care about our injustices. That nobody outside of our community will ever go to bat for us or speak up for us when it matters most. And I get it—I do. I agree with that sentiment wholeheartedly. But let's be real with one another for a moment. If we don't speak up for ourselves, how can we expect outsiders to do the same? How do you care about someone who seems to not care about themselves?

I don't mean to sound condescending in what I say next, although I am sure it will come off that way. Nevertheless, I shall persist. I am perplexed by the silent members of our community. Knowing all that our people have been through, how do they sleep at night?

Whether your knowledge of our history is limited or vast, it is engrained in every single one of us how hard our people have fought to survive, how our ancestors battled persecution, antisemitism, and worse. Granted, not everyone is going to learn about their ancestors from an eighth-grade textbook, but we all come from greats—from prolific Jews who stood up for what they believed in to those who stood in the face of adversity for the sake of religious freedom. We may not know their names, but we should be incredibly proud of what they did. We wouldn't be here without them.

***

It is so important for us not to forget that we are living in the Jewish Diaspora. Look at our history and you will see how much worse things could be for us. While living in a concentration camp, Rabbi Oshry came up with answers on how to observe Jewish laws while living in filth and being starved by Nazis. During Passover in the camp, when Jews were not supposed to be eating bread, they went to him and asked how to observe the holiday properly when the only food the Nazis gave them each day was a single piece of bread. Rabbi Oshry gave them answers; he wrote them down and buried them in the ground. He retrieved them after the war and then published them to remind the world that the possibility of history repeating itself always exists. He wanted to remind us to learn from our past. Even in the darkest of times, our ancestors were staunchly committed to keeping the faith.

Where is that energy now? The bar for us to be good and proud Jews has been sufficiently lowered, and yet so many of us are not rising to the occasion.

So, why did I choose comedy? In a strange way, I feel like choosing a career in comedy was a way to honor my history.

Humor might just be the greatest asset of the Jewish people. After all the Jews have been through, our ability to still laugh and bring joy to others is what truly sets us apart. The way I see it, humor and joy are the ultimate expressions of Jewish pride. It's how we have won and continue to win. It's how, no matter what we face, we continue to thrive. What's a better response than to *laugh* in the faces of those who seek to destroy us? While they plot and plan, we laugh, we dance, we sing. We celebrate all that we are.

Because who are we? *We are the Chosen People, bitch!* We are amalgamations of every Jew who came before us. Every Jew who didn't have it as easy as we do. I chose to celebrate that by spreading and sharing joy, by making others laugh in the way that only a proud Jew can. I can't think of a better legacy to leave.

38

STRONG INDIVIDUALS MAKE STRONG COMMUNITIES

Why We Can't Have One Without the Other

FANIA OZ-SALZBERGER

HAVE YOU EVER NOTICED the sheer number of people appearing in the Hebrew Bible? Men and women, old and young, rich and poor, leaders and drifters, the wise and the foolish, the righteous and the sinner are all invited to join the narrative. They are almost always named and identified by family, tribe, or town. They belong very strongly to the Israelite collective (even if they are foreigners like Zipporah, Yael, and Jezebel), but within it, they assert their individual personalities and sometimes change history by their sheer

Fania Oz-Salzberger is Professor Emerita at the Faculty of Law and Center for German and European Studies, University of Haifa, Israel.

strength of character. It sometimes feels like more than half of all ancient Israelites somehow managed to push their way into the story, competing for the reader's attention, like Israelis queuing for a bus.

Many of them are depicted as talking, arguing, opining, making individual choices, and acting upon their choices. If the Bible is essentially the tale of the Israelites' agreements and disagreements with their God, a parallel drama keeps unfolding: the Israelites'—and later the Jews'—disagreements among themselves. Jewish argumentation has always had faces, names, and individual voices. They debated almost everything, but it was the Talmudic civilization that made argument into an intellectual art, drawing on both sharp logic and strong personalities. A civilization of individuals, each with a name and a personal story, fighting over the future of the community to which they are deeply devoted.

"Individualism-in-community" is how we might describe a very ancient Jewish tradition that is curiously, and I think crucially, important for today's Jewish and non-Jewish political conflicts. It suggests a way out of the seemingly hopeless divide between conservative Right and liberal Left, in and beyond Israel and the United States. It stresses the value we should place on fellow Jews and fellow humans with whom we profoundly disagree. It also shows the limits of tolerance, the edges of our common ground. Finally, individualism-in-community underscores the long Jewish legacy of passionate but (mostly) non-violent debate.

***

As a historian, I reserve worldviews ending in "ism" to modern times only, but in the present context, it is useful to understand "individualism" as a concept derived from the biblical idea that every single human being was created in the image of God, and is therefore entitled to some social and economic standing in his or her community. The best metaphor for this sense of personal value within societal bonds appears in the Mishna: "Whereas humans make many coins from a single mold and they all come out the same, the King of Kings mints all people from the mold of Adam, and yet none of us are alike." Jews have never seen themselves as a herd or a faceless mass; we are, and have almost always been, a culture of interlocutors, a public spectacle of dramatis personae, deeply self-conscious women and men united and divided by a common story.

This helps explain the bewildering variety of opinions among major Jewish thinkers in modern times. As it secularized, modern Jewish thought spilled out dramatically across the full spectrum between socialism and capitalism, and between progressivism, liberalism, and conservatism (or neo-conservatism). From Karl Marx to Milton Friedman, from Isaiah Berlin to Jacques Derrida, this broad gamut kept faith with the major Jewish commandments of debate: think independently, argue wisely, and use words, not weapons.

But lines must be drawn, and let it be clear: The Jewish social-minded valuation of each single persona is neither the selfish individualism of the modern libertines nor the economic individualism of modern libertarians. The biblical and Talmudic individual is not defined by his or her personal needs and appetites alone, significant as they are. Nor is the individual entitled to a full and unscathed possession of private property and wealth. Quite the opposite: Being created as a unique personality in God's image, he or she never fully owns property but is obliged to share some of it. Ancient Jewish individualism is a strain—perhaps the earliest strain—that nurtured the modern theories of civic-minded respect for the individual.

The power of the individual man or woman within the close-knit community is one of the oldest Jewish longitudes. It runs along Israelite and Jewish history along with several other prevailing cultural habits, such as argumentativeness, humor, and daring criticism of self, leader, and even God. Individuals have proclaimed their independent thinking all the way from the matriarch Sarah to the comedian Sarah Silverman; from Hannah, Samuel's brave mother, to the philosopher Hannah Arendt; and from the prophet Moses to the philosopher Moses Maimonides to the Enlightenment thinker Moses Mendelssohn and to the socialist groundbreaker Moses Hess. Unlike the historical spheres of Christianity and Islam, where imperial or national values often subdued private voices and lives, Jewish values allow and encourage self-assertion and stand-alone individuals. It is the only culture and the only religion that encourages bar mitzvah boys (and, increasingly, girls) and bridegrooms (and sometimes brides) to celebrate their happy day with a *dvar torah*, an innovative take on the ancient sources.

This Jewish longitude is seldom discussed. Today's world is filled with the individualism of self-proclamation, indeed of self-advertising. My point is that the Hebraic and Jewish cultures held a version of this tenet—self-proclamation engaging with national tradition—long before the rest of the world caught up. There is no pre-modern civilization, including the highly verbal and literate ancient Greece and Rome, which has produced the same number of women and men inserting themselves into the historical narrative.

* * *

We are a nation that began its history, by its own light, as an extended family, transformed into a tribal federation, went into exile but kept within the folds of the congregation and within the walls of Jewish quarters, *mellahs,* and shtetls, and today inhabits its revived nation-state as well as a global, intersecting network of communities. Being Jewish, whether one deems Judaism as a religion, a culture, a peoplehood, or a nationhood—means grouping together. Orthodox prayer requires at least ten men. Jewish life requires constant cooperation. Jewish homes are often clustered together, whether this proximity is imposed from the outside, as in the medieval Venice Ghetto, or freely chosen, as in present-day Florida's assisted-living resorts.

Moreover, while the antisemitic caricature of Jews networking to rule the world is a slander, there *is* a sense of familiarity among Jews meeting each other across geographical and cultural lines. From academics attending international conferences to backpackers in the Andes and on the Mekong, chance encounters often raise a sense of distant cousinhood. The love of argument and the sense of humor, as I have often noticed, are similar across cultural and political boundaries. But we may rest assured that if Jews ever attempted to team up and rule the world, the plot would easily succumb to the internal divisions ignited by differing worldviews and powerful personalities.

Ever since Abraham and Sarah—or, if they were mere legends, since the birth of the Israelite culture that invented Abraham and Sarah—Hebraic and Jewish legacy has been filled with named, assertive, striving, active men and women. When they don't appear in a biblical story's dramatic narrative, at the very least they appear in those endless lists of names, catalogued by household and tribal ancestry, that crisscross the five books of Moses.

Thus, the Book of Exodus is titled, in the original Hebrew, Sh'mot (names), and begins with a list of Jacob's family members. Many chapters in the Book of Numbers look like a cut-and-paste job of ancient genealogies, roll calls of weapon-wielding men, and lists of land-owning heads of families. But even in those seemingly mundane inventories, surprises can crop up. Some figures practically walk out of the list, demanding that we hear their particular stories.

At times, we have to reimagine the story: How did a woman, Serah, daughter of Asher, get to be listed among the combat-worthy men just prior to the settlement of the Land of Israel? What's the story of that Israelite Amazon? We may never know; but a hint comes from five other women stepping out of line and into the limelight, the five daughters of Zelophehad, who demanded their fair share in the future allotment of land, as none of their male relatives had survived. Out of the tribal crowd, flying off the page from lists and family trees, rise some of the most daring individual voices in the Hebrew Bible.

This, as early modern Christian thinkers discovered with great fascination, was a republican culture, working along democratic lines centuries before the words "democracy" and "republic" were coined in Greece and Rome, respectively. The Israelite narrative and legal norms sought to allot every head of family, usually male and rarely female, entitlement to a smallholding in the promised land, based upon their belonging to an Israelite tribe and family. Here was the source of the concept of citizenship: *ezrach* in Biblical Hebrew meant a pure-bred vine and, metaphorically, a person of Israelite origin; it precedes *politikos* in Greece and *cives* in Roman. (In Modern Hebrew, ezrach takes on the Roman focus on one's legal persona rather than ethnic origin). As citizens, Israelite men (and, rarely, women) were also called to war when any part of the tribal federation suffered enemy attacks. Even more importantly, they had a voice in the nation's political conversation, albeit usually in an impromptu manner and not in a permanent assembly; institutions, if any existed, are only vaguely recorded, notably the "Elders" sitting at a city's gate. Nevertheless, early modern thinkers such as Petrus Cunaeus and John Milton regarded the ancient Israelites as the only civic society that existed prior to the Greek *poleis* and the Roman Republic.

"Notice the link," I wrote together with my late father, Amos Oz, in our 2012 book *Jews and Words*, "between naming, entitlement, landed property, and belonging. Note that the new Israelite state, soon to be conquered and settled, is conceived as a veritable republic. By this we mean a polity where numerous citizens, all propertied on a fairly equal basis, none too rich, none too poor, form the backbone of a stable civil society."

The gist of the "Hebrew republic" was equality before the law, extended as a matter, of course, to all Israelites, and as a matter of emphasis to the foreigners [gerim] living in their midst: "The same law applies both to the native-born [ezrach] and to the foreigner [ger] residing among you" (Exodus 12:49, cf. Ezekiel 47:22).

Yet Jewish individualism goes even deeper than equal rights before the law and political participation. It demands the acknowledgment and celebration of thousands of specific persons in constant mutual engagement. It grasps history as a huge interplay of individual human (alongside divine) wills in the flow of time. It offers a model for verbal and argumentative cohesion. It balances respect for the common hub of faith and belonging with a healthy disrespect for kings and grandees. And, in modern times, it offers a sense of people-based nationhood that can evade the totalitarian horror of crude nationalism.

Instead of crude nationalism, the Jewish legacy offers a pre-Greek and pre-Roman concept of civic republicanism or civic liberalism: The individual is of utmost importance, but part of being an individual is the sense of belonging to a group and contributing to its well-being. Very few can practice individualism in an empty desert, and even Moses and Elijah faced God in the wilderness only to return to their nation and act out their individual personalities upon it.

* * *

For a people so spellbound by its collective story, its common creed, and public spirit, this Jewish emphasis on individuals is remarkable. Patriarchs and slaves, prophetesses and kings, the righteous and (often more interestingly) the sinners, are displayed in the biblical narrative as strong-willed, often highly verbal, affecting the course of history by the force of their personality and decisions.

The Hebrew Bible's capacity to mix the intimate, private story with the greatest of national turning points is almost singular in ancient literature. There is a constant refocusing of many of its narratives, zooming in to domestic interiors or private conversations and zooming out to crowd scenes—battles, religious ceremonies, national celebrations, and calamities. Figures such as Miriam, Tamar, Jephtah, and Deborah actively change the course of history, and their own characters shine through the annals. Hannah, Isaiah, and Amos create formative texts, reflecting and at the same time forging their nation's values and collective memory out of their own private passions and principles, mobilized by their personal courage, passion, and pain. The women's strong presence is no accident; like prophets, they rise and speak regardless of their social status, and their words can be life-changing. Ever since God's creation of the world by the word, speech-acts have been crucial to the Jewish narrative.

The Talmudic system of large-scale, interactive scholarship lasted for generations, in two different lands and under very unfavorable national conditions of diaspora, occupation, and war. From the perspective of social history, it is an astounding human achievement, the closest thing to a democracy of philosophers, a feat even Plato did not have in mind. The Talmud intellectualized the biblical individualism-in-community, using the biblical content itself as its subject matter. A different freedom became available, not the Israelite sovereign liberty, but a freedom of the mind. This freedom continued in the medieval era, when individual rabbis stood out through centuries of debates and texts—and then into the modern era, well beyond the confines of traditional rabbinic Judaism and into the secular realms of literature, philosophy, science, and historiography.

The people of Israel have never been sticklers for privacy. I know this all too well, having grown up on a kibbutz. We have lived typically close together, sharing a certain physical and emotional crowdedness. This is true for present-day affluent Jewish neighborhoods almost as much as it was in the tent shared by Leah and Rachel and Bilha and Zilpa. When Baron Maurice de Hirsch built Jewish settlements in the broad pampas of Argentina in the late nineteenth century, the homes were huddled together as if the enormous grasslands around them were a den of hostile gentiles. The Jewish sense of togetherness, especially but not only in tough times, is more than instinctive peoplehood: It is a text-based bond, a vast human affinity of readers-responders to a common textual legacy.

The family table accommodated several generations, men and women and children, as they read and passed on written and oral texts that were themselves multivocal. The Halacha and many of the mitzvot, too, are pointedly social and community-oriented. In modern times, this bond was partially navigated toward Zionism and nation-statehood. Beyond the State of Israel, modern Jews now have greater capability and more tools to connect to their origins and develop a sense of identity, often within congregations. But we have retained individualism-in-community: At the Jewish family dinner, in Israel's Knesset, and in Jewish gatherings everywhere, vociferous individuals vie with each other in robust, open debate. The attachment between modern democracy and modern Judaism is so strong that the weakening or fall of democracy, in Israel and elsewhere, would deal a debilitating blow to the Jewish principle of fearless multivocality.

The principle of individualism-in-community comes from the depths of Jewish humanism. In its Orthodox form, it is the idea that each person, Jewish or otherwise, is coined, and coined *differently*, by God and in the image of God. This is the groundwork for every Jewish law and mitzva *bein adam l'chavero*, "between person and fellow-person," guiding social relationships. This is the gist of the second tablet of the Ten Commandments as well as the Yom Kippur atonement liturgy: Do not kill, hurt, rob, or cheat your fellow person. All this amounts to what my father called the "Eleventh Commandment": Thou shalt not, if at all possible, inflict pain.

* * *

Why is the idea of individualism-in-community important today? Because being part of an ethnic, national, or cultural group is a crucially important human right. Because the world is lacking a good balance between the value of individuals and the joys (and dangers) of belonging. Because the Jewish formula of balancing strong-willed, debating, critical souls with collective decision-making has proven to be a success. Historically, it has stood its ground. Here we are, divided by our common legacy, but almost always in a good or at least creative way: orthodox, traditional and progressive, pious and secular, capitalist and socialist, conservative and liberal, managing to kill each other only in words.

Take the rabbinic arguments of the Middle Ages and early modern times: They were not angelic by any means. They often became personal and spiteful. Rivals were sometimes harassed and, albeit rarely, even ostracized and turned out of the fold. But physical violence, especially in the context of intellectual debate, has always been alien to halachic culture.

This legacy is poignantly relevant to Israel today. Since the dawn of Zionism, Jewish national thought has been fraught by mighty disagreements. It took leaders on the scale of Theodor Herzl and David Ben-Gurion to channel debate into organized decision-making. But there was very little political violence. During almost a century and a half of Zionism, including the seventy-five years of the State of Israel, only a handful of Jews were murdered by other Jews for political reasons; the handful of assassinations was of course very meaningful and traumatic. The Altalena killings and the murders of Israel Kastner, Emil Grunzweig, and Yitzhak Rabin shamed and troubled the Israeli conscience for decades to come. Those were the horrific exceptions, however. As a rule, the fiercest of Israeli political controversies rarely led to violence.

However, Israel's present-day public debate could easily, in another country, ignite a civil war. Evading civil war, Israelis keep shouting at each other at the tops of their voices but respect the human value and civil membership of their political enemies. Will this bond last? It has come under dangerous strains during the last decade. Political discourse has deteriorated into expletives, rivals are labeled traitors, and critics are branded not as latter-day prophets but as full-blown and doomed heretics, like the biblical Korach and his ilk.

The value of individual human dignity has been one of the most enduring assets of the Jewish legacy as it went through modernization and secularization. Its relationship with modern civic liberalism is mutually nurturing: John Locke and his contemporaries gleaned inspiration from the Jewish scriptures as they politicized the Western idea of individual value. The modern Jewish permutation, more communal than its non-Jewish equivalents, can afford respect and civic equality for atheists and "leftists," LGBTQ persons, and the non-Jewish minorities among us. It is a moral wake-up call not for Israeli society alone but for communities—Jewish and otherwise—everywhere.

I have suggested two points of reflection. First, that from ancient Hebrews to modern Jews, our legacy supplies excellent source materials and arguments for individualism within the community and for belonging without losing one's personal uniqueness. Second, that a long line of Jewish interlocutors has created an intricate culture of oral and textual, adamantly non-violent, benevolent controversy.

As the poet John Donne, a Christian fascinated by Jews, wrote: "No man is an island entire of itself; every man is a piece of the continent, a part of the main." My father, a Jew fascinated by humankind, offered a gentle correction: No man is an island, but every person is a peninsula, one half belonging to the continent and the other half jutting into the sea. This, I suggest, is a time-honored Jewish thought. May it be a present-day Jewish priority.

39

TZEDAKANOMICS

The Power of the Haredi Social Safety Net

ELI PALEY

THE JEWS ARE A DIVIDED PEOPLE, separated by religion, geography, language, and politics. But perhaps the sharpest divide of all, one that feels almost impossible to overcome, is that which separates the Haredim (or "ultra-Orthodox") and the rest of the Jewish world—including secular, Reform, Conservative, and "just Jews."

This division is not just one of theology and ritual. It is above all an enormous cultural divide: The differences run from dress and values to politics and fundamental approaches to history, education, traditional authority and texts,

Eli Paley is chairman of the Jerusalem-based Haredi Institute for Public Affairs and publisher of *Mishpacha* magazine.

the role of women, democracy, parenting, the relationship between individual and community, and more.

This is *the* great Jewish divide. It goes back hundreds of years, beginning with the Jewish Enlightenment, or Haskalah, in Europe in the eighteenth and nineteenth centuries. As more and more Jews abandoned millennia of traditional ritual and textual study with the aim of achieving acceptance and equality in the new democratic world order, a countermovement arose in Europe, which became what is today called the Haredi world. It was a force that pushed toward isolation, even a kind of separatism, from the modern, secular world. It also pushed radically in the direction of textual study and halachic practice (or, in Haredi terms, "Torah and Mitzvot") above all other values.

It also may be the most important divide to bridge. Given the enormous difference in fertility rates between the two Jewish worlds, what is today a fairly small Haredi minority will represent an increasing percentage of Jews over time. If these two worlds do not find a way to understand and learn from each other, we face the prospect of an irreparable schism into two separate Jewish peoples—who speak different languages, live in different realities, and have very little to say to each other.

Most of us reading this book have seen the Haredi world only from the outside. As a result, we have a hard time telling truth from fiction. There is a broad narrative that is widely believed but only partially accurate: Haredim, it is said, are mired in poverty, foregoing advanced professions or employment in general in favor of endless Torah study. Their world, it is said, is economically unsustainable, dependent on handouts from donors and taxpayers. Haredi schools deprive their children of the tools they need to function in the real world, creating generations of dependency. In the narrative's nastiest versions, Haredim are seen as parasites, morally dubious, loose with the law, oppressing of women, and covering up abuse.

There is much the Jewish world as a whole can gain from looking beyond the stereotypes and hostile narratives, however, and understanding why so many Jews continue to prefer this way of life.

At a minimum, such understanding may foster a more fruitful dialogue that could help bridge the great Jewish divide. But it is also possible that the

Jewish people, in all its variations, could actually learn something from the Haredi world. Understanding the strengths of the Haredi way of life, we may look for ways to translate its positive elements into insights, programs, or institutions that may deepen and enrich the Jewish world without necessarily taking on the Haredi world's perceived weaknesses.

To explain what I mean, let's begin with a story about cannabis.

* * *

A neighbor of mine was grappling with multiple health burdens in her family. Her husband was diagnosed with oral cancer. One of her daughters had severe autism. Another daughter suffered from severe epilepsy—including seizures that regularly landed her in the hospital. To deal with the epilepsy, my neighbor secured a license for medical cannabis, which became a lifeline, saving her daughter from severe attacks and hospitalization. The cannabis was subsidized by the government through their healthcare fund.

Not long ago, the cannabis bottle broke. The healthcare fund was hesitant to provide a replacement, and this became an urgent crisis. She called me.

I started by turning to my Haredi friends. One works in the healthcare system. Another was an associate of Yaakov Litzman, the Haredi former minister of health. The vast gears of the Haredi social-support machine started turning.

Within an hour, I found myself on the phone with a senior police officer (because cannabis is a controlled substance) who quickly understood the situation and started directing the operation. Within two hours, an entire network had been activated to try and track down enough medical cannabis in the form she needed, until things could be worked out with the healthcare fund. Within an hour after that, a broader network identified a bottle in Bat Yam, south of Tel Aviv, and worked on getting it quickly delivered to Jerusalem. By that same night, the replacement bottle was in her hands.

This informal Haredi rapid-response social-support network spans the world. It can spring into action and deliver solutions quickly from as far away as New York, Melbourne, Paris, or Hong Kong. It is flexible, creative, energetic, and, above all, effective to a degree that is impossible to compare with anything else in the Jewish world or outside of it. Such a network requires a high degree of communication, mutual trust, creativity, and a widespread willingness to drop what you are doing to help someone in need.

It is hard to describe the impact of this system on the quality of life of Haredim, for to do so requires adopting a decidedly non-Western understanding of quality of life. One cannot, however, understand the Haredi world without first understanding this.

A study conducted by Nitsa (Kaliner) Kasir and Dmitri Romanov called *Quality of Life Among Israel's Population Groups: A Comparative Survey*, published in 2018 by the Jerusalem-based Haredi Institute for Public Affairs, which I lead, explored a whole array of quality-of-life indicators as expressed in the Haredi, non-Haredi Jewish, and Arab sectors in Israel. One of the most amazing things it revealed were the quantitative markers of such a powerful social-support network on Haredi life—many of which can be similarly found among Haredi communities outside of Israel, as well.

***

First: charitable giving. Despite the myth that the masses of Haredim are living off the government or a small number of wealthy Jews, the reality is radically different. In fact, it is the Haredi *masses* who themselves are giving charity, or *tzedaka*, to an astonishing degree, even those who have relatively little to give. The result is that Haredi society operates under a completely different economic model from the non-Haredi world.

The Haredi economy begins not with receiving handouts from without, but extremely generous giving within, by almost all segments of the population. According to the study, approximately 74 percent of Haredi households in Israel give to charity, averaging NIS 548, or about $158, per month. This compares with just 27 percent of non-Haredi Jewish households who give to charity, averaging about NIS 199, or $57, per month. On a per-household basis, in other words, Haredim in Israel donate almost triple the average of non-Haredi Jewish households. But when the figure is seen as a percentage of disposable income, the difference jumps even higher—to 4.6 percent for Haredim versus 1.2 percent for non-Haredi Jews. In other words, despite having far less money, Haredim are giving three to four times as much as non-Haredi Jews, depending on how you measure it.

So yes—the Haredi world benefits from the philanthropy of the rich (as does the non-Haredi world) as well as government support (as does the non-Haredi world). But this external support exists on top of a robust substructure of charitable giving, a core value inculcated throughout the community that translates into a vast foundation of charity extending well beyond the wealthy, through the middle class, and even among lower-income people.

A thriving social-services sector requires more than money, however. It requires manpower. Here, too, we discover higher rates of volunteering among the Haredi population, with 32 percent of Haredi adults volunteering their time, compared with 23 percent of non-Haredi Jews. Yet this tells only part of the story. Of those who volunteer, almost half of Haredim volunteer for ten or more hours per week, compared with only a third of non-Haredi Jewish volunteers. Haredim also spend a disproportionate number of those hours volunteering privately, rather than through an organization.

It is hard to imagine the number of formal and informal organizations a Haredi is likely to encounter daily, whether as a giver or a recipient. Every conceivable need—whether Shabbat meals for the poor, mother's milk for nursing babies, the sale or mending of clothes or appliances—has people and systems in place ready to provide, free of charge, to those in need. Very few people are left behind; the Haredi community takes upon itself the basic material needs of all its members.

Most of this activity, admittedly, is directed inward—its beneficiaries are mainly Haredim. In Israel, however, there are areas where Haredi volunteers have identified a need outside their own community, a hole that needed to be filled. Haredi paramedics volunteer for Hatzalah, the extremely effective first-response organization that deploys hundreds of motorcycles to shave crucial life-saving minutes off an emergency response—usually arriving well before an ambulance. In horrific moments such as a terror attack or other mass casualty event, it is the Haredi volunteers from the ZAKA organization who deal with human remains, preserving their sanctity and integrity at the scene of a disaster. Organizations like Yad Sarah, which offers free loans of medical equipment and is the largest volunteer organization in Israel; Matnat Chaim, which facilitates kidney donations; and Ezer Mizion, a far-ranging health-service organization that includes the world's largest bone marrow registry—all offer powerful examples of the nationwide impact of Haredi volunteerism.

The result of all this charitable and voluntary activity is that communal life is sustained to a degree of human satisfaction that is hard to imagine.

* * *

Poverty statistics, too, tell an important part of the story. According to the Central Bureau of Statistics, 52.6 percent of the Haredi community lives below the poverty line—compared with 8.7 percent of non-Haredi Jews. Yet when asked in 2016 whether they had "felt poor" over the past year, only 8 percent of Haredim answered in the affirmative, compared with 7 percent of non-Haredi Jews. And when asked if they had *ever* felt poor in their lives, the relationship reversed—with just 28 percent of Haredim saying they had, compared with 36 percent of non-Haredi Jews.

As anyone who has tasted poverty knows, the subjective experience is far more significant and traumatic than the objective measures of economists. People above the poverty line can experience that hardship—when unusually high expenses or mishandled finances bring people to ruin. But it is also the case that people living below the poverty line may be blessed with the ability to avoid that hardship—especially when communal structures ensure their minimal standard of living including food, shelter, clothing, and utilities. The radical disparity between objective and subjective poverty in the Haredi world is indicative not of a delusional way of life, but rather of the extremely robust system of communal support that most Haredim not only enjoy but also contribute to. Indeed, when asked whether they were "satisfied with their economic situation," 71 percent of Haredim answered in the affirmative—compared with 63 percent of non-Haredi Jews.

Other subjective indicators, too, suggest a comparatively high quality of life in the Haredi world. Only 11 percent of Haredim report feeling lonely, for example, compared with 23 percent of non-Haredi Jews. Sixty-four percent expect their economic situation to improve in the future—suggesting an optimistic outlook—compared with 45 percent of non-Haredi Jews; whereas 98 percent report being "satisfied" with their lives, compared with a still-high 90 percent of non-Haredi Jews in Israel.

Israel is well known as a happy country, routinely making the list of the top twenty countries in overall happiness in the world. Yet among Israelis, none are as satisfied, optimistic, and un-lonely as the Haredim.

* * *

None of this is meant to claim the overall superiority of the Haredi lifestyle, but rather to underscore the importance of getting beyond the stereotypes and understanding that alongside its perceived disadvantages, there are also notable advantages that may be learned from.

How do we account for these advantages? The Haredi world is successful in part because it is guided by a different set of values, expectations, and aspirations. A good life, to the Haredim, is above all a holy life—one of Torah and Mitzvot. And it is a life where the community takes precedence over the individual. Far from being suppressed, creativity, innovation, and self-starting are highly valued—but they are applied to the provision of social goods and services rather than money-generating start-ups and stardom. What is seen from the outside as dependency—with all its pejorative connotations—is seen by Haredim as a constant flow of both giving and receiving, a system of effective mutual care, in which some are blessed with the ability to give more, and others less. For the Haredim, there is no success like sanctity, nor is there shame in poverty, only in profanity.

It is a different world, but one worth knowing about, both at the pragmatic level and at the level of values, aspirations, social awareness, mutual trust, habits of mind, and the inner workings of the Jewish people's ancient wisdom.

And the entirety of it rests on a single central principle, around which Haredi life revolves and without which all the charity, voluntarism, and other benefits are difficult to make sense of: It is the foundational concept of *talmud torah* or Torah study.

Torah study is not the same as formal education, parenting, studying for exams, reading for leisure, teaching, therapy, or self-help—even though in an important sense it includes all of these. "And you shall teach them [the Torah's precepts] over and over to your children," we read in Deuteronomy, "and you should speak of them as you sit in your home and as you walk on the road, when you lay down and when you rise up" (6:7). Engagement with the Torah's teachings is meant to be habitual and enveloping, and its value is infinite. "These are the things that one eats their fruit in this world," the Mishna teaches, "but the core is preserved for one in the world to come: Honoring one's parents, generosity, making peace between neighbors—and Torah study is as great as them all" (Pe'ah 1:1). Torah study is understood as a kind of "meta-value," the source for the inculcation of all other values.

From an early age, Haredi children are inculcated in an entire world of texts and rabbis, of stories and laws and prayers, aimed at translating the words of the Torah into the practicalities of living—not just in a technical-ritual way, but especially in the area of instinctive values, aspirations, and dreams. It is a world in which fathers and sons, mothers and daughters—and, of course, schools—are forever undertaking a grand project of endless inquiry through textual study, formal teaching, casual conversation, role models, and storytelling. It is a life of constant and immersive devotion that is at once intellectual and spiritual, cognitive and emotive, and active.

But it is also social: The ethos of Torah and Mitzvot engenders a deep trust across the community, which expresses itself in efficient business relations, in people offering their homes to host families needing a place to stay or to hold events, and in the system of mutual social support that spans the world. Of *course* Haredim volunteer to help at the drop of a hat, because we already know that this is what the Torah demands. It is a mitzvah, an opportunity for sanctity, such that when the opportunity arises, you don't think twice.

And even if what we call the "Haredi world" is a reaction to Enlightenment and thus a product of the modern era, the spiritual-intellectual core of it all—from Bible to Mishna and Talmud to the vast ocean of kabbalistic, halachic, exegetical, philosophical, liturgical, homiletical, and midrashic works spanning thousands of years—is not new at all. It is from there that the Haredim draw their vision of a "society of learners," in which the entirety of life is held together by the study of Torah.

***

Most Jews, both in Israel and the Diaspora, do not wish to become Haredim—for such a lifestyle, whatever its benefits, requires giving up on much of the sense of freedom, individualism, ambition, and material prosperity on which modern life is based. But this doesn't mean a great deal cannot be gained from a deeper understanding of the world that lies behind the curtain.

A significant investment in mutual understanding between the two worlds could lead to a very different relationship between them—one built less on stereotypes and mutual animosity, and more on a kind of symbiosis in which each derives fundamental benefits from the other. In ancient Israel, according to our tradition, the tribe of Levi was charged with the duty of teaching Torah to the Israelite masses. A subset of that tribe, the Cohanim, served as the priests in the Temple in Jerusalem. Both groups saw themselves as providing a service to the Children of Israel, and the Israelites in return not only sustained them economically but also took advantage of the services they offered. It was a win-win.

How much stronger would the Jewish people be if, instead of Haredim and modern Jews seeing each other as strangers and adversaries, we saw each other as partners in an age-old journey together through history and into the future? Such an achievement is far more possible than commonly believed. It begins with casting off stereotypes, engaging in mutually respectful dialogue, investing in mutual understanding, and always remembering that despite our enormous differences, we are still one people, divided but destined to remain together through history.

40

SAVING THE JEWISH-
PROGRESSIVE ALLIANCE

Why We Must Fight for the Soul of the Left

CARLY PILDIS

AFTER EVERY MAJOR ANTISEMITIC INCIDENT, I am asked by friends, family, and readers if I have an "exit plan." No, I tell them, in my house, there is no special suitcase under the bed with passports, documents, and cash. There is, instead, a burning desire to fight back.

Carly Pildis has spent fifteen years as a writer, organizer, and advocate, and currently serves as Director of Community Engagement at the Anti-Defamation League. She was named as one of the 2019 Forward 50 in *Forward*'s annual list of influential American Jews.

These too-frequent conversations bring up important questions about maintaining stability, dignity, and prosperity for Jews in the Diaspora. Why do some Jewish communities thrive for hundreds of years, only to be suddenly consumed by raging violence? If we acknowledge that hatred of Jews will persist, as it has for millennia, how can we keep that hatred from taking hold in society with catastrophic consequences? How do we ensure antisemitism remains at the fringes of society?

We can turn to the work of social psychologist Amy Cuddy for some initial answers. While exploring hatred throughout various societies and eras, she identifies minority groups that are viewed warmly or coldly, so-called "in-groups" and "out-groups," but explains that this isn't the whole picture. There are two important axes: "warm" versus "cold" and "competent" versus "incompetent." As she put it in her 2013 *New York Times* op-ed, "The Psychology of Antisemitism":

> Insofar as a group is seen as good-natured, sincere and trustworthy, it is considered warm; insofar as it is seen as lacking those qualities, it is considered cold. Likewise, if a group is seen as ambitious, intelligent and skillful, it is considered competent; if it is seen as lacking those qualities, it is considered incompetent.

There are groups that are viewed as warm and competent—these are in-groups and cultural reference points, such as Christians and middle-class families in America. Then there are those that are viewed as cold and incompetent, such as the homeless; or warm and incompetent—like the elderly.

Jews, according to Cuddy, fall into a fourth category: cold and competent.

Cold but competent groups are generally deemed productive members of society—ambitious, intelligent, skillful. But they aren't an in-group that innately belongs. This can lead to more subtle and complex patterns of discrimination. In times of scarcity or upheaval, this type of minority is suddenly a competitor for in-groups as opposed to a societal asset. Political, social, and economic instability can spell disaster. Any success elicits resentment and jealousy, as though the cold and competent group has stolen from the cultural reference group—a phenomenon she dubs "envious prejudice." With this type of prejudice, cold-competent valuation becomes potentially deadly during times of economic, political, and social crisis. Her examples include the Cambodian genocide, Rwanda, and Germany after World War I. In all these cases, minority groups were seemingly tolerated, stable, and prosperous, but suddenly faced extreme and exterminatory violence.

So, knowing that we are most likely to be tolerated, even admired, but never fully accepted, how do we guard against antisemitism? Knowing that even in the best circumstances, we may never truly belong—and that in the worst circumstances, we could easily become the scapegoat—how do we keep our communities safe?

Think of the status of any global Jewish community as a house. If your basement is dark and damp, the mold will grow and sicken your household. If you want to avoid mold in your house, you can't just kill the mold where you see it. You need to protect the whole structure. You waterproof your basement. You seal it from cracks. You ensure that your house is not a friendly place for mold to grow.

If you want to fight antisemitism, you can't just call it out when you see it. You need to address the societal conditions that allow antisemitism to flourish. Where there is great inequality in society, Jews are vulnerable. Where there is poverty, racial injustice, economic instability, and political strife—antisemitism has the dark damp basement it needs to grow. If our home is built on top of a moldy basement, we will always be vulnerable.

We can never fully inoculate our societies from antisemitism, just as a flu shot won't guarantee you don't catch the flu. But when a society is more just, more equal, more prosperous, we can significantly reduce the likelihood of the virus of antisemitism turning deadly.

But this means that we cannot fight antisemitism in a silo, solely focused on Jewish well-being. We will need to join with allies to fight the underlying conditions of inequality and injustice that allow antisemitism to thrive. Antisemitism is a conspiracy theory that transforms itself to address any economic, political, or societal injustice. If we try to fight antisemitism alone, it is as if there is a fire raging through our house, but we are trying to put it out in only one room. The flames will still consume us.

* * *

How do injustice and inequality lead to antisemitism?

When you lose your house because your child is ill, and you cannot afford to save both her and pay your mortgage, you will look for someone to blame.

When your family is trapped in generational poverty, and, despite relentless effort and back-breaking work, you cannot escape poverty to meet basic needs, you will be angry and look for someone to blame.

When you are worse off economically than your parents or grandparents, you will want to know why.

When your brother is beaten by the police, when your public school is crumbling, when lead in the water poisons your children while others drink champagne, when you work sixty hours a week and still cannot pay your bills, you will be angry. You will want to understand why society has made you suffer.

This is where antisemitism thrives. There will always be someone, somewhere, saying, "Blame the Jew." Given that we are less than 0.2 percent of the global population and many people will never meet, much less know and understand, we make a convenient scapegoat. They may say it for money. They may say it to deflect blame. They may say it in a quest for power. To the Jewish community that suffers, the "why" will be immaterial, but the consequences we suffer can be deadly.

This is why leaning into "Tikkun Olam" makes sense as a strategy for fighting antisemitism. If we embrace our role as people commanded to repair the world, and we fight for social change, we can contain antisemitism while improving outcomes for our whole society.

* * *

How can we put this into practice? There are three pillars I suggest.

First, show up for the community—the whole community. Jews are few in number, and it's important that people get to know us, meet us, and see that we are their allies, not their enemies or oppressors. There is a portion of the Jewish community that is consistently present at every protest, every rally, for every civil rights or social justice cause. These activists are fighting antisemitism in a real and tangible way. It is harder to be scapegoated for societal ills when you are publicly proclaiming, through your actions, that the Jewish community opposes oppression.

How does this work in practice? Let me introduce you to my friend, Charlotte Clymer. Charlotte has built an enviable public platform, nearly 400,000 Twitter followers, regular television appearances, and a Substack contract. She is one of the most vocal transgender rights advocates in the country and was named one of Forbes 40-under-40 in Politics. Charlotte also cares about antisemitism. She has used her platform to decry growing violence against Jews, to commemorate the Holocaust, to urge Congress to confirm Deborah Lipstadt as the U.S. envoy against antisemitism and to ask her followers to donate to the Anti-Defamation League (ADL).

Recently, I had Charlotte over for brunch and we talked about hatred. I asked her how and why she got interested in fighting antisemitism. It was a very simple answer. Jews were always at LGBTQ rights events. They were always at transgender rights rallies. She hadn't known many Jews, or much about Judaism, but Jews were always there in allyship for her. It was only natural, when antisemitism began to rise, that she in turn advocated for them. When we advocate for each other, we keep each other safe.

Another example: My friend Manilan Houle is such an outspoken advocate for Jews that he is often mistaken for a Jew. He has worked for the American Israel Public Affairs Committee (AIPAC) and ADL and is a constant voice against antisemitism—especially when it bubbles up in left-wing circles. What makes a Native American man from Minnesota decide to be so passionate about antisemitism? He met many Jews when fighting for expanded access to social safety nets like the Child Tax Credit, Supplemental Nutrition Assistance Program (food stamps), and similar programs. Those programs were critical to him as a child and remain essential for his community. He met me, and many other Jews, engaged in fighting poverty. We became friends. When his local Jewish Community Center had a bomb threat, he saw pictures of babies being evacuated from the daycare in cribs. He called me in tears, heartbroken to see antisemitism. He asked a simple question: How can I help?

These are only two examples of many. Each of these people are one tiny patch trying to keep our foundation from rotting. Each one got there because they know us to be on their side, fighting for justice.

Traumatic history can stunt our ability to build allies. Every Jew has grown up with stories of betrayal—with deadly consequences. I can't promise you that no one will betray you or hurt you. But the alternative is fighting antisemitism alone—a fight we can never win.

* * *

Second, fight for policies that strengthen the whole community, enrich the whole nation, and dismantle inequity—and in doing so, make Jews safer. Jewish organizations should endorse policies that fight antisemitism in part by fighting societal ills that fan the flames of Jew-hatred. Disinformation and access to knowledge, pervasive and systemic racism, economic inequality and rampant generational poverty, political turmoil and attacks on democracy— these are all the kindling for violent antisemitism. Every Jewish organization can't take on every cause, but we can strategically couple our activism against antisemitism with the struggle against the conditions that allow it to thrive.

Take hate crimes. Hate crimes have been rising throughout America, and there has been a particular and frightening rise in hate crimes against Jews. As troubling as that is—can you imagine how much worse it would be if there were no hate-crime laws? There would be no legal recourse for the particular heinousness of crimes designed solely to intimidate and frighten a community; the swastika on your child's preschool would only be charged as graffiti. Hate-crime laws have become one of the most essential tools the Jewish community uses to fight violent hate. But they would never have been passed if Jews were engaged in fighting hate against Jews only. A coalition of Black Americans, gay Americans, and many others joined together and fought for decades for stronger federal and statewide hate-crime laws. If we had simply siloed off violence against Jews as a particular problem and the only lens we considered, it is extremely unlikely we would have hate-crime laws as a tool now.

Another example is the expanded Child Tax Credit. This may not seem like a Jewish issue, but if one in seven kids continues to wake up living in poverty, their parents will inevitably seek to understand why they live in one of the wealthiest countries in the world and yet their kids are hungry. Those kids will wonder why this is happening to them, and they will seek answers. Some portion will find the answer in Louis Farrakhan or Tucker Carlson or David Duke or the Goyim Defense League or Aryan Nation. Anytime we shrink that percentage, and make clear our role in it, we fight the mold in the basement.

America briefly flirted with an expanded Child Tax Credit and over 61 million children benefitted. Child poverty was cut by 30 percent in just six months. The best part was that it reached the most impoverished kids first and was overwhelmingly spent on food, rent, school supplies, and utilities. Tragically, the expanded Child Tax Credit expired only six months later, due to partisan politics. This type of simple policy, giving money to families struggling to raise their kids, is the perfect type of policy we should all be embracing to waterproof that basement.

Jewish organizations should be on the frontlines fighting for laws against hate crimes, and the expanded Child Tax Credit—both because it will lift millions of kids out of poverty and because any time we defeat inequity, we defeat antisemitism.

* * *

Third: Never let the antisemites kick you out of the fight.

Let us be clear. Antisemites never have our best interests at heart. When the antisemite says to get out of feminism or leave the racial justice movement or that we are the oppressors so we cannot fight poverty, they are only seeking to benefit themselves and their twisted aims. So why on earth would we take their counsel, pack up our stuff, and walk away?

Inevitably, you will encounter antisemitism. Wherever you are fighting for change or holding public office or are a public persona as a Jew, you will occasionally encounter antisemitism. Not the kind that comes from ignorance and is willing to learn or quick to dialogue, but the kind that is entrenched, inherited, and fully formed, full-scale hate.

I remember marching against the war in Iraq with my friends, and a group approached me, looked at my Jewish star, and told me to get out. That I didn't belong because Jews started this war, and all wars. Did I go home?

Hell no. I laughed, turned around, and kept right on marching. People tried to kick me out of Dyke March too, but I stayed, locked arms with the gay Jewish women I came to support, and refused to yield. They caved and let us in, where we were greeted by many people who were happy that we came. People have tried to kick Jews out of feminism, racial justice, economic justice, and environmental movements. I did not move. I did not yield. I quickly found plenty of people, Jewish or not, who were more than happy to stand beside me. They wanted me there.

So, while you are out there, fighting for a more just and equitable world, working for change, and in doing so, making a better and safer society for Jews and for everyone, you may encounter hate. I wish I could change that reality. You will encounter people who are not sorry, who do not want dialogue, who impose impossible litmus tests that are designed to make you fail and you shouldn't even dignify with a response. They want you gone. Guess what? If you are not at the table, you are on the menu—you're what's for lunch. Never let the antisemite kick you out. If they tell you to leave, you know you are exactly where you need to be.

* * *

The Jewish voice in the fight for global change is powerful. From labor movements and LGBTQ rights to feminism, racial justice, economic justice, and fighting poverty, Jews play a key role in fighting for a better world. We need these movements, and they also need us. You will find far more people who want the Jewish community in the fight than those who want us gone. Stand your ground, and you will find support.

The need to fight antisemitism is urgent and overwhelming. Nearly every Diaspora community worldwide is facing increased threats. We cannot fight in silos. We must band together and fight for everyone, fight the conditions that create fertile ground for antisemitism to grow, build new allies while standing tall for all, and embrace policies that fight antisemitism by creating a more equitable society. We can and should do that while continuing to push relentlessly for Jewish safety, dignity, and freedom from discrimination and hate. Liberation for all does not mean antisemitism is at the bottom of the list; it means that antisemitism can't find its shoes in the morning because the conditions for it to flourish are simply not there.

Most every Jew has heard the stories. Maybe they started with your grandmother, in the kitchen, when you asked about her family and she flinched for a moment. Maybe you heard them in Hebrew schools. Maybe, like me, you have known and heard these stories for so long, you can't even remember a time not knowing about the threat of antisemitism. In times of trouble, with antisemitism spiking across the globe, it is natural to want to batten down the hatches, shut down, and focus on just Jewish safety.

That instinct must be overcome. Instead of turning inward, when we fight antisemitism we must turn outward. We must build new coalitions and strengthen old ones, make our voices loud in defense of our fellow historically marginalized communities, and demand economic, social, and racial justice for all in our society.

In this way, we kill the mold in the basement, before our house, our whole of society, collapses in on us. Too often, Jews who are focused on "Tikkun Olam" are belittled by portions of our community as being distracted, or worse. The opposite is true. Jews who have focused on making a better neighborhood, country, and world for us all have been doing some of the best work to fight the conditions that allow antisemitism to flourish.

This is the true meaning of "Tikkun Olam." When we stand together and refuse to be deterred in the cause of an equitable and just society, we all win. When we save the world, we are also saving ourselves.

41

STUDY THE TALMUD THE OLD-FASHIONED WAY

Forget Viral Videos. Find a Teacher. Open a Book.

URI PILICHOWSKI

A MIDDLE-AGED MAN once found himself in a used bookstore in Jerusalem. Browsing the shelves, he found some interesting works, but nothing that excited him. Finally, he found an old book, worn but intact, on a top shelf in the corner of the store. It was a commentary on the Talmud by a scholar he had never heard of.

Rabbi Uri Pilichowski is a senior educator of Zionism and Torah at educational institutions throughout the world. He lives with his wife and six children in Mitzpe Yericho, Israel.

He opened it and was soon fascinated by the author's introduction. The book was first published four centuries ago, but this particular edition was published three centuries ago in France. Excited over his find, he was surprised to discover a lengthy inscription, written by hand, on the inside of the front cover:

> To my family: While most heirlooms passed from generation to generation are usually jewelry or Judaica, our family has passed this book down from father to son for generations. It is filled with the most wondrous Talmudic insights written by our great-great grandfather hundreds of years ago. Treasure this work, share its words and teachings with your children, and when your time to leave this world comes, leave the work with your youngest descendant. If, God forbid, someone from outside our family has found this book, an unthinkable tragedy must have occurred to our family. I beg of you to take care of this work and allow it to be passed from generation to generation in your family, as it was in our family.

By the time he had finished reading the inscription, his hands were shaking. He immediately understood that the "unthinkable tragedy" had indeed come to pass. Like so many families, the family of the book's owner was, in all likelihood, destroyed in the Holocaust. None had survived. The tradition of passing the book from generation to generation had come to an end.

He committed to renewing the tradition in his own family. He would study the book's insights, teach them to his children and grandchildren, and eventually pass the book down to his youngest descendant.

* * *

The Torah in general, and in particular the Talmud, cannot be properly studied without the traditional methods of study that have long accompanied it. The text is obscure and lives in a vast context of other texts, oral teachings, and methods of study.

Traditional Torah study, and in particular Talmud study, is thus more than just a personal endeavor. When a person studies Torah, he or she is connecting to the infinite and to God. "Why should one study Torah?" asks Rabbi Israel Chait, noted scholar and author of the book *Philosophy of Torah*, and answers:

> Because it is only through Torah that one can fulfill the one commandment that is the end goal of the entire Torah—the love of God. Why should one study Torah? Because the study brings man close to the source of all reality—the Creator of the Universe. Why should one study Torah? Because through the study of Torah man attains the highest possible state of human existence—the very purpose for which he was created. It is for this reason he was endowed with the *tzelem elokim*, his divine element. All else that a person may do in life is only a means for the state of mind derived from the learning of Torah. It is the most satisfying state of human existence attainable; one that gives man his true happiness. According to Judaism man's psyche was specifically designed for this experience. In it, all psychic energies are involved in a sublime joy and appreciation of intellectual beatitude. As such it is the most gratifying experience possible for man.

Although today there is more Torah being studied than ever before, there is one aspect of the study that is often not understood but is absolutely vital to the "Torah experience": studying Torah the old-fashioned way, with a teacher who is suffused with the ancient traditions and methods of our people.

Torah study is a religious act, a mitzvah by nature, but it is also so much more. Every nation has its own unique culture and traditions. There is a tendency to relegate Jewish culture and tradition to Yiddish theatre and matzo-ball soup, but Jewish tradition is much richer. It starts with the biblical stories of Adam and Eve, Noah, the patriarchs and matriarchs. It continues with Talmudic tales and philosophical lessons. Above all, Jewish tradition is based on the halacha or Jewish law. The main body of work where halacha is found is the Talmud. It is through the study of halacha that Jews can fully connect to their identity and culture.

Moses Maimonides, quoting a teaching of Rabbi Shimon in the tractate of the Mishna known as *Ethics of the Fathers*, wrote that every Jew can study Torah; there is no special class of Jews on whom this responsibility falls:

> Three crowns were given to the Jewish people: the crown of Torah, the crown of priesthood, and the crown of royalty. Aaron merited the crown of priesthood, David merited the crown of royalty, and the crown of Torah is set aside, waiting and ready for each Jew....

Torah study is an important part of Jewish practice. Elsewhere in *Ethics of the Fathers*, we read that "Rabbi Tarfon used to say: It is not your duty to finish the work, but neither are you at liberty to neglect it." Maimonides wrote that Torah study is the most important mitzva: "None of the other mitzvot can be equated to the study of Torah. Rather, the study of Torah can be equated to all the mitzvot, because study leads to deed. Therefore, study takes precedence over deed in all cases." (Maimonides, Laws of Torah Study 3:1)

The heart of the study of halacha is the "Oral Law." Maimonides described the process through which, according to tradition, Moses received the commandments from God in writing, along with their explanations transmitted orally. He then passed those on to the elders, beginning a long tradition of unwritten explication:

> Afterwards, the people reviewed with one another what they had heard from Moses and wrote down the verse on scrolls. Scholars would visit the people to teach and review the verse until everyone knew it accurately and was well-versed in it. They then taught the people the explanation of the God given mitzvah in all its many details. The wording of the mitzvah would be recorded in writing, while its oral tradition would be learned by heart. (Maimonides, *Introduction to the Mishna* 2:13)

Over a period of generations, as the world changed, disagreements arose about how the laws applied to new realities and situations. He continues:

Some of the laws…were undisputed and were unanimously agreed upon. Other laws gave rise to controversy. Depending on the precedent to which he compared the case at hand, one Sage would make a statement based on his logical reasoning insisting that he was right, while another Sage would just as vehemently insist that his rationale was right. When such disputes occurred among authorities, they would follow the majority opinion. (Maimonides, *Introduction to the Mishna* 2:26-27)

Eventually, after the destruction of the Second Temple, many of the core precepts and rulings of the Oral Law were codified in the form of the Mishna. But this did not change the fundamental dynamic—for alongside the Mishna, a vibrant discourse of interpretation continued for centuries, an ocean of stories, disputes, and rulings around it, all of it unified through a methodology carried by tradition. This became the Talmud.

With the passing years, differences of opinion arose about the interpretation of some laws. Whenever scholars studied together, invariably they probed and delved into the Mishna, discovered new insights, and increased their knowledge in general. This process of research and analysis continued up to the time of Ravina and Rav Ashi, the last of the Talmudic Sages. (Maimonides, *Introduction to the Mishna* 16:6)

The rabbis used a methodology to decide their position and to discover new insights. This methodology is the heart of the study of halacha.

Every area of study is enhanced by a methodological analysis. All studies, whether literature, science, or math should be more than just random thoughts—Torah more so than all other subjects. Rabbi Chait explained the importance of methodology in the study of the Talmud:

Although the Oral Law has been committed to writing for fear of it becoming lost, the particular method of analysis has always required verbal transmission from teacher to student to this day. In order to become a Talmudic scholar one has to have studied personally under the guidance and tutelage of another Talmudic scholar. The unique method of Talmudic analysis with all its intricacies requires years of personal tutelage and cannot be acquired from written words.

When studying Talmud, the use of a received methodology, carried to you through generations of teachers and students, is the minimal requirement for success in study. This is the "old-fashioned" way of studying the Talmud.

* * *

The objective of Talmud study is not just amassing knowledge and memorizing it. Talmud study aims to understand the mechanics of halacha. Like any chemical compound, each halacha is a compound of different elements. The goal of the student of Talmud is to break down the compound to its essential elements and to understand how the elements interact with each other to generate the law under study.

The analogy to chemistry is no coincidence. Just as the scientist studies a chemical compound to explain its mechanics, develops a hypothesis, and tests it against previous scientific principles and conclusions, the Talmud student also studies the halacha, develops a theory about how it operates, and tests it against previous Talmudic principles and conclusions. It is not enough for a student's explanation to sound appealing or meaningful, it must explain how the halacha operates. A halacha in the Talmud is best analyzed with a methodology taught by an expert who has been taught a methodology by a previous scholar, and so on back to Moses. The passing of the methodology from teacher to student through the ages is the true Oral Torah. It can't be written down—although some have tried.

The old-fashioned study of the Oral Law, the halacha, through the Talmud, is the traditional methodology. Its results can be found in the most scholarly works published in every generation over the past 1,500 years. When a scholar trained in this methodology picks up a commentary on the Talmud and reads the explanations of the Talmud contained in it, the scholar immediately recognizes the methodology used in its analysis.

The benefits of the traditional study of the Talmud far surpass the learning itself. The methodology of analysis permeates every aspect of life. From the Talmud student's business affairs to their relationships, the student can apply the methodology they have learned to new situations and understand them better. Instead of reacting reflexively to events happening in his life, the student can break down each situation and understand what has led to the particular circumstances they are facing. Challenging situations are simpler to break down and easier to handle. Complicated relationships become less complicated, business deals become faster to execute, and the world becomes easier to understand. The Talmudic methodology makes Talmud study easier, but it also makes life far more enjoyable.

Just as the man in the bookstore committed to passing down the insights of the old book he found to his family, Torah students are charged to pass on a methodology to their families and students. This, more than anything else, is what continues Jewish tradition. More than the warm chicken soup of the Friday night Shabbat table or the sweet *charoset* of the Passover Seder, the tastiest part of Jewish tradition is the explanation a Talmud student develops applying the patterns of thought they learned from their teacher.

Nothing compares to the joy experienced from one's first *chidush*, the novel explanation to a halacha found in the Talmud. The old-fashioned study of the Talmud has been passed from generation to generation, and although the Jewish people have faced tragedy after tragedy, it is still alive today. All are invited to partake of its wondrous experience.

42

WHY JEWS NEED A COMMON LANGUAGE

A Plan for Universal Hebrew Literacy

VARDIT RINGVALD

THE UNIQUENESS OF THE MODERN HEBREW LANGUAGE is its revival. A language found mainly in the Bible, liturgy, and centuries-old rabbinical texts was transformed more than a century ago into one spoken in everyday life. The "secularization" of the language is a product of the Zionist enterprise, the return of Jews to the Land of Israel, and the establishment of the Jewish state.

Vardit Ringvald is the inaugural Director of the Consortium for the Teaching of Hebrew Language and Culture and a research professor at the Mandel Center for Studies in Jewish Education at Brandeis University. She was a founder of the School of Hebrew at Middlebury College and is the leading expert in the Proficiency Approach for teaching Hebrew as an additional language.

There has long been agreement among Diaspora Jewish educators and policymakers in both formal and informal educational frameworks regarding the importance of teaching Classical Hebrew for participating in religious rituals and studying Jewish texts. There is less of a consensus about the study of Modern Hebrew, the language of Israeli daily life and culture.

The question of the relevance of Modern Hebrew study has become more acute in an era of global communications in which interactions between people of different languages take place through the English language, the lingua franca of the modern world. This new reality calls into question the need to invest in the acquisition of foreign languages at all.

Yet there are good reasons for Jewish education today to invest in Modern Hebrew—reasons that go far beyond the benefits of studying other foreign languages, and which are no less valid in an era of automatic online translation and the widespread use of English.

Modern Hebrew is today a crucial Jewish value, a powerful tool for strengthening Jewish identity, and a window into an entire Jewish world of life, creativity, and culture. In an era when Jewish engagement in the Diaspora is a seemingly endless challenge, now is the time to invest dramatically in Modern Hebrew language study.

***

The most obvious reason to study Modern Hebrew has to do with the nature of language itself. Mastery of a language opens a window into cultures that would otherwise be alien to us. By studying Modern Hebrew, Diaspora Jews may understand, empathize, and personalize the experience and feelings of the most important, active, and consequential Jewish community of the twenty-first century: that of the State of Israel.

Since the eighteenth century, scholars have been fascinated by the essence of language, and it has continued to be the focus of inquiry in fields as diverse as psychology, linguistics, philosophy, sociology, anthropology, and the life sciences. While each addresses this issue with its own special tools, they all seem to agree that language is essentially a system of signs that allows human beings to communicate with each other in a sociocultural context that is unique to its speakers. Claire Kramsch, a linguist and founder of the Berkeley Language Center, put it this way in her 1998 book *Language and Culture*:

> Language…is bound up with culture in multiple and complex ways. To begin with, the words people utter refer to common experience. They express facts, ideas or events that are communicable because they refer to a stock of knowledge about the world that other people share. Words also reflect their authors' attitudes and beliefs, their point of view, that are also those of others. In both cases, *language expresses cultural reality.*
>
> But members of a community or social group do not only express experience; they also create experience through language…. The way in which people use the spoken, written, or visual medium itself creates meanings that are understandable to the group they belong to, for example, through a speaker's tone of voice, accent, conversational style, gestures and facial expressions. Through all its verbal and non-verbal aspects, *language embodies cultural reality.*

Kramsch echoes what generations of scholars have argued dating back to the eighteenth century. "Absolutely nothing," wrote Wilhelm von Humboldt in 1797, "is so important for a nation's culture as its language."

Mastery of a language allows one to understand deeply the worldview of the people who speak it and the different layers of their cultural behaviors. This in-depth level of understanding that results from gaining proficiency in the target language allows those who acquire it to engage meaningfully in the discourse of the native speakers. It allows them to use the language to exchange written or spoken messages and ideas, while integrating in the native speakers' cultural-social conventions. The quality of this level of proficiency requires participants to develop empathy toward each other, understanding their feelings and life experiences, which is a necessary first step toward real interpersonal relationships.

A study conducted among participants in a summer Jewish day camp, coordinated by the Kayitz Kef organization, which develops Modern Hebrew immersion programs for educational and camp curricula, showed that campers who were intensively exposed to the language by interacting in Hebrew with Israeli counselors developed a more positive attitude and stronger emotional connection toward Israel and Israelis compared to those who experienced the Hebrew language in a lower dosage.

The acquisition of Modern Hebrew among communities in the Diaspora will make it possible to create direct meaningful relationships with Israelis and to understand their realities. True, advanced technology along with the basic study of English by many Israelis allows for some degree of communication between English-speaking Diaspora Jews and Israelis. But only through the mastery of Modern Hebrew will it be possible for Diaspora Jews to understand their world in depth and to develop genuine empathy, which is the key to creating real and sustainable relationships. Such mastery also offers Diaspora Jews the opportunity to take part in the Israeli discourse as an equal among equals, to become an active member of the native speakers' world.

* * *

Yet even if one leaves aside the benefits of connecting Diaspora Jews with Israelis on the deepest levels of life and culture, there is a second argument for the large-scale study of Modern Hebrew in the Diaspora: to create a common language, a lingua franca, connecting Jews around the world.

It is no surprise that the process of the rapid disengagement of Jews in the last half-century coincided with the demise of the Yiddish language. For centuries, having our own language meant enjoying the benefits of our own signs and symbols, our own internal dialogue expressed not only in daily life but in literature, newspapers, theater, and more—all of which created an automatic and even intimate connection of Jews to one another. Perhaps it did not include all Jews (only those from central and eastern Europe), yet it was spoken by a very significant portion of the Jewish people.

Today, we Diaspora Jews have no single language of our own. But we could. Modern Hebrew is there for the taking—and it is the most obvious choice, the only language that has ever connected *all* Jewish communities. According to the Israeli philosopher Rachel Elior, Hebrew always played a central role in the life of Jews around the world. While Jewish schoolchildren studied Hebrew to have access to the ancient texts and the liturgy, as adults they also used it in a variety of ways, including any context requiring communicating with Jews who did not speak their native tongue, such as in international trade. Hebrew was never, as is often claimed, a "dead" language: To the contrary, it lived as the language of Torah, prayer, and intercommunal communication throughout our long history.

It should be understood, moreover, that this was a large part of what many early Zionists had in mind in reestablishing Hebrew as the language of the Jews.

The poet laureate Hayim Nahman Bialik and the Zionist leader Ze'ev Jabotinsky, to take two prominent examples from the early twentieth century, both argued that the aim of reviving the Hebrew language was not merely to serve as the basis for the culture of the forthcoming Jewish state, but no less importantly as a common denominator for the whole Jewish people. "You, who completely believe in the gathering of the exiles," asked Bialik rhetorically, "what is the means by which we bring in our scattered sparks? Tell me, if there is another means besides the Hebrew language?"

For Jabotinsky, the integrity of the nation and its people depends on mastery of the Hebrew language. We "must make Hebrew the only language that controls all parts of the life of the Jews of the world," he wrote. "The Hebrew language will be my tongue and the language of my sons," he concluded, "whether in the Land or in the Diaspora."

While it is fashionable to think of early Zionism as a movement that believed in eliminating or "negating" the Diaspora, the reality was far more nuanced. For many key architects of the Zionist project—including Theodor Herzl, Ahad Ha'am, and others—building a homeland and resurrecting the Hebrew language would insert a creative vitality and living spirit across the Jewish people around the world.

Today we have a powerful Jewish state, but the Jewish people as a whole is far more splintered and distant from each other than ever before. Only the widespread adoption of Modern Hebrew can create the necessary platform for uniting Jews everywhere into a single conversation and a single people.

* * *

Yet there is something else that mastery of Hebrew offers, something far more profound than the benefits of relationships with Israelis or a common language for Jews. It is about connecting with our Jewish past.

For when Kramsch referred to language as providing a "stock of knowledge about the world that other people share," she was not just talking about the present. In the case of the Hebrew language, that "stock of knowledge" is nothing less than the vast birthright of our collective past—the history of life in Europe, North Africa, Babylonia, the Land of Israel, and around the world; our medieval history, our ancient rabbinic history, the Second Temple period, and going back all the way to biblical times. Hebrew, Bialik wrote in his 1917 essay "Nation and Language," is nothing less than the repository of our people's intellectual core:

> Language is the "living soul," the murmuring spirit, it weaves the national "I." The words determine the national self of the people. Precisely this is the sole determinant of the shape of the nation; and it is also the sum total of its spiritual treasure, the emotions and changing moods of a people. Language is what differentiates one people from its neighbor, and it is the thread on which are strung so many experiences of their soul—the "I" of the people is woven through it. Everything shifts and changes, everything can be stolen, robbed, taken, even land may be stolen—everything but language. Its contents (religion, mitzvot, deeds, thoughts, beliefs, opinions, practices) are vessels that come and go, while the form—language—remains. It is eternal and forever.

For this reason, Bialik described the Hebrew language as "a writ of our inheritance and all our national assets, a deed embedded in our blood and organs." In other words, only those who have internalized Hebrew as part of their being have rights to the cultural treasures of the nation. He concludes:

For this reason I would divide the nation not by its religious or political divisions, but according to the degree of their distance and proximity to the Hebrew language. There are "original" Jews who are connected to the soul of the nation, and there are "translated" Jews, who live their lives not in their own language, but in foreign tongues.... One who knows Judaism in translation, it is as if he is kissing his mother through a handkerchief.... It is as if he sees it through a blurred, distorted lens, and cannot feel all the flavor of it and all the essence of its soul, because language, only language, is the language of the heart and soul.

In addition to historical contents that are stored in in the language, Modern Hebrew also reflects linguistic aspects taken from the past.

Contrary to the fashionable statements of various scholars, Modern Hebrew is built almost entirely, in its deep structure, on the precedents of classical Hebrew—whether in its grammatical structures, vocabulary, or syntax.

According to the linguist and writer Rubik Rosenthal, the renewal of Hebrew fulfilled the vision of Eliezer Ben-Yehuda, who is credited with reviving the language and compiling its first dictionary. Modern Hebrew took elements from both biblical and rabbinic Hebrew. The different forms of the older Hebrew "were fused together, they enriched each other...alongside a significant contribution of the medieval language. The new language is therefore also properly called a 'fusion language.'"

As Rosenthal points out, the process of the development of today's Israeli Hebrew was mainly an expansion of vocabulary due to the need to adapt the ancient language to contemporary life. The renewal of words, which continues today, is based on roots and linguistic forms taken from the different versions of classical Hebrew: "The new Hebrew vocabulary," he points out, "contained over 50 percent classical entries, and alongside them, almost without exception, were new entries based on classical roots."

Obviously, there are many terms in Modern Hebrew, especially as it is spoken in a variety of fields, that are borrowed from foreign languages—just as there are in all living languages. Not every Modern-Hebrew neologism successfully took hold in the face of easy and compelling foreign imports like "telephone" and "television." But even as such terms enter Hebrew, they nonetheless are conjugated and declined according to the rules of the Hebrew language.

In a sense, those who choose to ignore Modern Hebrew, and invest only in the study of Classical Hebrew, do not have access to the entire story. Those who acquire mastery of Modern Hebrew, on the other hand, gain access to the vast treasures of our collective past—both ancient and recent and through the ages in between—as well as our Israeli present. As a result, they can take ownership of the accumulated knowledge of the Jewish people and of the Jewish state that has become so central to who we are.

***

So, how can Diaspora Jews gain mastery of Modern Hebrew?

To be able to communicate fluently with Israelis and other Hebrew-speaking Jews, and claim ownership of the Jewish national "inheritance," students of Hebrew need to become independent users of the language.

The Proficiency Guidelines published by The American Council on the Teaching of Foreign Languages (ACTFL), which is the largest language teacher's organization in the United States, created a framework that articulated the proficiency level of students at each stage of their linguistic development. These guidelines were modified for measuring proficiency levels in Modern Hebrew by a team of Hebrew-language teachers and scholars in the early 1990s.

According to these guidelines, students at the advanced level can freely communicate and interact with native speakers and with native authentic written and spoken materials on a variety of topics. This ability is because at the advanced level, students gain control of the core of the Hebrew language's grammatical and pragmatic structures and its core generic vocabulary.

The main challenge in achieving this level is that it requires a significant amount of time. Adults need to spend around 700 hours of Hebrew study in an intensive setting to achieve this level, and around 1,300 hours for those who start their Hebrew education at a young age in a non-intensive setting and typically become advanced users of Hebrew in their late teens. High-functional Hebrew achievement also requires additional institutional resources, both human and financial.

The challenge of achieving widespread proficiency in Modern Hebrew may seem daunting, but it is far from impossible. Facing these challenges, however, will require major changes in how we—as a broad community and as individual Jews—relate to the language.

First, responsibility for Modern Hebrew language education cannot fall on any single institution. Instead, it needs to be shared across the community—day schools and part-time programs, summer camps and Jewish Community Centers, Israel trips and college-age programs including Hillel, Jewish fraternities, and more. All have a role to play in helping young Jews develop their ability and desire to learn the language. Only by sharing the load will diverse audiences be able to make choices about how to study Modern Hebrew, either in formal or informal settings.

Second, investment must be made in producing materials for students and teachers as well as pedagogical tools, based on the discipline of language acquisition, that are inclusive and can effectively accommodate all students.

But perhaps the most important investment—before questions of accessibility and availability can be properly addressed—is the training of thousands of professional Hebrew educators, teachers capable of making informed decisions in real time to support the students' acquisition process for the purpose of internalizing the language. This training should be done in academic settings by experts in the field of second-language acquisition, with an emphasis on topics related specifically to the teaching and learning of Modern Hebrew.

Such an effort requires the creation of standards for the profession, as well as the recruitment of an array of institutions of higher education that will create the pipeline of future teachers and offer academic programs to train Hebrew educators.

To this end, Brandeis University has recently established a consortium for the teaching of Hebrew language and culture that will support academic institutions in developing degree-granting programs in Hebrew language and culture, as well as in teacher training. The consortium will also help establish frameworks for learning the language in Jewish and public education in both formal and informal settings.

Modern Hebrew is an essential thread of the fabric of an active Jewish life. As such, it needs to be cultivated and practiced like any Jewish ritual. And like any ritual, it should become a lifelong commitment embraced by individuals and institutions to ensure its continued presence and success.

There is a great deal the Jewish people—as embodied in its institutions, philanthropists, and the State of Israel—can do to facilitate the study of Modern Hebrew across the Diaspora. But ultimately, it will rest on each and every one of us. Mastering a language takes dedication and time over a period of years. It therefore requires, above all else, the decision to make it part of our lives and our communities. It requires making it a priority.

43

ONLY THE JEWS CAN SAVE EUROPE

Why We Shouldn't Quit the Continent

SIMONE RODAN-BENZAQUEN

A FEW YEARS AGO, in late 2014, I sat in the office of then French Prime Minister Manuel Valls. I had come to see him to discuss antisemitism in France. Fears within the Jewish community were at a record high, notably after the horrific demonstrations known as the "Day of Rage," in which thousands had shouted "Jews, France is not yours," and after attacks on French Jews and Jewish sites had taken place amid the Israel-Hamas war that summer.

Simone Rodan-Benzaquen is the Managing Director of American Jewish Committee Europe. She writes regularly for French, German, and English-speaking publications. She lives and works in Paris with her family.

While I had prepared myself for what I expected to be a usual, diplomatic, somewhat dry conversation, I was surprised to face a sincere and caring interlocutor for whom this was clearly more than just another issue to deal with. After a short discussion about the latest hate-crime figures, Valls asked me about our state of mind, both my own and that of the Jewish community.

I explained that most Jewish families I knew were seriously asking themselves whether they had a future in France. "Jews are scared," I told him. "They feel abandoned and lonely, and some consider leaving."

His face looked somber. "This is more than concerning," he said in a deep and sorrowful voice. "It is catastrophic. France without its Jews would not be France anymore."

Valls repeated this sentence publicly many times after our conversation, including in his famous speech after the murderous jihadist attacks against *Charlie Hebdo* and Hypercacher in January 2015—and it has stuck with me ever since. Why would half a million French Jews, who represent less than 1 percent of the entire French population, mean anything to the future of the country?

For Valls it was clear. As he explained in an interview with Jeffrey Goldberg that appeared in *The Atlantic* in April 2015, which I had organized and sat in on: "The choice was made by the French Revolution in 1789 to recognize Jews as full citizens," he told Goldberg. "To understand what the idea of the republic is about, you have to understand the central role played by the emancipation of the Jews. It is a founding principle."

As I continue to reflect on antisemitism, Jewish life in Europe, and the future of the continent, I find myself going back to these words.

***

I am the product of Jewish and European history. I was born into a family that suffered both from Nazism and Communism. My parents, who originally wanted to emigrate to Israel or the United States, had fled Nicolae Ceausescu's Romania in 1974 to Germany. Growing up in "the country of perpetrators," my identity was torn. The presence of history and the Holocaust in particular gave Sigmund Freud's concept of *(Un)heimlichkeit* in the mind of a Jewish teenage girl a whole new meaning. Germany was home, German my mother tongue, yet I could never entirely embrace it. So, I started to "escape": first to Switzerland, then to the United Kingdom, and ultimately to France.

I was a wandering Jew, a cosmopolitan Jew, a truly European Jew. My identity was fluid. Just as for my ancient Hebrew forebears, it was based not on where I came from, but on the journey. I was drawn to an idea: that of Europe, its liberal promise, and its intrinsic link to Jews. Jewish personalities had made Europe: from Freud and Albert Einstein to Karl Popper to Robert Oppenheimer to Léon Blum—and particularly in France, it seemed to continue. I had read the writings of Bernard-Henri Lévy, Alain Finkielkraut, and André Glucksmann. I had followed the life paths of Simone Veil, Laurent Fabius, and Dominique Strauss-Kahn. It was that idea that felt like home. Jews and liberalism were, as Yuri Slezkine wrote, "in my mind, almost entirely indistinguishable."

My beliefs were enshrined both in the values that had carried democratic nations since the French Revolution and in the idea of a shared project: that of an emancipating modernity and the forms it had taken since the eighteenth century. Despite the Holocaust and deep-rooted antisemitism in Europe, Jews had conceived a particularism whose ethics opened to the universal and a universalism that was supposed to affirm its respect for the particular. That was at least the idea that I harbored.

But as I moved to France in the early 2000s, I started to be confronted with a new reality—or one whose signs I may have willingly ignored until then. As the second Intifada unfolded in the Middle East, the Twin Towers fell, and a world of conspiracy theories exploded online, antisemitism started to raise its ugly head again in Europe. In France, in particular, it had found multiple outlets and sources—including through the mask of anti-Zionism and the rise of radicalism in its Muslim communities. It could be found on the far-Right and the far-Left and even among those who pretended to be anti-racists, human rights defenders, or anti-colonialists. In some European countries, ritual slaughter and circumcision were being debated and even banned, leaving the often-small Jewish communities with little choice but to either abandon their practice or leave. Jews were killed, from Toulouse and Paris to Brussels and Copenhagen, for no reason other than being Jewish.

Unsurprisingly, all of this coincided with a profound crisis in Europe. Political polarization was on the rise, and so was the distrust in the European model and in European governments, leading to Brexit and talks of other "exits." Europe's societal models of integration were famously questioned by German Chancellor Angela Merkel and British Prime Minister David Cameron. "The doctrine of state multiculturalism had encouraged segregation and failed to supply a vision of society to which people want to belong," said Cameron at the Munich Security Conference in 2010.

Each side of the political spectrum was starting to lean toward a search for purity and authenticity—where the temptation to find a sense of completeness was creating a system of thought. Islamist ideology and networks, which grew across the western continent, followed the same pattern and faced little resistance from politicians, or sometimes even were embraced. Ultimately, our continent seemed to be at war with modernity.

To make matters worse, taking advantage of Europe's weakness, foreign authoritarian countries and entities started to attack and manipulate Europe. Whether through the financing of political campaigns, political parties, think tanks, nonprofit organizations, fake environmental projects, or the use of propaganda on traditional and social media; whether through the spread of fake news and conspiracy theories or the financing of religious institutions, countries like Russia, Turkey, China, Qatar, Saudi Arabia, and Iran had identified Europe as the perfect battlefield to wage their hybrid war against the West.

***

The idea of Europe I had cherished was crumbling in front of my eyes, and Jews were paying a heavy price. Politicians and government leaders were slow to respond, making the situation worse and leading to inevitable questions being asked. This was the case of the president of the Conference of European Rabbis who questioned, right before the recent European elections, whether the outcome would constitute the ultimate signal for Jews to determine whether they could stay in Europe. It was a litmus test for Jews, so to speak—in living memory of the Holocaust—and a frighteningly realistic prospect that one day Europe could be deprived of its Jews.

It was the same question that Valls and I had discussed and had also been posed by Goldberg in the 2015 interview, leading to the piece he published in *The Atlantic*, entitled "Is it Time for the Jews to Leave Europe?" Goldberg's conclusion was clear: There was no future for us Jews in Europe. Too few Jews were left on the continent, and the situation had become simply too serious to be resolved.

I would be lying if I said I had not thought about leaving, imagining myself living in Tel Aviv, New York, Toronto, or even Sydney. I would be lying if I said I had not asked myself if I was a responsible parent, letting my children grow up on this continent.

Statistics only exist about Jews who have made Aliyah, with numbers ranging from 3,000 to 7,000 leaving France to Israel alone. None exist about those who have emigrated to other countries nor for those who have decided to return to Europe after having lived in Israel. It is, therefore, inaccurate to speak of an "exodus," as some journalists, commentators, and even the Israeli government sometimes have. The reality is far more complex.

But even the prospect of emigration and the conversations around it have far wider-ranging societal and sociological consequences. In a survey conducted by the American Jewish Committee and Fondapol in 2022, fully 46 percent of French Jews indicated that they had already considered leaving the country. Just before the last general election in the United Kingdom, 47 percent of British Jews stated they would consider leaving if Jeremy Corbyn became prime minister.

For many European Jews, the idea of Aliyah carries mixed emotions. On the one hand, it is a source of obvious comfort, because Israel represents, after centuries of persecution, an invaluable safe haven. On the other, it can be a source of tension or unease. The very thought of emigrating to Israel for other than spiritual and religious reasons means that European-Jewish identity is already in the process of becoming "deterritorialized," placing Jews, against their will, somewhat on the margins of society. "The real exile is not to be torn away from one's country, it is to live there and to find nothing more of what made one love it," wrote Edgar Quinet when he left France after the coup d'état of Louis Napoleon Bonaparte in 1851. The real exile is thus internal: It proceeds from the feeling of being alienated from one's own country.

This feeling is even further reinforced by the way the rest of European societies can view European Jews because of that very state of mind and the perception of dual loyalty that arises from it. When Benjamin Netanyahu stated, as he did after the Hypercacher attacks in Paris, that French Jews should abandon France and move to Israel, it not only created discomfort among France's Jewish community but also revived the ancient doubt in parts of French society that Jews somehow do not fully and completely belong.

The sentence in Michel Houellebecq's book *Submission* also rings a bell, when the main character's Jewish girlfriend informs him that she is leaving France for Tel Aviv, and the narrator (who is desperate about the state of affairs in France) notes: "There is no Israel for me."

At a time when Europe is crumbling, when Islamism and populism are raging, antisemitism being their first and most visible indicator, the possibility of "escaping" elsewhere suddenly distinguishes Jews from their fellow citizens, making them appear privileged.

All of this has led some European Jews to feel alienated, nearly incapable of reconciling their Jewish and European identity. This has notably been illustrated by the small but noteworthy celebrity status gained by the far-Right politician Éric Zemmour in parts of the French-Jewish community, where he is seen as the only one capable of dealing with rising Islamism and antisemitism. On the other side of the spectrum, a small minority, mostly younger people, feel that their French identity and values clash with what they perceive modern-day Israel to be: a right-wing, religious, colonialist endeavor. This leads them to ignore, or even reject, their Jewish identity.

* * *

I myself have chosen a very different path. Despite my doubts, I continue not only to hold on to my cosmopolitan European-Jewish identity, but (for now) not to leave Europe, and instead to make it my life's work to fight for the soul of the continent. The reason for this goes back to Manuel Valls's pronouncement almost a decade ago: That Jewish destiny is entirely intertwined with that of France, of Europe, and of liberalism.

If Europe without its Jews would no longer be Europe, giving up on Jewish life there would mean giving up on Europe itself. Such a prospect cannot be taken lightly. A world without Europe, as the most ambitious project of peace and democracy since World War II, would have far-ranging consequences for the world and for Jews alike. Autocracies like Russia and China, but also Iran and North Korea, are testing the West's resolve as I am writing these words, with the aim of bringing us back to a world that had previously produced two destructive world wars—and Europe's role in maintaining the resistance is crucial.

Moreover, in a liberal, globalized information world, no democracy is safe from going through the same experience Europe has. Back in 2015 when many, like Goldberg, considered Europe a lost cause for Jews and believed that the United States, alongside Israel, was the ultimate safe haven, I took a very different stance. I warned publicly that antisemitism and the crisis of liberal democracy would not be confined to Europe. Ideas travel—in the information age more so today than ever before. Signs of polarization and radicalization soon appeared in the United States as well, due to rapid technological changes, inequality, mass migration, institutional sclerosis, and the rise of new ideologies. My dire predictions have proven to be sadly true.

The fact is that today Jews are not only killed in Paris, Brussels, and Copenhagen anymore, but also in Pittsburgh, Poway, and Jersey City. Today Jewish students are no longer just dealing with anti-Zionism and antisemitism on campuses in Paris, London, and Oxford, but also in New York, Los Angeles, and Boston. Today it is not only the antisemitic propaganda of the French "comedian" Dieudonné that is terrorizing Jewish communities—but also that of Kanye West and Kyrie Irving.

Today in the United States, and not just in the British Labour Party, a member of Congress can play on antisemitic tropes of "Jewish influence and money" and ultimately get away with it, just as a former American president can host a dinner for two of the worst American antisemites while still being considered a viable candidate for the next elections. Today in America, movements that were supposed to be about women's rights and the fight against racism have been infected by the virus of identity politics where Jews are excluded or even vilified because of their supposed "Zionism" or "Whiteness."

Not just in Paris, but also in America, Jews are the symbolic victims of extreme polarization and the radicalization of the political spectrum and are starting to be deprived of their cosmopolitan Jewish-American identity that has made today's modern America.

If the United States is indeed going down the same path as Europe, does it mean we should be giving up on Jewish life in America as well? And again, because Jewish destiny is entirely intertwined with liberalism, does it mean we should also be giving up on America as the greatest liberal democracy in the world? And what does that mean for Israel—a country facing so many enemies, one that until recently has unquestionably been embedded in the alliance of democratic nations, on which it depends and with which it has shared not only interests but also values? And finally, speaking of Israel, which seems to have been infected by the exact same virus other democracies have, what does the current internal crisis about judicial reform and its Jewish and democratic character mean, not only for the state itself, but for Jews all over the world?

There are no easy answers to all these questions, but to me, the only way to help the world order as we know it survive is to make sure that liberal democracies resist. That means safeguarding the foundations on which they were built. For Israel it means salvaging the classical-Zionist vision of a Jewish state. For Europe and the United States it also means necessarily protecting their Jews.

44

THE SATMAR ART OF NOT GIVING A F*CK

Hidden in Brooklyn, a Surprisingly Vibrant Communal Model

ARMIN ROSEN

IN A CITY OF ETHNIC ENCLAVES, few feel as total as Brooklyn's Lee Avenue. It begins at Flushing Avenue, in the strange frontier between Bushwick hipsterdom and the historic black community of Bed-Stuy, under the dual mystery of a whitewashed, old Pfizer factory and a menacingly blank-faced Woodhull Hospital. When Lee ends at Division Avenue, three quarters of a

---

Armin Rosen is a Brooklyn-based writer for *Tablet* Magazine, as well as a frequent contributor to the *Washington Examiner* and *Al Arabiya*. He has reported from throughout Africa, Europe, and the Middle East for a range of American publications.

mile later, you are steps away from Peter Luger Steakhouse, the Williamsburg Bridge, a forest of million-dollar one-bedroom condos, and every yuppie amenity known to American capitalism.

In between is the Hungarian shtetl, an image of European Jewry before its destruction.

There are no chain stores on Lee, unless the kosher butcher Satmar Fleisch counts as a chain. There are almost no non-Jewish-focused businesses, period. English retreats: The newspapers and the ads on the bus shelters are in Yiddish, which is the language of daily speech among men with white stockings pulled up to their knees, women in ankle-length dresses, and seemingly hundreds of unattended and unworried children, with the boys often on scooters or little mountain bikes, and the girls pushing their younger siblings in strollers. Perhaps the largest retail business on Lee, closer to the Willoughby end, is an off-brand toy store, secular in its inventory but packed only with Haredi Jews. Everything on Lee is packed. It is lively even by Brooklyn standards, as swarming with activity as the blocks around the Bedford station on the L train, less than a mile away.

There are hatters and clothing shops but the only luxury goods on conspicuous display are silver kiddush cups and candlesticks. There's a wonderful Hungarian-style kosher sit-down deli nearby, dating from the 1940s, although the cholent and pastrami at Gottleib's aren't quite good enough to attract tourists, and even kosher foodies from other parts of town tend to ignore the place. "Town" becomes an abstraction on Lee Avenue, where nearly everyone sticks to the Satmar dress code, speaks the Satmar language—these are some of the last Jews in New York whose primary language is Yiddish—rides Satmar buses to Monsey and Kiryas Joel, studies in Satmar institutions, works in Satmar businesses, shops only at Satmar grocery stores, and reads Satmar newspapers. (There are other Haredi communities in Williamsburg, including significant populations of Pupa and Breslov Hasids, but they are a fraction of Satmar's size.)

Lee Avenue isn't like Kingston Avenue, the rambunctious Chabadnik main street, a global Jewish hub where it's normal to hear Hebrew, English, French, and Spanish; or Thirteenth Avenue in Borough Park, the Judaically diverse crossroads of Brooklyn's largest Orthodox neighborhood. Lee is somehow more austere, more inward-facing than the borough's other main drags. No one dances in the middle of Lee during any holiday.

The Satmars are a bit of an austere bunch in general. They read the weekly haftarah in an undertone; the few Satmar apartments I've been to are kept almost spotlessly clean. Satmar weddings are not drunken or effusively joyous affairs. It is not an unwelcoming place, but in contrast to the city's more celebrated ethnic high streets, there's nothing on Lee that's pitched toward people who don't live nearby. A visitor quickly realizes they are in a place that belongs to people whose lives and priorities appear to have little in common with their own, one that exists almost in defiance of everything surrounding it.

I am always seized with the disquieting suspicion that the people around me on Lee, however bizarre and cloistered they seem, are in fact living lives more serious than mine, organized around the most sublime possible objectives: God, family, the transmission of eternal truths, and survival into a future so certain that that they can see it right in front of them.

The energy of some underlying holy purpose begins to dissipate well before the other side of Broadway, such that by the time I reach the Bedford Avenue Whole Foods, it feels as if the city has reverted to its default level of frivolousness. Lee's isolation is not just sociological, but spiritual. I always feel as if I have found it by accident.

* * *

The Satmar Hasidim of Williamsburg are the most openly scorned group of people in New York City. Brooklyn's gentrifiers, which is to say much of the rising professional class, often know them as inscrutable landlords making unpleasant demands in difficult-to-place accents. The *New York Times*, the city's establishment guide to the boundaries of acceptable thought, accuses Satmar schools of being Dickensian indoctrination factories where children are beaten. Members of the community are routinely harassed on the streets—they are sucker-punched, or have their black hats knocked off. Few consider the rash of violent antisemitism against them to be any kind of a crisis. They are objects of silent, sneering curiosity the moment they board a subway car. New Yorkers barely think of them as fellow members of reality.

To their many critics, the Satmars are a misogynistic, pre-modern inconvenience, angering even to look at or think about, habitual defrauders of the government who conspire to use the public housing system to keep black and Hispanic people out of their neighborhoods. They tend to annoy Jews because of their opposition to the existence of the State of Israel. At a superficial glance they seem like throwbacks to a quietist past, specters of the Old-World Jews who failed to stand up for themselves—convinced, perhaps, that *golus* required them to be weak and oppressed.

Whether they actually believe any of that remains unclear. The Satmars are notably uninterested in openly pleading their case to mainstream society or even to their fellow Jews, including on pressing matters of communal safety. They often seem uninterested in their fellow Jews, period, at least the ones that are not also Haredi.

American Jews are, in turn, uninterested in them, except insomuch as they manifest an unenlightened and supposedly inferior way of being Jewish. For the numerous New Yorkers whose Jewish identity is mostly shaped in reaction to one or another allegedly gross and backwards type of Jew, the Satmars are a godsend.

And yet a resident of north Brooklyn notices after a while that the Satmars are everywhere—the footprint of their community is physically massive and constantly growing, their families are large, their school buses are full, and their wedding halls are filled nearly every night of the week. One eventually discovers, with some astonishment, that the building right above the Flushing Avenue stop on the G train has a very large mikveh in its basement. Even a curious observer sees only a fraction of the Satmars' total communal infrastructure.

It is true enough that the Satmars lack the openness and access to secular culture that metropolitan liberals believe to be the only possible criteria for living under humane conditions. But the Satmars have also shut out some of the most corrosive tendencies in modern society. Newfangled social-justice dogma has not crippled their education system. They have successfully resisted the onslaught of an omnipresent internet and many of the horrors that come along with it. The Satmars actually have kids—unlike the majority of my adult friends in Brooklyn—and those kids can read somewhere between two and three languages and have many of the same answers to life's big questions that their parents do. That the Satmars have transmitted both their values and an ethos of multilingual literacy to their children is a significant accomplishment within a culture—American as well as Jewish American—where God and the written word are rapidly losing their status.

The Satmars, in other words, are one of the only segments of the American Jewish community that has really nailed the continuity thing. Even more impressively, they did it in north Brooklyn, a short walk from the William Vale hotel and the House of Yes.

How? And more importantly, why? Perhaps it is brainwashing that is keeping the Satmar community so much stronger than its secular, liberal Jewish neighbors, and they sustain themselves only because their rabbinically dictated communal norms are so ruthlessly enforced. Or maybe Hashem is right, and adherence to the mitzvahs really is the price of Jewish flourishing, even if it's one that most of us don't have the inclination to pay, myself included.

I don't think mind control or the inherent truth of Haredi Judaism really explain it, though. I am no expert, but after years of occasionally reporting on the Williamsburg Satmars, I have another, more reassuring explanation for their relative communal health: They just want it more than we do.

The Satmars are American Judaism's starkest manifestation of what it takes for Jews to survive the centripetal forces of a secular society. Luckily for the rest of us, what it requires is pretty straightforward. We have to actually take being Jewish seriously, rather than treating it like a hobby or weird personal trait or a costume that can be taken on and off at will. We have to fight for a Jewish life—even and maybe especially in America. We have to want it as much as the Satmars do.

* * *

History helps explain why the Satmars are so motivated to protect their way of life. The Satmars of Brooklyn were Hungarian survivors of the Holocaust—the Satmar *dayan*, or chief judge, whose Covid-era public funeral provoked such outrage in late 2020, had a number from Auschwitz tattooed on his arm. Joel Teitelbaum, the Satmar rebbe, made it on the Kastner Train of Hungarian

Jewish notables who were spared death upon arrival at Bergen-Belsen. He then reconstituted his community in the hottest-boiling part of the American melting pot: Brooklyn, right on the East River.

In the generations since the Satmar arrival, nearly all former evidence of any kind of mass Jewish presence has disappeared from the Lower East Side, once the largest Jewish community on earth. That is not the case across the river in Williamsburg, where survivors of the European horror arrived in a neighborhood that was about to be sliced apart by the construction of the Brooklyn Queens Expressway.

The Satmars stayed even as a concrete trench tore through the neighborhood. Even as the city got worse, they stayed. In the grimy and violent 1970s, they launched Brooklyn's first *shomrim* neighborhood watch. With the encouragement of their rebbe, Satmars began purchasing distressed industrial real estate in neighborhoods like Bushwick, where they opened light factories and warehouses—and, later, rental properties and condos. They did not leave for the suburbs, expanding into Rockland and Orange Counties only when their Brooklyn *sh'chuna* ran out of space or grew in ways that threatened always-delicate relations with nearby black and Puerto Rican communities. They did not disappear into the larger society, the way other mid-century groups of New York Jews did. They refused to change who they were, and they refused to care that they were refusing to change.

The most notorious instance of their refusal to change touches on the issue for which the Satmars are best known within the Jewish world. Despite briefly settling in mandatory Palestine in late 1945, Teitelbaum was one of Haredi Judaism's most passionate opponents of Zionism, a position that still keeps him and his movement far outside most of the rest of Jewish life (even though frequent Satmar travel to Israel and a near-total lack of interest in geopolitics separate them from the BDS crowd). Celebrating the political reality of Jewish statehood would have been a risky theological capitulation.

I have always found Satmar anti-Zionism to be a forgivable quirk, perhaps even proof of intellectual and spiritual integrity. And of all the things the Satmar can teach us, the most important is to embrace discomfort and not to be ashamed of ourselves.

They can teach us a great deal more than that, too. They can teach us not to be too delighted with our own prosperity. On average, the Satmars are some of the poorest people in New York. But the community has its multimillionaires—a half-in, half-out Satmar once told me the number was about fifty—most of them made rich from the real estate and construction sector, who subsidize almost all Jewish infrastructure. For the most part, the wealthy spend their money on perpetuating *yiddishkeit* rather than on fancy houses or cars. There are numerous Satmar families in public housing, but no one goes hungry on Shabbat. I know of one Williamsburg charity, with a skeletal website and few professional staff, that spends an eye-watering $12 million a year buying kosher groceries for disadvantaged families in Haredi communities around the world.

The Satmars, like other Haredi groups, consider education intrinsic to their way of life. The Satmar yeshiva system might not meet secular American standards, but it seems to meet Satmar standards nicely, in the sense that the community thrives within a social and political environment where their success should be impossible. They have made obvious what many Americans would rather forget: That there is a direct relationship between what a community values, what it teaches its children, and whether it endures at all. They know that education is survival; the schools are the largest and best-maintained buildings in Jewish Williamsburg.

Unlike Israel, New York is not built to accommodate Jewish observance, and Haredim are a tiny minority in a quasi-hostile society. Intense political discipline means that Satmar concerns are taken seriously among elected officials, giving the community some loose form of official protection. In contrast to much of the rest of America, they are arch-pragmatists politically, voting not on ideology but on relationships and communal imperatives, supporting social liberals when it serves their interests. Such a nakedly transactional politics can look baffling and even paradoxical. But the Satmars understand that the world doesn't exist to make them feel at ease.

It is the Satmars' willingness to endure social ostracization and carry out difficult choices in the name of sustaining their community that explains why there are now Satmars in Jersey City. Over the past decade, Williamsburgers displaced by the high cost of living in Brooklyn created an outpost of a hundred families in a depressed section of the first city across the Hudson, complete with shuls, a school for young children, and a single kosher grocery store. That community suffered a deadly attack in the fall of 2019, when two black nationalists set off a hostage crisis at that grocery store, killing its owner, a rabbinical student, and a non-Jewish employee.

I reported from the neighborhood the day after the attack, in a run-down corner of an already unattractive city, where the non-Jewish residents seemed to share the views of a local school board member who later called the killings a justified response to "the assault on the Black communities of America." The Satmars haven't left Jersey City. They are not leavers. They care about having lives more than they care about their lives being easy.

What is "life" to a Satmar? They showed us during Covid. The community happily paid a $15,000 fine for holding a wedding that thousands of people secretly attended in the fall of 2020, when the city was still under lockdown. Mass funerals, such as the dayan's, scandalized the New York tabloids. The Satmar leadership didn't seem to care very much, or even at all. Satmar yeshivas and summer camps were open for much of 2020 while the secular world cowered from the pandemic. For the community, celebrating a marriage and the promise of new life, honoring the dead and reinforcing the connection between the living and the eternal, and educating and socializing the young are imperatives that override respect for state authority or the strict need for physical well-being.

It was as if the Satmars had decided there was no point in sustaining one's body in a society where the truly essential things could no longer be done.

I am not sure they were wrong. During the pandemic, the Satmars took on the risk of being scorned for living out values that made perfect sense to them and should have made perfect sense to the rest of us, too. Standing alone is a common experience for the Satmars, just as it has been for Jews throughout our 3,000 years of documented history.

***

There is much to admire about the Satmars, if we care to look at them with something other than self-satisfied judgment. Satmars do not leave cities or change their way of life when things start getting difficult, they orient their entire lives around a rigorous and text-heavy version of Jewish education. They have filtered out many of secular society's worst excesses, and they don't shriek about their own supposed victimhood. American Jews should learn from their example.

Yet a reasonable observer could also look at the many less edifying aspects of Satmar society—the position of women, the lack of emphasis on English, math, and science in the education system, the outsized power of a small all-male religious leadership, the extremely limited range of life paths that don't require leaving the community, the coldly instrumental view toward the rest of the world—and wonder if Jewish survival in America is even possible or desirable, if *this* is what's needed to secure it.

We should know better. Non-Orthodox American Jews once had proud examples of what it means to take Judaism seriously here—of what it means to really, actually want it. Then, over the course of a century or so, nearly all of them either disappeared or failed. Yiddish vanished. Distinctively American Jewish religious movements dwindled into irrelevance. Israel advocacy and Holocaust commemoration built formidable political operations and left a vast physical and organizational legacy, but they were inevitably an expression of a specific era's anxieties. The "Tikkun Olam" ideology—the orthodoxy that social justice is our special Jewish American destiny—is too generic and earthbound to keep us engaged at any kind of scale.

That the Satmars and American Haredim in general are now among our most visible avatars of intense, uncorrupted Jewish commitment is not a sign of their extremism, but of everyone else's lack of imagination. Judaism is limitless enough to contain sources of meaning and cohesion that don't require adherence to a mystical, self-segregating way of life. None of them come easy—Hebrew and Torah are tough, *shacharit* is very early in the morning, Israel is controversial and far away and sometimes ugly, children hate going to Hebrew school on weeknights, kosher meat is expensive, camps and schools and youth groups are hard to organize and even harder to make affordable for median-income families, and there's enough to read and see and care about in the world without feeling the need to crack open Dara Horn, never mind the Rambam.

But we must embrace the difficulty. The real gift of Judaism, and a key source of its survival across thousands of often-bloody years, is that it forces us to grow familiar with the constant discomfort that is intrinsic to human existence. The Satmars understand this. And if we don't, they will be all that's left of us in the future.

45

ZIONISTS ARE MADE, NOT BORN

The Fight for Israel's Image Can Be Won. Here's How.

ROZ ROTHSTEIN

IT WAS MAY 14, 1948. Ann Lautenberg and her mother were living in a Displaced Persons (DP) camp in Milan, Italy. They had survived the horrific years of the Holocaust and were refugees. Eighty of their relatives had been murdered. Ann also lost her beloved father, who died of disease and the cold of Siberia, where Ann and her parents ended up after running from the Nazis during the six years of World War II. Ann was nine years old when the war began, and fifteen when it ended. All the survivors knew it was dangerous

---

Roz Rothstein is the CEO and co-founder of StandWithUs International, which is now working on six continents. A daughter of Holocaust survivors, Roz was named twice by *Forward* and twice by the *Jerusalem Post* as one of the most influential Jews in the world.

to try to return to reclaim their homes. The DP camp was full of people just like her, who had lost everything and had nowhere to go.

But on this day, their world would forever change. At a time when Holocaust survivors had nothing and nobody, they suddenly learned that there was a Jewish state in a cold and heartless world. Ann said that after hearing of Israel's rebirth, she danced and sang all night with all the other survivors in the DP camp, overjoyed by the news that there was now a recognized Jewish home in the land of their Jewish ancestors.

Ann Lautenberg was my mother. She told this story to my brother and me with tears in her eyes, recalling the moment when people who were lost and profoundly traumatized, many beyond hope, suddenly had a Jewish country. It meant everything. And whenever she told her story, it was always the same. She could throw herself back in time, to that night, when she first learned there was a Jewish homeland. You could see that faraway gaze in her eyes, looking to another time and place.

Fast forward to 1967, when the Six-Day War broke out. My mother and grandmother were sitting on the couch in front of the television, all hours of each day, hanging on every word coming out about the war between Israel and Egypt, Syria, and other Arab states. I would come home from school and find my mother crying on the couch, convinced that things would go badly and the precious Jewish homeland would be forever lost. There was no reassuring her. The same was true for the Yom Kippur War in 1973. For my mother, Israel was a symbol of the safety and future of the Jewish people. A special gift. A jewel in all our lives to be treasured. And while we had very little money, she always sent what she could to Israel, feeling personally connected and responsible for its well-being.

Shortly after the Yom Kippur war, Ann remarried another Holocaust survivor, Jay Shalmoni. The number on his arm was A7661. His family had been rounded up in Uzhhorod, Czechoslovakia, in 1944. He was the sole survivor of his family, who were all murdered in Auschwitz.

Jay was an extraordinary man. When the war ended in 1945, he was only seventeen years old. He helped survivors from all over Europe get on ships bound for British-ruled Palestine through a group called the Bricha. After a year of working to move Jews across Europe to the rickety ships bound for the Promised Land, he, too, boarded a vessel, the *Shabtai Luzinski*, filled with over 800 Holocaust survivors. Sadly, as the vessel approached the shores of what would become Israel, nearly all the weary passengers were arrested by the British authorities, refused entry, and sent to Cyprus. A disturbing fate, considering that the refugees had just survived an unfathomable war.

Jay evaded the British roundup, jumped ship, swam to shore, and mingled with the Israelis who were already there, waiting to help any survivors who might jump from the ships. He was immediately inducted into the Haganah— the predecessor to the Israel Defense Forces—along with other Holocaust survivors, and he fought for Israel's independence in 1948. He watched many of his survivor friends die in that war.

Ann Lautenberg, my dear mother, and Jay Shalmoni, my beloved stepfather, were Zionists to the core. And they never hesitated to share their profound love for Israel as the precious priority for the Jewish people. The other Holocaust survivors that I grew up around had similar, tragic stories, and all of them cherished Israel. In addition, the rabbis I grew up with, and the youth group that I was a part of, Bnei Akiva, all fostered a Zionist atmosphere that promoted clarity and conviction. I became a leader within Bnei Akiva, and later a leader at the Jewish Centers Association in Los Angeles, always wearing my Zionism proudly on my sleeve so that everyone could see and feel it. So that anyone who had questions about Israel could ask me. So that if I were ever in a position to help someone understand the existential threat faced by the one Jewish country or the extraordinary humanitarian aid Israel provided to people worldwide almost from its inception, I would proudly do my best to educate and inspire.

I am a Zionist born and bred and have made it a priority to make sure that others have the benefit of my passion, inspiration, and knowledge about Israel. This should be a central priority for the Jewish people. Unfortunately, far too often, it is not.

***

Zionists are not born Zionists. They must be inspired by the people around them; they must be created. So, if it is our goal to bring up children who care about Israel, our strategy for the end goal must be intentional.

I am one of the founders of StandWithUs, a rapidly expanding international, non-partisan Zionist organization. Our mission, which has not changed since our inception more than two decades ago, is to support Israel through education and to fight antisemitism. When we opened our doors in 2001, the rising antisemitism and misinformation being promoted about Israel was frightening. It has become worse today.

I was motivated to help start this organization precisely because I grew up knowing exactly who I was, and understanding only too well that hate and misinformation about the Jewish people and Israel can, and do, lead to violence. What our co-founders Jerry Rothstein and Esther Renzer recognized at the time was the need to create a movement of people all over the world who would make it a priority to teach their communities about Israel, speak up for Israel when it is misrepresented, and stand up against antisemitism. But getting there would be quite a journey, and it still is.

What we noticed during the early years of StandWithUs was that there were many students and community members who were willing to help fight the growing war for hearts and minds. However, they were missing huge chunks of information and lacked the tools to educate and support their friends and communities. So, while the desire was there for many, the background was not. For all those people who had the heart for Israel and needed a supportive network and tools to share with their communities, we began producing colorful small booklets that were free and downloadable online, covering a variety of topics. We also sent out speakers who gave timely lectures about Israel. Providing information to communities was relatively easy, and we have been doing it for the last two decades in a variety of ways and in different languages.

What also became clear during the early years of StandWithUs, however, was that far too many Jews lacked an emotional connection to Israel and Zionism. Some felt that the war for hearts and minds was someone else's problem. In retrospect, it is shocking and beyond disappointing that so soon after the Holocaust and expulsion of Jews from Arab states, there were so many indifferent, disconnected Jews who were unconcerned about the misinformation being promoted about the one Jewish state in the world. We needed to figure out creative, vigorous, and efficient ways to inspire the masses of those who were uninvolved. We also began, almost immediately, working with friends and allies who were not Jewish, and who loved Israel. We immediately began working with students to bring Israel programming to campuses, high schools, and middle schools, always with the goal of inspiring Zionism.

Inspiring Jews and non-Jews to care, learn more, and, eventually, stand up for Israel, was to be the most important task facing the founders of StandWithUs. Because without inspiration for Israel as a modern Jewish state in the ancestral home of the Jewish people, without a consensus that Jews, like all peoples, have a right to self-determination, we would not have our essential network of international educators. We recognized immediately that without the network telling Israel's story and pushing back against blatant misinformation, both Israel and the Jewish future were at risk. We realized that in order to inspire tomorrow's Zionists, we needed a knowledgeable network today.

Where to begin? How do we create a sense of connection, concern, and responsibility? How do we move the hearts and minds of masses of people? Who is the first target? The second? Is there agreement in the Jewish world that this is even a priority? Or did we, at StandWithUs, stand alone with lofty, unrealistic goals about the need to create knowledgeable, active Zionists?

Truth be told, we had no clue about where to begin. That is the funny thing about beginning anything. One literally just needs to begin.

**

As the first couple of years unfolded, the evolution of this organization took on a natural rhythm. It began with the squeakiest wheel: the college campus. Students from California universities came to us with horrific stories about rising antisemitism, which was often tied to anti-Zionism. Many of the students felt threatened, frightened, and alone.

Back in the early days of StandWithUs, there was no network of students supporting one another against antisemitic rants by professors or radical Islamist student activists hosting extremist speakers who promote one-sided narratives and hate. Students not only lacked the network, they also lacked the ability to engage in rich conversations about Israel, and they had no organizational or community support.

So, we began with the lowest hanging fruit: students across the country who wanted to come together to discuss their campus experiences, challenge the new rising antisemitism, and learn how to organize inspiring educational programs about Israel for their peers. They knew intuitively that as students who cared about Israel, they could be helpful. It turned out that approximately one-third of the students who came to us every year at the beginning, and even today, are descendants of Holocaust survivors, just like me. Many others come from families that had fled oppression and violence in Arab states, Iran, the Soviet Union, and elsewhere. And some got involved simply because they had personal or educational experiences that inspired them to care.

Our work on college campuses grew rapidly. Zionist students, both Jews and non-Jews, self-identified and became our early student leaders. The same was true for our early staff. Self-identified Zionists came to us to volunteer, hoping that we would one day be able to afford to employ them.

Each student became a universe of influence. They were not only able to do the work, they were empowered to inspire others to join a new, growing Zionist movement. We soon recognized that we needed to pick up our pace and grow even more quickly because the anti-Israel network was also growing rapidly. By 2010, the anti-Israel movement began to include antisemitic boycott campaigns against Israel—BDS. StandWithUs began to attract the support of major donors who agreed that our mission was a priority, and they began supporting us with significant funding. We became an international platform for Zionism.

We also launched a high school program to prepare Zionist teens for the challenges they might face in college. Like our campus program, approximately one-third of the talented student leaders who came to us are descendants of Holocaust survivors and many others descend from those who escaped anti-semitism in other parts of the world.

The beautiful thing about the high school program was that the teens who came to us were not only preparing for college, but also organizing inspiring programs in their schools and youth groups during their year of training. So, these young Zionists were already affecting a new generation of their peers in their high schools and youth groups all over the United States and Canada. We also began educating through social media platforms, promoting interesting information about Israel and correcting misinformation being promoted by those who want to see Israel eliminated from the world of nations. In a few short years, we became a leader on social media platforms that reach millions of people each week.

Our success and popularity on college campuses and in high schools, combined with our rapid growth on social media, made it clear that we were on the right track. Soon there was demand for our support in cities around the world including Johannesburg, Sydney, Toronto, São Paulo, and London. And each year we found increasing numbers of willing organizational partners around the world who would work with us to meet our mission.

We opened a middle school program that offers curriculum to teachers helping inspire students to develop their own personal connection to Israel. We opened a legal department that has over 250 pro-bono attorneys who are prepared to help students, faculty, and community members facing bullying, harassment, or discrimination because they are Zionists. We opened a Holocaust Education Center because antisemitism, anti-Zionism, and Holocaust denial have become conflated during the last few years of rising bigotry against Jews.

***

I am a Zionist, and I believe Israel is a safety net for world Jewry. To me, the need to intentionally inspire more Zionists who feel love and responsibility for Israel is clear. I recognize that not every Jew agrees, but for the purpose of this essay, I direct my comments to those who believe that Israel and the future of the Jewish people should be a priority.

For those of us who care about Israel existing as a safe and thriving Jewish homeland, how do we inspire massive amounts of people to feel the connection we feel?

We need to regain the moral clarity of the 1950s and 1960s, when we didn't take the Jewish state for granted and understood how precious it is.

However, we also need to adapt to the present to effectively inspire a groundswell of love and support for Israel.

Big-picture studies have shown that a strong sense of Jewish religious and/or ethnic identity is often tied to having a closer connection to Israel. On the flip side, those who live in relative comfort and do not directly encounter antisemitism may be more likely to believe that Israel is not important. We need a wide variety of approaches to meet young Jews where they are, foster Jewish pride, and educate about the Jewish past and present.

That education must include a strong focus on Israel as the birthplace of Jewish language, tradition, culture, religion, and peoplehood, and a modern state where people are building a thriving Jewish future. It must also cover the oppression and violence Jews have experienced across the Diaspora. While we live in an unprecedented era of Jewish empowerment, we cannot forget that many of the worst antisemitic episodes in history came during a time of very successful Jewish communities in Germany, Poland, Spain, Iraq, and elsewhere.

We also need more Jews in the Diaspora to get to know Israelis on a personal level. That means Israel must invest more in *shlichim*, or Israeli emissaries. When selected and trained properly, these emissaries serve as role models and inspire young Jews in the Diaspora to develop their love for Israel. More synagogues and Jewish institutions should request these Israeli emissaries and make them a part of the fabric of their community, and their regular programming.

Some have chosen to avoid the topic of Israel because it can be controversial. However, the reality is that many young Jews are hearing anti-Israel narratives on social media and elsewhere, anyway. Silence has never served the Jewish people well. It is crucial to push through any discomfort and address difficult questions and topics head-on. Education about the Israeli-Palestinian conflict should be done in a way that is factual, age appropriate, recognizes the humanity of all its victims, and helps students understand different perspectives. We can do all of that without compromising on core values or legitimizing misinformation about the Jewish state.

Instead of shying away, more rabbis should bring Israel into their sermons and holiday celebrations to remind their members of Israel's importance. For rabbis, we have created a non-denominational network, called Rabbis

United. Rabbis can even organize StandWithUs virtual tours to Israel. More day schools should bring better programming to their children about Israel. More Jewish federations should put money into Israel programming catered to a variety of Jewish audiences with different levels of knowledge and involvement. And Jewish institutions should empower parents with resources that can help them educate their children about how Israel and Zionism fit into their Jewish identity.

As Jewish children grow up and enter high school, college, and the professional world, we can connect them with Israelis who are working on issues they care about. That can include social justice projects inside Israel, humanitarian aid missions worldwide, and Israeli companies that are using unique technologies to solve problems across the United States and beyond.

There is no silver bullet to fix apathy, neglect, division, and hate. It will take many different approaches, often tested through trial and error, to overcome these challenges and inspire young Jews with Israel and Zionism. The single thing all of us can do, however, is to simply decide that this is a priority, commit to taking action, and begin doing the work.

46

RAISING INQUISITIVE CHILDREN

Educate Kids to Ask Better Questions

JODI RUDOREN

WHEN OUR TWINS STARTED KINDERGARTEN, my husband sent them off each day with a simple but profound mandate: "Ask great questions!"

He would call it out cheerily as their little feet bounded down the stairs of our apartment in Jerusalem, where I was working harder than I ever had to fulfill that very mandate as bureau chief for the *New York Times*. In later years, he would say it as the kids slumped out of the car, embarrassed at the possibility that any of their little friends might hear. We'd try to remember

Jodi Rudoren is editor-in-chief of the *Forward*. Before coming to the *Forward* in 2019, she spent twenty-one years as a reporter, editor, and digital innovator at the *New York Times*, including a stint as Jerusalem bureau chief. This essay is adapted from her weekly column, "Looking Forward."

to inquire, at dinner or bedtime, about the questions they'd posed, mindful of the story the great physicist Isidor Isaac Rabi told about how his mother had paved his path of discovery:

> Every other Jewish mother in Brooklyn would ask her child after school: "So? Did you learn anything today?" But not my mother. "Izzy," she would say, "did you ask a good question today?" That difference—asking good questions—made me become a scientist.

Questions fuel science, of course, but also society. They are the backbone of my profession, journalism—and the beating heart of Judaism. The Talmud is basically a series of questions interrogating the Torah. The best rabbis pose provocative questions in their sermons rather than preaching some predetermined gospel. The Passover Seder is framed as the answer to four seemingly straightforward but actually quite layered questions—and, throughout our Jewish calendar, throughout our Jewish existence, we are encouraged to ask, ask, ask.

Why do we cover the challah during kiddush? How come the official mourning period for a spouse is so much shorter than that for a parent? Which is the more perfect Jewish food, latkes or hamantaschen? What is the purest form of tzedaka? Is quinoa kosher for Pesach? Do we light the newest or oldest Hanukkah candle first? Why do bad things happen to good people?

Great questions prompt great stories, and storytelling is key to human understanding. And yet, instead of asking great questions these days, too many of us are spending too much time pontificating about what we think we already know; dismissing or even demonizing people who disagree with our hardened ideologies; ignoring evidence that does not support our points of view.

My kids are sophomores in high school as I write this. It is nearly two years after the January 6, 2021 insurrection at the Capitol, four since the massacre at Pittsburgh's Tree of Life synagogue, six months after the Supreme Court overturned the constitutional right to an abortion, a century after the first American woman became bat mitzvah, eighty-four years since Kristallnacht, seventy-eight since Rabi won the Nobel Prize in Physics. As my son and daughter balance their heavy backpacks while staring at their smartphones, as they navigate a world burbling with hate and division and disinformation, as they gain independence and take on responsibility, Izzy's mother's voice is ringing in my ears. Ask great questions. Ask. Always ask.

* * *

Seems easy enough. Most of us ask questions all day—how are you, what's the weather outside, how much does this cost, where's the nearest bathroom, what do you want for dinner? We have been doing it since we ourselves were kindergarteners bounding down the stairs. What's seven times six, can I stay up late, why is the sky blue, when will the yelling stop? Now we can ask Google—How long do I cook chicken thighs in the air fryer? How many Jews live in Georgia? Is Elon Musk Jewish?—or Siri or Alexa.

But not all questions are created equal. "Ask great questions" means inquiring from a place of true curiosity. We must ask honestly, openly, without judgment—and we have to actually want to hear the answers.

Nearly thirty years ago, I was invited to a dinner in Los Angeles featuring Michael Dukakis, the former governor of Massachusetts, where I grew up. After an hour of cocktails and chitchat, the forty-some guests settled around a large square table, where Dukakis led a conversation.

Remarkably, he recalled the name of and some salient detail about every person he had spoken with during the schmooze. And when I introduced myself, he asked about a second cousin who shared my surname and had, apparently, given $500 to his disastrous 1988 presidential campaign. I understood that in Dukakis's business, remembering names can quickly translate into valuable support, but his recall was nonetheless astonishing. So, I asked him about it afterward.

That moment when you meet someone and ask their names, he explained, is usually fraught and tense. You are nervous, worried about how you'll find a connection with this stranger, what they might think of you, whether your handshake is too soft or too long or too sweaty. Your mind is racing ahead to form the *next* question—what do you do for a living, where do you live, why are you here; essentially, what do we possibly have in common. So, you don't really listen to the name, which feels superficial anyhow, basic; you'll pay attention to the substantive stuff once they get to it.

In contrast, Dukakis suggested, think about when you walk into someone's home and see an antique or artwork you admire and inquire as to its provenance. If you are a collector—or, to take it down a notch, if you love someone's hairdo and have been looking for a new stylist—you really hear the answer because the information matters to you. Dukakis said he simply brings that kind of focused attention to the routine introduction moment that most people rush through.

I have been telling that story ever since. It hasn't made me any better at remembering people's names, but it has given me deeper appreciation for the art of asking questions and actively, truly listening to the answers.

The dirty little secret of journalism is that most of us do not have enough people in our lives who truly listen to our answers, our stories. Why else does the surviving spouse of a terror victim—or the parent of a terror suspect—let us into their living rooms and pour their hearts out into our notebooks? We must honor their vulnerability by asking serious, respectful questions with a truly open heart, ready to digest and engage the answers, whatever they may be.

"How do you feel?" is not a great question to ask the relative of a victim of a terrible crime. Better: What was her favorite book or song or food? "Why do you think he did it?" is likewise not a great question for someone close to someone accused of something abominable. Better: What did you talk about the last time you spoke?

What's your earliest Jewish memory? One thing you always do on a given holiday? A food you remember a grandparent making? Something that's keeping you awake at night?

Great questions are specific, but also open-ended. Because the goal is not gotcha, but a conversation that might yield some greater understanding of the other, of our complicated world. Do not ask a person who voted for someone else, "How could you?" Better: I'd love to hear about why this candidate appealed to you, was there something they said or did that sealed the deal? Or was it something the guy I supported did or said that pushed you away?

Trial lawyers, especially prosecutors, are taught never to ask questions they don't already know the answer to. That's the opposite of what it means to ask great questions. We need Jews (and other humans) who are always asking questions hoping to be surprised by the answers, hoping to learn something new, think something different, discover a nuance. That means asking questions of people who live and work and think and pray and vote on the other side of whatever aisles you live with; asking earnest, real, substantive questions, great questions, questions worthy of Izzy Rabi, and of all our forebears, and of future generations.

* * *

The Passover Seder outlines four categories of questions, from four gross stereotypes of children, each of whom we should imagine as if they were our own kids bounding down the stairs to kindergarten. As with all kids' questions, we should take them seriously, meet them where they are, and answer in ways that prompt the next great question, that nurture true curiosity.

The wise child asks for all the details. This may seem like a tedious question, but it can be a "great" question. Because people often get overwhelmed or insecure when facing a big, broad question, like "Why did you become a doctor?" or "How do you understand God?" or even "How are you?" I like to ask people what they had for breakfast, and if they say something vague like "cereal" or "eggs," I ask "What kind?" or "Who makes them?" Talking about something specific and factual is easy, and it often leads to an interesting anecdote about an unusual thing that happened that morning—or an insight about the person's approach to routine, maybe even a complex relationship with food. It is how I found out the priceless detail that Jerry Nadler, the dean of the Congressional Jewish Caucus, starts his day with gefilte fish.

The wicked child asks, "What does this mean to you?" The sages find this question to be seditious, but I think it is actually kind of great. Sure, he's deflecting, he's testing, he's trying to separate himself from the experience. But he's also giving you the opportunity to frame the conversation and create pathways to connection.

The simple child asks, "What does it mean?" and the text advises giving a basic summary of the story. I protest. That's how people talk past each other, when they simply state facts as though the meaning should be obvious because shared priorities are presumed. It is an awfully good question: *What does this mean?* We should all ask it more.

Then there's the kid who doesn't even know how to ask. I'm guessing few Seder-goers identify with this character. We Jews are inveterate hand-raisers, challenging authorities and husbands alike. And yet, it feels like a lot of us have lost our ability to ask great questions of people we perceive to be different from ourselves. Or maybe we have lost our desire to hear the answer.

Take abortion, which the vast majority of American Jews agree should be legal in all or most cases. How many of us have honestly, openly, curiously, and without judgment asked anti-abortion activists about their backgrounds and beliefs?

Or Israel. When we visit, we should ask all kinds of people—Haredi women, Mizrahi immigrants, Palestinians, soldiers, cab drivers, settlers—about their family histories and their relationship to the land and their thoughts about the government and their hopes for the future. And, you know, what they had for breakfast.

I like to ask couples how they met—it is interesting even just to watch who tells which part of the story. I like to ask people what their parents did for a living—you learn about education, role models, ambition. My new favorite job-interview question is: What is your superpower that would never be listed on a resume? The colleague who introduced me to that question—it is also a terrific icebreaker—is excellent at killing flies with her bare hands. Another colleague is a good parallel parker and can put any baby to sleep. One reporter-candidate said he makes the perfect smoothie, which led to a key trade secret regarding bananas: freeze with peel on, then cut in half, then quarter them lengthwise—the peels come off seamlessly. A young woman, talking over Zoom, revealed, "Well, I'm 6-foot-1 and have the wingspan of a professional basketball player, so I like to help people get things down off high shelves at the supermarket."

My husband's favorite question is: "What if?" What if I'd become a lawyer instead of a journalist? What if we didn't look at our phones on Shabbat? What if we made this highway go through this mountain rather than around it? What if he had quit his job and we had moved to Jerusalem when the twins were not quite five years old?

He is an architect, a playwright and director, an author (*Comedy by the Numbers*), a dad and brother and son, an improviser, and, starting at age fifty-eight, a high school teacher. "Everything I've ever thought about creating starts with questions," he says. But not all questions are created equal.

He explained: An architect might ask a client, "What size bedroom do you want?" A better architect would ask, "What do you want to see out the window when you wake up?"

Once, when he asked a client about the bathroom of her dreams, a whole story spilled out about her struggles to shave her legs in the shower. So, he designed her the ideal leg-shaving shower—and later did the same for me, with a built-in tiled bench that is the perfect height for propping an ankle at the right angle.

He has this workshop he leads called, "Dream Up Your Dream Room," where kids or adults draw, or collage from magazine cutouts, their fantasy bedroom and then tell a story about it. Once, a little girl who loved ice skating filled her paper with a huge rink. It was pink, her favorite color, and there were bleachers so her parents could watch her skate. Her bed was plopped in the middle of the rink, and she said she was allowed to sleep with her skates on so she could jump right out of bed in the morning and start skating.

Off to one side of the paper were a series of little marks. "What are those?" my husband asked. It turned out to be a really great question.

"Oh, those are the pipes," she said. Pipes? "There's an orchestra in the next room," she explained, "that plays music to help me fall asleep."

* * *

It is always funny to me when someone I'm talking to says, "Good question." Given all of the above, I take this as the highest of compliments. And yet, this is what I do for a living. More than that, it is where I stand in the world, who I am. I question.

The investigative reporter Jodi Kantor, the Jewish half of the duo that broke the Harvey Weinstein sexual misconduct story and led the *New York Times* team that won the 2018 Pulitzer Prize for Public Service, traces her craft back to her childhood as the grandchild of Holocaust survivors.

"This is a really common third-gen thing," she told me. "You're always trying to redeem what can be redeemed, ask the big questions. How could something like this have happened? What was the system? What were the mechanics? Why didn't anybody try to stop it? How could people have thought this was okay?"

We were talking around the premiere of *She Said*, the movie based on the book Jodi wrote with her reporting partner, Megan Twohey, about the Weinstein investigation and all that followed.

"I don't want people to think that in the *New York Times* newsroom I go around seeing the world through Holocaust-related eyes, because I don't," Jodi added. "I'm not a big fan of overciting something so sacred. But later, when I became an investigative journalist, it all made a kind of sense."

Because those are the questions that drove the Weinstein investigation and so many others. What was the system? Why didn't anybody try to stop it? And, as Jodi put it: "Will there ever be any accountability?"

The greatest question my daughter has ever asked me—well, so far—came over breakfast on a weekend in the fall of 2018. She was eleven and just getting interested in politics. We had been looking at some midterm campaign videos, noticing the differences in how a race was framed by a local Democratic candidate (who happened to be the mother of a kid who went to her elementary school) and her Republican opponent.

"If you and Daddy had been born into the same families as you were," she began, "but raised in Red states instead of Blue states, do you think you'd have the same political opinions?"

My husband grew up on Long Island, I in suburban Boston—both, indeed, bright blue Democratic strongholds. We live now in the People's Republic of Montclair, New Jersey, where the rare pro-Trump sign in 2020 got egged on Halloween. This was indeed a great question.

We'll never know for sure, of course. But here's what I told her, what I think is true.

Some political opinions, like about abortion and Israel, are grounded in core values. I don't think those change depending on where you grow up; I can't imagine not believing in women's rights to make their own reproductive choices, and in Jews' rights to have a safe and democratic homeland.

But others—like taxes and gun control—I think are shaped more by your experiences, and thus by the particulars of your community, the neighbors you know and care about. I told her about my years covering the Midwest, including struggling industrial cities and rural small towns that were nothing like the well-off suburb where I was raised. I told her what I had learned from family farmers about the impacts of estate and small-business taxes, and from hunters about their relationships with guns.

We talked about the dangers of only really knowing one type of people, one race or ethnicity or religion, and, of course, one political perspective. We talked about how to seek out and build understanding of those different types of people no matter where you live, no matter what type of family you're born into.

It's simple, really. Just keep asking great questions.

47

THOU SHALT BE BEAUTIFUL

The Forgotten Jewish Ideal

LIZZY SAVETSKY

AS A CHILD, my father used to read me a book every night. One of our favorites was *Miss Rumphius*, a story by Barbara Cooney about Alice Rumphius, a girl who longed to travel the world and live in a house by the sea. Alice's grandfather told her that while those dreams were "all very well…. There is a third thing you must do: *you must do something to make the world more beautiful*." Alice spent her life trying to figure out how to do just that. Ultimately, she planted lupine flowers all over her town and in the surrounding hills and fields. She became known as "The Lupine Lady."

Lizzy Savetsky is a digital influencer and Jewish activist with a passion for fashion, Israel, and the arts. Her mission is to empower people to stand up for what they believe in. She lives with her husband and three children in New York City. You can follow her journey on Instagram at @LizzySavetsky.

My father, who is a gifted artist, reminded me through my childhood and beyond that I should not only internalize the message of *Miss Rumphius*, but I should live it as a mission. As a child I could not fully grasp the significance, beyond the immediate joy brought to the beholder of my father's incredible paintings or Miss Rumphius's beautiful lupines. Yes, these beautiful things are nice to see, but they are also a manifestation of our ability to enhance the world around us through our God-given talents, a vital tool for connection, and a vessel for important messages that can transform minds and make lasting change.

The Jewish people so often neglect the importance of beauty, not only in and of itself, but as a means to change the world. With an emphasis placed on intellect and success, our stereotypical culture does not prioritize the value of aesthetic allure. While we may subscribe to the significance of attractiveness, in whatever ways society defines it through the times, rarely do we embrace beauty in all its glory and its ability to have a positive impact on and for our people.

From a religious perspective, there are specific blessings we make to exalt God's creations that appeal to each of our senses. When we appreciate beauty in our world, it brings us closer to God. If human beings are made in the image of God, then there can be no greater beauty than human beauty. And if *we* are created in God's image, then should we not appreciate, value, and work to improve our own physical appearance?

* * *

People often say that "beauty is skin deep," but throughout the colorful journey of my life, I have seen how beauty can carry a much deeper message. Beauty, in that sense, comes with great responsibility and great opportunity. My first brush with this revelation occurred at a VA Hospital in a small town in Texas, where I was crowned Miss Teen Duncanville in 2001. Within hours of winning the title, my new pageant directors, Jim and Sherry, said to me, "Lizzy, the crown is your microphone. What are you going to use it to say?" I could not fully grasp what they meant, but I quickly discovered that my sparkling new accessory got people's attention and made them want to listen to me, a little girl not even old enough to drive. What could I possibly have to say?

My calendar was suddenly filled with appearances at schools, hospitals, and local events, where I was called upon to relay some sort of inspirational words. I have always been an old soul and a deeply passionate person, but just what was my message? I dug into my own life to find it.

To understand my passion for the Jewish people and the work I do today, one should know a bit about where I come from. There are no fewer than 1,200 churches in the Dallas–Fort Worth area where I was raised, but today there are only eighteen synagogues with mostly very small congregations (including one Messianic), which is at least double what there was when I was growing up in the 1990s and early 2000s. For most of my primary education, I was the only Jew in my class. And as I later discovered, I was the first Jewish contestant in the history of both Miss Texas and Miss Teen Texas.

Being Jewish made me different, but I was always very proud of my heritage and religion and was raised with a strong sense of self. From a young age, I felt like an ambassador for my people. When the Jewish holidays rolled around every fall and I had to miss school, I used the opportunity to teach my peers about Rosh Hashanah. I brought donuts every winter and talked about Chanukah. Being the lone Jew forced me to educate myself about my Jewish identity so I could confidently relay its teachings to others.

My Jewish identity also brought both implicit and explicit forms of anti-semitism throughout my life, but I just accepted it as the norm. I was constantly told I was going to hell because I did not recognize Jesus as my savior. I knew this wasn't unique and that Jews had been persecuted throughout history, but I couldn't understand why. I knew I was a good person, and my family was hardworking, honest, and philanthropic. Why would we burn in hell? I decided to use my personal experiences as a Jewish minority to form a message of love, tolerance, and self-empowerment. Not only was this the message my crown would carry, but it would ultimately become the grounding force of my life's mission as an influencer and activist. I went on my Miss Teen Duncanville speaking tour, and I saw how the crown captivated the eyes of crowds, and that through it I could penetrate their souls. The glitz and the glamour drew them in, and with their guards down, they were open to tough discussions about bias, bigotry, hate, and fear. As I used my personal stories to reach people, I saw their hearts and minds open before my eyes, not just about the Jews, but about the gay community, the black community, and anyone with any difference at all. My passion for my mission garnered me top scores in the interview portion of the Miss Teen Texas competition and I went on to place third runner-up. Although I did not win the title, I won an epiphany that paved the way for my entire life's path: It was the sparkle of the crown that created a path for me to make a real impact in the world.

* * *

It is no secret that the Jews do not have the best PR. Though we have the most innovative, inclusive, brilliant offerings, we so often neglect the packaging. Even though the Torah tells us many times just how important beauty is, we tend to think of it as frivolous and unnecessary. Like most Jewish families, ours placed the utmost importance on academic and business success, but we also greatly prioritized beauty. My great grandmother, Pesha Ita, for whom I am named, relished glamour, elegance, and the simple art of looking damn good. She passed it on to my grandmother, my Bobbie, who passed it on to me. To them, the finest clothing, jewelry, and makeup were a symbol of victory they proudly wore. It represented overcoming a dangerous Ukrainian childhood filled with persecution and constant threats to their lives. Bobbie took me to Neiman Marcus every year to buy me designer suits and dresses for the High Holidays. I knew my grandparents counted every penny, but no expense was spared when it came to fine clothes. She constantly told me, "Lizzy, you're very short but you have a presence. People notice you, and you'll want to embrace that. You have to dress to match your vivacious personality!" Every outfit had something special that shouted, "Look at me!" when I walked into the synagogue. My passion for fashion and beauty led me to start an accessories blog back in 2013, which quickly grew a devoted following. My audience tuned in daily to see my over-accessorized outfits, how I styled my way through my pregnancies, and how I dressed my growing family. Ultimately my blog shifted to social media, primarily Instagram, where the bulk of my followers are today.

In a pivotal moment, I made the impulsive decision to disrupt my highly curated beautiful content to publicly share my pregnancy losses with my followers. I was vulnerable. I cried. They cried with me. It was the beginning of something magical. I realized how many women felt similar isolation from this unnecessarily taboo subject, so I decided to start a movement on Instagram to destigmatize pregnancy loss. I called it "Real Love, Real Loss." Within a week, thousands of women and even a few men went public with their losses. Because pregnancy loss is an invisible loss, it can cause incredible pain. We have nowhere tangible to put our pain—no grave to stand beside and mourn. I had a realization that we could raise funds for a Torah scroll in memory of the souls we never got to meet. We could dedicate it to the Israel Defense Forces soldiers on the front lines and even provide a bullet-proof casing. Our lost souls could protect their living souls. I was once again reminded not to underestimate the power of glittering accessories to open the door to change the world. My little accessories blog raised $57,000 in under a year for this Torah scroll, one $18 to $1,800 donation at a time. Today my crown is metaphorical. I use my platform as a social media influencer to support my people and my homeland. I do this with the same formula I learned as Miss Teen Duncanville. I draw the audience in with beautiful pictures, glamorous outfits, and charming videos. I package up the serious message, whether it be in the realm of education or activism, and sprinkle a hefty amount of glitter on top. This approachable and palatable method is incredibly effective. My 225,000 followers may come for the sparkle, but they stay for the inspiration.

* * *

The comparison to the story of Queen Esther is not lost on me. There, too, a beauty pageant leads a young, innocent girl to become a moving advocate for the Jewish people. It was her crown that gave her the power to convince the king to save her people from Haman's evil decree to murder them all. No crown, no Jewish people.I learned later in my life that Bess Myerson, the first and only Jewish Miss America in history, had also taken a page from Queen Esther's playbook. She was crowned in 1945 at the height of global antisemitism, as news of the horrors of the concentration camps and gas chambers was just reaching America. She refused the pageant director's request to change her last name to something that sounded a little less Jewish. She wanted her impoverished neighbors in the Shalom Aleichem housing project of the Bronx to know that one of their own had won the title. It was Bess's exterior beauty that allowed her to win, but it was her message, "You can't be beautiful and hate," that became her legacy. When she was crowned, she looked out into the audience and saw so many Jews who attended because they heard one of their own may win. As she walked the runway, she saw the Jewish attendees turn away from her to embrace one another. She knew then that she represented so much more than the title of Miss America. She represented the possibility of the rise from ashes to royalty for her persecuted people just emerging from their darkest hour. She became iconic. Bess continued to boldly take the controversial stance to embrace fully her Jewish identity throughout her reign. The Miss America program lost sponsorships, and Bess was denied entry at many places on her national tour, because she was a Jew. Instead of filling her year with the typical Miss America swimsuit appearances, Bess used her crown as a microphone. She spent her reigning year in partnership with the ADL on a national lecture tour, speaking out against bigotry. Bess had the chutzpah to be a proud Jew in a moment when many wished the Jews didn't exist at all. Her bravery gave hope to many and has been a tremendous inspiration to me. Taking a controversial stance is terrifying. Queen Esther wavered, knowing her own life would be endangered by going to the king to plead on her people's behalf. Mordechai told her that the entire reason she had been blessed with the crown was to save the Jewish nation. I keep this in mind every time I stand up for the Jews only to encounter misunderstanding, unpopularity, hate, and even death threats. When I receive messages from my followers about how my work inspires them to stand up proudly in the face of adversity, I am empowered to keep going. I see the impact before my eyes every day. That is how I found the courage to wrap myself in an Israeli flag and post the truth about our beautiful nation to my Instagram followers as celebrities and mainstream media pummeled Zionists during the 2021 conflict in Gaza. That is why I was able to put myself in the line of fire to take the stage at a pro-Israel rally where a massive pro-Palestinian contingent became violent and aggressive. That is where I find the courage to take the risk of losing jobs, friends, and followers, when I stand up for the truth. This is my duty. If I don't use my voice and my sparkle for the future of my children and their children, what is the point of it anyway?

We all have the power to make real change when we can take the time to seek out our purpose, but without a crown we have no microphone. We have nobody to listen. We have no impact. We cannot neglect the sparkle. In some ways, as we have seen in countless examples of evil propaganda throughout history, the packaging is even more critical than the message itself. We are up against more and more incredibly attractive and dangerous misinformation than ever with the growth of social media. They may have the crown, but the message is an evil one that threatens our very existence. We, as Jews, are never going to win the numbers game. We have to put more attention on bedazzling our urgent message to reach the world, but especially to reach our own, whom we continue to lose to apathy, and worse yet, to the sparkle of the alluring evil they encounter in vulnerable places like college campuses.

✴ ✴ ✴

How do I put my method into action? I take my own life experiences—like my Birthright Israel trip, my journey to Poland to visit the concentration camps, our march against antisemitism across the Brooklyn Bridge, my success in Jewish matchmaking, my weekly Torah classes, and my one-on-one interactions with people who impact me—and I use my platform to bring my audience along in my own glamorous, entertaining, passionate way. My visit to a factory in the West Bank that manufactured air conditioning filters allowed me to educate my audience about how, contrary to popular belief and media portrayal, Israelis and Palestinians work together beautifully. I intentionally wore a neon pink knit set as I interviewed the Israeli factory owner. Let me tell you, it opened him up to conversation in a different way than if I had come dressed in black. It also grabbed the attention of my followers. First, they wanted to know where my striking outfit was from, but then they were shocked to learn that they had been deceived by the media. They took home the message that boycotting Israeli products in fact only hurts the Palestinian employees of the factories.

People can be greatly affected by that which appeals to their senses. External, tangible beauty can therefore be used as a vessel to instill a far deeper beauty, something unshakable and infinite. The Talmud says, "Three things broaden a person's mind: a beautiful house, beautiful possessions, and a beautiful wife." When people enjoy physical beauty, it enhances our spirituality. It also opens us up to receive important messages. First, we appeal to the eyes, and then to the minds and hearts.

As an adult I see now that it was not only Miss Rumphius's lupines that made the world more physically beautiful, but it was also her internal mission to "do something to make the world more beautiful" that left a lasting mark. She understood that purpose and beauty are intrinsically intertwined.

48

DON'T TAKE DEMOCRACY
FOR GRANTED

Why We Must Not Be Politically Complacent

DAHLIA SCHEINDLIN

HOW LONG have the Jewish people been democratic? In one view, the Jewish tendency toward democracy predates democracy itself. "Perhaps Jewish party politics began with the rivalry of Jacob and Esau," quipped the scholars Gerald Pomper and Miles Pomper in their 2004 essay "Movers, Shakers, and Leaders," on Jews in American political life. H.H. Ben-Sasson, in *A History of the Jewish People*, found elements of a "primitive democracy" in the period of Judges:

Dahlia Scheindlin, Ph.D., is a political scientist and a political advisor who has worked on nine national election campaigns in Israel and studied public opinion regarding the Israeli-Palestinian conflict for twenty-five years. Her book about the history of democracy in Israel is forthcoming in 2023.

an alliance of tribes led by a general assembly, or "representative institutions" with legislative and military authority, rather than by judges or kings.

In 1985, the Israeli Likud lawmaker Michael Eitan captured the primordial Jewish democratic theory in a Knesset discussion: "The Jewish people, the Jews, according to their characteristics—individualism, thinking, development, unwillingness to submit to inflexible frameworks—cannot exist without democracy."

Alas, neither ancient Judea, nor ancient Athens for that matter, would count as democratic by any modern understanding of the concept. By contrast to the Israeli legislator's lofty assertion, most of Jewish history existed without democracy.

Democracy as we know it today emerged only in the late eighteenth century, in areas where most Jews did not live. It grew legs alongside liberalism of the nineteenth century and came to fruition in the twentieth; the Jewish and democratic trajectories only began to converge alongside cataclysmic changes in Jewish life of the same century.

A panoramic look at the modern, postwar relationship between Jews and democracy shows a mixed and complicated picture. Democracy thrives among Jews under certain historic and political circumstances, but curdles in other contexts. No inherent Jewish democratic gene will save democracy among Jews if they take it for granted.

***

For most of post-exile Jewish history, democracy in its current form, had it existed, would have been a lifeline. To state the obvious, from the destruction of the Second Temple onward, Jews everywhere were a minority. In the broadest sense, the two main aims of Jewish people from Kaifeng to Cork became physical survival and preservation of a common soul with no physical center or sovereignty. Jews adapted; the Hebrew word for exile, *galut*, shares its root, G'L'H, with the verb "discover" (*le'galot*), and exile drove the discovery of mechanisms to achieve both aims. Jews everywhere needed protection from persecution by both authorities and marauders, and they needed religious freedom. Emerging Western European liberal values of the eighteenth and nineteenth centuries, human and civil rights anchored in equality, were a great leap forward for Jews.

By the late nineteenth century, about three-quarters of all Jews lived in

Eastern Europe. The Israeli historian Alan Dowty observes that Jewish community organization of the shtetl displayed elaborate social and political organization, including participatory organizational life and community leadership. Jewish municipal councils raised taxes from Jewish communities, made laws beyond religious law, and held elections. Active participation in the shtetl was voluntary, but was understood as essential to both survival and preservation of the community and tradition. Consensus-building was key, as well as coalition-building, political bargaining, and rules (and rule-bending). Shlomo Avineri views these values as the foundation of democratic practice in Israel; the idea that Jewish tradition in general provided the roots of democracy in Israel is, in his words, "utter nonsense." Jewish political values of modernity were born of historic and sociological circumstances and evolved in response to needs, rather than an innate democracy gene.

By the early twentieth century, Jews were attracted to all manner of political philosophies. In eastern Europe, many were swept up by revolutionary socialism, with its promise of supra-national class-based equality. Cosmopolitan, polyglot, and assimilated Jews of central or western Europe were drawn to universalist liberalism of the nineteenth century, but were devastated when it gave way to fresh waves of violent antisemitism. The masses migrating to America rushed to embrace equality and opportunity as per the promise of American democracy. Finally, among the grand ideological forces of the twentieth century was nationalism, which ricocheted among colonial subjects around the world. As empires crumbled, nationalism, resting on the principles of self-determination, became the conceptual basis for the audacious and increasingly desperate Zionist movement.

When the ashes settled after World War II, the centers of Jewish gravity had entirely realigned. One pole of Jewish leadership lay in the United States, now representing about half of all Jews remaining in the world. The other nexus of Jewish leadership was Israel. What Israel lacked in numbers (barely 6 percent of the world's Jews lived there in 1948), Israel made up for in symbolism—redefining Jewish history, identity, and aspirations.

Democracy was by now the global currency. By the late twentieth century, as Fareed Zakaria argued, that meant liberal democracy. Modern democracy requires representative governments elected in free and fair elections at regular intervals, with universal suffrage of citizens. To meet the "free and fair" condition, a democratic society requires the freedom to think, speak, and organize, as well as the means to educate itself through free press and information. Freedom of religion and from persecution must be guaranteed, alongside minority rights and protection against tyranny of the majority. Human and civil rights, equal treatment before the law, an independent judiciary, and an active civil society are essential conditions; these in turn can only be guaranteed by a separation of powers and agreed limitations on the power of any one branch.

In the postwar era, Jews in both the U.S. and Israel claimed to be the torchbearers for democracy. But the two centers of Jewish life had fundamentally different, possibly irreconcilable aims.

Put simply, Jews in America wished for equality of opportunity and the freedom to be Jewish; they needed rights, freedoms, and equal treatment before the law. The Jews of Israel had one overpowering need above all else: sovereignty. When historic circumstances diverged, it turns out, so did the Jewish relationship with democracy.

* * *

The American Jewish community came to be associated with, even inseparable from, democracy. Writing in 2002, the Jewish historian Rafael Medoff has estimated the Jewish voter turnout in presidential elections to be ten points higher on average than the total American turnout rate. Jews participate enthusiastically in public life in all branches of government.

Jewish Americans threw themselves into civil society, and with good reason: They needed social organizations to fight antisemitic discrimination in housing, education, and employment, to help immigrants and fight injustice. Those groups grew, collaborated, and won victories, contributing to the secure standing that has catapulted the Jews of America to material success and social influence. And as their hard-won struggles helped them reap the benefits of America's professed values, American Jews did not cease their activities but applied these civic skills to others. For many activists, rights and freedoms were inseparable from solidarity with other minorities in need.

In the early twentieth century, Anna Strunsky's horror at the Kishinev pogrom of 1903 fused with her disgust at the lynching and violence against African Americans, according to the historian Steven J. Zipperstein, drove her to play a key role in the establishment of the National Association for the Advancement of Colored People (NAACP) in 1909. The Hebrew Immigrant Aid Society (HIAS) served Jewish immigrants to the U.S. for over one hundred years. Today it serves refugees and immigrants from over a dozen countries and works in other countries as well, illustrating the direct link from the Jewish experience to universal rights.

New York attorney Kathleen Peratis, drawn to Jews from her childhood, related that she was launched into political activism by Jewish friends in high school, joining struggles against the death penalty and the House Un-American Activities Committee and in favor of free speech. In the 1970s, she worked at the American Civil Liberties Union (ACLU) with mostly Jewish colleagues, where she "could hardly distinguish 'ACLU' from 'Jews.'" Peratis then said, "It dawned on me. These Jews were—Jewish." Peratis converted to Judaism in the early 1990s, illustrating that democratic civic activism became a defining and even magnetic trait of American Jewish life, bringing newcomers into the fold.

This is not about partisanship. Although most Jews vote Democrat, for most of American history voting Democrat or Republican was a disagreement over opinion, policy, or perhaps certain values, not about democracy itself. That would change with Donald Trump, whose presidency was, it seems, committed to dismantling American democracy. But only a minority of Jews voted for Trump (18 percent reported supporting Trump in an American Jewish Committee poll after the 2016 elections). Exit polls showed some rise in Jewish support for the GOP under Trump's influence in 2020 and 2022, mainly from conservative religious communities who prefer Republican policies on Israel. Democracy in America, at least, remains a unified commitment of Jewish life in America.

***

Israel took a different path.

From its earliest days, the deepest and perhaps only unifying premise of Zionism in its myriad forms was Jewish sovereignty. In which land, within which borders, when and how to achieve it, and how much power to share—these were the famous and enduring cleavages within early streams of Zionism, and many of them remain today.

In the early twentieth-century Zionist literature, the word "democracy" often appears as shorthand for majority rule, something David Ben-Gurion and other top leaders were wary of promising. Jews, after all remained a minority in Palestine right up to the eve of statehood.

Ben-Gurion's socialist ethos may have been anchored by a parliamentary democratic system and electoral framework held over from the pre-state institutions established at the World Zionist Congress. Yet, he also, ultimately, brought the most powerful institutions under effective one-party rule, and those same institutions wielded highly centralized control in the early decades of statehood. Israel has hardly any structural limitations on the power of government. Even the judiciary, which is independent, has only an ambiguous basis for authority to oppose other branches, eventually leading to the current crisis of judicial legitimacy. And even Ben-Gurion's socialist ideology was secondary to his true, singular aim of sovereignty, according to his biographer Tom Segev. By contrast, it was Ze'ev Jabotinsky who articulated the most developed proposals of liberal, constitutional democracy, including even Arab national minority rights and elaborate power-sharing that would scandalize his political successors of modern-day Likud. But Jabotinsky's more liberal vision emerged alongside his ultra-nationalist militarism insistence on maximal land in what was, by his own logic, effectively a Jewish-dominated colonial project. Religious Zionism opposed the very notion of secular law supplanting the Torah and halacha—thereby rejecting both equality of all citizens and the civic backbone of democracy.

With irreconcilable democratic differences, the emerging national leadership of the nascent state cut major corners on democracy. In 1948, in a triple blow, the new Israeli Constituent Assembly failed to pass a written constitution, and the first Knesset abandoned the task to slow incremental constitution-building; religious authorities were given authority over major areas of public and private life in the new state and kingmaker-level power in governing coalitions, even as Israel's chief rabbis boycotted the establishment of the Supreme Court; and most of Israel's Arab citizens were placed under martial law, suffocated by a military regime that would dominate their lives for the next twenty years. Moreover, politics in Israel's first thirty years were dominated by one party, which won elections largely through intense party patronage, funneling voters into its institutions that dominated social services, labor rights, and opportunities, and the information environment in those first three decades. The corrupt, coercive political environment generated so much anger that its effects still hover over Israeli politics today.

By 1967, Israelis had never experienced a country of civic equality free of religious interference; they had accepted a two-tiered legal regime, one grounded in military rule, for the country's entire history, and still knew only one party in power. There was little reason therefore to imagine that Israelis would suddenly oppose undemocratic rule over the new populations in the territories conquered in 1967. Those who did oppose it, practically from the earliest hours, remained marginal figures in the decades that followed.

The vast majority of Israeli Jews would tolerate occupation that flowed not from a parallel authority in some other land, but from the very same civil institutions that governed Israeli life, from tax authorities and government ministries to the Supreme Court. When the Labor movement eventually came to oppose ongoing occupation, it flourished in the 1990s but collapsed incrementally over the next few decades.

Israel demonstrates a selective and dismissive approach to the law when there are opportunities to expand settlements, confiscate Palestinian land or destroy homes, or soft-pedal proceedings against law-breaking and even violent settlers.

The country still has no constitution. The only stand-in for a bill of rights, the two Basic Laws passed in 1992, are bitterly divisive. Critics argue not just over their interpretation and status vis-à-vis regular laws, but over their very legitimacy as well. If the arc once seemed to be bending toward liberal democratic values in the 1990s, Benjamin Netanyahu became the symbol of, and catalyst for, Israeli illiberal nationalist populism.

But it would be wrong to give him all the credit: Netanyahu merely built on the historic weakness of Israel's commitment to democratic norms that left it particularly susceptible. The military government over Arab citizens officially ended in 1966, but some of its practices continued; a slew of undemocratic legislation in the 2010s attacked the status of Arabs in Israel, such as a law constraining the right to observe the Nakba, or to call for political boycott. These efforts culminated in the 2018 Nation-State Law effectively elevating Jewish citizens above all others. Attacks on one minority never stop with one: The populist Right fought feverishly to constrain and demonize left-wing organizations, civil society, and the media. In 2022 the third-largest party leader called human rights organizations an existential threat. The populist Right has mounted a dark, sustained attack on the legitimacy of the Israeli judiciary itself.

* * *

The diverging trajectories between Israeli and American Jews are symbolized aptly by one man. A decisive majority of American Jews rejected Trump at the ballot box, but in Israel, the longest-serving prime minister embraced Trump and brandished his image in his political campaigns. Surveys by the Pew Research Center from 2019 showed Israelis held among the highest view of Trump (regarding global affairs) among all countries surveyed. Jewish Israelis—and some American Jews—were clearly pleased about Trump's blank check and boost for Israeli settlements, including his willingness to recognize Israeli sovereignty over all of Jerusalem, the Golan Heights, and parts of the West Bank—representing support for the most undemocratic policies of Israel, its violations of international law and human rights. In 2022, the American Israel Public Affairs Committee (AIPAC), one of America's most influential Jewish political organizations, endorsed lawmakers who refused to certify America's democratic presidential elections of 2020, prioritizing Israel's policies even over American democracy.

American Jews should resist the influence of Israel's ambiguous relationship with democracy and recommit to the long history of Jewish American support for democratic values. Israel could use some recommitment as well.

There is no Jewish democracy gene. The events that have transpired since the Israeli elections of 2022 mark a new low in attacks on democratic institutions and values, and show that nothing can be taken for granted. All Jews must make a conscious choice to rededicate themselves to democracy by facing the flaws and threats to democracy in Israel, the U.S., or wherever Jews live—and working to repair them.

49

WANTED: A JEWISH TOLKIEN

Why We Need a New Mythology

JOE SCHWARTZ

"ARE YOU THE TOUR GUIDE?" a kindly woman asked my nine-year-old yesterday, as we wandered through the Acropolis. Zev smiled at her with impatience and went back to explaining to his long-suffering younger sister about Poseidon and Athena, and how they vied to be the patron god of Athens.

We flew from Tel Aviv to Athens for the weekend because ever since Zev discovered Rick Riordan's Percy Jackson series this summer, his thirst for Greek myth cannot be slaked. He tore first through the five-book series and

Joe Schwartz is an attorney, rabbi, and Jewish entrepreneur. He serves as Director of Educational Innovation and Director of Makom at the Jewish Agency for Israel. He lives in Tel Aviv with his wife, Avigail, and their children, Zev, Paz, and Shai.

moved on to the follow-up, The Heroes of Olympus series; he listened and re-listened to every episode of the *Greeking Out* podcast (to which he falls asleep at night); read and re-read *D'Aulaires' Book of Greek Myths*; delivered a presentation on the Greek pantheon to his fourth-grade class; constructs Lego models of Charon ferrying souls across the Styx; and never desists from quizzing me on the curse of the House of Atreus, the parentage of Heracles, the career of Daedalus, and on and on. Since landing in Athens, he has dived into learning Modern Greek on Duolingo.

Before Riordan's young-adult adventure stirred his passion for Greek myths, Zev spent two years at Hogwarts, memorizing the catalogs of fantastic beasts and explaining to anyone who would listen the difference between hexes and curses.

I write this not to kvell in public about my son (well, not *only* to kvell), but to point to a great hole: Seeing how these stories of adventure and danger kindle my son's imagination, I have been trying to nudge him toward things Jewish. He is, after all, living in the Jewish state, in the ancestral home of the Jewish people, spending his days and nights in Hebrew, among Jews of every color and variety.

And yet the bookshelf of works of Jewish imagination that might win his interest is bare.

I don't mean to say there exist no works of imagination featuring Jewish protagonists—there are many, including some that are excellent (special mention here goes to Adam Gidwitz's 2018 *The Inquisitor's Tale*). Only a few books drawn on Jewish folklore have been written for children. And, of course, there exist compilations of Aggada (Jewish legend), including some edited for younger readers. What has not been produced, however, is anything approaching the work of J.K. Rowling or even her imitators—to say nothing of J.R.R. Tolkien or C.S. Lewis, universes as elaborate as Middle Earth, built out of and inspired by the Jewish past and the Jewish present and the vast trove of the Jewish imaginary, as deeply informed by our histories, stories, legends as Harry Potter's world is by Britain's, or C.S. Lewis's Narnia series is by Christian myth; no stories full of wonder and adventure, involving protagonists who confront great danger and overcome their own terror and limitations to achieve what they believed impossible, paying a terrible price in the process. These are the elements, after all, that grip our imagination on the deepest level, moving not only Zev but his middle-aged father.

Above all, I search in vain for a work of the Jewish imagination that would open the door to the great saga of the Jewish people. We live forty-five minutes from Jerusalem, but nothing my son has read or watched draws him there. Instead, here I am, seated in a café in Kolonaki.

* * *

This is not a minor lacuna. The Jewish people, like any people, is not a natural but a social fact. A people is what the scholar of nationalism Benedict Anderson has called an "imagined community." Though most members of a people, writes Anderson, "will never know most of their fellow-members, meet them or even hear of them, yet in the minds of each lives the image of their communion." It is through this imagined communion that a people summons itself into existence. To the extent a people can be said to exist at all, its existence transpires upon a landscape of its imagining, by and through the sagas of its heroes and their trials. By telling, retelling, and revising its shared mythic past, a people points the way toward a shared mythic future. And in the absence of this imagined communion, no people—including the Jewish people—possesses any existence at all. Indeed, much of what preoccupies and alarms the organized Jewish world—declining affiliation, declining literacy, declining attachment—is downstream from this impoverishment of the Jewish imagination.

And imaginations are forged early. The rabbis well understood this, which is why they placed so great an emphasis on winning the imaginations of children. The Passover Seder, perhaps the central ritual of rabbinic Judaism, takes shape in response to a threat foreseen by the Torah: If it was the shared experience of the Exodus from Egypt that forged the Jewish people, what will become of future generations who did not experience the Exodus first-hand? What will bind them to one another and to generations gone by? The Torah's answer is: The recounting of our great national saga. "And when, in time to come, your child asks you, 'What is this?' you shall reply to him: 'With a mighty hand the Eternal brought us out of Egypt, the house of bondage'" (Exodus 13:14). Even if the child is so estranged from the community that she cannot formulate the question, the Torah commands us to recount the story to her unprompted: "And you shall tell your child on that day, 'It is because of what the Eternal did for me when I went free from Egypt'" (Exodus 13:8). From the word used for "tell"—*vehiggadeta*—we get the Haggadah—"the telling"—which lies at the heart of the Passover Seder.

But merely telling the tale is not enough. Instead, the rabbis adjure us to succeed in enthralling the imaginations of those to whom it is told. "In every generation," in the words of the Haggadah, "a person must imagine himself as though he is leaving Egypt." That is, the Jewish community is charged with bringing the saga of the Jewish people to life for them and for the next generation, making the Jewish story into the story their imagination inhabits.

This is a very high bar, which in our day has only gotten harder to reach.

When Jews lived in tight-knit Jewish communities, their curriculum was exclusively Jewish sacred text and their lives were structured by Jewish ritual. As a matter of course, then, Jews' imaginations belonged to the community. As the great historian of Jewish thought Eliezer Schweid wrote, "The religious myth that had formed the collective historic memory of the Jewish people throughout the generations [was] nurtured by the Bible, the legends of the sages, the prayer book, the poetic hymns and kabbalistic literature of the Middle Ages." And yet, already by the close of the nineteenth century, this great mythic collective consciousness had been progressively undermined by modernity. Into that vacuum stepped poets and writers like Hayim Nahman Bialik, Micha Josef Berdichevsky and others, who sought to reshape the religious inheritance into a "historic myth of the Jewish people on its path through destructions and exiles toward redemption in its own land." The attempt was only partially successful in its day. Today, these historic national myths have lost much of their hold on the popular imagination, even here in the Jewish state.

In our time, for all but the most traditional, collective identity has become a voluntary affair, and competition for the minds and attention of young Jews is fierce. Imaginative universes abound, and with them ever more imagined communities. More and more Jews belong primarily to these, straying further and further from the historic myth of the Jewish people. But without stories of our own to fascinate young Jews, their fertile imaginations will yield only foreign crops.

We do not want for source material. In 2010, Michael Weingrad observed in the *Jewish Review of Books* that biblical and rabbinic literature, Jewish folklore, and the wondrous world of the Kabbalistic tradition contain "all the elements necessary for classic fantasy—magic, myth, dualism, demonic forces, strange worlds." If anything, Weingrad understated the sheer volume of material ready to be transfigured into fantasy. Is any story as deeply affecting as that of our people, banished from its home, scattered across the globe, preserving its ancient traditions and languages under conditions of almost unendurable hardship, yearning day and night for return to its land? The long history of the Jewish dispersion—to Spain, Russia, Turkey, Libya, Syria, Yemen, Uzbekistan, India—contains endless episodes and incidents ripe for exploration. Jews have been mystics and warriors, poets and scholars, revolutionaries and saints.

It is more than surprising, then, that according to Weingrad—who has spent the better part of the past two decades keeping abreast of Jewish imaginative fiction in the *Jewish Review of Books* and on his blog, "Investigations and Fantasies"—no book or series has yet been written that manages to "plumb the theological depths like Lewis" or even "thrill Jewish preteens with tales of Potterish derring-do." To be a Jew is to be heir to a story more remarkable and more filled with incident than that of any other people. Indeed, echoes of our story run through the work of Tolkien, who took inspiration from it. Why then do we have over a dozen anodyne children's books about potato pancakes and none about the mystic Abraham Abulafia, who set out alone on the quixotic quest to convert the Pope to Judaism?

The material is there for the taking. Why have such works of imagination not already been written?

***

The first, most obvious reason has to do with literacy: The overwhelming majority of Jews living outside of Israel cannot read Hebrew, Aramaic, or any other classical Jewish language; and few Jewish artists in Israel (alas) take a deep interest in Jewish lore and myth. Just as Tolkien could not have created Middle Earth without being steeped in Old English, Germanic, Celtic, and Norse literature, so our own Jewish fantasists will need to discover their inspiration in Hebrew midrash, in Aramaic mystical literature, and in older Near Eastern myth.

A second reason, as Yehezkel Kaufmann and other scholars have noted, is that Israelite religion was distinguished from other Near Eastern religions by its tendency to strip its stories of mythological elements. The Pentateuch contains no pantheon, no demigods, few monsters, and almost no magic. One can detect traces of earlier myth in our corpus, but these have been muted and rationalized. God performs miracles; human beings, including even those with second sight, remain firmly human. It is for this reason that Weingrad is skeptical about the possibility of Jewish fantasy literature. There is something in the Jewish imaginary, he argues, that resists fantasy: "Whereas fantasy grows naturally out of Christian soil, Judaism's more adamant separation from myth and magic render classic elements of the fantasy genre undeveloped or suspect in the Jewish imaginative tradition."

A related challenge is Judaism's historicizing element. While Jews retell and relive great events from our mythic past, we have always been aware that our story is ongoing and looked expectantly toward messianic redemption. Judaism is a historical faith. Rather than departing for a parallel realm, the Jewish imagination has tended to occupy itself with this world and with our fate as it unfolds in history.

To create a Jewish fantasy universe, then, will demand that our artists work against the grain of normative Jewish religion and culture, and push against mainstays of the fantasy genre. Jewish fantasy will need to differ in its very essence from non-Jewish fantasy. Not for us the stories of knights, dragons and wizards, or simple tales of good triumphing over evil. Something else will be needed to light our children's imaginations. Those who choose to cultivate the fields of the Jewish imaginary will have to work harder to sow the ground and make it bear fruit. We cannot know what this will be like until it is done, of course. But it has been done before: Those mythic elements of Jewish religion that were suppressed in the Bible spring up in rabbinic legend and explode into a riot of exotic imagery in medieval Kabbalistic literature.

The chief obstacle to the creation of such works is the damage that has been done to the Jewish imagination by our own historical experience: first by exile, and then by political Zionism.

Jews living in the West for over a millennium as a coldly tolerated and often despised minority were cast in certain roles and not others. And in being so cast, we learned to imagine ourselves only in profoundly limited ways.

The Jew appears in pre-modern English literature, according to the critic Leslie Fiedler, only as "the Usurer, the Jew with the Knife, the Jew as Beast": "half-comic, half-hideous, with red wig and grotesque false nose, who meets us, bloody knife in hand, to call us *chaver*, fellow-Jew: Shylock, Fagin, Isaac, Barrabas, Ahasuerus, Cartaphilus, Colleoni—his momentary labels do not matter." In the modern period, the Jew with the Knife gave way to more benign figures. From Gotthold Ephraim Lessing's *Nathan the Wise* (1779) until today, the Jew appears as a paragon of liberal virtue: broadminded, benevolent, harmless, and sexless—think Judd Hirsch in *Independence Day*. And what of Jewish women? Though in the 1970s Barbra Streisand and Erica Jong had their moments (which coincided with Dustin Hoffman's and Elliott Gould's turns as sex symbols), in general to identify a woman as a Jew is still to mark her out as loud, shrewish, and undesirable. And yet in its revolt against these and similar constructions of Jewishness, political Zionism too often stripped its protagonists of any meaningfully Jewish traits: Jewish and "exilic" were, for it, one and the same, and so Jews would have to become stolid Hebrew warriors and farmers without a history, speaking a Hebrew uninflected by the 2,000 years that transpired since the fall of Betar. The ideal type of the Second-Aliya pioneer is all but indistinguishable from any other proletariat, except that the field he plows is in the Land of Israel. To mine the Jewish past for distinctly Jewish stories, in which heroes display distinctly Jewish virtues, would require the artist to shake off both her "exilic" and her narrowly Zionist conditioning. It would demand that we reenter our own history with an ear toward its uniquely Jewish music. Early cultural Zionists began this work. It falls to us to continue it.

***

How might this be accomplished?

The project I envision draws inspiration from Tolkien, Lewis, Rowling, and Riordan, but is different in important ways. Tolkien's Middle Earth was not just a flight of fancy, but something more serious. He aimed at least in part to imagine what a British saga on the order of the Finnish Kalevala or the Norse Edda would be like; and by the time he completed *The Lord of the Rings*, he had created an allegory for a Britain transformed by industrialization, war, modernity, and much more. Lewis, for his part, embedded Christian themes in his tales of Narnia. And Riordan, of course, uses his tales as an opportunity to teach his young readers about Greek and Roman myth. The project or projects I am calling for can resemble these or be something entirely new. What is important is that they arouse fascination with things Jewish and prompt further exploration.

What themes might our Jewish Tolkiens, Lewises, Rowlings, and Riordans draw on? It seems to me that they should seek to tap those veins of the Jewish imagination that have been the most vital and enthralling over the millennia.

The messianic idea and messianic hope, as Gershom Scholem famously argued, has animated and propelled Jewish history. Jews throughout history have awaited their redemption in the midst of exile, holding fast to promises of restoration at our lowest ebb—or else despaired of divine aid and sought to force the end through mystical and political activism. The idea has led in many different directions—here toward secret rituals aimed at repairing the divine fabric of the universe, there impelling Jews to revolt against their fate through political activism, and still elsewhere channeled both into exalted ethical ideals and antinomian orgies. This great electric conduit of Jewish history and all that it has yielded are a powerful current to be tapped.

Another central and idiosyncratic feature of Jewish history has been our tendency toward discord, dissension, and debate. The Jewish people has always been at war with itself because we contain diametrically opposed tendencies: mysticism against rationalism, radicalism against conservatism, utopianism against realism, particularism against universalism. The way Jewish controversies give expression to deep and eternal tensions is rich ground for narrative as well.

Finally, the vast scope and sweep of Jewish history and literature offer a tremendous opportunity. Jewish writers must look beyond small and well-worn incidents and settings: beyond Anatevka, beyond America, beyond even the Holocaust. The stage of the Jewish saga has not been a single land, like Narnia or Middle Earth, but the entire world: Egypt, Babylonia, Rome, Persia, Spain—we were there, of and apart from the greatest imperial powers. Jews lived in Baghdad and Yemen for more than 2,000 years. There is so much that remains untapped. Jewish history and literature remain in many ways a vast and undiscovered continent. Melila Hellner-Eshed of the Hebrew University has only recently made available in Hebrew and English an entire metaphysics—the theology of the *partzufim* found in the Idras of the Zohar—utterly unlike anything we know in Jewish mysticism. A Jewish writer of imaginative literature must be an explorer.

Above all, the importance of the endeavor must be recognized. Our writers and artists and dreamers are our most precious resource. Supporting their work, helping them build worlds to enthrall the Jewish imagination, should be among our highest priorities. We need a Jewish Creative Trust overseen by our leading scholars, artists, and visionaries. Big, expensive, and ambitious products should not be the enemy of smaller and more targeted efforts. There is no earthly reason why a Jewish equivalent to the *Greeking Out* podcast has not been produced, nor a beautiful and strange illustrated retelling of Torah that approaches the D'Aulaires' Greek Myths and Norse Myths. Bringing these smaller efforts to market could spark larger visions.

As much as I kvell over my children, they are not unique. There are today millions of bright, curious Jewish children whose attentions and energies could be turned to things Jewish. My son, after all, is eagerly teaching himself Greek, on his own initiative, on account of a book and the spell it cast. Imagine what is possible, what talent might be enlisted to Jewish causes, what energies could be harnessed for a rebirth of Jewish culture and civilization. This Jewish future must be dreamed into being—and it begins with the dreams of children.

50

STRENGTHEN THE CHRISTIAN-JEWISH ALLIANCE

The Urgency of Overcoming Our Prejudice

FAYDRA L. SHAPIRO

MOST OF US WOULD AGREE that a deeper understanding of one another, and of each other's particular cultures and beliefs, contributes to human flourishing in a pluralistic world. Abraham Joshua Heschel's assertion that "no religion is an island" is certainly correct, and therefore interfaith engagement is a vital tool for promoting a society of dignity and tolerance

Faydra L. Shapiro, Ph.D., directs the Israel Center for Jewish-Christian Relations. She is a senior fellow at the Philos Project and a research fellow at the Center for the Study of Religions at Tel Hai College in northern Israel.

without abandoning a sense of personal religious integrity and commitment.

But while interfaith understanding is essential, we Jews have a unique and particular—and particularly difficult—responsibility to engage with Christians. Among the many priorities the Jewish people face, this one probably doesn't seem obvious. Not only *may* we engage with Christians (some Orthodox Jews might think otherwise), but we absolutely must learn how, and actively seek out opportunities to do so. I say this not at the expense of other interfaith relations, but to argue that our Jewish obligation toward a dialogue with Christianity constitutes a special responsibility.

The relationship between Judaism and Christianity is unique among world religions. Rightly, college courses in World Religions schedule Judaism and Christianity on different weeks, and textbooks have different chapters for each faith. Judaism and Christianity have—among other things—different beliefs, different Scripture, different rituals, and different authority structures.

But the relationship between the two is qualitatively different from the relationship between any other religious traditions. The entanglement between Judaism and Christianity runs deep, and in many ways the two emerged in relation to one another. So, while Jewish-Hindu relations or Jewish-Buddhist relations or even Jewish-Muslim relations are valuable, Jewish-Christian relations are uniquely so.

I am often asked by Christians active in building better Jewish-Christian relations why it seems that there are so few Jews who are equally dedicated to this project. The reasons why Christians need to understand Jews and Judaism are pretty obvious. The simple fact that Jesus was Jewish, raised by Jewish parents, surrounded by Jewish followers, and participated fully in Jewish rituals and communal worship, means that Jewishness is foundational to Christianity. At a very deep level, it behooves Christians to dig into Judaism to understand Jesus and the foundation of their own faith. Thus, to argue that Jewish-Christian relations is a Christian priority is pretty straightforward. At some level, Christians *must* engage Jewishness and Judaism.

But there is no equivalent need for a Jew to dig into Christianity to understand Judaism. Jews can (and do) lead completely faithful, robust, and authentic Jewish lives without ever having to engage Christianity as a theological category. So, it's not immediately obvious to us Jews why Christianity should be of any special interest.

Plus, let's face it: Christians make us kind of nervous. Or rather, different kinds of Christians make different kinds of Jews nervous. Differently. Liberal Jews, for example, are often put off by evangelical Christians—by their conservative social agenda, their Messianic Zionism, and their absolute conviction that Jesus Christ is indeed the Way, the Truth, and the Light. Orthodox Jews might appreciate the social values, Zionism, and active faith (while disagreeing with the content) of Evangelicals but are profoundly uncomfortable, on the other hand, with the history and ostensible idolatry of Catholics.

The relationship between Christianity and Judaism might be unique, but it is also uniquely difficult: Jews are extremely aware of the painful history that stands between us. The very real discomfort of many Jews due to a long history of Christian anti-Judaism cannot just be ignored. For many of us, almost everything we know about Christianity is where it tragically intersects with the history of our own people—in places like the Crusades, the Inquisition, charges of deicide, blood libel, and host desecration. And while that is undoubtedly only a partial view, it means that many Jews are at the very least uncomfortable with Christianity. And let's face it, discomfort, negativity and suspicion are hardly a strong platform for developing mutual understanding.

So, then—why should we? Why should Jews prioritize an active engagement with Christians today?

***

First, around half of the Jews in the world today live in what are at least nominally Christian countries. To understand the texts, beliefs, and practices of our friends and co-workers in the Diaspora, we should know the basics of Christianity, some of its different articulations, and how it might affect the priorities, ideals, and politics of the people around us.

But even in Israel, where the other half of the Jews in the world today live, we have an obligation to seek out engagement with Christians. While Christians comprise only a very small portion of the Israeli population (about equal percentage-wise to the proportion of Jews in America), as a Jewish majority we have a special responsibility to understand and develop respect for the minority religions and ethnicities in the Jewish state. It is especially because Christians are so easily overlooked here as a minority within a minority that Israelis must be intentional about learning about local Christian culture and religion.

Related to the importance of understanding our neighbors is a second reason: the need to understand and participate in the West in general. Christianity has been foundational to the development of Western civilization. And while secularization and modernization might have rendered that influence less obvious today than it was in the past, it can hardly be underestimated. To understand the West—whether as political theory, art, literature, philosophy, architecture, or history—we need to understand something about Christianity. For Jews to be responsible, active citizens of Western countries and participants in shaping modern Western civilization, we need know something about the basic narratives, values, and history of Christianity. It is an essential piece for our ability to engage shared challenges together, as citizens of an increasingly pluralistic and secular West. If we want a voice at the table, we need to at least understand the language being spoken there.

Third, it is important for Jews to remember that the State of Israel—which is so important to us for reasons that can be at the same time theological, cultural, communal, and emotional—also elicits a great deal of complex response among Christians. That Christian response strives to understand the State of Israel, but with different lenses from our own, those of Christian categories, scripture, historical experience, and anxieties. On the ground it also means that the State of Israel finds at the same time both its staunchest supporters and some of its strongest critics from within the Christian world. If Jews want to understand or engage with how Christians think about Israel, which includes everything from Christian movements pushing for boycott and divestment from Israel (BDS) to active Christian Zionist support for Israel, we need to know something about Christianity. And equally if we wish to communicate something about Israel to Christians—about our own hopes and dreams and fears for the Jewish state—we need to be able to do so in a way that can make sense for a Christian audience. That requires both knowledge and some real understanding.

Fourth: The relationship between Jews and Christians, and between Judaism and Christianity, has been active for 2,000 years. It has been a challenging and even bitter relationship, one that has included persecution and significant mutual hostility. Yet we stand now in a new kind of relationship that has emerged over the last century: one of growing trust, education, understanding, engagement, and alliance. It is by no means a perfect relationship. Nor can we rush to call something this young a "revolution," notwithstanding the revolution that has indeed taken place within much Christian theology and teaching concerning the Jews. But I do believe that this change, taking place little by little, allows room for significant optimism. Both Jews and Christians need to become better acquainted with the deep, careful, respectful kind of Christian re-thinking about Jews and Judaism that has characterized Western Christianity, especially in the wake of the Holocaust. If Jews and Christians can learn something about resolving our long-standing, deep-seated mutual hostilities, then we might turn to that as a positive model for other communities and ideologies in conflict.

***

Finally, a modest theological argument: We should remember the big picture. Jews are entrusted with the essential mission of being God's chosen people, to be the particular node of the single, universal God.

Without doubt, Jews thinking, talking, worrying, educating, and engaging with other Jews is an essential part of this. We must know who we are and be stable enough, both in numbers and in identity, to fulfill our mission. But we should also not mistake the need to survive quantitatively and qualitatively with the mission itself. Survival is indeed necessary, but it is not sufficient. We are, in the image of the prophet Isaiah, to serve as a guide to humanity, a "light to the nations," so that a knowledge of the one true God can reach all peoples.

That is a tall order, and the re-entry of the Jewish people onto the world stage, as an actor and not just an entity that is acted upon, is still pretty recent. How do we engage the world, as Jews?

For us to envision the possibilities and dangers along that path, we can usefully look to Christianity. It is in Christianity that the basic narrative, categories, expectation, scripture, worship, and hopes of the people and God of Israel have met the non-Jewish world, so far in history. In many cases that meeting went tragically wrong, most especially when Christianity forgot its Jewish roots. But in our time, attention to Jewish-Christian relations can help us imagine what that encounter might look like—and what it must *not* look like—when the People of Israel, the Torah of Israel, and the God of Israel are understood to be in dialogue, communion, and engagement with the rest of the world.

51

THE RIGHT WAY TO COMMEMORATE THE HOLOCAUST

By Using It to Reclaim Our Nationhood

NATAN SHARANSKY & GIL TROY

A FEW YEARS AGO, mid-career professionals from Israel and the American Jewish community met in Auschwitz. The Israelis wrapped themselves in the blue-and-white flag, emphasizing the "Never Again" message they learned in school, that Jews would never be helpless again.

Natan Sharansky was a political prisoner in the Soviet Union, served in four Israeli cabinets including as deputy prime minister, and served as the chairman of the Jewish Agency for Israel. He is a recipient of the Congressional Gold Medal, Presidential Medal of Freedom, and the Israel Prize, and author of the New York Times bestselling The Case for Democracy: The Power of Freedom to Overcome Tyranny and Terror (PublicAffairs, 2009) and Fear No Evil (Random House, 1988).

Gil Troy is a distinguished scholar of North American history at McGill University, an American presidential historian, and a Zionist activist. He is the author or editor of nine books on presidential history and four books on Zionism, including Theodor Herzl (LJP, 2022) and The Zionist Ideas (JPS, 2018). Sharansky and Troy also co-authored Never Alone: Prison, Politics, and My People (PublicAffairs, 2020).

The Americans bristled. They wondered why so divisive a nationalist symbol like a flag should be imposed on such a holy place—reflecting the "Never Again" message *they* had learned, which was that never again should the world let nationalism degenerate into evil.

In our either-or world, the 300-year-old power struggle between universalists and particularists has become particularly heated. Those who imagine themselves as citizens of the world dismiss proud nationalists as bigoted xenophobes, while those who see themselves as grounded patriots mock universalists as naïve traitors.

This tension, indeed, underlies the most serious internal clashes among Jews today. Israelis often see liberal American Jews as too universalist, while Israelis are deemed too particularist, too provincial. Reform Jews see Orthodox Jews as too narrow-minded, while Orthodox Jews fear Reform Jews are so open-minded their brains will fall out. And within Israel, voters on the Right sneer at left-wingers as unpatriotic saps, while left-wingers mourn the mainstreaming of demagogic bigots.

In truth, when any one of these combatants veers too far to one extreme or the other, they often prove their critics to be right. In an increasingly divided Jewish community, more and more battling zealots fail to appreciate the balanced, nuanced, 3,000-year-old Jewish teaching, reinforced by modern Zionism: that if we look out for ourselves in just the right way, we not only help ourselves—we help others too.

In what follows, we refer to this balanced form of particularism as "good nationalism." It lies at the heart of the Zionist enterprise, but it exists in other nations and contexts as well, and offers a model that can help us find a way out of some of the most acute narrative conflicts in our world.

***

Every new attempt to commemorate the Holocaust raises the same fundamental question: How do we acknowledge the unique horrors of this crime, which so clearly targeted the Jewish people, while drawing broader lessons for all of humanity? It is clear that the Nazis launched a war against the Jews, making the Shoah a uniquely Jewish story. But it is equally clear that the

Nazis committed crimes against humanity, which some bad actors, refusing to learn the obvious lessons, have mimicked—in Rwanda, Bosnia, and Darfur. In short, most Jews understand that we cannot keep this story to ourselves, even though it is about us.

Thousands of miles from America and Israel, this dilemma has haunted the complicated $100-million project that began in 2016 to commemorate the mass slaughter of more than 33,000 Jews in just two blood-soaked days at Babyn Yar just outside Kiev.

The machine-gunning of so many innocents on September 29 and 30, 1941, ranks as one of the ugliest of Nazi crimes. Over the next two and a half years, the Nazis and their Ukrainian henchmen added at least another 70,000 corpses to their Satanic pile, making Babyn Yar the Holocaust's largest mass grave. And yet, the Soviet Communists covered up these monstrous crimes, even starting to build a stadium on that sacred site.

Over the decades, Babyn Yar became a powerful symbol of that universalist regime's desire to bury the Holocaust, so as not to stir up any Jewish nationalism. This blatant erasure effort was characteristic of the Soviet approach to history, identity, diversity, and free thought. Eventually, the Soviets did build a monument on the site—but failed to mention the Jews, even though over 90,000 of the people the Nazis murdered there were Jews.

The leaders of a now free, independent Ukraine understand the importance of remembering the Holocaust and specifically commemorating Babyn Yar, but it's complicated. Alongside the questions of universal versus Jewish narratives, any Holocaust museum must also engage with its host country's own particular national narrative—and nowhere is this more sensitive than in the countries Adolf Hitler conquered.

In 2016, one of us (Natan) was asked to chair an international board to build the Babyn Yar Holocaust Memorial Center, which is still on track to become the world's largest Holocaust museum. The committee has worked hard to keep the narrative clear. Every future visitor to this site must learn that this Einsatzgruppen massacre, this Holocaust by bullets, was one of the many ugly expressions of Hitler's antisemitic war against the Jews.

At the same time, while honoring the 2,600 righteous Ukrainian gentiles who saved Jews, the museum also must acknowledge the many Ukrainians who collaborated with the Nazis. The problem of how to cope with the legacy of collaborators continues to stick in European throats, be it in Poland, Lithuania, or France.

Many Ukrainian politicians and public intellectuals said they were willing to engage in the required historical accounting, but they insisted that their nation's story be told in context. Initially, the Nazis appeared to many Ukrainians to be liberators who would save them from Soviet Communism. "You cannot understand why many nationalists collaborated in Nazi crimes against the Jews without acknowledging Communist crimes against us," they explained.

To Ukrainians, perhaps the cruelest of many Soviet crimes was the Holodomor, the infamous terror-famine that began in 1931. Josef Stalin's collectivization campaign penned tens of millions of peasants into unproductive, unfree Kolkhozes, and triggered mass manmade misery. Some estimate that as many as six million Ukrainians starved to death, died from disease, or were purged by the KGB. Since 2006, at least fifteen other countries have joined Ukraine in recognizing this horror as an intentional genocide, seeking to break the Ukrainian people's independent spirit.

"We understand the trauma of the Holocaust," some leading Ukrainians explained, "so let's have one museum exploring and commemorating these crimes together." These Ukrainian nationalists also challenged the museum's original vision, saying, "It's hypocritical to cry 'Never Again,' but then reduce the Holocaust to an exclusively Jewish story."

They were half right. "Never Again" is a call to the world, not just a battle cry for Jews. It is a challenge to the future more than it is an interpretation of the past. There are important moral lessons to teach the world—lessons that too often have been ignored.

Still, those of us on the Holocaust Memorial Center's international committee had to explain why this false equivalence was misleading. Although both Nazism and Soviet Communism were criminal, they were different kinds of awful. Clumping both evils together risked distorting Hitler's crimes— and Stalin's. Such historical sloppiness minimized the racist nature of Nazi genocide, which determined who could live and who could die based on the purity of their blood. It also minimized the totalitarian nature of the supposedly egalitarian Communist dictatorship, which determined who could live and who could die based on class and cooperation with the regime. So, yes, we acknowledged to the Ukrainian parliament, in the media and elsewhere, that both crimes must be unmasked and dissected—but each in its own way.

The Ukrainian leadership accepted this argument. Eventually, we developed a common vision for the Holocaust memorial, which is slated to have nearly thirty exhibits reflecting different dimensions of the Nazi war against the Jews. A final exhibition will broaden the story to explore subsequent attempts at genocide in the decades since the war.

**

Vladimir Putin's brutal invasion of Ukraine in February 2022 shook that common vision, while also shattering the museum's timetable. As evidence of Russian soldiers' mass rapes and mass murders accumulated, as the international community launched formal inquiries to clarify whether Russia and Putin were guilty of genocide, the pressure for the museum to highlight these crimes against Ukrainians intensified.

It became obvious to all of us that once the war ended and the project resumed, it would indeed be difficult not to spotlight Russian barbarism as proof that so many failed to learn the Holocaust's most compelling moral lessons.

In the spring and summer of 2022, the museum made two dramatic moves that reflected the "good nationalism" Jews have long lived by—and which helped the Zionist movement succeed.

Good nationalism begins with the understanding that you fight for freedom throughout the world by fighting for your freedom as a nation. And so, this Holocaust museum-in-formation decided to help document this Ukrainian-genocide-in-the-making. Software developed to track Jewish martyrs who were killed eight decades ago would now be used to track new Ukrainian victims today. And at the same time, the museum enlisted Father Patrick Desbois, who had spent decades looking for Nazi-era Jewish mass graves in the former Soviet Union, to help find and document evidence of

Russian-inflicted genocide in Ukraine, building a case against the perpetrators.

And so, while the Russian invasion made it harder to keep the Babyn Yar memorial exclusively Jewish, it made it easier for the Western world to distinguish between the good nationalism that motivates people to defend themselves and others—and Putin's bad nationalism.

For too long now, many on the Far Left and Far Right have misread nationalism as exclusively a tool of mass aggression. The new populists in Europe and the United States indulge in self-sanctioned xenophobia; their illiberal rivals on the Left repudiate nationalism in general, charging all Western nationalists with the intersecting crimes of racism, imperialism, and colonialism.

The division, however, is not as clean as the shouting matches make it sound. The Far Left has embraced identity politics—an inherently particularistic endeavor—quite aggressively. In practice, many progressive extremists somehow justify certain forms of nationalism they deem sacred, from Black Lives Matter to the Palestinian cause, as well as other particularist causes like trans rights.

These faux-universalists rationalize their particularisms by simply not associating the word "nationalism" with their causes. Increasingly, the Far Left only uses the word as a slur against Donald Trump and other enemies—while adding modifiers, as in "white nationalism," "populist nationalism," or the boogeyman of the moment, "ethno-nationalism."

But when, in February 2022, as so many in the West cheered Ukrainian nationalism when pitted against Russian aggression, the Ukrainians' valiant resistance gave new life to the word "nationalism." Outnumbered and outgunned, the Ukrainians impressed the world by not being out-motivated. They demonstrated once again that you cannot defend freedom purely in the abstract; it has to be done country by country, repelling border attack by border attack.

Scrambling, many observers ended up trying to universalize this kind of nationalism. Their verbal acrobatics helped rehabilitate the term—but mischaracterized both Ukrainian nationalism and what made it constructive. The "Responsible Statecraft" blog, written by a former U.S. intelligence official named Paul R. Pillar, praised "the nationalism that Ukrainians are displaying today in resisting Russian aggression." But Pillar defined this "good" nationalism as "loyalty to the entire nation-state rather than any one demographic group within it. It is inclusive rather than exclusive." And in March 2022, the veteran *New York Times* reporter Steven Erlanger condemned Putin's "ethno-nationalism," as "an idea of nationhood and identity based on language, culture and blood" in "contrast to the Western idea of a multicultural state built on civic responsibility, the rule of law and individual rights." To "Putin's opponents in Ukraine and the West," Erlanger claimed, "nations are built on civic responsibility, the rule of law and the rights of individuals and minorities, including free expression and a free vote."

True, liberal-democracies protect rights and freedoms, but they often have a tribal dimension, too. Ukrainian nationalism, like most nationalisms today, is deeply rooted in Ukrainian nationhood. It is indeed based, at least partially, on "language, culture and blood."

Human beings are tribal. Most like to feel connected to a place, a story, a culture, a people—essentially, their home and their community. The democratic challenge is not to negate tribalism, but to make tribalism transcendent.

Tribal nationalisms—rooted in pride, history, identity, language, culture, and geography—can be constructive or destructive. They need to be exclusive enough to help the majority bond and inclusive enough to give the minority not just rights but dignity. The true test for liberal-democratic nationalism is not whether it connects with a specific people and land, but how much freedom and how many rights the people enjoy within the national entity, regardless of their connection to the defining national story.

For dictators like Putin, nationalism is a tool for imperial aggression and internal repression; for democracies like that of Ukraine in recent years, nationalism is a tool for national liberation and internal satisfaction, as citizens exercise and defend their freedom in their homeland. That is why the Ukrainian fight for good nationalism is in the interest of the Free World.

And that is why the Ukrainians invoke the Israeli example of fellow good nationalists fighting for freedom against unfair enemies. As President Volodymyr Zelenskyy himself put it, "If Israel can do it, we can too."

***

Nationalism is a neutral tool. Jews themselves experienced nationalism at its most murderous in the 1940s under Nazism, and at its most liberating in 1948 through Zionism. The liberal-democratic nationalism developed in the United States overlaps with the younger form of liberal-democratic nationalism developed in Israel. Both are inspired by the story of the ancient Israelites, a single coherent nation that would, in the words of Leviticus, "declare freedom in the land to all its inhabitants."

But they are not the same. At its purest, American nationalism emphasizes what is called civic nationalism, giving everyone individual rights, creating "one out of many." Nevertheless, American nationalism has long been fueled by a passionate commitment to "America" and "Americanism" that often approximates ethnic nationalism.

Similarly, at its purest, Zionism seems to be ethnic or Jewish nationalism, committed to building a Jewish state by the Jews for the Jews. But the diversity of the Jewish people, the mix of Jews and non-Jews enjoying equal citizenship in the State of Israel, and the broad democratic rights all Israeli citizens enjoy puts Israel more in line with civic nationalism.

Ultimately, both Americanism and Zionism are constructive forms of liberal-democratic nationalism, because they have created countries that are part of that small, mostly-Western club of democracies producing leaders responsive to the people's needs rather than peoples enslaved to a dictator's demands.

Judaism has long intertwined identity and freedom—what today we call particularism and universalism. The call of Sinai is to look out for one another, and to create a model society for humanity. Every Friday night, Jews bless the wine by remembering the God of Creation, who rested after six busy days of creating the world; and the God of Israel, who made the Jews a free people by delivering us from slavery in Egypt.

When he formally launched the Zionist movement at the First Zionist Congress in 1897, Theodor Herzl built on that delightfully mixed legacy. "We are a people, one people," he had written in his 1896 manifesto *The Jewish State.* And clearly, he saw the Jewish State as a refuge, a response to the endemic antisemitism that Europe's Enlightenment and Emancipation had made worse. But as a romantic liberal-nationalist, he demonstrated just how liberal nationalism could synthesize, redeeming both a people and the world. Calling patriotically for Jews to be proud, modern Maccabees, he concluded: "We are to live at last as free people on our own soil and die peacefully in our own homeland." Then he soared, as every liberal-nationalist should, building up universal hopes and values: "The world will be freed by our freedom, enriched by our riches, and made greater by our greatness."

Forty-four years after Herzl's tragic death at the age of forty-four, Israel's Declaration of Independence echoed that same balanced message. The 1948 Declaration, pulsating with particularism, anchors Israel in the Bible, the homeland, and the Jewish story. But, at the same time, resonating with universalism, the Declaration offers equal rights to all its "inhabitants"—both Jewish and non-Jewish. And the second line defines the Bible as both a national and international treasure, saying that in the Land of Israel, the Jewish people "first attained to statehood, created cultural ideas of national and universal significance, and gave to the world the eternal Book of Books."

More recently, both of us have championed a Zionism that fights broadly for freedom by embracing our identity. And when one of us (Gil) created a Zionist anthology, *The Zionist Ideas*, in 2018, he searched for a single Zionist text that was purely defensive, that just sought a kind of narrow-minded normalcy—but failed to find even one. Jewish values, the Zionist ideas, are so catalytic, so idealistic, they can never leave the rest of the world as is. In the Bible, this vision challenged the Israelites to be a "light unto nations," which, of course, first required a strong sense of nationhood to generate that light. The traditional Aleinu prayer calls for "repairing the world within God's kingdom," which also challenges Jews to go forth and repair the ills of the world, while remaining true to their own tradition. And Israelis today often translate that rich dueling but essentially reinforcing heritage into a vision of developing a *hevra l'mofet*—an exemplary society.

Here, then, is a pressing mission for the Jewish people, too. It starts with preserving the historical integrity of the Holocaust, emphasizing that it was a uniquely anti-Jewish crime teaching powerful lessons for all to learn.

Every one of us benefits by staying rooted in our story, proud of our land, committed to our people, ready to defend and perfect our country. But a healthy patriotism, a constructive liberal-democratic nationalism, naturally bubbles over, offering a model to the world, inspiration to others and, ultimately, protection to all who value freedom.

Nations are like people: If you don't stand up for yourself, you have no spine; but if you don't stand up for others, you have no soul. We all need both.

52

THE JEWEL IN THE CROWN OF JEWISH EDUCATION

The Power of History to Shape Our Kids' Identity

LAURA SHAW FRANK

IT WAS TIME to teach the Uganda Plan. As a young Jewish history teacher at a large American Jewish community day school, I was teaching our required twelfth-grade History of Zionism and Israel course, and I was troubled.

Laura Shaw Frank, Ph.D., is the National Director of the William Petschek Contemporary Jewish Life Department at American Jewish Committee (AJC) where she works on the thriving of the American Jewish community. Laura completed her doctorate in Jewish history from the University of Maryland and has undergraduate and law degrees from Columbia University.

On the one hand, Theodor Herzl's fleeting idea in 1903 to accept a British offer for land in East Africa as a temporary Jewish homeland to save the endangered Jews of Eastern Europe was a mere blip on the radar screen of Zionist history. On the other hand, it loomed large for me because it represented an enormous question that seemed to come up over and over again in Jewish history: Should we save Judaism or should we save Jews? While the two usually did not contradict, in some particularly heart-wrenching situations like the case of the Uganda Plan, they did.

What was more important in 1903—continuing to work on the elusive goal of obtaining the Land of Israel, the Jewish ancestral homeland, for the Jews, or obtaining an immediate solution that might save the lives of the Jews of the Russian Empire in the immediate moment?

Teaching the Uganda Plan felt important, but I knew from past years that the students had little patience for the topic. As safe and secure twenty-first-century American Jews, they could not imagine the dire circumstances in which early twentieth-century Russian Jews found themselves. On top of that, living in a world in which Israel was an established fact, they simply could not understand why Herzl would think it was a good idea to establish a Jewish state on a piece of land to which the Jews had no connection. No matter how I tried to explain the context, their eyes would glaze over and they would simply tune out.

I decided to throw my teaching notes out the window. I divided the students into groups and gave them primary sources to read. I tasked them with coming up with speeches to defend their positions. The students huddled together, reading the sources, the room humming with their preparation.

When I called on them to present, magic happened. As students began to make their arguments to the class, they became so impassioned that they, just like those early Zionists at the Sixth Zionist Congress in 1903, literally began yelling at each other. One group insisted that we hold out for the Land of Israel, another insisted that the highest priority of the moment had to be saving Jewish lives. The third group, representing the voices of most of those endangered Russian Jews, was the most powerful: Despite their precarious situation, they objected with all their hearts to the Uganda Plan. They wanted only the Land of Israel. Nothing else would suffice.

At the end of the class, I explained that in the end, the objections of the Russian Jews won the day, scuttling the Uganda Plan once and for all. "It's complicated," one student told me as she walked out the door to her next class. "I actually think the Russian Jews needed the hope of the Land of Israel even more than they needed the safety of an immediate place to go."

I understood at that moment that my students got it. They had stepped into the shoes of the Jews of the past with empathy. Their understanding of those complicated circumstances long ago would no doubt inform their understanding of similar complications in their own times.

*　*　*

The magic that occurred that day in my twelfth-grade classroom was not a one-off. Over the nearly twenty years I have spent as a Jewish history educator, I have seen again and again the unique power of Jewish history to connect Jews of all backgrounds and beliefs to Judaism and the Jewish people.

In the Jewish history classroom, young Jews see how the Jewish past helped shape their Jewish identities today. Students learn that their difficult questions about Jewish identity were asked by others in the past. They see that their questions do not remove them from their people, but rather are part of a vibrant Jewish conversation that is centuries old. Students bring their difficult questions about religion and faith and examine them from a less emotionally charged and more dispassionate perspective through situating religious thinkers in historical context.

Most of all, students see the resilience of their people, who have been knocked down countless times over millennia but continue to get up again and offer the world brave new ideas and staggering creativity.

The Jewish history classroom helps students see themselves as part of something larger than themselves, something we now know is intrinsic to emotional health and well-being. It speaks to the religious and the secular, the activist and the scholar, even the Zionist and the anti-Zionist. Whatever type of Jew a student is, Jewish history has riches to offer them.

An email I received from one of my Jewish history students years ago says it all: "I learned more about being a Jew in the contemporary world than I have in any other class," he wrote. "You have single-handedly eradicated any indifference I had toward my Jewish identity." Jewish history is the silver bullet of Jewish education. It has unparalleled power to engage a new generation of young people with Jewish peoplehood and tradition.

The examples leap from the curriculum. When students study the Roman destruction of the Second Temple in 70 C.E., they come to understand the elasticity and resilience of a Jewish religion that morphed from being Temple-based to being synagogue- and study-based, while remaining firmly rooted in and connected to its origins, rituals, and beliefs. This idea is reinforced again and again as they study the emergence of movements such as Hasidism, Reform Judaism, and Zionism, each of which answered in different ways questions of what Jews needed to keep Judaism alive. Learning about these movements cannot help but sow the seeds of students' own creativity when it comes to keeping Judaism vibrant in the twenty-first century.

Similarly, when students study the *conversos* of the fifteenth and sixteenth centuries who secretly held onto their Jewish identities, sometimes for generations, before being able to live openly as Jews again, they see a version of themselves—Jews who circulate in a non-Jewish world with Jewish identities that are often private. The seeds that are planted in their minds to consider actively what it means to have a Jewish identity that is private rather than public is instrumental to their self-conception as adult Jews.

These are only a handful of the countless ways that Jewish history invests our students with the knowledge, critical thinking skills, and drive to be a part of the Jewish future.

And yet, Jewish history is a severely neglected subject in Jewish education, at least in America. Most Jewish educational institutions—whether supplementary schools or day schools—teach little to no Jewish history, focusing curricular time instead on Jewish text study, Hebrew language acquisition, and prayer skills. If Jewish history is taught at all, frequently the only periods that receive attention are the Holocaust and the founding of Israel.

What a terrible, shortsighted mistake. To right the ship of Jewish education, to make it relevant and captivating for students, we must teach Jewish history in all its fullness, covering the grand sweep of millennia and enabling students to see its powerful relevance to their lives today.

***

Why is Jewish history so absent from our classrooms? When pressed, Jewish education administrators give several reasons.

First, many note the lack of time in the schedule. They already don't have enough time for the subjects they do teach, they argue. Second, they don't have the faculty. In supplementary schools, finding faculty is itself challenging, but at least the requisite knowledge needed to teach the very basic Judaism and Hebrew in the curriculum is fairly minimal; educators who live reasonably active Jewish lives and attended Hebrew school themselves can probably do it.

Jewish history, by contrast, requires background that most do not have. In day schools, Bible and Talmud faculty typically have studied these subjects intensively in yeshivot, midrashot, or rabbinical schools. Hebrew-language faculty are typically native Hebrew speakers who utilize well-thought-out standardized curricula like NETA. Where should a school seek faculty who have studied Jewish history?

The real fundamental barrier, however, lies in administrators' ambivalence about the importance of teaching Jewish history.

It is true that time is in short supply in Jewish education. North American supplementary schools have their students two to four hours per week at the most, and the vast majority of those students leave after their bar or bat mitzvahs. Educators in these programs focus on basic knowledge about Jewish holidays and Israel, and on teaching how to read Hebrew so their students can chant a portion of the Torah or Haftarah for their bar or bat mitzvahs. As American Jewry becomes more and more assimilated, Jewish children are not receiving mimetic Jewish education in their homes, and the only space where they will learn about prayer, ritual, and Israel is in supplementary school.

Day schools obviously have more time in their schedules for Judaic studies, but many day school administrators still maintain that there is no time in the curriculum for standalone Jewish history courses. Day schools are tasked with turning out highly educated young Jews while still offering rigorous college preparatory secular studies, all during a school day that already ends hours after public schools dismiss their students. Once they have devoted three to six hours a week each to the Bible, Talmud, and Hebrew, they simply cannot squeeze in another "Jewish" class. The Bible and Talmud are the "real" Judaic subjects in the eyes of most Jewish educators; Jewish history does not make the cut. Some day schools integrate Jewish history into general history classes, which is better than nothing, but does not allow for substantial conversations about Jewish identity and Jewish communal concerns to take place. The one place where robust Jewish history education can be found, in the form of standalone required courses, is in a select few non-denominational community Jewish day schools, who alone have learned the importance of Jewish history in fostering enduring Jewish identity for their diverse student body.

Administrators are correct that there is, indeed, a serious lack of Jewish educators who have the background and familiarity with Jewish history to teach it. Finding supplementary school teachers of any stripe is challenging. The wages and prestige are low, and the task is incredibly difficult. Day school teachers know what a Bible or Talmud classroom looks like because they, too, had such classes growing up. Not so with Jewish history. Unless they studied Jewish history in college, or even better than that, pursued graduate work in the subject, teachers generally feel ill-equipped to teach Jewish history. Not only that, but even with some background, educators struggle with understanding the how and why of the Jewish history classroom: What purpose should the class play in the curriculum? The lack of familiarity feeds on itself; no one learned Jewish history growing up, so no one has thought about how to teach Jewish history to the next generation.

These issues are challenging, to be sure, but are easily solved with rebalancing curricula and offering robust and high-level training on a national level for Jewish history educators. But the fact remains that even if time and available faculty were in abundance, many Jewish educational programs would not include a standalone Jewish history class because they feel that Jewish history is simply *not as important as other subjects.*

This attitude is rooted in ignorance of the power of Jewish history to forge enduring Jewish identity. True, Bible and Talmud study transmits our people's foundational stories, rich traditions, and profound culture of intellectual and moral inquiry. Learning Jewish prayer and cantillation is central to feeling a sense of comfort and belonging in synagogue. And, of course, the study of the Hebrew language connects us to our textual tradition as well as to our homeland of Israel.

But many students, particularly the non-Orthodox—or frankly anyone struggling with Judaism as a faith-based religion—may have trouble connecting with the Bible, Talmud, and liturgy; and Hebrew, without the input of history and culture, is just another foreign language. Only dedicated Jewish history education has the unique power to root our students in the story of the Jewish people and foster in them the passion to be a part of that story.

I am not suggesting that Jewish history be taught in a moralistic fashion, with pat conclusions served pre-packaged to students. Quite the contrary; the Jewish history classroom can and must represent a space for critical thinking. As the master history educator Sam Wineburg put it:

> The study of history should be a mind-altering encounter that leaves one forever unable to consider the social world without asking questions about where a claim comes from, who's making it, and how time and place shape human behavior.

Jewish history students should learn to examine the Jewish past and present through these critical lenses, asking themselves how to interpret the past and how to understand the present.

Never has this been more important than today, when students face a constant barrage of rhetoric on social media that not only oversimplifies historical events related to the Jewish people and Israel, but actively seeks to brainwash and indoctrinate. Jewish history studies give them the skills they need to think critically about what they see and the ability to contextualize and interpret it for others in their communities. Investing our students with the critical thinking skills of the Jewish history classroom will nurture their ability to be the Jewish leaders of tomorrow, leaders who can assess our challenges and strengths, and think strategically about fostering a thriving Jewish future.

***

It is for this reason that it is not only insufficient, but actually detrimental, for the only Jewish history in the curriculum to be the study of the Holocaust and the founding of Israel.

I understand the impetus to focus on these two monumental events in Jewish history. They each had an immeasurable impact on the Jewish people that continues to reverberate today, and they are recent enough that students feel more of a direct connection to them.

But we make an enormous mistake when we think that teaching the Holocaust and the founding of Israel fulfills the goal of teaching Jewish history. Leaving aside the dubious educational decision to focus on a mere fifteen years out of millennia of history, teaching only these two seismic events presents a story of the Jewish people that is unlikely to resonate with young Jews: The Jewish people are the people who is tortured and killed, and because of our dark history, we need a State of Israel to escape to when things get bad.

If all we can say about Jewish identity is that being Jewish means being a victim, why would anyone young want to be Jewish? And if all we can say about Israel is that it is a refuge for endangered Jews, why should it have meaning to American Jews today?

In addition, teaching the State of Israel as an answer to the Holocaust, which is so often the implicit or even explicit narrative that emerges from a narrow focus on these two events, eradicates the incredible history of the rise of Zionism in the nineteenth century and the idealistic young Jews who fought for a Judaism that was not rooted in victimhood. It also begs the question: Now that there is no more genocide being perpetrated against the Jews, do we really need a state of our own?

A full and rich Jewish history curriculum that exposes students to the connections that Jews maintained with the Land of Israel over nearly two millennia of exile and to the emergence of complex philosophies of Zionism fosters students' ownership of their own relationships with Israel. At a time when the very term Zionism is increasingly misunderstood, criticized, and even rejected, we owe it to our students to give them an education that will allow them to process the discourse around them from a position of knowledge and understanding.

Jewish history must be studied in all its fullness. Jewish children who learn about the history of our people see a people that has unbelievable creativity and resilience, a people who have brought so many of the central ideas of humanity to the world, who have held on to their faith and tradition against truly unbelievable odds. A people who resurrected a language not spoken for 2,000 years and made it dance with the vitality of modern life, with sentences made up of Arabic slang and ancient Biblical terms all mashed up together. Who wouldn't want to be a part of this history?

If we want to keep our young people connected to Judaism, if we care about the vibrancy of the Jewish future in America, Jewish history should be the jewel in the crown of Jewish education. Prioritizing the teaching of the Jewish past is critical to a thriving Jewish present and future. It is time to think broadly and holistically about Jewish education. It is time to be brave and visionary about what our students need. It is time to train teachers, rearrange schedules, and insist that our students receive the education that will help the Jewish people flourish for millennia to come.

53

LET'S GET BACK TO SMASHING IDOLS

The Worship of Power Is More Dangerous Than Ever

SCOTT A. SHAY

ACCORDING TO ANCIENT LEGEND, the story of the Jews began with Abraham smashing idols. In the various rabbinic retellings of the story, Abraham's contemporaries saw his toppling of these objects of worship as unbelievable, astonishing, liberating, revolutionary, and most of all, so threatening to the existing power structure that the king of the realm thought Abraham should be executed. According to the legend, Abraham spent thirteen years in hiding trying to evade capture.

Scott A. Shay is the author of *Conspiracy U: A Case Study* (Wicked Son, 2021) and *In Good Faith: Questioning Religion and Atheism* (Post Hill Press, 2018).

Abraham's destruction of idols is a seen as a turning point in world history—the Bible is nothing if not a thousand-page assault on polytheistic idolatry, and Abraham is the father of all monotheists. Yet the rejection of idolatry has lost its meaning to most Jews and most people today. Unlike injustice or racism, it is not something that we think needs fighting. It is not in the repertoire of our noble aspirations. It is disregarded in the halls of the academy as well as in the voting booth and the streets of protest. The Bible's primary message sadly no longer has any resonance. This is a tragic and colossal failing of both Jewish education and Jewish intellectual life in our time.

Most people, including those who should know better like our public intellectuals and political, economic, and cultural influencers, cannot define idolatry. If anything, it is ignored as a judgmental misunderstanding of traditional cultures, a remnant of a Western imperialism with its zeal of assimilating indigenous peoples. Yet we misidentify idolatry at our own peril.

Idolatry is not about outlawing other cultures or about ceremonial protocols like bowing down and chanting in front of statues. Idolatry is a profound statement about the nature of the world and of good and evil. Idolatry has always been and remains the most divisive and dangerous ideology in the world.

Simply put, idolatry is a set of lies about power. It falsely attributes superpower and super authority to finite beings. Left unchecked, it leads to all the injustices we identify more commonly like chattel slavery, racism, oppression, and totalitarianism. In fact, idolatry is the conceptual root of all this evil.

For those who are willing to read it, the Bible's primary theme is describing the dangers of idolatry in an accessible and yet multifaceted way. Rather than define the concept in philosophical jargon, the Bible, as it often does, offers us vignettes of idolatry in action.

For example, in the story of the Exodus, the Bible stresses that the pharaoh could enslave whomever he wanted, kill whomever he wanted, and terrorize his own population by reproducing the plagues simply to show he could. He did all this because in his own eyes and that of his people, he was a god. Above other humans, he was not accountable to or responsible for them. The lie of his superpower was maintained through pomp, song, parades, assemblies, and all manner of festivals (the midrash even recounts that he would relieve himself in the Nile to conceal this very human action). This theater persuaded the masses of his power. Of course, his fictitious superpowers were also buttressed, as the Bible describes, by real power in the form of an army, a network of secret informers, and court magicians. But loyalty from all these groups came from the foundational lie of his special status, as well as the pharaoh's own willingness to kill anyone who got in his way. This belief affected not only Egypt; it served as the justification for conquest and war. As a self-imagined god, the pharaoh declares in the Bible that he is not subject to other powers, as he exclaims: "Who is the Lord that I should listen to him and let Israel go? I don't know about the Lord, nor will I let Israel go!" (Exodus 5:2).

Jewish tradition demands that on Passover we internalize having personally left Egypt, not as a folkloric exercise, but as a warning. The fantastic violence and intensity depicted in the Exodus story can be understood only in the context of the power of idolatry as a force in the world. Some commentators have asserted God did not harden the pharaoh's heart to take away his free will, but rather to strengthen it, to give him the resolve that aligned with his conviction of his own godly place in the world. In following through with his convictions, he destroyed his own country. When my father, a Holocaust survivor, would sit at the Passover Seder table, I was deeply aware that the exercise to imagine that we have personally left Egypt was not an arcane request. He knew what it was to be a slave laborer, and to have his family murdered at the whim of a god-king.

Pharaohs have resurfaced throughout history and, most recently with technology, have evolved into being ever more terrifying. Hitler was deified by even his closest in command, who, as one historian describes it, tried to anticipate his will. He appeared in posters and postcards with the iconography of Jesus or a god. His elevated status was confirmed by great parades captured by Leni Riefenstahl on film. With this superpower attributed to him, he enslaved and murdered tens of millions of people and willingly let Germany itself go down in flames. Josef Stalin, another pharaoh, had the Soviet space agency project his image into the sky. His rivals in the Communist party were liquidated in the Great Purge, and the NKVD, Red Army, and bureaucracy were subordinated to his will. Like Hitler, with no checks on the power he was granted, he created camps of slavery and death such as the Gulag. The North Korean dissident Yeonmi Park describes how the word "love" in Korean is now limited to description of the citizens' relationship to the supreme leader Kim Jong-un, who is represented in a giant statue in Pyongyang, and who does not hesitate to starve his population and endanger the world through nuclear war.

Yet despite these open references to the supernatural, we use terms like "tyranny," "totalitarianism," or "dictatorship" to describe these regimes, and "mass murder" or "genocide" to denounce their heinous deeds. The closest we have come in calling these regimes what they are at the root is through words like "cult": the cult of the Fuehrer, Stalin's personality cult, or the cult of the Kims. But we fail as Jews to point out the deification, the lies about power, the in-your-face pervasive, inescapable, idolatry of it all.

* * *

The Bible, again, can be summed up as a revolutionary teaching against idolatry. In contrast to the myths of old, or the propaganda of modern totalitarian regimes, the Bible describes Adam—the prototypical human being—as created in God's image. This is the foundational opposite of idolatry. Man is both created and like God. He can partner with God, but is not a god.

The message God gives to Noah after the Flood elaborates on this point in the simplest but most profound terms. God commands him: "Whoever sheds human blood, by humans shall their blood be shed; for in the image of God has God made mankind" (Genesis 8:6). In other words, God affirms that man is equal and subordinate to a higher law governing his relations. The antithesis of idolatry is thus recognizing the image of God in each other and that none of us are gods. This is the social order of equality before the law that we should aspire to achieve.

I don't know many Jews or readers of the Bible who brandish this passage for the revolutionary meaning it conveys. But the Bible's emphasis on this is more foundational that the American Constitution or the Universal Declaration of Human Rights. It describes with unmatched precision the conditions under which these rights can exist. Indeed, if we were to take this message to heart, that we are truly created in the divine image, it follows that we are all brothers and sisters, which means we could admonish our fellow human beings but we could never oppress or dehumanize them. We would genuinely appreciate that each person has their unique contribution to make. But most of all, we would be armed against charismatic figures and cult leaders who wish to take away our freedom and our lives.

While the Bible expresses the truth about power—that omnipotence, omniscience, and omnipresence are God's alone—it also bears witness to the appeal of believing lies about it: the mirage of participating in being a god oneself, of escaping the justice and morality that the true God demands of us. The prophets who rail against the idolatry of the time from Amos to Jeremiah also bemoan the injustice and cruelty of their society. The appeal of Nazism fits this pattern perfectly. How intoxicating it is to believe that one is part of a superior race who then has the license to rule and use, abuse, and eliminate others as one pleases. There are plenty of historians who describe Nazism's enduring popularity among Germans even in the years after the war.

* * *

Idolatry is bad for everyone, but it is worth taking a moment to understand why its many adherents so often attack the Jews. Idolaters all know in their heart of hearts that there could be a bigger god somewhere that could topple their god. The ubiquitous censorship in idolatrous regimes is the direct result of this fear. Unsurprisingly, the Bible has often been among the first books to be censored or attacked, since it says that the God of Abraham is the One God of the entire world. In other words, if there is a Jewish God that is really big, *that* God needs to be defeated. What better way to achieve this than to defeat his people?

This reasoning appears in the Bible itself. The snake character of the third chapter of Genesis wishes to challenge God, but since he cannot do so directly, he goes after God's people, Adam and Eve. While Jews most often fail to live up to the ideals of the Bible, they still represent them at a basic level. This is why Jews have been persecuted by idolatrous leaders from antiquity to the present, even though Jews are rarely large enough in number to pose an actual threat to any nation.

The Bible's prohibition against idolatry is as timely a message as ever. While the defenders of Hitler, Stalin, and the Kims are relegated to the fringe, understanding worrisome trends in our global society through the lens of idolatry remains essential.

One of them is the issue of monopoly. The relationship between monopoly and idolatry is not accidental: A god-king must control or seem to be in control of everything. The god-king's monopoly goes hand and hand with his status of being above or the source of the law. A revolutionary feature of the biblical polity is the separation of powers between the kings, the prophets, and the priests. A king in biblical Israel could never be a god because he was subservient to the law like all other humans. By the time of the Second Temple, an independent judiciary had been added in the form of the Sanhedrin and its lower courts.

We are living in a time of an unprecedented monopolization of power in the economy. Some obvious examples are the concentration of dozens of industries, from banking and airlines to tech, in the hands of a few companies; or more classic examples like the Chinese Communist Party's control over huge sections of the world economy through their Belt and Road Initiative and their investments in Africa, or Putin's power (as of this writing) over the oligarchs of Russia. Some readers might find this comparison spurious since the CEOs of large American (or other) corporate monopolies don't seem to be taking over government functions and leading us to dictatorship. Nevertheless, their size and wealth are a cause of concern. As monopolies or oligopolies, they can leverage states to do their bidding on matters of regulation in addition to the impact of lobbying. As a result, citizens are less and less able to limit their abuses by laws and more likely to be victimized by them. Corrupt politicians naturally like having industries with few competitors. It is more profitable for such politicians to strike mutually enriching deals with a few massive firms than to do the hard work of devising and administering health, safety, and environmental policies for the best of all citizens. Citizens in democratic, free-market societies are repulsed by crony capitalism, since it kills both competition and voter power; whereas dictatorships, whatever their stripes, require economic monopolies.

Too much power concentrated in too few firms is something the biblical prophets would have vociferously opposed. They would have recognized that the over-concentration of economic power fundamentally stems from idolatry. None of the behavior of these state or corporate actors makes sense for people who believe that everyone is made in God's image. It is, however, entirely consistent with a view that some people should become god-like in their exercise of power and authority.

Other arenas of creeping idolatry that should frighten us include the academy and the media. An indispensable feature of idolatrous regimes is their promotion of propaganda and suppression of truth. Indeed, since lies underpin the very power of the leaders, the entire regime is born of lies. While there are no supreme leaders in the West—unlike in North Korea, China, and Russia—there is a growing preference for ideology over truth on both sides of the political spectrum.

Here the biblical institution of the prophet was the essential countermeasure to any royal delusions, in addition to the priestly class. In modern democratic life, the press and the academy are in many ways supposed to carry out this critical function. And yet they are less and less independent or critical in the ways that they should be. Many journalists lack the courage or even desire to speak truth to power, but rather prefer to lead or follow the partisan party line. Stunningly and worrisomely, some are even actively working against the freedom of those who wish to express themselves. And while we have thankfully yet to see mass political killings (and hopefully never will), we live in a time when people find it perfectly acceptable to use the media and the academy to destroy someone's career, reputation, or permanently exclude them from an institution or group based on what they say.

In the context of an increasingly propagandist media and partisan academia, we are now witnessing the rise of conspiracy theories, another fundamental feature of idolatry. Idolatrous societies always devise conspiracy theories. These serve to demonize actual opponents of the regime as inhuman to deflect anger toward the regime to bystanders or perceived enemies. The key feature of conspiracy theories that idolatrous leaders love so much is that they cannot be falsified; evidence to the contrary is simply evidence of a cover-up. Thus, they are the perfect weapon for idolatrous power, because they demonize those who denounce them as simply part of the conspiracy.

The truth can't actually be true. Today, conspiracy theories not only populate the dark web; they have also moved to the mainstream in academia, the very institution that is supposed to guard against such lies. Idolatry fosters and is fostered by a climate of lies. As the Talmud states, "The seal of God is truth." As Aleksandr Solzhenitsyn emphasized, the totalitarian regime is characterized by the pervasiveness of lying even to oneself.

I certainly do not argue that we are in a full-blown totalitarian regime. But the matrix that makes up the world of idolatry has many parts, and too many of them are visible in our society today. The rising hatred against Jews means something is desperately wrong with the discourse in our society.

That is why the Jewish mission of exposing idolatry and idolatrous ideas is as urgent as ever. The Bible remains the most insightful road map to identifying the telltale signs. Foundationally, Judaism is about truth. It demands we tell the truth even when those truths are difficult.

It is my great hope that as a community we will return to closely reading and studying the Bible with ethical and philosophical passion. And through what we learn, we challenge ourselves and the greater world. Let's get back to smashing idols.

54

A WESTERN WALL FOR EVERYONE

Why Was I Arrested for Praying at the Kotel?

HALLEL SILVERMAN

THE SUN ROSE in a pink and yellow sky above the Old City of Jerusalem early on a crisp February morning. We stood with our Jewish sisters for the morning prayers of Rosh Hodesh, celebrating the new month of Adar. Many of us wore prayer shawls and *kipot*, and some donned tefillin. As the sun grew hotter, so did the energy around us: ultra-Orthodox women shouting nearby in the women's section of the Kotel, men across the *mechitza* in the men's section, standing on chairs to cast down their judgmental gaze. It was, at that time, illegal for a woman to pray at the Kotel wearing a tallit.

Hallel Silverman is an American-born, Israeli-raised activist, content creator, and blogger in Tel Aviv. She has created content for dozens of major organizations and has been a leading voice online for liberal Zionism. She is an associate at the Tel Aviv Institute. Follow her on Instagram, Twitter, and TikTok.

Mom and I were arrested. Along with eight other women, we were taken to the police station: fingerprints, mugshot, and all. A month later, the case was taken to the Supreme Court of Israel, where the law was finally overturned. We took one step forward in the battle for religious freedom in the Jewish state, but the avalanche it caused also took us one step backward in the relationship between ultra-Orthodox, Conservative, and progressive Jews. It also did its part to widen the gap between Israel and the Diaspora.

This experience at the Kotel was my first lesson in learning what it means to love Israel. Loving Israel means fighting for the ideals in our country that we ourselves value. I also learned that day that the Kotel is more to me than simply the holiest site in Judaism. For me, it also serves as a monument to Jewish power—and to what brings Jewish power to its knees. It seemed ironic that those at the Kotel, cursing their fellow Jews for thinking differently, had not considered that such division of brothers and sisters was what lost us the Temple in the first place. History was repeating itself before my eyes.

* * *

When Jewish children ask their parents why the Second Temple was destroyed, they are often told the Talmudic story of a man in Roman-occupied Judea who had a friend named Kamtza and an enemy named Bar Kamtza. One day, the man sends his servant to invite Kamtza to a feast. When the day of the celebration arrives, it becomes apparent that the servant made a mistake, for Bar Kamtza shows up instead of Kamtza. The host sees Bar Kamtza and reacts by throwing him onto the street, despite his pleas to stay in order to avoid public humiliation. Later, in a rage of vengefulness, Bar Kamtza falsely reports to the Roman authorities that his host was treasonous, and that he and other Jews were conspiring against the Empire. Only then, according to the legend, did Rome resolve to destroy Jerusalem.

The lesson, according to Jewish tradition, is that our destruction was the result of *sinat chinam,* or baseless hatred.

The month after our arrest, Yitzhak Yiftah, one of the three paratroopers who helped capture the Western Wall from Jordan in 1967, came to the Kotel with Women of the Wall, the organization that routinely demonstrates for egalitarian holy space.

"I decided to come here to show my support for all those who wish to pray at the Western Wall whatever way they wish, so long as they are not doing anything immoral," said Yiftah. "It breaks my heart that the ultra-Orthodox have decided the Western Wall belongs to them."

Similar expressions of support came from across Israel, the Diaspora, and on social media. It was in the aftermath of my arrest that I realized the value of people like Yiftah, people who express an *ahavat yisrael,* love of the Jewish people, which is the opposite of sinat chinam, the opposite of the Kamtza and Bar Kamtza story. It is the love of fellow Jews, love of nation, love of family, that strengthens the foundations of the Temple walls. It is exclusion and grievance that send them tumbling down.

These, I'd like to think, are the liberal values that Israel was built upon. Our founding mothers and fathers believed in a progressive society. They believed that Israel would, in the words of our Declaration of Independence, "ensure complete equality of social and political rights to all its inhabitants irrespective of religion, race or sex; it will guarantee freedom of religion, conscience, language, education and culture."

The State of Israel was founded on looking to the future. Its leaders were committed to the process of constantly bettering their homeland. Obvious mistakes were made along the way, but it was the adherence to a set of principles that mattered. That is what ultimately made it a successful endeavor.

Yet, like many of the world's democracies, Israel has not been successful enough. The Declaration of Independence should have protected my religious freedom to pray at the Western Wall with a tallit. But we as a society are not where we could—really should—be. We still have to wade through our fair share of sinat chinam, or what I call "cracks in the Kotel."

Of course, there are two parts to the story of how and why the Temple fell. Yes, it was infighting and sinat chinam, but it was also the military superiority of the Roman Empire, external on top of internal threats. But if these stories teach us anything, it is what our first step should be when confronting foreboding external threats.

Today, there are countless efforts to fight antisemitism from a variety of people, organizations, and institutions. And yet the squabbles that arise among these bodies, often found in entertaining threads on Twitter, make the fight seem at best difficult and at worst hopeless. If the Jewish world were united in ahavat yisrael, it would be far easier to fight the growing hatred of Jews in the Diaspora.

Put simply: If we can't get past our own sinat chinam toward each other, why do we have some illusion that we can defeat the sinat chinam against us?

***

I feel passionately about overcoming internal strife within the Jewish community. As a content creator with an online platform, I saw firsthand the viciousness that came during the May 2021 Gaza conflict. I saw the memes with millions of likes and comments and statements from celebrities that were incorrect at best and downright bigoted at worst. I know how scary it is, which is why I want the home front in tip-top shape.

Take what happened to my aunt, the comedian Sarah Silverman, as a sign of the shifting battleground. She was brutally harassed and threatened on her social media accounts when she wished my baby brother, Adar, a happy birthday. She had used a photo of him in his Israel Defense Forces uniform on Twitter. She was tormented for weeks solely because of where her family lived and their national and religious background.

Our world is increasingly intolerant of our demand to live as a sovereign state. In the Diaspora, it may not come in the form of tanks and guns, but it can come in the form of ridiculing comments and incitement just for existing. There is a consistent flow of false information circulating about Israel online. It is easy to write #FreePalestine and harass Jewish people who defend Israel, simply because you see it from many other people you deem respectable. It is easy to join in the crusade. It is much harder to learn the history and nuance of an issue or a people. The minimization of any complex issue more often than not is extremely harmful to those most in need.

My good friend, Blake Flayton, a columnist at the *Jewish Journal*, recently faced a wave of antisemitic online harassment when he posted a picture of himself at Ben Gurion Airport on his first day as an Israeli, having just moved from New York City. Like what happened to Blake, we now face an environment where Jewish college students are forced to transfer schools or are removed from student government positions and liberal organizations simply because they support Israel's existence and are unwilling to go along with the Boycott, Divestment, and Sanctions (BDS) rhetoric.

* * *

At the Kotel, I learned that in order to stand up for ourselves, to make some noise against this tsunami of antipathy, to start convincing the masses of our story, of our legitimate self-determination, and of our indigeneity to the land of Israel, we must bridge our own divides. Kamtza and Bar Kamtza are *so* 66 C.E.

The Women of the Wall protest at the Kotel is the issue most personal to me, but there are many other things that bring sinat chinam to the forefront of the national conversation. When Israel denies refugees from Darfur and Eritrea safe haven in the Jewish state and threatens to deport them, that is hatred that makes us weaker in the fight for our defense. When Israel elects to the government parties that have expressed support for canceling gay pride marches, that is hatred that dims our flame. When parents send their children to conversion therapy to erase part of who they are, thankfully illegal in Israel but still commonplace in the Diaspora, that is undoubtedly an expression of baseless hatred that distracts us from the real issues at hand. And finally, when Jews in the Diaspora internalize hatred of Jewish peoplehood and of Israel, it is completely without basis, completely without logic or a sense of truth, and like it has been throughout the centuries, it is a threat to our security. Sinat chinam would appear to be everywhere.

The answer, I am pressing, is more love, more trust, and more egalitarian thinking when it comes to fellow Jews.

I still go to the Kotel quite often. I go there comfortably, and always with a tallit on. My mother, a rabbi, wears a kippa. We still make our pilgrimage to this hallowed ground, despite the dark memories of Jew against Jew that it releases in both our memories. We still come because we know that our presence there acts as a sort of glue in the cracks in the Kotel.

Our prayers keep the wall standing, I have learned. And if it is true that in every generation our enemies rise to destroy us, then the walls of our third attempt at a Temple had better be sturdy enough.

55

LIBERATE OUR INSTITUTIONS

A New Organizational Paradigm

ANDRÉS SPOKOINY

A JEW who went to sleep in 1923 and woke up in 2023 would recognize very little of the world; but she would see the same Jewish organizational landscape, operating in more or less the same manner. The federation would still solicit her for its annual campaign, the Hebrew Union College and the Jewish Theological Seminary would still be training rabbis, the Joint Distribution Committee would be assisting Jews overseas, and the Jewish Agency would be talking about Aliyah.

Andrés Spokoiny is a long-time Jewish communal leader. Currently the CEO and president of the Jewish Funders Network, he held senior positions in Canada, Europe, and South America. Andrés has a multi-disciplinary academic background that includes business, Jewish education, rabbinic studies, and organizational behavior.

At certain inflection points, during times of massive change and disruption, organizational paradigms become obsolete. Communal organizations then needed to be redesigned to continue being relevant. We are now at one of those inflection points.

It is not just that circumstances have changed; the individuals that are the "customers," the "members," the employees, or the leaders of communal organizations have also changed. They have a different view of themselves as "hyper-empowered" and "hyper-connected" individuals who demand much more choice and agency in every aspect of their lives.

To continue thriving, Jewish communal organizations will therefore need to evolve and adapt. Communal institutions have changed many times in our long history, performing a delicate dance between change and continuity, evolution, and preservation. But such change is becoming more urgent with each passing year.

***

The beginnings of the modern organization can probably be traced back to the Prussian Army in the eighteenth century. Frederick the Great's idea was that every movement of the army had to be precise and predictable, like that of a timepiece. Every soldier had one commander, and every individual had a clearly defined role. The line of command was vertical, and following orders was the key value.

The army became the metaphor by which companies and other enterprises were organized. The "Taylorist" model, named after the nineteenth-century American engineer Frederick W. Taylor, was based on high specialization, efficiency, division of labor, and clarity of orders. It became the central model adopted by the industrial organizations of the nineteenth and twentieth centuries.

These companies had a pyramidal structure and a vertical flow of information. They were centralized and bureaucratic and had strong structures of control (remember punch cards?) and straightforward mechanisms for reward and punishment. They relied on employees being predictable and, in many cases, not creative, because you don't want a worker deploying creativity in the assembly line.

Throughout the twentieth century, the centralized, pyramidal organization produced goods and services with remarkable efficiency and low costs, allowing the explosion of consumer goods and the comfort that we enjoy today. But with the advent of the information era and the growth of automation, the pace of change accelerated, and traditional organizations discovered that their strengths could easily become liabilities in a fast-changing market that required rapid response, quick flow of information, and creativity at all levels. In a world of hyper-empowered individuals, Henry Ford couldn't say, "You can have a car of any color as long as it's black."

By the turn of the twenty-first century, it became evident that the organizational model of the industrial revolution was beginning to outlive its usefulness; the centralized decision-making mechanism became too slow. The obsession with control and "discipline," so useful in the assembly line, proved an obstacle to creativity and innovation. And the vertical flow of information prevented rapid response and sharing of information across the system. Maverick companies emerging from the garages of college dropouts proved nimbler and more adaptable than the big, industrial-era organizations. The "Open Source" movement changed the way we look at intellectual property, and the new "sharing economy" undercut traditional organizations by monetizing interactions between users and customers. As the "command-and-control" model started to crumble, organizations moved toward a "collaborate-and-connect" paradigm. They understood that organizations needed cross-pollination both inside and outside their boundaries.

Like all twentieth-century organizations, Jewish institutions, from synagogues to Jewish Community Centers, specialized in producing and distributing proprietary goods and services. Yet, we have failed to adapt. Indeed, our institutional structures and leadership models are twentieth-century ones. Information is considered a source of power both inside the organizations and in relation to potential competitors. Jewish institutions are designed to discourage creativity and risk-taking. Consequently, there is a malaise in the world of Jewish organizations, which may be seen in dropping affiliation numbers, fundraising problems, and employee dissatisfaction.

Every organization is unique, and the fields in which they operate are different. But there are a number of core challenges that the next generation of Jewish organizations will have to address.

The first and most obvious is the creation of *networks instead of pyramids*.

* * *

Jewish organizations have become complex systems that operate in complex environments. A complex system is one in which the autonomous components interact in non-linear ways and create patterns of self-organization amid upheaval and messiness. Thus, organizations should seek to restructure themselves along a network model, one that distributes leadership, democratizes the flow of information, and provides flexibility and nimbleness.

Google, like many hi-tech organizations, has some elements of the traditional organization but also has a network architecture, where independent groups work on projects and products, alternatively separated and connected from the totality of the organization. Liberated from the straitjacket of the traditional org chart, these working groups innovate, create, and experiment.

Designing and running a network is not easy or simple. For example, in a network, the flow of information is much richer, but it's also messier, so one needs to create systems that capture and distribute that information. There's a good reason why social networks depend on algorithms to analyze, organize, and distribute enormous amounts of data. Without that, the richness of the network may be lost.

Operating as a network also implies changing incentive systems. During my years at IBM, we tried to encourage employees to work across department boundaries, but bonuses were set by each department. To win the bonus, one department needed to outcompete another. When one adopts a new organizational paradigm, other systems and processes need to be transformed as well.

Imagine a federation or large synagogue that created semi-independent innovation teams that are less constrained by organizational hierarchies or can engage users in a more direct way. Imagine if organizations rotated their employees and lay leaders among departments to help them discover hitherto unknown connections. Imagine a federation that, instead of having a rigid division between allocations and fundraising, operated in ad-hoc task forces that jointly designed programs and engaged donors.

In a communal organization, the most valuable member or employee is not the one higher up in the hierarchy, but the one with the largest number of connections, the one who can tap into many different nodes of the network.

But once we rid ourselves of our Prussian-style pyramids, a question necessarily arises about the relationships *between* organizations. These, too, need to become less rigid and proprietary. Nowhere is this more urgent than in the sharing of data.

Our organizations are not very adept at sharing information and resources. Everything is seen through a proprietary lens, from donors and population research to program design. The Jewish community generates vast amounts of data about its members, but it isn't used or leveraged. Think about the amount of data generated by Birthright Israel or PJ Library or the religious denominations—programs and institutions that collectively touch millions of individuals over long periods of time.

Our community needs a "data commons" and a protocol to share information for the benefit of all. Having access to data and the technology to analyze it properly also allows us to identify potential or actual connections between nodes. In my work at the Jewish Funders Network, information about what different funders fund allows us to generate connections that result in philanthropic joint ventures. Knowing that two funders care about the same issue becomes the beginning of a partnership that benefits the community. A new platform called JLife offers a shared platform to connect individuals to all Jewish events in a given city, enacting the proverbial rising tide that lifts all boats.

Finally, organizations need to rethink the classic role of "intermediation"—acting as a go-between between donors and members on the one hand, and causes, experiences, and impact on the other. Part of this is practical. In the age of hyper-empowerment, we have little need today for organizations to arrange our travel or tell us about nonprofits we can give our money to. But it is also conceptual and ideological: I want to be directly involved in my choices. I don't want to outsource them to somebody else.

That doesn't mean all intermediating organizations should be dissolved, but they must clearly explain how they add value to a process that the client feels he can do alone. Telling a contemporary Jew to give through Federation "because we know better where the needs are" may or may not be factually true, but it will sound patronizing and disempowering. Instead, if we said, "Tell us what your goals are, and we'll use our resources to help you do it better," donors will feel ownership of the process. This will make community leaders and service providers into excellent "concierges"—folks who know you and can enrich every experience you have, without taking it over.

* * *

We also need to reconceive our idea of organizational leadership. New organizations require a new kind of leader.

In the traditional model, the leader was in charge of setting strategy, distributing resources, and managing the operation. Leaders were supposed to incentivize good performance and maintain the hierarchy. In the new paradigm, the leader retains many of those functions, but their relative weight changes and diminishes.

In a world of hyper-empowered individuals who want to self-organize, a leader needs to be a *catalyst*. Leaders do not have to come up with all the answers or produce the best program ideas. Instead, they need to harness and direct the creativity and energy of the system. As on Twitter or YouTube, users will self-organize; as with Google, employees can form de-facto groups to produce innovation.

The crucial question then becomes: How can Jewish leaders improve and add value to the self-organization of their clients, members, or employees?

Imagine if fifteen people in a Jewish Community Center got together to create a theater troupe, and the JCC provided them with space, a qualified director, and visibility in the marketplace. Imagine if a federation made an open call for anybody who wants to "do something Jewish" and facilitated their access to capital, connections, and professional support.

In the Detroit Jewish community, the Jewish Federation acted as a catalyst for the self-organization of young Jews who were moving to the city. A federation professional helped identify connections with local business leaders, provided resources, gave a small push when needed, and, in general, tried to speed up and add value to emerging groups of Jews who were benefitting from the resurgence of the city.

Many of our federation CEOs, rabbis, and other leaders follow the "alpha male" paradigm (even if they are female). That style of leadership now becomes a hindrance, because it fails to capitalize on the creativity and entrepreneurship of the hyper-empowered individual.

Much of the creativity of today's economy depends on serendipitous encounters and a certain alchemy that occurs when diverse people get together. True, even in a top-down environment, one can *hope* for serendipitous exchanges that create new ideas. But what's needed now is the deliberate creation of frameworks that facilitate the emergence of those ideas—a kind of "engineered serendipity."

This is already happening to some degree. Many organizations have embraced the idea of community "hubs" to encourage spontaneous collaboration. The Leichtag Foundation, for example, has converted a building into a hub for young adult organizations. By being all in the same place, those organizations develop relations and eventually, joint programs. The Charles and Lynn Schusterman Family Foundation's ROI Program gathers young Jewish leaders from different organizations and, while the program is rich and diverse, its key is the opportunity for serendipitous multi-disciplinary encounters. In the United Kingdom, the Pears Foundation has launched "JHub," a co-working space for Jewish organizations that aims to discover and create new synergies. The "central square" in the Palo Alto JCC serves as a space for casual encounters; like the square of a Spanish town in which citizens conducted business, created connections—and even plotted revolutions.

Such a change in leadership will also mean taking a completely different approach to our failures. Much has been written about the need for companies to embrace intelligent failure. Yet while the discourse has changed, the practice hasn't. We still like to boast of our successes and rarely talk about—or learn from—our failed experiments, let alone reward those who try to innovate and fail.

Embracing failure is critical. Every day, we confront new situations without a handbook and sail through uncharted waters without a compass. A culture that penalizes trial and error will inevitably repress innovation. What is necessary is not just a change of attitude, but structures and procedures that capture the wisdom gained from failed experiments. At every JFN Conference, the Rothschild Foundation organizes a "F*ck Up Night," at which the community's most renowned philanthropists present their biggest mistakes and what they learned from them. Could something like that be done at the communal level?

* * *

Finally, we need to release ourselves from bondage to our own physical assets.

Over many decades, Jewish organizations created an impressive array of physical assets; buildings, campuses, JCCs, Hillels, Chabad Centers, and so on. Those buildings were important both practically and psychologically, conveying a sense of strength and permanence for a people of whom many were immigrants and refugees.

But in a time when individual Jews are highly mobile and virtual engagement grows exponentially, physical assets can become a ball and chain. Their management and maintenance devour resources, while linking programs to a specific location limits our thinking. Many successful organizations treat the city as their campus: they meet in coffee shops, museums, homes, and even the basements of churches. An organization like Moishe House (through which young Jews share living space and do home-based Jewish programming) has no central base. PJ Library (which distributes books for young children) is completely home based.

At any given moment, there are both a shortage and an over-abundance of space in the Jewish community, because the assets are not efficiently distributed. People move, patterns of utilization change, and new needs emerge. Looking at community assets with a comprehensive mindset allows us to optimize space for the community as a whole, and helps individual organizations manage their real estate. For that, yet again, a sharing mentality is needed.

The Jewish Federation of Montreal once created a multi-layered map of the city. One layer showed the demographic distribution of Jews by age, purchasing power, level of observance and engagement, and so on. On another, one could see the locations of Jewish institutions. This eye-opening exercise led to a thorough rethinking of the community's physical infrastructure.

Communal architecture can be planned to maximize connection, innovation, and serendipity, as with the Palo Alto JCC. In other words, it's not only the number of buildings but the kind. Many communal buildings are planned like office complexes and neglect the creation of spaces for interaction and connection. A new space in Boston called The Lehrhaus calls itself a "Jewish Tavern and House of Learning." As of this writing, it has not yet opened. But I foresee its success, for it incorporates many of the principles described above.

* * *

These are only a few of the ways in which Jewish communal organizations must reinvent themselves. Beyond lie additional hard questions: Do organizations place too much emphasis on loyalty—for both staff and donors—at the expense of impact, creativity, results-orientation, and flexibility? Should we be placing greater emphasis on platforms rather than specific products and services—more like AirBnb and Uber, less like Marriott and medallion cabs? At a time when products are commodified, true value lies in the platform.

The Jewish organizational world is overdue for such a revolution. We need to rethink the entire scaffolding of Jewish life to make it relevant for the realities of our time and meaningful for the hyper-empowered individual. We need to rethink our leadership paradigms and create organizations based on sharing and partnership, leveraging self-organization, and co-creating with our clients and users. Like our forefathers before us, we need to give a new organizational template to the timeless idea of community.

56

A NEW PANTHEON OF HEROES

Without Stories of Courage and Sacrifice, We Can't Have Jewish Pride

MICHAEL STEINHARDT

IN JANUARY 2022, an armed gunman walked into a synagogue in Colleyville, Texas. After an eleven-hour siege, in which he held the rabbi and three others hostage and demanded the release of a notorious al-Qaeda terrorist, the rabbi threw a chair at the gunman and told the other hostages to flee. The gunman chased them out of the building and was gunned down by FBI agents.

Every Jew should know that rabbi's story. His act of selfless sacrifice and courage deserves to be remembered and celebrated. Yet, how many of us even know his name? (His name, by the way, is Rabbi Charlie Cytron-Walker.)

Michael Steinhardt is the co-founder of Birthright Israel and author of *Jewish Pride* (Wicked Son, 2022) and *No Bull: My Life In and Out of Markets* (Wiley, 2001).

Our failure to commemorate this act of heroism is part of a larger and worrisome trend. We—I mean the Jews of the non-Orthodox Diaspora—are reluctant to venerate our heroes. True, we celebrate individual Jews, but they are usually either philanthropists or great scientific, cultural, political, or business figures, revered more for their success than their personal qualities.

This is a fairly recent development, an unconscious decision seemingly taken in the last generation. The consequences are difficult to fathom. Without individual Jewish *heroes*, our children will have few vibrant historical Jewish examples to draw upon in charting the course of their lives, or even a sense of how important being proudly and defiantly Jewish really is.

Fortunately, it is the kind of problem that, once we put our finger on it, presents a clear solution.

I propose an ambitious communal effort to create a "pantheon" of Jewish heroes, including the institutional, educational, and cultural apparatus necessary to tell our children about the many heroic Jews who have lived through the ages and who still live among us today. This effort can include museums, curricula, scholarly and literary books, and even films or TV series.

If this talk of "Jewish heroes" sounds old-fashioned or outdated, that is largely a symptom of the problem we need to address. Among Diaspora Jews, Jewish heroism has indeed fallen out of fashion. In reclaiming it, the "How" is much more obvious than the "Why."

* * *

Anyone who has spent time in Israel will be struck by the number of museums and historical sites commemorating the heroes of early Zionism— from the Palmach and the Underground to the illegal immigrants who came on ships like the *Exodus*. Israeli children learn about how Theodor Herzl drove himself to an early death to build a Jewish state that might forestall the coming catastrophe in Europe; they know about the Zionist pioneers who braved disease and hunger to drain the swamps; they know the names of Jews like Abba Kovner who led the Vilna Ghetto uprising, or the poet Hannah Senesh who parachuted into Nazi Germany to help the partisans. Israeli parents and schools take kids to memorial sites and retell their stories.

Israelis grow up knowing a great deal about Jewish heroism. But the issue I raise is not about Zionism or the building of a successful Jewish state against all odds. It is about the need of non-Orthodox Jews in the Diaspora for a tradition of Jewish heroism that we can encourage our children to admire and emulate.

Ultimately it is about fostering a proper pride in the tremendous historical achievement of the American Jewish Diaspora, built by generations of immigrants who faced struggle, hardship, prejudice, and exclusion to create the largest, most powerful and influential Jewish community in history.

First, of course, we must define what is meant by "Jewish heroism." Heroism is different from success or individual accomplishment. When I speak of a Jewish hero, I am referring to something very specific: Someone who, through *courage and a willingness to sacrifice*, dedicates himself or herself to the betterment and welfare of our people.

Jewish history is full of heroes, and for most of that history, we made sure our children knew about them. Indeed, until quite recently, we have *always* believed that being a great Jew required qualities of character that we consider heroic.

Of course, there are the biblical heroes—starting with Abraham and Moses, who braved the wilderness to lead their people to a new life in the Promised Land; to the prophets who challenged the power of kings, to Queen Esther and the Maccabees. Great rabbis of old, too, risked the might of the Roman empire to teach and practice Judaism—and many were put to death for it.

To the extent these ancient stories are familiar, we often fail to see the risk and drama they involved. We need to recapture this sense of original Jewish risk-taking so we can appreciate the qualities of faith and perseverance they required. We need to bring these individuals to life not as musty icons but as heroes who risked everything to found, uplift, and preserve the Jewish nation.

The modern era offered Jewish heroes as well, from Benedict Spinoza, who challenged the authority of rabbis and tradition, risking excommunication to pave the way for a non-Orthodox Jewish identity, to Rabbi Mordecai Kaplan, the once-Orthodox rabbi who endured excommunication and public censure for his efforts to craft a Judaism that would appeal to the modern lives of less-traditional Jews. In living memory, we have seen Soviet refuseniks like

Ida Nudel, Natan Sharansky, Roman Brackman, and Joseph Bigun stand up to the most powerful totalitarian empire in history.

What these heroes had in common were the risks they were willing to take to affirm their proud identity as Jews. And we made sure that our kids knew their names.

***

But now, it seems, we do not. We don't have museums or curricula to commemorate them. We don't focus on the heroism of Moses or the prophets or the rabbis who stood up to the Romans and the Inquisition. We venerate successful Jews, famous Jews, award-winning Jews, but not necessarily heroic Jews.

Growing up in 1950s Brooklyn, I, too, had Jewish heroes. Their names were part of my childhood. Louis Brandeis, the Supreme Court justice who fought for civil rights, and also for Zionism, at a time when neither was particularly popular. Mickey Marcus, an American Army officer who volunteered for the Israel Defense Forces and became Israel's first general, tragically killed by friendly fire in the War of Independence. Even Sandy Koufax, who refused to play major league baseball on Yom Kippur, risking his career, added a whiff of the heroic to his Jewish success story. And, of course, Albert Einstein, who openly espoused his Jewish and Zionist beliefs in the face of the rise of Nazi Germany.

We in the U.S. don't have a Jewish museum dedicated to Einstein. The government of Israel, however, is building one in Jerusalem.

To be clear, I am not suggesting that heroic Jews don't exist. On the contrary—we know they do. We just haven't made an effort to identify and hold them up for praise and emulation.

The Orthodox world, of course, has its pantheon, made up of great, usually late, rabbis. Although many of them indeed showed heroism in their lives, they are revered far more for their wisdom, learning, and communal leadership than for their deeds.

As for non-Orthodox Jews, our heroes exist but they are missing from our lives. We have stopped *looking* for heroes, praising heroes, commemorating them, or teaching our children about their deeds. Worse, we have stopped associating heroism with Jewish identity altogether. The absence of a sense of Jewish heroism is one of the most striking changes in Jewish life of the last generations—and it happened without our even noticing it.

*　*　*

Why has Jewish heroism fallen out of fashion?

The most obvious reasons have to do with the decadence of our time: American Jews are supremely comfortable; we don't think we really need heroic sacrifice. The Civil Rights movement of the 1960s—in which heroic Jews like the murdered Freedom Riders Andrew Goodman and Michael Schwerner, or Rabbi Abraham Joshua Heschel who marched with Martin Luther King, played an important part—brought equality not just to African Americans, but also to Jews themselves, who no longer could be legally excluded from hotels, higher education, or jobs. A level playing field allowed Jews in America to succeed beyond their wildest dreams in almost every field.

But living off the heroism of those who came before us, we apparently saw little need to cultivate it in ourselves or our children.

Perhaps this was a natural result of the relative security and success of American Jews. But what about now? We live in a time when antisemitism is rising. More and more young Jews are being forced to choose between hiding their identity and incurring the wrath of anti-Israel and antisemitic forces on campus and elsewhere. Do our children have the spiritual resources required to stand up for their Jewish identity? Or will they be intimidated into silence?

We have also embraced the Holocaust as a central pillar of our identity. We talk about it constantly, building curricula and museums to keep its memory alive. We habitually focus on our victimhood, the scale of the destruction, and its universal moral implications. We talk more about Anne Frank—who is relatable as a victim but not as a hero—than we do about the resistance fighters of the Warsaw Ghetto. The hero of Steven Spielberg's blockbuster Holocaust movie, *Schindler's List*, wasn't even Jewish.

Through our almost exclusive focus on the Holocaust without a comparable focus on Jewish heroism, we have crafted an identity that is antiheroic in its essence.

We also live in a cynical time, one that is far more sensitive to the sins of past heroes than to the virtues that made them heroic. Perhaps we are afraid to put anyone on a pedestal for fear of drawing attention to their flaws. But this is a mistake.

True heroes, because they are great, are also greatly flawed. King David was not allowed to build the Temple in Jerusalem because, the Bible teaches, he had "spilled much blood." King Solomon amassed wives and riches and lost sight of the divine cause, setting the stage for the rupture of the kingdom. If anything, it is their flaws that make them human, relatable, and therefore useful models for young people.

Many of us have come to believe that heroism itself is not a Jewish trait. They do not realize how crucial it has always been to Jewish identity. The rabbis teach that there are certain laws which Jews must be willing to die rather than violate, such as not committing murder or idolatry. But there is another principle we must uphold: One must be willing to die rather than do *anything* that non-Jews interpret as repudiating Judaism.

Elie Wiesel tells the story of a man whose father was murdered in a concentration camp by a Nazi officer. The officer offered repeatedly to spare the man's life if he only repudiated the Jewish God. The man repeatedly refused, saying only "The Lord is God!" The officer shot him to death.

"You know," the son added, "my father was not a believer."

The life of Jews in America and other wealthy, free nations today does not demand the same sacrifices as the Holocaust, or the early decades of Zionism, or the time of the Soviet refuseniks. But when we deprive our children of the very concept of courage, sacrifice, and risk for the sake of our people, when we remove heroism from the curriculum and recognize only success, generosity, and Jewish victimhood, we rob them of something that affects every aspect of our lives. We, therefore, put our collective future at risk.

***

Why are heroes important? Simply put: It is only through demonstrated courage and a willingness to sacrifice that we discover the price a person is willing to pay for their Jewish commitment. In business terms, heroism is an act of *valuation* of one's Jewishness. A Jewish hero is not merely a successful person who is Jewish; and not even a hero who happens to be Jewish. A Jewish hero has put his or her Jewishness on the table. And by focusing on such individuals, we are sending a message to the next generation: Heroism teaches our children how important being Jewish is; its absence similarly teaches us how unimportant it might be.

In a world where the valuation of Jewish identity is low—where Jewish commitment is something that may be hidden or abandoned under pressure—should we be surprised at the assimilation of young Jews? Should we be surprised that antisemites feel comfortable rearing their heads? Should we be surprised when non-Jews fail to come to our defense?

Ultimately, the absence of heroes has the effect of cheapening Jewish identity and providing oxygen to the incendiary hatred of Jews that still smolders and is never extinguished. For if being proudly Jewish does not require courage, risk, and sacrifice, then it must not be all that important to us. Why then should anyone else respect it?

* * *

Today, we have many tools for fashioning and elevating heroes if we want to. Books and films and TV series can capture heroes in their complexity, exploring not just their greatness but also the flaws that make such men and women compelling and real. Hollywood, despite the prominence of Jews in the film industry, has mostly chosen to ignore the Jewish heroes of the ages, from Bar Kokhba and Spinoza to Herzl, David Ben-Gurion, and the refuseniks. But we do not have the luxury of waiting for market forces to supply Jewish heroes for our children.

Jews of the Diaspora have the resources to create our own heroic pantheon. We can choose, say, eighteen or thirty-six heroes from across our history to the present era, to symbolize the Jewish life they affirmed through their courage and sacrifice. We can imagine creating cultural projects that recognize their qualities of courage, sacrifice, responsibility, resistance, and above all, Jewish pride. We can imagine a museum and educational center dedicated to them, a fund to subsidize screenplays and books and educational curricula about them.

Because we are Jews, we will, of course, disagree about who should be included. Some may argue that only great religious leaders should be commemorated. Others may feel that we should focus on figures who took risks and sacrificed on behalf of the whole world, not just the Jews. Some may wish to include Alfred Dreyfus, whose 1894 trial and imprisonment brought attention to the antisemitism rampant in French society, while others may object that he was not a hero but a victim. Such a process will naturally engender a good deal of healthy debate.

But the goal is not exclusion: If various Jewish communities in the U.S. and abroad choose to add their own heroes, this would further the goal of rediscovering Jewish heroism overall.

Just having such a debate would be immensely valuable in itself. It would force us to focus on heroism and to ask difficult questions: What are the kinds of courage and sacrifice we *want* our children to emulate? Is it enough to voice unpopular opinions, to speak out when others will not? Must it involve risk to life and limb, such as we saw with the rabbi in Texas, or is reputational risk sufficient to merit inclusion in our pantheon? Must their intentions be entirely selfless? Must they be limited to serving Jews or Judaism alone?

However we answer such questions, the bottom line is this: Our kids need heroic exemplars. Specific Jews who made sacrifices and took personal risks to preserve their identity and their people. If we want young Jews to place a high price on their Jewish identity, they need to be shown examples of such heroism.

They need to know it is possible, even desirable, to care about being Jewish so much that it is worth sacrificing for, taking risks for, fighting for—even dying for. Because as Dr. King famously put it, "If you've got nothing worth dying for, you've got nothing worth living for."

57

THE POWER OF "NO"

Judaism Began with an Act of Refusal.
We Still Have a Lot More Refusing to Do.

BRET STEPHENS

MY YOUNGEST CHILD used to be obsessed with the Meghan Trainor hit, "No." The signature lyric: "My name is 'no,' my sign is 'no,' my number is 'no,' uh, you need to let it go…. Nah to the ah to the no, no, no."

The song is about telling boys to buzz off. In a way, it also expresses the high calling of the Jewish people.

No to the gods of seas and rivers, war and love, the sun and moon.

Bret Stephens is a columnist with the *New York Times* and editor-in-chief of *Sapir*. He won the Pulitzer Prize for commentary in 2013 and was banned for life from Russia in 2022.

No to theft, adultery, murder, graven images and taking the Lord's name in vain.

No to child sacrifice. No to work on Shabbat. No to boiling a kid in his mother's milk. No to the consumption of blood and unclean animals and swarming things and fish without fins and scales.

No to promises of eternal salvation, in this world or the next. No to emancipation from our peoplehood via the French Revolution, or to emancipation from our faith via the Russian Revolution, or to emancipation from our past via assimilation, or to forfeiture of a Jewish state via the suicide pill of binationalism.

No to the pharaoh, the emperor, the grand inquisitor, the czar, the commissar. No to Greece and Rome. No to Christ, Mohammad, Luther.

All our Noes go far to explain our enduring unpopularity. We are, in our distinctiveness, an obstacle to consensus and uniformity; in our rules-bound morality, a rebuke to "whatever-floats-your-boat" individualism; in thinking for ourselves, a rebuttal to prevailing orthodoxies; in our faith, a rejection of other deities and the priests and princes who worship them. It is why so much of the world has spent so much of its energy trying to convert, exile, ghettoize, assimilate, or murder us.

I don't mean to suggest by this list that Jewishness is a mere matter of negation. The religion itself records 248 positive commandments in the Torah, and Moses's final instruction to the Children of Israel before publicly transferring the mantle of leadership to Joshua is to "Choose life" (Deuteronomy 30:19). Nor is Judaism at all a religion and culture at war with everyone and everything. On the contrary, we have been remarkably able to make our peace over centuries with our social and cultural surroundings. But our Yeses to those cultural surroundings remain predicated on the Noes, and what we affirm also requires the courage to reject. It is a form of courage the Jewish people, most of all those outside the Orthodox fold, will need to find ways to practice, reinforce, and pass on if we are to survive.

What are the Noes that Jews—secular American Jews in particular—need now? What follows are *communal* imperatives, many of which may clash with our personal desires or circumstances but are essential to maintain a thriving Jewish life outside of Israel in the decades to come.

***

No to intermarriage. Sixty-one percent of American Jews who married in the last decade did so to a non-Jewish spouse. Some of these marriages will lead to conversions, and many religiously mixed couples will choose to raise their children as Jews. But many others will not. Today, there are 8.6 million American adults who have at least one Jewish parent, but only 4.3 million consider themselves culturally and religiously Jewish. That is an overall attrition rate of 50 percent. If non-Orthodox American Jews are alarmed by their dwindling numbers or discomfited by the increasingly Orthodox cast of what remains of the Jewish community, they need to muster the courage to reject intermarriage as an unobjectionable personal choice.

No to choosing childlessness. The number of children born to the average American is 2.3, according to a 2020 Pew Survey. For non-Orthodox Jews, it is a demographically catastrophic 1.4. (For the Orthodox, the figure is 3.3.) Pew also found that Jewish women between the ages of forty and fifty-nine—that is, beyond childbearing years, or nearly so—are "twice as likely as U.S. women overall to have no children." Secular American Jews are compounding their cultural self-erasure via intermarriage with generational self-termination via a refusal to procreate or adopt.

No to Jewish illiteracy. "Continuity," Daniel Gordis has noted, "requires content." For secular American Jews, content cannot boil down, as it so often does, to lighting candles on Hanukkah, being conscious of the Holocaust, and simply not being Christian. Jewishness—a category that includes religion but is hardly limited to it—is 3,000 years of culture: history and myth, literature and languages, ideas and beliefs and practices. To be ignorant of this culture is to be incurious about the methods by which Jews have been able to survive over millennia when so many of our sibling civilizations have vanished.

No to "Tikkun Olam" as the central Jewish value. In many ways, Judaism gave birth to the idea of social justice and its core tenets: care for the needy, a belief in equal justice, and a commitment to human dignity. But to reduce Judaism to a form of social justice is to strip the faith of its full meaning and make it hostage to the whims of progressive movements that, historically, have an ugly habit of turning antisemitic. The essence of being a good Jew means putting the commandments of personal decency ahead of the dictates of ideology. Repairing the world is important, but only after one fulfills one's primary obligations to God, family, community, and nation.

No to radical and revolutionary ideologies. There have always been Jews who are drawn, like a moth to a flame, to various kinds of utopian politics, most catastrophically Soviet totalitarianism and its offshoots. But Jewish political thought is generally anti-radical in its leanings: meliorative and incrementalist, working with the grain of human nature rather than against it, as concerned with process as it is with outcomes. As Rabbi Yitz Greenberg has observed, Jews care more than just about *tzedek tzedek tirdof*—"justice, justice you shall pursue." We also seek to "pursue justice justly" as a check against our own fallibility.

No to anti-Orthodox bigotries. Secular Jews, including me, may find much to dislike about the personal and communal demands of strict religious observance. But we should be mindful that the prospects of the Jewish people would be dim if it rested on our non-Orthodox shoulders alone. Before we deride the Orthodox for their supposed backwardness, let us at least acknowledge how much they do to preserve the Jewish life we claim to cherish. Large families. Thriving yeshivas. Spoken Yiddish. The rekindling of customs and communities was nearly extinguished in the Holocaust. Daily examples of strict observance from which we are free to depart—but which at least furnish the examples by which we measure our departure. All this should be a source of gratitude, not scorn.

No, never, to anti-Zionism. There is a debate of sorts as to whether anti-Zionism is a modern form of antisemitism. Answer: Yes, it is. But the question misses the larger point: Anti-Zionism is a malignant bigotry irrespective of its connection to classic antisemitism. If the Jewish state were to vanish, the world's largest population of Jews would be left stateless. And if it were to be submerged into a "binational state for all its citizens," as the more naïve or disingenuous anti-Zionists claim, it would be a catastrophe for Jews unmatched since World War II. Under the best circumstances, Israeli Jews would become the new Christians of a second Lebanon. Under the worst, they would be captives and victims of Hamas. Anti-Zionism represents the single greatest ideological threat to Jewish lives in the world in our day. For American Jews to pretend it is anything else is an unforgivable moral and intellectual failure.

***

There are readers who may strongly object to, or take personal offense at, some of these suggestions. That's okay: There is no more force behind them than the force of persuasion.

But I have yet to see a serious argument for how American Jewish identity as we have generally experienced it for the past century or so—distinctive but integrated, proudly American *and* Jewish, faithful to our heritage but modern and open to adaptation—can otherwise be maintained. Secular Jews are tacitly relying on Orthodox fecundity and Israeli resiliency to guarantee a Jewish future, while often disparaging both. What offer are we putting on the table to avoid the near-extinction that likely awaits us in fifty or a hundred years if we refuse to change?

Beyond the specifics, there is a matter of attitude. Much of the failure of the secular American Jewish community over the past several decades is that we have moved, sometimes helplessly but often happily, with America's broad cultural currents.

We have learned to be strictly non-judgmental. We have been taught to bite our tongue about other people's choices, however objectionable we might privately find them. We have asked little, Jewishly, of our children, and gotten even less in return. We have allowed much of Reform Judaism to devolve into a kind of insipid do-gooderism. We have tolerated, and even participated in, the incessant slanders of Israel as if we have no stake in its survival.

Above all, we have failed to muster the courage to reject lest we seem intolerant. But rejection does not imply intolerance. It merely says that some things aren't good for us; that we are willing to make some sacrifices, to abide by some limitations, to say No to certain things, for the sake of our collective future; that being Jewish is a precious inheritance and a priceless bequest and that we will do what we must to hand it down.

If that takes courage, it is nothing next to the courage it took for our forebears to hand it down to us.

58

THE CASE FOR JEWISH GUILT

Why Feeling Bad About Our Non-Observance
Is Crucial for Passing the Torch

DAVID SUISSA

I FELT THAT TINGE OF GUILT as I saw friends walking back from synagogue
as I meandered over to a lunch that promised an exquisite brisket and lots of
meaningful schmoozing.

But before I got to indulge in that special joy of the three-hour Shabbat
lunch, I had to deal with that pesky feeling of guilt. Why was I not in synagogue with my friends that morning? Yes, I was exhausted, not just from a long
week but from a Friday night dinner that lasted past midnight and included

---

David Suissa is publisher and editor-in-chief of the *Jewish Journal* of Greater Los Angeles, host of *The David Suissa Podcast,* and an award-winning weekly columnist since 2006.

one too many servings of cabernet. But that's an explanation, not an excuse that God, or my conscience, would or should accept.

So, where does this guilt come from, and why am I so weirdly attached to it? Why would such a negative sentiment give me such a feeling of comfort?

The answer, I believe, is that I was raised to embrace Jewish guilt, in particular the guilt associated with observing our tradition. Growing up in Casablanca, rituals like going to synagogue on Shabbat were the community's default position. We were all expected to go to shul and follow standard rituals. We hadn't yet discovered that thing in America they call freedom of choice.

It helped that we weren't surrounded by alternatives. There were no Reform or Reconstructionist shuls in Morocco that may have aroused our curiosity about doing things another way. Observing rituals was not an Orthodox thing, it was a Jewish thing. We also weren't distracted by more global concerns like "Tikkun Olam." The world we looked after was our own neighborhood, and keeping our traditions and rituals alive kept everyone plenty busy.

This communal focus on rituals defined our Jewish identities for centuries. Observing these rituals, in other words, was the one way we knew to express our Jewishness. Seen through that lens, a sense of guilt for *missing* a ritual became a poignant way of staying connected to those very rituals, to our very Jewishness.

That feeling of guilt I felt that Shabbat morning, when I saw my friends returning from synagogue, represents not an emotional annoyance but a precious attachment to my Judaism. I *want* that guilt. I *need* that guilt. I never want to feel okay about not honoring tradition.

Guilt is sharper than just a sense of obligation. Guilt has tension, electricity, even pain. When all else fails, guilt keeps me in the game.

* * *

For many Moroccan Jews who left the cozy nests of their Moroccan neighborhoods for the free-for-all of America, that tradition of guilt has come in handy. Among those who make it a habit to miss rituals, there's even an expression: "non-practicing Orthodox." It is a light-hearted label that captures the serious respect for the traditional Judaism we grew up with, a Judaism where one is expected to follow the laws handed down at Sinai 3,300 years ago.

Indeed, our ancestors kept those laws and rituals alive for millennia. Respecting these rituals keeps us connected to our past. Guilt is a way of showing respect even when we fail to practice. For those moments when we stray, we tolerate the sting of guilt for the comfort of staying attached.

For many of us, it is a decent bargain.

But it's hardly an obvious one. Guilt can be a destructive emotion; it is not something we want to wallow in. As any shrink will tell you, hanging on to guilt can be paralyzing. If anything, in Judaism guilt triggers a process of repentance so we can flush it out.

The popular cliché of "Jewish guilt" is just that—a cliché that provides material for standup comedy. The stereotypical Jewish mother who makes her kids feel guilty about everything is an adorable shtick, but it is not serious. It's comical. It's a way of diffusing the tension of real guilt.

Secular American Jews may feel guilty about many things, but not about ignoring the Jewish tradition. After all, why feel guilty about abandoning something that the great majority of Jews have already abandoned, especially when observing tradition is generally seen as the domain of the Orthodox?

While the "Casablanca guilt" I feel when I miss shul on Shabbat is a lifeline to my Jewish identity, most American Jews may not feel they need that lifeline, or, to be more precise, they may prefer alternate lifelines.

These other lifelines usually revolve around "Jewish values." The word *value* is one of those flexible terms that can encompass many virtues, from social justice and being a mensch to repairing the world, being kind to strangers, and living with humility and dignity.

The fact that those values are universal and humanistic, however, raises a vexing question: How solid and long-lasting is a Jewish identity based on humanistic values? If a Jew follows mostly universal ideas, how necessary is his or her Judaism? Visiting a homeless shelter or fighting climate change may be worthy pursuits, but how do they nourish Jewishness if they are not uniquely Jewish?

These questions are most relevant in the Diaspora but not in Israel, where "uniquely Jewish" is the oxygen that one breathes. Beyond all the challenges of modern-day Israel, beyond the security threats that never seem to wane, beyond the societal and political divisions that dominate its public discourse, if there is one iron-clad accomplishment of the Zionist project, it must be the forging of an instinctive Jewish identity.

Put simply, whether one observes religious rituals or not, it is a lot harder for a Jewish identity to evaporate in the Jewish state. Whereas America can lure Jews with a multitude of non-Jewish lifestyles in which to assimilate, in Israel, regardless of lifestyle, you always feel Jewish. It is in the air.

We don't have that luxury in the Diaspora. Being a tiny minority in a secular country, Jews who hope to forge a strong Jewish identity must look beyond fighting antisemitism and remembering the Holocaust. Above all, they must open their minds and hearts to the uniquely Jewish rituals that have sustained us for millennia.

＊＊

My kids like to say that the strongest argument I have ever made about Judaism and Jewish identity is the image I sometimes offer them right before reciting the Kiddush on Friday night.

"Just imagine," I tell them, "in some little village in Morocco a thousand years ago, your great-great-great-great-great-great-great grandparents were probably gathered around a table doing the same thing we're doing, lighting the Shabbat candles and reciting the same Kiddush."

I occasionally add my amazement that after the destruction of the Second Temple, the Jews were scattered around the world for 1,900 years, and still, after all these centuries and after all the pogroms and persecution, we all still read from the same Torah scroll on Shabbat today.

"How is that not a bigger miracle than the splitting of the Red Sea?" I wonder.

In the Diaspora, the quaint Jewish rituals of my Casablanca childhood have become more than rituals. They have become tools of memory, instruments of connection to my past. Attending synagogue or reciting the Kiddush or learning the Torah or building a succah are no longer just commandments. They are invaluable links to my ancestors, to my people's story, and to my Jewish identity.

I have a close Ashkenazi friend who shares my attachment to the collective Jewish story. We like to say that we have been "friends for 3,300 years," since we were all at Sinai to receive the Torah. We used to joke about it, but over the years, we have come to enjoy the idea so much that now we totally believe it.

If we want future generations of the Diaspora to forge a lasting Jewish identity, a good starting point is the miraculous Jewish story itself—the story of how, against all odds, our grandparents kept the Jewish tradition alive for so long so that we can do the same and pass it on.

"To be a Jew," the late Chief Rabbi Jonathan Sacks wrote, "is to inherit a faith from those who came before us, to live it and to hand it on to those who will come after us. To be a Jew is to be a link in the chain of the generations."

But just as our ancestors had to overcome obstacles to keep that flame alive, we have our own obstacles to deal with. Away from the tight bonds of Jewish neighborhoods, awash in the pleasurable sea of secular assimilation, one of those obstacles is the very absence of Jewish guilt about ignoring tradition. For all too many Jews, confident in their adherence to Jewish values, feeling guilty about, say, not lighting the Shabbat candles must be the last thing on their mind.

* * *

I once heard a rabbi say, "You don't give to someone because you love them; you love them because you give to them."

We are more likely to love our tradition if we give to it. The power of rituals is that they force us to give. Even something as simple as schlepping to buy Shabbat groceries is a form of giving. It is an investment in Jewish identity. Embracing Jewish values in our heads is one thing, but nurturing a real Jewish identity, building a succah or hosting a Shabbat meal, is on a whole other level.

When I think back to my Casablanca neighborhood, that is pretty much what we did—we gave to our Judaism. The whole rhythm of the community revolved around the rituals of being Jewish. We forged a Jewish identity through the simple act of giving to it. We didn't debate, analyze, or agonize. We gave.

What pulls at my heart is what lies behind this giving. When I see Shabbat candles in the corner of our dining room as I prepare to recite the Kiddush, it is not just candles I see. It is the countless Shabbat candles that our ancestors have lit every Friday night.

When we read from the Torah on Shabbat, I see the same Torah scroll that is opened and read across the world every Shabbat morning, from Casablanca to London, to Warsaw to Johannesburg to New Delhi.

When we huddle in our succah every year, I see the succahs where our ancestors gathered to learn the lessons of gratitude and humility.

When I gather with my family at Passover, I see the Passover Seders that Jews celebrated annually century after century, learning the lessons and responsibilities of freedom.

In each ritual, I feel an attachment—to my past, to my story, to my people.

And when those moments inevitably arise when I fail to do those rituals, I make sure to embrace my Casablanca guilt. That guilt is a little voice that reminds me I am still connected no matter what, that I must never abandon the tradition my ancestors fought so hard to keep, that I'm still as proud to be Jewish as ever.

Next time I miss synagogue on Shabbat, I know that guilt will rescue me.

59

HOW TO BEAT THE
NEW ANTISEMITISM

It's Not About Human Rights. It's About Soviet Propaganda.

IZABELLA TABAROVSKY

IN JULY OF 1970, Soviet Ambassador to Washington Anatoly Dobrynin sent a cable to his superiors at the Ministry of Foreign Affairs in Moscow entitled, "On Fighting American Zionist and Pro-Zionist Circles' Hostile Anti-Soviet and Anti-Socialist-Bloc Activities." In it, he provided his analysis of Zionists' success at penetrating the American establishment.

Izabella Tabarovsky writes about Soviet Anti-Zionism, contemporary Left antisemitism, and the links between the two.

Dobrynin wrote about the all-powerful Israel lobby; the "excessive public activity" of more than three hundred Jewish organizations; the presence of a large number of Jews in influential positions in American media, business, and the AFL-CIO leadership; and the Pentagon's supposed pro-Israel position. He noted that the Zionist element "had struck deep roots in the American soil" and that fighting it successfully required "a unified and carefully coordinated plan."

The language and assumptions of the report fully aligned with Moscow's belief that a mighty Zionist conspiracy operated against it in Washington. His superiors responded by directing Dobrynin to study closely the American Jewish community and American Zionist organizations, and pay particular attention to the ways Zionists "manipulated American public opinion" in general and members of Congress in particular. The embassy was to work to undermine harmful Zionist influence among Republicans and Democrats; investigate Zionist connections with "American monopolistic capital"; and study financial and industrial enterprises controlled by "Jewish capital." It was tasked with taking note of any disagreements among American Jews regarding the Soviet Union, Israel, and the Nixon administration, and to use these "to discredit and weaken the unity of anti-Soviet Zionist forces."

If you sense a whiff of the *Protocols of the Elders of Zion* emanating from this exchange, you are right. In the wake of Israel's victory in the Six-Day War over Soviet-trained and Soviet-armed Arab states—an unexpected and traumatic defeat for Moscow—the Soviet propaganda and security apparatus developed an elaborate theory about a shadowy, omnipresent, and omnipotent enemy operating against the USSR around the world. It dubbed this enemy "International Zionism." Among the sources of inspiration for this conspiracy theory were the *Protocols*, Russian pre-revolutionary pogromist literature, Nazi literature, and Arab antisemitic propaganda, rewritten to fit the Soviet Marxist-Leninist framework.

Guided by this *Protocols*-based logic, the Ministry directed Dobrynin to play up the trope of Zionist treacherousness—an easily recognizable counterpart of the right-wing idea about the perfidy of Jews. He was to demonstrate to the American public that Zionists were hostile to American national interests; to try and divide the Jewish community by working with progressive American

Jewish and mainstream press to expose Zionist anti-American actions; and to report on antisemitism in the United States, particularly among political elites, while suggesting ways to use such instances in Soviet propaganda.

When Dobrynin wrote back, he informed his superiors that the embassy had established a special propaganda council tasked with aggravating divisions among American Jewry along the Zionist-Israel fault line as well as between Zionists and the non-Jewish population of the United States. The council's task, he wrote, was to raise questions among key American constituencies about Zionists' loyalty to Israel; to help deepen disagreements between American and Israeli governments; and to expose ordinary Americans to "the brazen face of the leaders of the newly-minted Zionist 'higher race' from Tel Aviv."

We don't know whether the propaganda council in fact was established, or if it achieved its objectives. Window dressing was an essential part of Soviet bureaucratic culture. An experienced bureaucrat, Dobrynin would have known exactly what to say and how to say it to please his superiors. But the fact that pleasing Moscow meant playing into its anti-Zionist and antisemitic conspiracy fantasies says much about the climate in Soviet corridors of power at the time.

Dobrynin's correspondence also points to some of the tactics Moscow used to fight its imaginary Zionist bogeyman. One crucial strategy, for example, was to induce American Jews to end their support for Israel. Convinced that Zionists ran America, Moscow calculated that once American Jews turned away from Israel, the American establishment would do so as well, draining Zionism and Israel of their magic powers. One of the ways to achieve this objective was to turn Zionism and Israel into moral outcasts.

Soviet propaganda worked tirelessly to achieve this goal. It equated Zionism with Nazism, claimed that Zionists collaborated with the Nazis in the annihilation of their own people, and painted Zionism as a colonial project serving the interests of imperialism and monopolistic capital. It engaged its Academy of Sciences and the full power of its press, domestically and internationally, to equate Zionism with racism and paint Israel as an "apartheid state" akin to South Africa.

It is astonishing to me that American Jews remain blind to this history—or how it continues today, more than three decades after the collapse of the Soviet Union, through a range of institutions and movements. What makes it especially bewildering is that American Jews had been at the forefront of the fight for Soviet Jewry and understood that what the Soviets called anti-Zionism was but a rebranding of old antisemitic conspiracy theories. They knew that the antisemitism experienced by Soviet Jews was inextricably linked to the anti-Zionist propaganda that the state engaged in at home and abroad. Yet today, when the very same tropes appear in the American environment, American Jews seem blind to the toxic history and charge.

Yet the antisemitic effects of these tropes are already evident. We see Jewish students and professors in America being harassed and silenced on university campuses. We see pro-Israel Jewish authors being shut out of mainstream American publishing. We see Jewish organizations being excluded from progressive circles on account of their failure to denounce Israel and Zionism. Conditioned to worry about right-wing antisemitism, third- and fourth-generation American Jews are sleepwalking through this latest iteration of Jew-hatred, which comes at them from the Left, which many consider their political home.

Debates about whether anti-Zionism is or isn't antisemitism play out in the pages of the Jewish press and scholarly journals. Some have acknowledged that it is antisemitism but dubbed it "new," and possibly more benign than the right-wing kind. But there is nothing novel about this form of antisemitism. We have seen it all before. We know how it ends.

***

Today, when these Soviet themes resonate across American university campuses and are part and parcel of American political discourse, it is instructive to trace their history and evolution.

Take, for example, the slander equating Zionism with racism and Israel with South African apartheid. To understand its origins, let's turn to a 1959 KGB memo, which reported on the agency's effort to analyze Jewish religious writings to better understand Zionism. With no religious background, and none in Jewish religious thought, KGB personnel ploughed through the

Hebrew Bible and a dozen Russian-language Jewish prayer books. Their conclusion: Jewish religious writings are "permeated throughout with a spirit of militant nationalism and 'spiritual racism,'" expressing "the racist conception of exclusivity and superiority of the Jewish people" and enabling Jews to "disseminate hatred toward those of different ethnicity."

Claiming that these "racist" ideas "constitute the foundation of Zionist ideology," the KGB raised particular alarm over two prayers: Aleinu and Kol Nidre. These, they wrote, openly propagated "Zionism, the 'exclusivity' and 'superiority' of the Jewish people, and the final victory of the Jewish people over the entire world."

What is striking about this analysis, besides its utter ignorance, is the extent to which it parallels right-wing antisemitic thought. The obsession with supposed Jewish superiority, predicated on the religious concept of "chosenness," is central to the fear and loathing of Jews on the far-right. But this parallel did not stop Soviet propaganda from turning it into the centerpiece of its anti-Zionist defamation and, ultimately, into the well-known trope about Zionism as racism. Here, for example, is the Soviet ambassador to the UN Yakov Malik in a 1971 speech to the Security Council:

> The Fascists advocated the superiority of the Aryan race as the highest among all the races and peoples in the world…and the Zionist does the same. The chosen people: is that not racism? What is the difference between Zionism and Fascism, if the essence of the ideology is racism, hatred toward other peoples?

The same logic guided Soviet propaganda's defamation of Israel among African states to which Israel had begun to make diplomatic outreach, peeving Moscow in the process. Here is a quote from a 1974 book *Against Zionism and Israeli Aggression* published by the Soviet Academy of Sciences:

> Both Zionism and Afrikaner nationalism propagandize the idea of the "chosen people," especially created by God…. It's no wonder that Zionists consider the theory of separate development (apartheid) a

sensible solution to the racial problem in South Africa. This is precisely how they would like to solve their "Arab problem." Zionists and white South Africans find common ground in their attitude to people of color.

The same gross distortion of the biblical idea of chosenness lies at the core of one of the most infamous Soviet tracts: Valery Skurlatov's 1975 *Zionism and Apartheid*. "Racial biological doctrines, according to which people are divided into 'chosen people' and goyim," he wrote, "have been turned into official ideology and state policy in Israel and South Africa, where the 'inferior' are forcibly separated from the 'superior.' That is what apartheid is."

Efforts to paint Israel and Zionism as racist culminated, of course, with the adoption of the UN "Zionism is a form of racism" resolution in 1975. Countless well-meaning progressives and anti-racists around the globe took this monstrous propaganda exercise at face value, ignorant of the fact that it was built around a fundamental element of right-wing antisemitism. Moscow's endless protests that anti-Zionism is not the same as antisemitism helped thwart potential criticism. Yet antisemitic outcomes quickly followed the adoption of the resolution for Jewish communities across the globe. For example, British Students' Unions began restricting the activities and funding of Jewish societies on campuses and even banning them. As British author Dave Rich noted in his *The Left's Jewish Problem: Jeremy Corbyn, Israel and Antisemitism*: "When you use the 'Zionism is racism' idea as the basis for practical politics, you can end up with an antisemitic campaign."

But for no other group were the outcomes of Soviet anti-Zionism as damaging as for millions of Soviet Jews. Anti-Zionist fear-mongering limited Jewish educational and professional opportunities. Convinced that Jewish religious and cultural institutions served as channels of Zionist influence, the state increasingly banned those, along with Jewish religious texts, literature, and the Hebrew language.

The effect was more insidious than one might imagine. An academic council failing a Jewish Ph.D. candidate might do so not because its members were antisemitic or got a specific directive to fail the Jews: They might do it because they understood instinctively that it was a safer choice, for their institution and their careers. A manager of a television station might harbor no personal animus toward Jews but choose to keep a Jewish journalist or performer off the air—just in case. With Zionists declared public enemy number one, avoiding adding Jews to a workplace or keeping them out of the public eye was simply the sensible approach.

***

Among the tools Moscow used to undercut the Zionist power it imagined ruled America was to work with the American press. And here, the Soviets' biggest success was a piece they managed to place in the *New York Times* in January 1971. From a secret Soviet memo, we know that the authors of the piece, which was published under the title "A Soviet View on Jews," had proposed a different title: "The Fuehrers and Storm Troopers of Neo-racism." Their objective was to expose "the spiritual kinship of Zionism and fascism."

The piece was framed around condemning Meir Kahane and the Jewish Defense League, which at the time were busy terrorizing Soviet offices and cultural productions in the United States in the name of freeing Soviet Jewry. The framing was clever and offered a surefire way for Soviet propagandists to earn an agreement from most American Jews. But the real point of the piece was to introduce Soviet "Zionism-is-Nazism" smears to the *Times'* massive readership. While ostensibly focused on Kahane and the JDL, it ultimately tagged every American Jew identifying with Israel as a "Zionist fanatic" and member of a fifth column standing in the way of peace between the United States and the USSR.

Another approach was to work with Western leftists sympathetic to the USSR. One way to do so was to finance these groups and to get them to toe the Soviet line in return. According to the historian Harvey Klehr of Emory University, in 1958–1980 the American Communist Party (CPUSA) alone got $28 million in subsidies from Moscow. Subsidies grew each year after that, to reach $3 million in 1988 alone. Millions more were spent on European groups.

One example of how this cooperation played out in practice is evident from the story of Hyman Lumer, editor-in-chief of CPUSA's *Political Affairs* journal. In 1971, Lumer went to Moscow to attend a symposium on Trotskyism. He used the opportunity to request help from highly-placed Moscow comrades to prepare "materials to unmask the Zionist anti-Soviet campaign." He promised that the materials would be distributed widely in the U.S. His liaisons arranged the necessary meetings. The material Lumer collected appeared in his 1973 book *Zionism: Its Role in World Politics* as well as other writings that circulated among the American and, presumably, British far-Left.

People like Lumer were extremely valuable to Moscow. For one thing, having Soviet talking points on Israel coming out of the mouths of Western activists, thought leaders, and journalists helped endow them with greater credibility. Having first fed them these talking points, Moscow then translated and republished their writings and speeches at home, creating an illusion that all the world's "progressive forces" agreed with it on Israel and Zionism. This global anti-Zionist echo chamber was a classic case of circular reporting: Although multiple independent sources seemed to confirm the idea that Zionism and Israel were evil, the real source of this idea was the same—the KGB and Soviet propaganda.

Soviet anti-Zionism left behind a rich written legacy. Soviet anti-Zionist books circulate on the internet and live in libraries around the world—in English, Spanish, French, German, Arabic, and Farsi.

More importantly, it left behind a legacy of political conviction. Soviet tropes about Zionism are part and parcel of Palestinian discourse vis-à-vis its Western supporters. (We only have to recall that Mahmoud Abbas defended his dissertation at the Soviet Institute of the Oriental Studies and turned it into a book to understand some of the channels through which Soviet ideas traveled to the rest of the world.) Portions of the Western Left adopted the conspiracist perspective on Israel and Zionism in the 1970s, when the Soviet influence was strongest, turning it into their default position.

* * *

Does this history really matter? Even if contemporary demonization of Zionism has antisemitic roots dating back to Soviet propaganda and the *Protocols of the Elders of Zion*, the argument will be made that Israel is still a problematic state and Zionism a problematic ideology from the left-wing perspective. Why can't a well-meaning anti-racist denounce antisemitism while feeling free to use these slogans to communicate their very valid concerns?

The best way to answer this question is to use an example that is closer to home. It comes courtesy of the British philosopher Quassim Cassam. In his book *Conspiracy Theories*, he asks: Could a white Southerner raise the Confederate flag over her porch to express pride in her Southern heritage without it connoting racism and slavery?

Most progressives would intuitively answer this question with a resounding negative. Cassam agrees and explains why. What the flag symbolizes, he writes, "isn't determined by the beliefs and intentions of the individual who chooses to display it. The flag has a life of its own, its own history and meaning." It does not become "politically benign" just because the person displaying it is a good person or "doesn't think of it as a symbol of slavery and racism." The flag's history and meaning are independent of those who raise it. Which means that "people who display the flag are, wittingly or unwittingly, associating themselves with what it *in fact* symbolizes, regardless of their personal views."

In other words, a well-meaning leftist deploying Soviet anti-Zionist tropes inevitably dips into the toxic legacy of Soviet antisemitism—a fact that is obvious to any Jew who, like myself, had been subject to that form of Jew-hatred. This legacy includes persecution and murder of religious and Zionist Jews. It includes a physical destruction of Jewish cultural figures and intellectuals. It connotes an eradication of Jewish culture and religion and restrictions on educational and professional opportunities for Jews. For Jews from the socialist bloc, it brings up memories of humiliations—from what we would today call micro-aggressions on the part of friends and colleagues, to open taunts and even beatings in the streets.

When we recall what toxic right-wing antisemitic brew went into the construction of Soviet "left-wing" anti-Zionism, the picture looks even bleaker. The simple truth is that when well-meaning progressives say that Zionism is racism or equate Israel with apartheid, they evoke an intellectual heritage that is responsible for the deaths of millions of Jews in pogroms and Hitler's genocide, and for a spiritual and cultural annihilation of millions more. I can't imagine that any genuine progressives would want to associate themselves with that—much less Jewish progressives.

Diaspora Jews, and especially American Jews, have failed to incorporate this part of history into our collective memory and to pass it on to the next generations. Today, we and our children are paying the price of this forgetting.

It is time to wake up. We *must* reacquaint ourselves with the long history of contemporary anti-Zionist demonization. We *have to* acknowledge that today's anti-Israel Left often draws on tropes, motifs, and explanatory logic of Soviet anti-Zionist discourse grounded in antisemitic conspiracy theory. We *must* recognize that politically weaponized anti-Zionism has left behind a long trail of antisemitic outcomes around the globe and will produce more—including and especially in the United States. It is our generational task to figure out how to stand up to it today.

60

IGNORE THE GLOBALISTS

Why Jewish Nationalism Drives Them Up a Wall

GADI TAUB

ANTISEMITISM HAS EVOLVED through a breathtaking dialectical leap: It is now expressed through the language of human rights. As a result, many liberals and progressives, many of them Jews, have been seduced into supporting NGOs that claim to promote human rights, but are in fact promoting their opposite: a racist view of the Jews. They do so by singling out the Jews as the one people not partaking in the universal right to self-determination, and Israel alone among the nations as the one state that has no right to exist.

Gadi Taub, Ph.D., is a historian, bestselling author of fiction and non-fiction Hebrew books, screenwriter, and faculty member at the Federmann School of Public Policy and Government at the Hebrew University of Jerusalem.

Singling out the Jews for special hostile treatment is, of course, the very definition of antisemitism.

How has this become a legitimate, even respectable position? And how did the idea of human rights, which purports to serve as a universal standard, get distorted so badly as to yield an argument for exclusion?

One part of the answer is that academia and the media have created an Industry of Lies," as the title of Israeli Left-leaning journalist Ben-Dror Yemini's book accurately called it. By using gross double standards, this industry portrays Israel as a monstrous violator of human rights. The actual egregious violators of human rights—China, North Korea, Cuba, Iran, and most of Israel's neighbors—don't receive a fraction of the moralizing attention that Israel gets.

But that is not the whole story. Another part of the answer lies in the way the human rights agenda has been channeled globally into undermining national democracies in general. This trend usually presents itself as a critique of nationalism, understood by the global Left as proto-fascism permanently poised to break into actual fascism at any moment.

The argument is admittedly catchy: If nationalism is particularistic and exclusive, then human rights, which are universal, are the answer. Catchy, that is, only if you conceive of nationalism as a "negation of others," as opposed to the particular manifestation of a universal right to national self-determination. But what is more troubling is that inside the velvet glove of the critique of nationalism hides the iron fist that is deployed against democracy. To "transcend" nationalism is to "transcend" the nation-state, and that, in turn, when those are democracies, means "transcending" democracy, too. It means undermining the effective framework by which citizens exercise control over their common fate.

Imposing a universal regime of human rights from above, through international institutions, is therefore a direct attack on civil rights, and above all on the right to elect the government under which one lives. This right is the single most effective check against tyranny, and therefore the linchpin of liberty and, consequently, all other human rights. This is how human rights arguments have been twisted into undermining our ability to defend them.

Both parts of the answer—the demonization of Israel and the attack on democracy—were clearly manifest in the Durban Conference of 2001, beginning with its Orwellian title: "World Conference against Racism, Racial Discrimination, Xenophobia, and Related Intolerance." The conference turned into a festival of blood libels against the Jewish nation-state—in the name of tolerance, of course. But the conference also exhibited the rising trend of using the idea of human rights to undermine democracy.

John Fonte was the first to point out, a year after the conference, that the new transnational globalist agenda was utilizing the UN and the conference to undermine the principle of government by the consent of the governed. Forty-seven American human rights activists, Fonte noted, sent a petition to the UN's high commissioner for human rights demanding calling for the UN to impose on the U.S. an agenda that the U.S. government had rejected. Fonte went on to write a book, *Sovereignty or Submission: Will Americans Rule Themselves or Be Ruled by Others?*, in which he detailed the many ways in which new globalist elites are bypassing democratic sovereignty in pursuit of policies that the citizens of democratic nation-states have not consented to.

The case of Israel is most instructive because the general trend of anti-democratic liberalism acquires special poignancy in the one case where a nation-state's very right to exist is questioned. The effort to undermine the Jewish nation-state has thus become explicit about both its aim and its means: the destruction of Israel in the name of human rights.

***

The argument against Israel's existence is multifaceted, but it does have a central theme, and that theme is not the occupation, though confusing it with the occupation is convenient for the purpose of propaganda. It is also not the issue of church and state, since despite some idiosyncrasies, Israel does not have an official religion or a state church such as the UK has, for example. Israel is Jewish in the national, not the religious, sense. It is Jewish the way Italy is Italian, not the way Italy is Catholic. And therefore, the question of nationalism is the heart of the argument against the existence of the Jewish state.

Israel cannot be fully democratic, the argument goes, so long as it remains a Jewish state, since by definition, a Jewish state is exclusive of all its non-Jewish citizens. Since the problem is Israel's national character, no provisions for religious freedom will solve the problem. Nor will a wall of separation between church and state alleviate it. At its extreme, this argument identifies nationalism with ethnicity, which gives it a racial ring, and then—though the Jews of Israel are one of the most multi-racial groups on earth—the argument proceeds to assert that a Jewish state is necessarily a racist state. The solution, those critics of Israel suggest, is de-nationalizing Israel, making it a non-national "state of all its citizens."

If, by these standards, Israel is "racist," or even just not democratic, then most nation-states are racist and not democratic. Most of them have national minorities who, by definition, by virtue of being *national* minorities, do not partake in the collective national identity of the state. Yet no one has demands of Italy to renounce its Italian national identity to accommodate the German-speaking minority among its citizens in the region of South Tyrol, nor does anyone ask Romania to renounce its Romanian character on account of its Hungarian minority.

In fact, the Council of Europe explicitly recognizes the legitimacy of national states when their national character is based on the majority's identity, as the Council of Europe made clear in its Framework Convention for the Protection of National Minorities. The Convention does not suggest to nation-states with national minorities to adopt a new inclusive identity that will encompass the minority (which would mean in one way or another, forced assimilation), nor does it seek to create a non-national state that is purely "neutral" toward all national identities among its citizens. Rather, it demands that nation-states with national minorities furnish national minorities with the means to protect their separate identities, such as schools in their native tongue, proportional share in cultural budgets, proportional access to support for religious institutions, and so on.

This is more or less the approach Israel chose from its inception, long before the EU existed, in its 1948 Declaration of Independence, which, beside proclaiming equal individual rights to all citizens, Arab and Jewish alike, also asserts the legitimacy of collective minority rights by proclaiming the right to "religion, conscience, language, education and culture."

Israel did not always live up to this standard, which is lamentable, though not entirely surprising given the bleeding national conflict with the very people to which Israel's Arab minority—or much of it—purports to belong. There are also ways in which Israel is more accommodating to its national minorities than most democracies are, and this, too, is not unconnected to the special circumstances of the conflict. Israel allows, for example, Arab parties who seek the destruction of the Jewish state, quite explicitly, to sit in its parliament, even though the law in Israel, like that of other democracies, forbids running on such platforms.

***

The only way to make Israel renounce its Jewish national character is to overthrow its democracy. As long as there is universal suffrage and a large Jewish majority that cherishes its Jewish culture, Shabbat will continue to be Israel's day of rest, Jewish holidays will structure its calendar, Hebrew will be its first official language, and its public symbols will draw predominantly on the Jewish tradition. This makes clear why the post-national Jewish elite (in Israel and no less importantly outside it) must work to undermine democracy if it seeks to make Israel a non-Jewish state. Nowhere is the connection between the critique of nationalism and the assault on democracy—through the use of human rights—as clear and explicit.

And it is not only clear in theory, it is also manifested institutionally. Consider the rise of Israel's Supreme Court to the status of an uber-government. It usurped power by means of reinterpreting two of Israel's semi-constitutional Basic Laws, which sought to secure "human dignity and liberty" and "freedom of occupation." These laws, the court argued—without any explicit authorization in the language of the law—granted it the power of judicial review over the elected executive and legislative branches, which it has used with increasing frequency and brazenness.

The usurpation of power took some decades to mature, but it has finally reached a state in which there is no formal limit to the court's power, no area of politics over which it does not demand jurisdiction, and there are no checks or balances to speak of that can counter its power. Of course, it also helps that the decidedly progressive court has effective veto power over the nomination of its own judges.

Courts, as Fonte noted, are the common portals through which the globalist agenda is imposed on democratic nation-states, often against the will of most of their citizens, via the endorsement of "international law" and international agreements. The original petition submitted by American human rights NGOs to the UN's high commissioner for human rights, with which Fonte opens his book, demanded that the U.S. "remove its restrictions" from full adoption of the UN Convention on the Elimination of All Forms of Racial Discrimination (CERD). Chief among these restrictions is the caveat that says the implementation of any international covenant is subject to the U.S. Constitution.

Increasingly, Fonte shows, U.S. courts have eroded this principle and began considering cases in light of foreign norms. This has brought about a subtle but important shift in American jurisprudence, where the authority of human rights, formerly derived from their endorsement by the American people who included them in the constitution, now resides above the people, in "international norms" poised to subdue the will of the people in case of a conflict between them.

But Israel has gone further down that road, as demonstrated most clearly by the court's repeated interception of any attempt by the state to curtail illegal immigration. Immigration laws are, of course, central to a society's ability to preserve its national identity. In Israel this is perhaps even more manifested because of its Law of Return, which grants automatic citizenship to any Jew arriving in Israel. The law is, of course, a cornerstone of the Zionist enterprise. Its logic is what originally animated the Balfour Declaration of 1917, as well as the Partition Plan adopted by the UN General Assembly in 1947. The UN Special Committee on Palestine (UNSCOP) understood that Jewish immigration was the heart of the controversy. Partition was designed to allow the Jews, a stateless people, more or less unlimited immigration to a Jewish state, to be created on part of the disputed territory, leaving the other part with a secure Arab majority. It can be said, then, that the Law of Return was the original intention of the UN assembly's Partition resolution.

Though the court has never dared to strike down the Law of Return, it repeatedly extrapolated from the idea of universal human rights a general principle of equal rights, which frowns upon attempts to insist on the difference between the rights of citizens and the rights of illegal immigrants. Social benefits are generously extended to people who broke the law entering the country, the definition of "refugee" is stretched, and even mild measures encouraging illegals to leave—such as a small deposit by both employer and employee, to be collected upon leaving the country—are off-handedly struck down.

* * *

In all this, the court is prodded on and cheered by NGOs, a good number of which deal specifically with illegal immigrants, offering them legal assistance, contributing expert opinions in the press, and taking part in agitation in the name of human rights.

There is a vast number of other NGOs that include "human rights" in their mission statements. As Swedish journalist Paulina Neuding aptly put it, Israel is a virtual Disneyland for NGOs. Many of these are bent on enflaming the conflict, defaming Israel by documenting in a strongly biased fashion the human rights violations of one side only, real and imagined, with the explicit intention of drawing outside pressure to force Israel's hand into concessions it does not want to make.

Inviting external pressure is the option preferred by a considerable part of the Israeli Left that has given up on promoting its agenda by convincing Israeli voters. Confident in the moral superiority of their stance, but lacking any clear plan to promote it after the unravelling of the Oslo process, which exposed the absence of a peace partner on the Palestinian side, their impotent rage morphed from a desire to save Israel from the dangers of the occupation into a hatred of Zionism itself.

In this way an organization like B'Tselem, originally devoted to documenting human rights infringements by the Israeli army in the disputed territories under military rule, eventually produces a report that rejects the very legitimacy of a Jewish nation-state, claiming Israel as a whole is an "apartheid state." A 2021 report by B'Tselem was entitled "A Regime of Jewish Supremacy from the Jordan River to the Mediterranean Sea: This is Apartheid."

The report clearly aims at world public opinion, which B'Tselem hopes would be able to bully Israel to do its bidding. This is not a hypothesis. B'Tselem's director, the activist Hagai El-Ad, has already taken the case against his own country to the UN Security Council in 2016.

The so-called post-Zionists are a minority in Israel but they wield influence far beyond their numbers. They are disproportionally represented, in some cases dominant, in academia, the press, the bureaucracy, and the courts. They are also supported by a seemingly limitless stream of cash from abroad from private donors, civil society funds and organizations, international institutions, as well as state governments.

This deluge of funding is aimed at changing Israel in the spirit of the progressive globalist elite, in ways its citizens have clearly rejected. Those include the usual anti-religious, anti-national, and anti-family goals, with the addition of fostering Palestinian nationalism and political Islam (and pushing Arab citizens of Israel in these directions).

Matan Peleg's book *A State for Sale: How Foreign Countries Interfere with Israeli Policy* documented the funding coming from states and groups of states into campaigns designed to change the social, political, and cultural fabric of Israel. Topping the list in the last decade are Germany (over $44 million), the EU (over $43 million), the U.S. (over $17 million), the UN (over $17 million), with the Netherlands, Switzerland, and Norway trailing not far behind. There is also Turkish money harnessed to foster a Muslim Brotherhood identity around which different stripes of Arab citizens can unite—against Zionism— and money from OPEC claimed to foster Arab "culture" but actually worked to preventing the civil assimilation of Arab citizens into Israeli society.

Make no mistake: All this money, and much more from private sources— including Jewish donors via groups like the New Israel Fund—are harnessed to attempt to destroy Zionism and undermine the right of Jews to self-determination in their own nation-state. For this, it creates levers that can subdue the democratic will of Israel's citizenry. This would have been unimaginable in any other country. It can only seem legitimate if you assume—together with the antisemites—that the case of the Jews is somehow unique.

* * *

Zionism and assimilation were always two alternative strategies for Jewish life that are in permanent tension. Jews who sought to assimilate into other national societies were never easy with the reformulation of Jewish identity in national terms. For if Jews are a nation, they would necessarily face the suspicion of dual loyalty, which had been such a useful trope in the hands of antisemites.

But Zionism, as Shlomo Avineri had observed, has also set Jews free not only within Israel, but outside it, too. For the first time in two millennia, Diaspora became a choice, not a fate. Yet the tension persists in other ways. The controversy survived the success of Zionism, though it may have metamorphosed: Progressive Jewish detractors of Zionism seem to be bothered less by the specter of dual loyalty accusations, since the same crowd that despises Israel's nationalism often sneers at expressions of American patriotism as well. One suspects that distancing oneself from Israel is a badge of progressivism not only among gentiles but among Jews seeking less to be accepted into American society and more to be seen as adherents of progressive internationalism. This, too, is not entirely new. There was a disproportional representation for Jews among the adherents of another kind of internationalism—that of Communism. And just like international progressivism, Soviet Communism wished to undermine the Jewish state in the name of lofty sounding ideals.

With a view to the future of the Jewish people, this rift—this cultural war turned political struggle—should be taken seriously. We will all be better off if, instead of kicking shins under the table, we put this controversy directly on the table, where we can debate it honestly and openly—ready, too, for the possibility that the rift may not be bridgeable.

In such a case, Israel will have no choice but to defend itself more vigorously against its Jewish detractors. It should protect its democracy from the antidemocratic influences of foreign money—Jewish or non-Jewish—respect the choice of Jews in the Diaspora to live their Jewish identity differently, and keep the door of the Law of Return open, even for those Jews who are now trying to deprive their own people of the right to self-determination—just in case progressive antisemitism forces them to flee, once again.

61

ZIONISM AS THERAPY

How the Movement's Founding Texts Offer an Answer to Today's Bullies

EINAT WILF

IN THE FALL OF 2021, I spent a semester at Georgetown University teaching a seminar on "Zionism and Anti-Zionism." When I wrapped up the final class, one of the students approached me. "The course was more valuable," she told me, "than dozens of hours of therapy."

Einat Wilf, Ph.D., was a Member of Knesset on behalf of the Labor Party from 2010 to 2013. Her most recent two books are the co-authored *The War of Return: How Western Indulgence of the Palestinian Dream Has Obstructed the Path to Peace* (St. Martin's, 2020) and *We Should All Be Zionists: Essays on the Jewish State and the Path to Peace* (2022).

I have spent my life thinking, writing, and speaking about Israel, Zionism, the Jewish people, anti-Zionism, the conflict, and the path to peace. But I had never taught this course before, and now I was both moved and baffled. Why did she feel the need for therapy, and what was in the course that offered it so powerfully?

The course argued that while Zionism is one of history's most successful revolutions, it has faced since its inception not only diplomatic and physical obstacles to implementing its vision, but also intellectual opposition to its very idea, which continued even once Zionism materialized in the form of the State of Israel. The course explored how every type of Zionist thought—political, social, religious—was opposed by a certain brand of non- or anti-Zionism. These would be presented through a set of pairs loosely paralleling historical developments.

The first section, under the theme of "politics," paired political emancipation, as a non-Zionist alternative of Jewish integration into European society, with the rise of political Zionism as a response, among other things, to the failure of emancipation. The second pair—under the heading of "labor"—explored the ideas of socialism, Bundism, and communism as non-Zionist utopian visions for Jewish equality, paired with Labor Zionism and the critiques each of them had towards the others for being either too universalist or too particularist.

The course then moved to Zionism and anti-Zionism as reflected in the three monotheistic theologies. Jewish theological anti-Zionism was paired with Jewish religious Zionism as the theological post-facto justification for the success of secular Zionism. Christian anti-Zionism presented the theological basis for Christian, and later Western, opposition to Jewish sovereignty. It was paired with Christian Zionism, exploring the later theological development of Christian support for Zionism. We then turned to the world of Arab Islam, exploring Arab anti-Zionism against the background of the establishment of the State of Israel—ending with discussion of Soviet anti-Zionism and the intriguing possibility of the rise of Arab Zionism.

The course syllabus consisted almost solely of primary sources. Following a short introduction of historical context for each pair, the students engaged directly with the original texts, learning what Zionists and anti-Zionists had to say in their own words. Much like yeshiva students, they became part of an inter-generational conversation by engaging with the arguments and counter-arguments from the time. They were asked to make every effort to insert themselves into the conversation, and so gain a sense of how the debate unfolded in real time, and how the success of Zionism cannot be understood as inevitable.

***

One unexpected outcome of the course was that the current tenor of debate was placed in perspective. When students were exposed to how Zionists wrote about emancipated Jews and how communists and religious anti-Zionists wrote about Zionists, the current discourse seemed tame by comparison. If anything, the late-nineteenth and early-twentieth centuries emerged as an era of Jewish disagreement and division far greater than our own.

But more importantly, the direct engagement with Zionist and anti-Zionist texts accounted for some of the therapeutic effects of the course. When reading what Zionists had to say in their own words, the toxic descriptions of Zionism as emblematic of the world's evils, from racism to genocide, melted away. Instead of a cabal of evil conspirators intent on wreaking evil in this world, these Jewish writers were desperately trying to carve a path for surviving as Jews in the modern era. Rather than powerful privileged Europeans seeking to dispossess another people, these were powerless and thoughtful Jews wrestling with how, against all odds, they could go about building a modern state in an ancient homeland that was mostly barren but in places also populated. Instead of the idea of Jewish nationhood and self-determination presented as a unique aberration in human history, Zionism emerged from the texts as no more than the Jewish manifestation of the concurrent global transition from empires to nation-based states.

In contrast, reading anti-Zionists in their own words exposed the total, often sinister, worldview that was the basis for their opposition to Zionism. When the deep roots of anti-Zionism were exposed, current justifications ostensibly tied to recent events revealed themselves to be nonsensical. Once the ancient Christian theological need for Jews to remain stateless and powerless was studied, its secularized western manifestation in the obsession with Israeli power became understood. Once the history of blood libels, with its particular emphasis on Jewish ritual lust for the blood of non-Jewish children, was seen, its secularized version in news headlines about the Israel Defense Forces killing children could no longer be unseen. Once Soviet anti-Zionism was studied as a scrubbed heir to the Tsarist *Protocols of the Elders of Zion*, the current academic discourse on Apartheid Racist Colonial Israel was traced to its original authors, long before post-facto justifications for those epithets were made. And once the ideals of political emancipation, Bundism, and communism were understood as genuinely believed utopian alternatives to Zionism, the verdict of history on the practical impossibility of these paths for Jews became tragically apparent.

Direct engagement with Zionist and anti-Zionist texts made the present clear—in the original sense of the word "clear," as transparent and see-through. Students acquired the ability, almost a superpower, to see through the current discourse and understand Zionism and anti-Zionism for what they are. Zionism emerged as something *normal*: a national movement of self-determination of a people with a historical connection to a specific land, at a time when many peoples rose to establish nation-based states to replace receding empires. And anti-Zionism emerged from the texts as *abnormal*: a unique, ancient theological obsession that presents itself to every generation as newly justified.

And so, students discovered that *nothing* being said today about Zionism, especially by anti-Zionists, is new. While they did not study directly about the present, by the end of the course they had acquired the tools to understand the present far better than most people who express themselves on the topic. The students had joined the ranks of a select few who had first-hand knowledge of the foundational texts of both Zionism and anti-Zionism.

***

It was that connection—between today's discourse and its ancient roots—that made clear to me why therapy was even needed, and why the course was effective in providing it. *Therapy was needed because anti-Zionism is but a recent manifestation of an ancient attack on individual and collective Jewish life. The course was effective in providing it, because Zionism itself was formulated as a therapeutic response to that ancient attack.*

Anti-Zionism in the West desperately tries to hide behind the claim that is nothing more than "criticism of Israel," but its targeting of Jewish students and faculty, its promotion of Jews who are most virulently as anti-Zionist, and its relentless dynamic of constantly moving the goalposts, mean that it is experienced by many Jews as incessant bullying—a dynamic I call the "pound of flesh." After all, William Shakespeare had it backwards: Throughout history, it is not the Jews who demanded the pound of flesh. Rather, it was the Jews who were bullied for a pound of flesh, usually metaphorically, but all too often literally.

When the pound of flesh is metaphorical, the demand is to mutilate one's Jewish identity as the price of social acceptance and toleration. Sometimes the mutilation is visual, demanding that Jews be less visibly Jewish in the public sphere. Sometimes it involves severing elements of Jewish identity, such as denying any special Jewish collective solidarity or the Jews' connection with the Land of Israel. Sometimes nothing less than a ceremony of exorcism, in which Jews mutilate their identity in public, is demanded.

These exorcism ceremonies require Jews to repeat with enthusiastic Amens any claims made about Israel, however outlandish. This is what I have termed the "placard strategy," equating Israel, Zionism, and sometimes just the Star of David on placards with the greatest evil du jour. And so, the ceremony proceeds: Zionism equals Racism. *Amen.* Zionism equals Apartheid. *Amen.* Zionism equals Nazism. *Of course.* Zionism equals genocide. *What else?* Oh, Zionism now equals White Supremacism. *That's a new one, but sure.* There is nothing natural and understandable in this progression. It is the pure expression of a relentless dynamic of bullying at work.

This bullying has ancient roots. The historian Tom Holland, in his excellent book *Dominion: How the Christian Revolution Remade the World*, which my students read, described this centuries-old dynamic as "a program for civic self-improvement that aimed at transforming the very essence of Judaism." Holland describes how Western ideas of enlightenment and human rights have, when it comes to Jews, been nothing more than a secularized version of the ancient Christian dream "that Jewish distinctiveness might be subsumed into an identity that the whole world could share—one in which the laws given by God to mark the Jews out from other peoples would cease to matter." Despite this being a dream that in modernity was "garlanded with the high-flown rhetoric of the Enlightenment," Holland explains, its roots go "all the way back to Paul." Faced with this all-encompassing, new-old campaign, "Jews could either sign up to this radiant vision, or else be banished into storm-swept darkness." Holland clarifies that "if this seemed to some Jews a very familiar kind of ultimatum, then that was because it was."

The ancient roots of the "pound of flesh" dynamic make it relentless. It always wants more, until there is no more flesh left. Either Jews are no longer Jews, or they are no longer alive. Throughout history, Jews have discovered again and again that no amount of flesh is ever sufficient.

* * *

This kind of bullying takes an emotional toll. It is not a matter of intellectual discourse. It operates at the deepest levels of one's being. Almost all Jews have been subjected to it at one point or another and recognize it viscerally. Even when students could not explain it, their emotional reaction to anti-Zionist attacks on campus was the typical response triggered by persistent bullying. Anti-Zionist bullying was taking its toll on those Jewish students who refused to join its ranks.

Even I, who study and teach Zionism and anti-Zionism, find myself at times exhausted after engaging with Western students on the topic, interactions that increasingly include personal attacks and charges of evil. It is not pleasant. It takes an emotional toll to be told that what you hold dear, even who you are, is evil. It would be much nicer to be lauded by students for concurring with them that Israel is evil. The temptation of being liked in a world of likes is powerful. I can understand why young students on campus would choose to either stay silent or even join the bullies in the hope of being left alone.

But what Zionist thinkers like Theodor Herzl reluctantly realized is that they would never be left alone. Herzl observed how antisemitism rose in the nineteenth century as a progressive idea, popular among students on campuses, such as the one in Vienna where he studied law, by giving a modern scientific-sounding façade to ancient ideas about Jews. This convinced Herzl and fellow

Zionists that as much as modern Europeans claimed to uphold ideals of equality, liberty, and fraternity, they could not bring themselves to apply these ideals to Jews. Observing nearly a century of European emancipation, Herzl and his fellow Zionists realized that no matter how much Jews strained themselves to be acceptable to their fellow Europeans—changing their clothes, their language, even their very conception of being Jews, away from a collective identity to a personal "faith"—Europeans would just come up with new cover stories to tell Jews the same old thing they had always told them: You do not belong.

Although they didn't call it bullying, Zionist thinkers understood Jews were prey to the "pound of flesh" dynamic. Often harsh in describing the Jewish condition under European domination, some of their criticisms could hardly be differentiated from those of antisemites. But whereas antisemites believed the Jewish "sickness" to be inherent to Jewishness itself, Zionists believed it was the result of European actions—situational and conditional—and the systemic powerlessness forced upon the Jews of Europe.

This was the seminal insight of Zionist thinkers: that powerlessness corrupts no less than power. That power corrupts is an ancient teaching shared by biblical writers no less than Greek, Roman, Hindu, and Chinese ones. But Zionism argued that *powerlessness* corrupts no less. Zionist thinkers observed that a people whose very survival depended on the frequently absent goodwill of others would inevitably be corrupted by the need to ingratiate itself with those in power.

***

At its core, then, *Zionism was a therapeutic project.* Zionism was about healing the Jewish sickness engendered by the contorting and corrupting effect of centuries of powerless exile. Since, in the Zionist analysis, this Jewish "sickness" was the result of living at the mercy of others, healing that "sickness" would require that Jews attain power of their own. Zionism sought to correct this corruption of Jewish existence by making Jews masters of their fate, powerful once again, normalized political actors among the nations. Zionism provided both the diagnosis and the cure.

But precisely because the cure was so effective, Jews had to be told it was actually toxic. Those who bullied Jews throughout the centuries needed Jews to believe the problem was with themselves, so that they would be amenable to efforts to make them no longer Jewish. Like an industry that profits by keeping people sick and therefore invests heavily in making simple, cheap cures appear toxic and unreliable, civilizations that required Jews to feel they needed to be less Jewish had to paint Zionism as so toxic that no Jew would want to touch it.

But touch it is exactly what the course did. Successful therapy taps into the molten lava that runs deep below the surface. Jewish leaders, rabbis, and organizations who thought they could escape the onslaught by avoiding discussions of Zionism and Israel discovered that the attacks never relented. The more they ran away, the more they were chased. Jews were told that Zionism was a sin and therefore they had to disavow it. In reality, Zionism was the cure that endangered the entire malignant project of de-Judaizing Jews.

This is why the course proved so therapeutic. Students discovered that their ailment had been diagnosed long ago, and an effective cure already found. Exposing the ancient roots of anti-Zionist bullying provided young Jews with understanding that while it appears tempting to disavow or contort Jewish identity to buy a reprieve from the bullies, this reprieve, if ever given, is at best temporary. Rather, Zionism already formulated a response to that bullying by refusing to play into its ever-increasing demands.

Bullies everywhere prey on weakness and shame. But if one is neither weak nor ashamed, they move on to easier targets. The course offered students the ability to understand the genealogy of attacks Jews face today while simultaneously generating an empowered appreciation for the vigorous debate and revolution that produced Zionism. It created excitement and confidence in the modern Jewish project and identity.

By robbing anti-Zionists of the power to shame them, students of these century-old texts discovered they had the power to rob their bullies of their prey. If anti-Zionists are met with Jews who are proud Zionists, who embrace their Jewish identity fully, and who understand the nature of the attacks against them, it is nearly impossible to shame them into handing over another pound of flesh.

What they realized by the end of the course was that the only effective, tried and tested response to anti-Zionism is, well, Zionism.

62

ON MORAL CONFIDENCE

How the Diaspora Lost Its Jewish Spine, and How to Get It Back

RUTH R. WISSE

THE FIRST TIME I recall using the phrase "moral confidence" was when planning a conference on the centenary of Zionism at Harvard in 1996–1997. Beyond the call to celebrate and commemorate the First Zionist Congress, I wanted to advance the study of this magnificent venture in the history of the Jews, who were too often associated with political failure and cultural assimilation.

Ruth R. Wisse is a Professor Emerita of Yiddish and Comparative Literature at Harvard University and a Fellow at the Tikvah Fund. Her latest book is *Free as a Jew: A Personal Memoir of National Self-Liberation* (Wicked Son, 2021).

Zionism was the most inspiring of all the world's modern liberation movements. I planned the conference on a grand scale in partnership with Israel's largest universities, and looked for sponsorship to support it.

When the donor whom I had identified said he doubted the benefits of academic gatherings, I explained that this one could help strengthen the "moral confidence" that I found so lacking among the Jews at Harvard. Why were many Arab and Muslim students ready to *attack* Israel in the name of their faith, whereas their Jewish counterparts could barely defend the Jewish national homeland, let alone refute those who denied its legitimacy? Why were Jews who had risen to important academic and administrative positions on campus unwilling to correct and repudiate obvious anti-Jewish and anti-Zionist calumnies? Why were Hillel House professionals afraid to champion Israel? Why, after antisemitism had almost disappeared in America, was it making such a comeback in the world of ideas where Jews were supposed to have an advantage?

Truth is said to be the best weapon in a free and open society, but the donor questioned whether several days of high-level presentations by even the finest scholars could affect the prevailing climate of opinion. Their value, I suggested, would be realized by disseminating their conclusions in the academy and, as much as possible, in the media. The attendees would learn from and be encouraged by an international gathering on the subject. Students would gain from exposure to these speakers and their ideas, and Zionism would be on positive display. Still skeptical, and insisting on anonymity, the donor wrote the check.

I believe the ensuing conference justified itself academically, but nothing more. There was little media coverage, even in the Jewish press. The longest item featured an interview with Benny Morris, the only participant to give a condemnatory talk—about Israel's actions in its War of Independence—a position he would later recant.

Since then, the problem I identified to our donor has intensified to proportions I could not have foreseen. The growing ferocity of the political and ideological attack on Israel and Jews has induced a corresponding collapse of morale among those who are sensitive to accusation. Jews of strong autonomous faith in Jewish values can withstand hostility to the point of death, but those without such commitment can fold like an accordion—one that is playing the enemy's anthem.

**

Moral confidence is essential to those who consider themselves a chosen nation. As the Torah records and tradition reinforces, the Jewish people were forged as a nation at Sinai when they entered into a contractual agreement with the Almighty, Lord of the Universe, and declared themselves ready and willing to stand before His judgment. The ark in the synagogue that I attended as a child bore the inscription, "Know Before Whom You Stand"—*da lifnei mi ata omed*—making every day Yom Kippur. Before there were "secular Jews," Jews held themselves to a strict code of law and custom, and felt personally accountable for the national fate when they failed to do so. The best minds and spirits of the Jewish people went into ensuring that Jewish civilization continued to preserve individual freedom within strict religious and social constraints.

Yet the drive for self-perfection also had its perils. The British editorialist Gerard Baker recently identified the central paradox of liberal democracy— "Since we are free to air our faults, we can talk about nothing else"—and warned that, when taken to excess, compulsive self-criticism destroys the system of accountability that it was intended to fortify. How much truer this dynamic is of the Jews, whose creative energy has always gone into self-accusation, including through their celebrated humor, much of which would be considered antisemitic if leveled from outside the community.

And whereas Baker was referring to major democracies like Britain and the United States, Jews lived as a minority by choice among nations that controlled their political fate. Jews defined their defeats as divine punishment for their actions, *theirs* and no others, so that when the Jewish homeland fell to the Babylonians in the sixth century B.C.E., then to the Romans in 70 C.E., they blamed themselves for having failed to uphold God's standard.

This same self-accountability then enabled the survivors to form dispersed communities with the confidence that they would be returned to their land whenever they *did* satisfy the terms of their contract. But what about the surrounding peoples who, in happy agreement that Jews were being punished for their sins, felt rightful in destroying them?

In my book *Jews and Power*, I tried to show how Jews paid with their lives for this moral solipsism. Modern Jews finally concluded that the cost was too high, and went about securing their homeland through all available means, in the face of what seemed insurmountable opposition. But still the old habits survived, and from the moment that the Soviet-Arab bloc succeeded in driving the Zionism-equals-racism equation through the United Nations and then into the academy, the media, and the politics of Western democracies, many liberal Jews began losing their confidence in the justice of their cause. Leftists in particular—Jewish and otherwise—led the lemmings into the resulting moral abyss, making common cause with "Palestinians," a term I put in scare quotes because Arab and Muslim leaders had deliberately forged Palestinian grievance into the excuse for denying to Jews what was *their own* land and no one else's.

* * *

A century ago, had I been asked about the priority for the Jewish people, I would have insisted on territorial and military self-defense. Adherents to the Torah customarily thank God for *not* having made us like all the nations, but at that point I would have joined Ze'ev Jabotinsky and those in the *yishuv*, the Jewish community in pre-state Palestine, who had decided to be enough like other nations to protect themselves from the worst of those other nations. Thankfully, though far too late for far too many, enough Jews adopted these priorities to create the State of Israel.

Having done so, Jews now confronted all the hard tasks of maintaining a sovereign state with the disadvantages of not having had to manage one for a very long time. What is more, the acute political asymmetry between Israel and the surrounding Arab and Muslim world had not lessened the political imbalance. Helped, however, by skills and habits of adaptation in the Diaspora, Israel became a successful "start-up nation" that dared not relax its vigilance for a millisecond. So, I salute those whose Jewish priority is the protection of the Jewish state.

Nonetheless, writing as I do from America, where the collapse of national will threatens this much larger and presumably already stronger democracy, I see that belief in a country's legitimacy and purpose must underlie all that is precious to its citizens.

Let future historians determine the reasons for the symptomatic erosion of faith in American democracy; I will merely cite some of its manifestations. At elite universities, academic ideologues antagonistic to "capitalist" America and to "unjustly privileged" Western civilization drive home the idea that the Republic is not worth preserving. Protests against the draft during the Vietnam War expanded into a ban of all recruitment or training on campus for what had now become a volunteer army. Under the euphemism "affirmative action," the school engineered racial and group preferences in admissions and hiring, defying the Civil Rights Act that called for equal treatment *irrespective* of race or creed. Women formed political action groups to disadvantage males and disparage allegedly patriarchal institutions like the family. By now, intersectional alliances of these and other grievance blocs dominate the culture even if they do not yet represent a majority of the people.

Unbelievably soon after Hitler's war against the Jews, yet with bleak predictability, the cause heading this March of Blames is the charge that Jews deprive Palestinians of their land. Ideological antisemitism that had attacked Jews in their dispersion is now anti-Zionism that attacks Jews in their homeland. The Arab League war to destroy the Jewish state is the most lopsided conflict in history, and the assigned role of Palestinian Arabs in this struggle is to remain its perpetual pretext and battering ram. Whereas all previous antagonists have vowed to expel, expropriate, or exterminate the Jews, Palestinian Arabs intend to *replace* the Jews without making any effort at self-rule until they do so.

That this asymmetrical, morally repellent aggression against the Jewish people should have penetrated the United States is bad enough; that the inversion of Jew killers claiming victimhood should have won the support of American academic and cultural elites is many degrees worse; but that Jews in the freest country on earth should have joined the ranks of their deniers is a great stain on human history. We see Jewish Studies professors signing petitions against an American embassy in Jerusalem, and rabbis trained in "advanced" seminaries protesting the Jews' right to their land. Jewish liberals march in parades led by antisemites and contribute to politicians who revile their people. Jewish leftists still follow the Soviet playbook that expects Jews to disadvantage themselves in favor of all other minorities to achieve the equity that communism seeks to impose. I will refrain from quoting the indignities that issue in times of stress from celebrities who expect that trashing Israel will cement their fame.

It was understandable that some Jews should have joined their enemies to escape the heel of Rome, the pyres of the Inquisition, and the secret police of Stalin. But that they should fail to mount in America an effective political counterforce as effective as the Israel Defense Forces insults America and the legacy of Sinai. History will never forgive them.

So, as against this blight, I single out the moral confidence of the many Jews who enjoy the blessings of Jewishness and of partnership in sustaining a Jewish state. Holding oneself to a higher standard of civilizing behavior results in a higher quality of living. If this proves enviable, let us explain and promote Judaism's advantages, for although we may not actively seek converts, anyone can become a Jew who genuinely wishes to. But let us never allow our depraved adversaries to redefine us in their image or to defame the soundness that Jews represent.

We owe it to those who received the law at Sinai and to those who guard the Western Wall not to kneel and scrape before the destroyers, but to know and to proclaim before Whom we stand, and why.

63

RESPECT YOUR OPPONENTS

In Great Disputes, There Is No Solitary Truth

DAVID WOLPE

LET'S START AT THE BEGINNING. People do not like to hear opinions that contradict their own, challenge their cherished beliefs, or offend their moral sensibilities. Contradictory creatures all, we do not seek to be contradicted. We wish to be affirmed. Few pleasures in life are as validating as being able to say, "You see—I was right!"

There is an old Jewish joke about two scholars dividing the world. First, they divide into Jews and non-Jews. The non-Jews know nothing of Torah. Then into religious Jews and non-religious Jews. The non-religious know

Rabbi David Wolpe is the Rabbi Emeritus of Sinai Temple, Visiting Scholar at Harvard Divinity school, and the author, most recently, of *David: The Divided Heart* (Yale, 2014).

nothing of Torah. Then they go through each sect, each Rebbe, dismissing the one that is not their own. Finally, one of them concludes: "Really, that leaves only you and me. And you *know* how little you know."

While the world is not quite so dogmatically individualized, there is a genuine threat to the spirit of disagreement in our culture. Almost no day passes without instances of people being attacked or dismissed from their jobs for views they hold or positions they have taken. Most alarmingly, a principal source of such intolerance is the college campus, which is traditionally a bastion of free speech. For too many, disagreement is not an invitation to engage but a demonstration of unfitness.

Yet at the same time, even the most dogmatic among us know that advancement is not won solely through agreement. The law of averages means most of us will be wrong about most things since there are infinitely more ways of being wrong than being right. Knowing this, we are nonetheless stubbornly insistent on our views, while claiming to seek a system that permits alternatives to be explained and explored.

Providentially, Judaism has just such a system. The Talmud enshrines argument. If Judaism had sacraments, debate would be one of them.

***

When the great rabbi Resh Lakish died, his brother-in-law and intellectual sparring partner, Rabbi Johanan, was inconsolable. The other rabbis, seeking to comfort Rabbi Johanan, sent Rabbi Eliezer ben Pedat, who was known as a very fine legal mind, to engage and perhaps distract him. It did not go well.

Every time Rabbi Johanan offered a teaching, the learned Rabbi Eliezer ben Pedat would say, "There is a teaching that supports you." Finally, Rabbi Johanan burst out: "Do you think you are like Resh Lakish? When I stated the law, he would raise twenty-four objections, which led to a fuller understanding. All you do is tell me there is a teaching that supports me." Rabbi Johanan teaches us the counterintuitive comfort of contradiction.

The Talmud is unclassifiable, but one would not go too far wrong to describe it as one long dispute. Unlike most books, the Talmud enshrines a large number of voices, and they disagree with one another. My Talmud teacher once said that learning Talmud in school as a child he learned that if the instructor asked a question and you weren't paying attention, you just said, "There's a *machloket* (dispute)" and you would almost always be correct. The back and forth continues among the later commentators on the page until, if the words could be suddenly vocalized, you would get a cacophony of intricate and often indignant argument.

There are limitations, of course. The equivalent of "fire in a crowded theater" existed in Judaism as well. Blasphemy exists as a prohibition, and there were things one was simply not supposed to say. You can imagine that insulting God was not allowed. But even there it was not so simple. The rabbis often found a way to express even seemingly forbidden ideas.

To take but a single example: Making a play on the verse "Who is like You among the gods?" (*elim*), the school of Rabbi Yishmael taught, "Who is like you among the mute?" (*ilmim*) (Gittin 56b). After all, God has a disconcerting habit of not joining in when the divine voice would be deeply appreciated. Still, labeling God as mute is pretty daring. Don't forget that Abraham, in the Book of Genesis, already questions God's justice when told Sodom is to be destroyed: "Shall the Judge of all the earth not do justice?" Blasphemy may have been interdicted, but the argumentative impulse found ingenious ways of expressing itself.

The verse in II Kings about "those who wage war" is taken by the author of Sifre, an ancient collection of midrash, to be those who engage in the dialogue and debate in the war of Torah. In other words, the arguers.

So how sad and un-Jewish it is to hear people shut down argument and debate. Name-calling and epithets are not debate. Insult is not argument. Increasingly there are certain points of view one is simply not permitted to voice, because they offend or disconcert others. We are all being tossed out the Overton window.

Several years ago, I was talking to an Israeli entrepreneur about the way ideas are presented at meetings. I mentioned that in most of the meetings I attended, when we were brainstorming, no criticism of ideas was permitted. He scoffed at the notion: "In Israel, if you don't criticize other people's ideas, everyone thinks you must be stupid." He laughed as he said it, but we both agreed that the legacy of Talmudic dispute found its way into Israel's corporate culture.

Being ready to criticize, however, should not just mean throwing grenades over the fence at others. True criticism entails self-criticism. Notice that Rabbi Johanan was not upset because Rabbi Eliezer ben Pedat wasn't criticizing other rabbis, but because Rabbi Johanan wanted his own ideas challenged.

Judaism holds that there is an objective truth, but at the very heart of the Jewish system is the difficulty of distilling that truth and the necessity of hearing different views to attain it. In other words, dispute is not an adjunct to Judaism, but central to its mission.

* * *

Like most rabbis, I often receive articles from my congregants that urge their point of view on political issues, Jewish religious issues, and Israel. For many of them, as soon as I see who penned the editorial, I know what the argument will be. Many writers are not analysts; they are polemicists.

To such writers—and you can easily make a list—the other side never makes a good point, does a good deed, or promotes an honest politician. If they are liberal, then the conservatives are prejudiced and narrow; if they are conservative, then the liberals are unpatriotic and foolish. The drumbeat of ideology is so loud I wonder how it doesn't give the writers themselves a headache.

Even some of our noblest spirits sometimes refuse to have their preconceptions challenged. We have many fine scholars and teachers who will not engage with other Jews who have "wrong" views on Torah, politics, or both. But this is a position that Jewish history and philosophy, with its plurality of incompatible views, flatly contradicts.

Preaching pluralism to the world and denying it at home violates the heart of our tradition. It is possible to be passionate and still open to debate, to acknowledge the merit in other views and still believe they are wrong. But to many, any concession is seen as betrayal of the tribe (or subtribe, or microtribe), so that you don't only risk losing the argument, but you risk losing your friends. Not only is it difficult to grant a point to those who stand opposite you; it is even more difficult to break ranks with those who stand with you. Conceding that the other side has a point is less likely to be viewed as open-minded than as betrayal, a question not of honesty but of loyalty.

Judaism has wise counsel for those who wish to do better. The Talmud in Tractate Eruvin says that the House of Shammai and the House of Hillel, the two great rabbinic schools, argued for years. A voice came from heaven and announced that "these and those are the words of the living God"—that is, in great disputes, there is no solitary truth. However, the Talmud goes on to ask, why then is it that the House of Hillel prevailed in most disputes? "Because they were kindly and modest, studied the views of the House of Shammai as well as their own, and not only that but quoted the views of the House of Shammai before their own."

Now there's a strategy: Be kindly, modest, and, rather than excoriate the opposing view, study your opponent's ideas and present them fairly before your own. That is the Jewish way. If you doubt the strategy can succeed, it is worth considering that it has, for 3,000 years.

64

A CURE FOR DIASPORA DELUSIONS

What We Can Learn About Ourselves from Soviet Immigrants

ALEX ZELDIN

THE FIRST TIME I encountered American Jews talking about a "shining city on a hill," I didn't realize they were talking about Israel. I similarly didn't understand what it meant, when Israel went to war, that a subset of the American Jewish community publicly declared that Israel was "losing them." I was not born an American Jew, but immigrated from Belarus, following the collapse of the Soviet Union. I had much to learn.

Alex Zeldin is a columnist for the *Forward* focusing on issues of Jewish communal affairs, Russian-Jewish politics, American foreign policy, and U.S.-Israel relations. Alex's work has been featured in the *Atlantic*, the *Washington Post*, *Tablet* Magazine, and others.

Repeated exposure over the course of years taught me the phrases and slogans American Jews were fond of deploying for an Israel that seemed nothing like the Jewish state I knew. The Israel of their imaginations was a high-minded place of scientific advancements, a champion of tolerance, and a place filled with reluctant warriors committed to achieving peace.

For years, I carried a deep insecurity—their Israel was a lot more inspiring than the one I knew spending my summers among Russian-speaking Israeli family members during the Intifada. What was I missing?

Since that time, as Israeli politics has shifted rightwards and the majority of American Jews continue to be left leaning, the difference between their vision of Israel and the realities of a Jewish state has caused growing tension. Is there a path to, if not agreement, then at least understanding each other on our own terms?

I believe so. Specifically: The ties that bind Russian-speaking Jewry, with over a million residents in Israel, half a million in the United States, and half a million in the former Soviet Union, offer a guide to a healthier Israel-Diaspora relationship.

* * *

It is important to understand where people are coming from. For Jews whose families have been in the United States for several generations, the relationship to Israel has been molded and sustained through Jewish institutions. Day schools, summer camps, JCCs, shuls, and other communal organizations offered, and continue to offer, a great deal of Israel programming. Much of it is rooted in the accomplishments of the Jewish state. The advancements in medicine and science. The cultural output of Israel in literature, music, film, and television. The unlikely rebirth of Jewish statehood in 1948 and America's swift diplomatic recognition of it. The miraculous accomplishments of the Six-Day War and even more miraculous survival of the Jewish state following the Yom Kippur war. The difficult road to peace with countries like Egypt that waged war with Israel five times.

All good information—but all of it taking the form of abstract appeals to higher values. This is an education, not a relationship with human

485

beings. It also omits key facets of life for Jews and Arabs in Israel and life for Palestinians living under Israeli military rule. Finally, it does not focus on the less inspiring reasons why so many Jews fled to the Jewish state. For most of the roughly three million Jews who fled to Israel since its founding, the decision was not made from ideological Zionist commitments, but for simple pragmatic reasons rooted in concerns that early Zionists understood deeply: Jews were faced with impossible circumstances and needed a place to go. For most of Jewish history, refuge was hard to come by. Much of this narrative is centered around or culminating in the Holocaust but this was also the case well after 1945 for hundreds of thousands of Jews trapped in former Nazi camps because their home countries opposed repatriating them. This was the case, as well, for Mizrahi Jews driven out of ancient communities in the Middle East and North Africa for the crime of being Jews after a Jewish state had won its war of independence against Arab armies. It was the case for Ethiopian Jews facing violence and extreme food insecurity decades later. It was also the case for my family in the Soviet Union. They never heard of Freedom Sunday or knew who Vladimir Slepak or Anatoly (Natan) Sharansky were until years after the demise of the Soviet Union. In the 1980s, my father was an *otkaznik* (refusenik) in Soviet Belarus. Like many other Jews who sought to resist and escape Soviet antisemitic persecution, he faced retaliation from the state in employment, travel, and education opportunities. One form of state retaliation against *otkazniki* was undermining activists' resolve by letting some leave while forcing others to stay. My mother's family was permitted to leave for Israel.

After the collapse of the Soviet Union, restrictions remained in Belarus, which as of this writing continues to be an authoritarian quasi-Soviet state. Soviet tyranny ended for many in 1991, but state restrictions against my father continued for years in newly independent Belarus.

The years after the collapse of the Soviet Union were challenging for many. Our material existence centered around state rations of bread, butter, and vodka. My father would trade the vodka for sources of protein on the black market. Diapers, baby formula, and other things a family with young children would need were difficult to come by. Medicine was, too.

This period also saw the end of Communist repression of far-right politics, and the return of Eastern European nationalists and the antisemitism so dear to them. Antisemitic mobs would make it known they would be marching through Jewish neighborhoods. To say the least, moral ideals are far higher up on Abraham Maslow's hierarchy of needs than were the concerns of two million Soviet Jews in the late-Soviet and early post-Soviet period.

In 1994, my parents were told by my paternal uncle, who was already in New Jersey, that if they were able to get to the United States, that they would be given asylum. We fled Belarus and never looked back.

* * *

While I grew up meeting many American Jews, I spent my time, as many immigrants do, among people of my own background. I also spent summers with my mother's family in Haifa. I saw the excitement they felt about being in the Jewish state.

I also saw the way well-educated Russian-speaking Jews would not have their credentials accepted for employment. The trope of physicists sweeping the streets wasn't an anecdote to me. My grandmother had an economics degree in the Soviet Union. She cleaned hotel rooms in Israel to make ends meet. Her daughter, my aunt, met her husband in the army when they were working on what became the Iron Dome. When they sought to get married, the Chief Rabbinate treated them as non-Jews until they could prove otherwise—a humiliating experience and a painful memory for some of the proudest Jews I know.

At the same time, I also saw the hope both American and Israeli Jews expressed in the late 1990s when peace talks were underway with Palestinian leader Yasser Arafat. I later witnessed what the violence of the Intifada did to transform my relatives and Israeli society more broadly in the 2000s, when I was forbidden from riding buses during my summers there.

It would have never occurred to me to describe the Jewish state as a shining city on a hill. Israel, like every other place I had lived in, was a real country with real accomplishments and real problems. I adored Israel and was grateful for the refuge it provided to my family, but I never imagined it as a moral beacon to humanity. Israel could not "lose me" for the choices it made—because I never expected more from it than what it was. What it was—a desperately needed refuge for millions of Jews—was good enough.

My approach to Israel is not unique to me or pioneered by me. It is one shaped by lived experience that will be immediately familiar to many Russian-speaking Jews who lived through these challenges. Our relationships are with each other—to human beings—not to ideals or institutions.

It does not mean we lack ideals. It simply means that discussions about Israel in many (not all!) Russian-speaking circles do not center around what it means for our personal identity. The Chief Rabbinate's hostility to non-Orthodox Jews is one our families have experienced for their most joyous life events. The military occupation Palestinians live under is one our friends and family members served in. The violence Israelis experience at the hands of Palestinian terrorists is not an abstraction appearing on the news—it is too often carried out on the bodies of our loved ones.

Does it mean we have no criticisms of the Israeli government and Israeli policy? Of course not. Jews are a stiff-necked and opinionated people. Russian-speaking Jews no less so. It does often mean that our criticisms are more concrete, rather than questions about our identity, labels, and inspiring but incomplete narratives.

Healthy relationships include frank conversations and the assertion of boundaries. They are not fixated on *the status of the relationship*. We are not going anywhere. Neither are our brethren in Israel. For better or worse, we are stuck with each other. It is not a bad thing to make an effort to understand each other on our own terms, even as we continue to disagree on important issues.

For American and Israeli Jews who want a healthier relationship, my advice is simple: Make it with actual people and talk about the problems and disagreements, not what it means for your identity. Comforting stories, all-or-nothing attitudes, and turning a military occupation into something that is about *you*, thousands of miles away, benefit none of us.

65

THE CITY OF OUR DREAMS

Why Tel Aviv Is the Model for Jewish Life in the Twenty-First Century

NERI ZILBER

THE ENTIRE BLUEPRINT for political Zionism and the establishment of the State of Israel was laid out by Theodor Herzl in his 1902 utopian novel, *Altneuland* ("The Old New Land"). The future home of the Jewish people would be, of course, in the Land of Israel. It would be modern, liberal, economically vital, and inextricably linked to the rest of the world. It would confer on its inhabitants not just physical and material safety from European antisemitism (the prescient reason for Herzl's Zionism), but also cosmic redemption: The entire

---

Neri Zilber is a journalist covering Middle East politics and culture, an adjunct Fellow of the Washington Institute for Near East Policy, and an advisor to Israel Policy Forum.

endeavor is termed, repeatedly and earnestly, "The New Society." A Jewish beggar in Vienna could become a wealthy civic leader; a lovelorn cynic could again become a romantic believer.

"A magnificent city had been built beside the sapphire blue Mediterranean," the narrator writes, in the first inkling to both the reader and the two main protagonists that something remarkable had been created by the Jews. This city was Haifa: the industrial and commercial heart of the new Jewish common-wealth, replete with the most advanced technology and public infrastructure, connected by fast boat and rail links to all corners of the globe, fundamentally cosmopolitan in its cultural offerings and attitude.

"There's been a miracle here!" exclaims Friedrich Lowenstein, the former cynic, as he takes it all in.

Nahum Sokolow almost immediately translated Herzl's novel into Hebrew. Seven years later, the first new Hebrew city in two millennia was founded about fifty miles south of Haifa, along that same sapphire blue Mediterranean coastline. How did Sokolow choose to render the word *alt-neuland*, the old new land, from the German? He called it "Tel Aviv." The new city that later arose fittingly took its name.

If Herzl's utopia laid out the vision for what a future Jewish state could be—and what it shouldn't be—then Tel Aviv is its closest realization in the here and now. The center of the Jewish world (demographically, culturally, religiously) has shifted from far-flung, disparate diasporas to Israel. With all due respect to Jerusalem, the real capital of the Jewish people is Tel Aviv: a city that has come to embody not just the modern Israeli ethos, but also that of twenty-first century Jewry.

For quite some time, Israelis have viewed Tel Aviv as both a real place and an idea. Similarly, the city has increasingly come to be not just a physical location but also a global brand, an economic player, a lifestyle—in short, a distinctly Jewish metropole, a mother city, around which the rest of the family aligns.

If Herzl expected this from his fictional grand city, then he may have been the only one. Tel Aviv's current status is a decidedly new development, at certain points over the decades unlikely, if not unthinkable. For much of its history, Tel Aviv wasn't considered the cool, self-confident, non-stop White

City on the Med. The story of Tel Aviv is, in this way, the story of the evolution of the Jewish people and state over the past century. There is no doubt today that the center of gravity for both can be found there.

***

The year 1909 was a seminal one in Zionist history and the Land of Israel. Just as Tel Aviv was being founded in the sand dunes outside Jaffa on the shores of the Mediterranean, a small group of pioneers to the north began to build the first kibbutz, Degania, on the swampy shores of the Sea of Galilee.

For much of the next century, the popular visage of the Jew living between the two seas was certainly not that of the Tel Aviv bourgeoisie—the suited, café-dwelling trader, banker, or insurance salesman—but the plucky, ascetic pioneer tilling the land, bucket hat on his head and sandals on his feet. It wasn't an inevitability back then that Tel Aviv would beat Degania, and that *Tel Aviv-ism* would come to dominate the future state.

"Tel Aviv is fated to spread across all the Land," Meir Dizengoff, Tel Aviv's legendary founding mayor, wrote in 1935. Dizengoff likely meant this as a literal model to emulate: As the first Hebrew city, Tel Aviv "was built by Jews, per the desire of Jews, and for Jews," he had said earlier.

Tel Aviv was the first Jewish settlement in the *yishuv* to give Hebrew names to its streets. It—and not, say, Jerusalem or Haifa—hosted both the first Maccabiah Games (1932) and the Levant Fair (1934). By 1939, at the World's Fair in New York, the Jewish Palestine pavilion had its own "Café Tel Aviv." The city at this time was home to banking and industry, the political party headquarters, the media, the military command, various proto-state organs, and myriad cultural institutions.

By the 1960s, and much to the chagrin of Israel's old-guard socialist leaders, Tel Aviv was the vanguard of Israel's Western cultural awakening—a trend that would only grow stronger in subsequent decades. But then the party stopped. Tel Aviv, as a city if not as an idea, began to erode and crumble like so many seaside housing blocks in the salt air.

In the 1970s and 1980s, people left Tel Aviv in droves to outlying satellite towns, due to the city's shabbiness, crime, and squalor. No one wanted to live in the first Hebrew city anymore. In the late 1980s, a scheme was introduced to actually pay young students and artists to move to Sheinkin Street. This may read like science fiction given that Sheinkin later turned into the hippest and most sought-after street in the entire city, with rents rivaling those in Manhattan. But it really did happen. By 1994, the city's population was still less than it was in 1962.

* * *

All of that has now changed. Tel Aviv has not only returned to its former glory but surpassed it, to the point where demand to live in the city far outstrips supply.

The Tel Aviv metropolitan area now stretches from Herzilya, Ramat Hasharon, and Netanya to the north; to Ramat Gan, Or Yehuda, and Petach Tikva to the east; and to Rishon Letzion, Holon, and Rehovot to the south. This vast concrete conurbation, clearly visible on any approach to Ben Gurion Airport, holds roughly half of Israel's entire population and is the country's overwhelming economic engine.

Dizengoff's prediction has, in a physical sense, increasingly been proven correct: Tel Aviv is spreading across the land. In Israeli-speak, there is the "center" of the country and the "periphery," by which is implied everything else. The center of this "center," of course, is the city of Tel Aviv itself.

Many have taken to calling this all the "State of Tel Aviv," a separate "bubble" distinct from the rest of Israel, living in its own self-absorbed beach community, untouched by the atavisms of the Middle East. This would be wrong.

In November 2012, during the eight-day mini-war between Israel and Hamas, the Palestinian militant group fired several rockets at Tel Aviv—the first time air raid sirens had gone off in the city for twenty-one years. "Let the rockets fall," a young man in the southern city of Ashdod told me as he watched Tel Avivis scurrying for cover on television. "They should wake up."

Yet later that night, 15,000 yellow-clad fans filled Tel Aviv's basketball arena to watch Maccabi Tel Aviv, a European powerhouse, host a game against a Spanish team. "Tel Aviv isn't a separate country," Maccabi's longtime president, Shimon Mizrahi, reminded the television audience. "In 1991 [during the First Gulf War, when Iraqi Scud missiles targeted the city] we practiced here with gas masks next to us."

Indeed, on any walk through central Tel Aviv, one will come across memorials and plaques commemorating bloody terror attacks of the past: Savoy Hotel, Dizengoff Center, Café Apropo, Mike's Place, Dolphinarium, Simta Bar, and many others tragically too numerous to list. Since 2012, Tel Aviv has been fired upon regularly from Gaza during every major escalation.

Tel Aviv isn't a separate country, and Tel Avivis aren't a separate people.

"At any [Tel Aviv] club, most of the people dancing around you to the sounds of a deep-house hit dedicated to peace and love have undergone extensive automatic-weapons training and a hand-grenade tutorial," Etgar Keret wrote in the introduction to his *Tel Aviv Noir* anthology. "This isn't a conspiracy...just one of the fringe benefits of a country that institutes mandatory military service."

Around the table at a weekly poker game in north Tel Aviv made up of thirty- and forty-somethings, you may find a restaurant manager originally from Beit She'an, on the Jordanian border; a tech executive originally from Kiryat Shmona, on the Lebanese border; a former undercover special forces operative originally from Haifa, in the north; a serving military officer, originally from Be'er Sheva, in the south; and so on.

The point being that the vast majority of people who live in Tel Aviv are not native to Tel Aviv.

They come from across Israel, usually after their military service, to work in the bars and cafés to save money for their post-army trips to Asia or Latin America. They come to enjoy the nightlife and to find their future wife or husband. Some may even stay for a while after marriage, and after the first child, until they begrudgingly decamp out of the city in search of larger apartments at lower prices. They may come back later in life, after retirement and all the kids are gone, downsizing into smaller apartments in the center of town from which they can walk to the theater or museum or restaurants.

They come for the bright lights and the big city, to fulfill their version of the modern Israeli Dream.

Which brings us back to the year 1909 and Degania. Look at Israel today: The kibbutzim are aging and have mostly privatized. Farming and most manual labor are done by foreign hands. The socialist ethos lives on only in the nationalized health system and other government programs—not in the hearts of the citizenry. The Israeli Dream today is to make it in tech, to own a spacious apartment in an urban tower, to eat at high-end restaurants, to vacation abroad. Tel Aviv as an *idea* has spread across the land.

***

The howls of protest coming an hour's drive east of Tel Aviv, from Jerusalem, are palpable. The cosmically significant seat of the Israeli government and heart of the Jewish religion may lay claim to the title of capital of the Jewish people. But is it really?

Jerusalem provides a crucial connection to the Jewish past. Yet Tel Aviv is the present and future. As Dizengoff once put it, "Tel Aviv is considered the first Jewish city, not because its population, homes and property are Jewish, but because she belongs to all the Jews." None of these are exclusively true of Jerusalem like they are of Tel Aviv.

Israel's "eternal and undivided" capital is, to even a cursory observer, highly contested and fragmented. Most of the world doesn't recognize Israeli claims to the eastern half of the city, and still maintains it should be divided politically. Billions of people globally—Muslims and Christians—also lay spiritual claim to the holy city. Demographically, 40 percent of Jerusalem's residents are Palestinian Arab (with this proportion growing), and the Jewish residents increasingly ultra-Orthodox. Jerusalem for several years has led Israel in net emigration—Israelis voting with their feet, choosing to leave.

Today there are entire swaths of Jerusalem where Israeli Jews dare not enter. Many other parts of the city, ever more religious, are utterly alien to most Israelis. Jerusalem, in other words, isn't representative of Israel, let alone the Jewish people writ large—both groups of which still overwhelmingly skew non-observant and socially liberal.

Yet Tel Aviv's connection to the Jewish religion per se is stronger than popularly imagined. Despite its well-earned reputation as Israel's "Sin City," Tel Aviv is not a godless Gomorrah. It may be the most secular city in the Jewish State, but it is still a Jewish city.

"Tel Aviv isn't a secular city," maintains long-serving mayor Ron Huldai. "It's a city that *both* Haredim and the secular can live in."

In this way, like everywhere else in Jewish Israel, the streets of Tel Aviv begin to thin out every Friday afternoon ahead of sundown; the usual cacophony of car horns and construction is muted; most shops do close. The "healing quietness" of Shabbat, as Alfred Kazin once described it in a different context, descends—yes, even on Tel Aviv.

In certain quarters of the city, well-dressed worshippers can be seen heading to and from shul. Surprising to some, one can easily find in Tel Aviv kosher sushi and hamburger joints and high-end restaurants run by celebrity chefs to feed those more observant. On Friday evenings, parking is for once readily available, since many residents are at family Shabbat dinners back home, out of town. The city's many bars stand nearly empty till later in the night, awaiting revelers finishing those dinners.

But if we are being honest, it's those Tel Aviv bars, and not the city's religious life, that have helped broaden Tel Aviv's appeal, which now extends well beyond Israel. And not just the bars, but what the bars and nightlife represent: liberalism, cosmopolitanism, vitality, modernity. Tel Aviv in more recent times has become not just a city, and not just an idea. It is now a global brand.

***

On Tel Aviv's fiftieth anniversary, in 1959, then-mayor Chaim Levanon quipped: "Haifa wakes up early, Jerusalem goes to sleep early, and Tel Aviv gets to bed very late and rises at dawn." The intriguing point here isn't the clichés, accurate as they may have been, but that he was comparing Tel Aviv to other Israeli cities at all. Even three decades later, PR copywriters created the "Non-Stop City" tagline for Tel Aviv to simply encourage *domestic* tourism.

Today the aperture has widened considerably, with the first Hebrew city coming to see itself in the same league as major international destinations like Berlin and Barcelona, New York and London. By nearly every metric that matters in terms of urban livability and happiness in the twenty-first century, Tel Aviv ranks extremely high.

Sunny weather and Mediterranean beaches. Outdoor sport and fitness and yoga. World-class DJs spinning and endless bars serving, but also idiosyncratic cafés pouring cappuccinos past midnight. Upmarket culturally, there are the theaters and art galleries and architecture, with UNESCO world heritage Bauhaus buildings returned to their former understated glory. And there is the sumptuous food scene, as Tel Aviv chefs increasingly export their modern Israeli cuisine to countries all around the globe.

Tel Aviv also consistently places as one of the most LGBTQ-friendly cities in the world, with a yearly Pride bash on the shoreline that draws a quarter million revelers. For the more local LGBTQ community—Israelis and Palestinians alike—Tel Aviv is a sanctuary, in the very real sense of the word: an open and accepting place, where most things are accessible and permissible, where one can come to fully live.

One would be remiss not also to highlight Tel Aviv's well-earned reputation as a global tech hub, the "Silicon Wadi" of the vaunted "Start Up Nation." There are few cities in the world that can compete with the amount of tech capital—people and money—found in Tel Aviv these days, in the co-working spaces all along Rothschild Boulevard and the new towers that have gone up on both sides of the Ayalon Highway.

Those glass-and-steel towers, nearly all of them built over the past fifteen years, are only the most conspicuous manifestation of Tel Aviv's newfound affluence and confidence. There are also the luxury sports cars on the roads and the impossible-to-obtain dinner reservations, with restaurants packed until late at night even on weekdays. The building boom in Tel Aviv is unmissable. There is construction everywhere: upgrading the city's signature four-story apartment blocks into modernist condos, a long-needed light-rail network, sleek office towers (to house all those tech start-ups) and opulent residential towers (to house all those new tech millionaires, along with foreigners seeking a holiday home).

Huldai, the mayor, says it is all meant to undo decades of neglect, especially in terms of transit, infrastructure, and housing. The urban regeneration underway, he said in his gruff way, is meant to move Tel Aviv "from a European city of the 1950s to a European city of the 1990s." The end result will be a much denser city built skyward, as in the United States or Gulf, but with the services and livability of a well-run European city.

There are those who wonder whether this sprawling program will demolish the charm and innocence of old Tel Aviv, especially for those who can't keep up with the spiraling housing costs. But no one can question that this facelift is long overdue. In physical terms, Tel Aviv isn't a beautiful city (despite the Mediterranean sunsets)—but it will be once the construction is finished.

"A shithole." That's how one well-known British photographer described his first impression of the city, before he made it his home. He then went on to publish an entire book highlighting the beautiful people of Tel Aviv, which likely gets at the core truth behind the city's global appeal. The great poet Hayim Nahman Bialik once said: "We will be a normal state when we have the first Hebrew prostitute, the first Hebrew thief and the first Hebrew policeman." Tel Aviv is an abnormal city, with those prostitutes and thieves and policemen, techies and hipsters, businessmen and artists, immigrants and sabras colliding with each other on the shores of the Holy Land.

It is often termed, simply, as the "vibe" of the place. Some cities may have the beach, nightlife, food, or tech of Tel Aviv; very few have all of them together in one place, in one walkable twenty-square-mile package.

It is the indescribable quality of the Tel Aviv boardwalk on a late summer day, with the sun setting and people strolling, taking in the fiery orange and crimson red ball disappearing below the horizon. The look on the faces of the people is one of contentment, security, even happiness. The Jewish people, they seem to be intimating without saying a word, are right where they want to be; they are right where they belong. A miracle has truly occurred.

AFTERWORD

Is This a Jewish Book? A Jewish Publisher's Priorities

ADAM BELLOW

ONE DAY MANY YEARS AGO, when I was still a young editor learning my trade, I got a phone call from a reporter at the *Baltimore Jewish Times*. "I'm writing an article about Jewish publishing," he said. "So I'm calling up Jewish editors and asking, 'What's a Jewish book'?"

To be honest, I had never really thought about this question. Yes, I had published books on Jewish subjects. But I didn't think of them as conforming to a particular set of criteria. As far as I was concerned, my choices were entirely personal and idiosyncratic. But I had to say something, so without thinking about it too much, I replied, "A Jewish book…is any book that a Jew wants to read."

Adam Bellow is publisher of Wicked Son Books and executive editor of Bombardier Books, imprints of Post Hill Press. He has previously been editorial director of *The Free Press*, executive editor at Doubleday-Broadway, and editorial director of Broadside Books and All Points Books. He is also the author of *In Praise of Nepotism: A History of Family Enterprise from King David to George W. Bush* and co-editor of *New Threats to Freedom* and *The State of the American Mind*.

We both laughed, and I hung up. But the brief exchange stayed with me and I have thought about it many times over the years. For it was not entirely clear, even to me, what I had meant by it, or whether it was true.

Throughout my career I continued to publish Jewish books. Even so, I did not think of myself as a "Jewish editor" until quite recently, when my partners and I decided to launch a Jewish imprint. And since imprints must have names, and a defining sense of purpose, we decided to call it Wicked Son.

The wicked son, as everyone knows, is not a respecter of pieties. Provocative and sly, he defines himself in opposition to his family and tribe, not necessarily embracing them or granting them authority. As if to say, "Oh really? *I'll* be the judge of all that." We thought the name would suitably evoke the irreverent attitude we wanted to project—and attract the sort of writers we wanted to publish. Informal market testing with our friends evoked appreciative laughter. This confirmed we were on the right track.

But what would it look like in practice? After all, we can't just publish any book that comes our way. We have to make choices, and those choices must be guided by some principle—some notion of what we think Jews ought to read at this moment in time.

This is all the more important given the many daunting challenges we face. The traditional Jewish readership is shrinking, aging out. Young Jews are increasingly disaffected from Israel. Jewish media is disaggregated, making readers hard to reach with specifically Jewish content. Nor is there a dearth of Jewish books. Indeed, it sometimes seems there are more Jewish books being published than there are actual Jews to read them. Meanwhile, outdated models of production, distribution, marketing, and reading itself are desperately in need of reinvention.

Given all this, one might think it quixotic to be launching a new Jewish publishing business. Why even bother? Why not just publish the occasional Jewish book and leave it at that? More to the point in this context, why assemble sixty-five essays on the Jewish future by writers and thinkers all over the world in an ambitious attempt to reset the whole Jewish agenda? Is that really any business of ours? Does the world need another Jewish publisher?

Apparently, we think it does. Explaining why necessitates a brief look back at our historical lineage—the story of Jewish publishing in America—to help us understand how we got to this point, and what our predecessors thought they were doing. What's really striking at this distance of time is how little interest most of them displayed in Jewish books.

***

There is in this country a vibrant Jewish publishing tradition going back to the founding of the Jewish Publication Society in 1888. The mission of JPS is to promote Jewish literacy and preserve the Jewish heritage. To that end it publishes books on Jewish observance; holidays and customs; history and theology; ethics and philosophy; and numerous Bible editions and study resources. For JPS, then, a Jewish book is one that transmits some core aspect of Jewish tradition. But this is where clarity ends. For as soon as we depart from preservation and literacy as Jewish publishing priorities, we enter the realm of sensibility, wherein each publisher makes choices based upon a unique combination of personal taste and visceral business instincts.

Take Alfred A. Knopf, the first and most distinguished Jewish American publisher. The son of a successful ad executive, Knopf was more interested in books than in becoming a lawyer; so his father got him a job in the ad department at Doubleday, and in 1915 gave him $5,000 to launch his own house. An assimilated version of a conventional WASP publisher, Knopf's idea was simply to publish the best works of European literature, including the English, Russians, French, and Germans. He also published Kafka and Babel, but he published them more as Europeans than as Jews, while rejecting books by I.B. Singer and Anne Frank. He probably thought they were too Jewish.

That said, Knopf was thoroughly Jewish as a businessman, both in the entrepreneurial energy he displayed and in the way he applied modern marketing methods that would have been considered crass by traditional publishers. Consider this brief sketch by editor and journalist Chip McGrath:

> He made sales calls himself, believing that he could do it better than any sales rep; he sent out direct mailings and even corresponded with

individual readers. He quickly embraced new advertising technology, buying ads on the radio, for example, and even on Times Square billboards. He wrote all the early ads himself, and the tone is partly that of a chatty confidant and partly that of a busker.

You have to love a guy like this, especially given his anglophile pretensions and noted sartorial flair (he favored tailored suits with wildly colorful shirts and ties). This type of larger-than-life Jewish impresario was to become a familiar figure in the twentieth century, including Sol Hurok, Leonard Bernstein, Mortimer Adler, and Joe Papp, who brought high culture to the American middle class.

A very different ethos was displayed by Simon & Schuster, a "Jewish" firm founded in 1924 by Richard L. Simon, a piano salesman, and Max Schuster, the editor of an automotive trade magazine. Their initial offerings were crossword puzzle books. But they soon developed a method for exploiting other popular fads and trends, often coming up with their own ideas and hiring writers to carry them out. S&S quickly became a mass-market powerhouse, employing many brilliant Jewish editors over the years. Few of them showed much interest in Jewish books per se. However, S&S did publish Will Durant's bestselling *The Story of Philosophy* (1926), followed by the eleven-volume *Story of Civilization*. They thus displayed a typical Jewish proclivity for mass educational uplift and boosting the Western heritage—while also selling tons of books.

A worthy successor to Knopf was the flamboyant and outspoken Roger Straus, co-founder (in 1947) of Farrar, Straus. A publisher of consummate taste who cleverly cornered the market in Nobel Prize-winning novelists, Straus (like Knopf) was more Jewish in his entrepreneurial flash than in his editorial priorities. Also like Knopf, he came by his defining mix of highbrow taste and mercantile commercialism honestly: his mother was a Guggenheim and his father's family owned Macy's. But he did publish Jewish authors of distinction, picking up Singer as well as Malamud, Roth, and Joseph Brodsky.

Salman Schocken has probably the best claim to be the premier Jewish publisher in America, and the world. An itinerant peddler who became the founder of a German department store chain and a leading collector, philanthropist, and patron, his eponymous press sought to publish the best of secular Jewish culture for both Jewish and German audiences. Forced to abandon his business empire during the war, he promptly founded two new houses in New York and Tel Aviv.

Thoroughly elitist in his tastes and social attitudes, the introduction to his first catalog grimly assessed American Jews as a "dark" uncultivated people, a people who lived "in empty houses—empty of books and of the spirit." Schocken undertook to fix this by exposing his benighted fellow Jews to "the treasures of thousands of years of our Jewish culture." His inaugural list included books by Kafka, Buber, Benjamin, and Scholem. It is a credit to his force of personality and vision that the house retains its Jewish focus. The jury is still out on the impact of his program on American Jews themselves.

Pantheon, founded by the legendary Kurt and Helen Wolff, was another "Jewish" firm that wasn't very Jewish in its content. Wolff, a well-regarded German publisher, was best known for "discovering" Kafka. But his tastes were more literary than Jewish. Fleeing to New York in 1941, the Wolffs launched Pantheon out of their living room in Washington Square, bringing out neglected European classics in first rate translations. They were almost priestly in their emphasis on publishing books that embodied transcendent cultural and spiritual values. But despite having excellent taste they were terrible businesspeople and eventually sold the company to Random House.

Their successor, André Schiffrin, was a born and bred publishing aristocrat whose French-Jewish parents—distinguished literary publishers—decamped from Paris to New York in 1944. There his father joined Pantheon, acquiring books by André Gide and Albert Camus before dying prematurely in 1950. Meanwhile, André grew up in the left-leaning New York literary world, working summer jobs at Pantheon while attending Yale and Cambridge. In 1962, he joined the company and spent the next 28 years making it the intellectual home of the New Left with books by Noam Chomsky, Edward Said, Michel Foucault, Studs Terkel, and Barbara Ehrenreich. Though there was nothing remotely Jewish about these books, the act of publishing them arguably was. Regardless, Schiffrin deserves high standing in the ranks of Jewish publishers for sponsoring Art Spiegelman's *Maus*.

We at Wicked Son would be proud to trace our lineage to any of these celebrated forebears. But we actually derive from a different branch of American Jewish publishing—that of The Free Press and Basic Books, which published serious nonfiction for the intelligent general reader. Neither went out of their way to publish books on Jewish subjects. But both were clear extensions of a broader Jewish intellectual and academic enterprise.

Founded in 1947 by Jeremiah Kaplan, The Free Press launched with titles by Émile Durkheim, Max Weber, and Bertrand Russell. In the '60s and '70s, its program was a roster of important books about society and culture. Most of its authors were Jews from immigrant backgrounds deeply concerned with issues of race, culture, economics, urban policy, and intergroup dynamics in a large multiethnic democracy. Later, the house acquired an emphasis on business and politics under its neoconservative publisher Erwin Glikes, who hired me as an editor in 1988. The Free Press under Erwin was a perfect hybrid of the Columbia graduate seminar and the garment center sweatshop. Brilliant, irascible, funny, a born showman, charming and high-minded when it suited him but hard and mercenary in his business dealings, Erwin (Jewishly educated in Antwerp before the war) consistently published Jewish books while helping to formulate the intellectual resistance to post-'60s liberalism.

Basic Books, founded in 1952 by the equally tough and charming Arthur Rosenthal, started out as a trio of academic book clubs. Through his connections to Freud's circle he acquired the three-volume biography of Freud by Ernest Jones, and went on to publish an impressive list of books across the social sciences. After he sold the company to Harper, Basic came under the direction of Martin Kessler, an owlish, bespectacled man with an impenetrable Viennese accent. Not noticeably Jewish in his tastes, Martin was a consummate intellectual who somehow persuaded his superiors to publish Douglas Hofstadter's *Gödel Escher Bach*, an 824-page tome on the esoteric connections among these three creative geniuses in mathematics, art, and music. The book became an international phenomenon. No publisher today would even contemplate such madness. But it was (I think) a very Jewish thing to do.

***

The first conclusion we may draw is that American Jewish publishers were traditionally divided into literary and intellectual wings. The literary publishers were frankly elitist and assimilationist, seeking to foster a taste for European culture in Jewish readers or introduce Jewish writers to the American mainstream. The more commercial houses embraced middlebrow American materialism but preserved the Jewish penchant for cultural uplift.

Jewish publishers also answered the question "what's a Jewish book?" in different ways according to their lights. Some published Jewish books as their defining mission; others as an adjunct; still others as an afterthought. Some manifested their Jewishness directly in the books they published; others through a commercial ethos that combined high-minded taste with garment district *sechel*. Intellectual publishers seemingly expressed it through a commitment to ideas and contrarian arguments.

Above all, they were clever and resourceful impresarios—inspired opportunists and promoters who operated by feel or instinct more than a set program. Time and again they acquired the books that they felt in their guts were important and figured out the reasons why afterward.

A charter member of this tribe was Barney Rosset, founder of Grove Press and a pioneering publisher of avant-garde countercultural books. An ardent communist and free speech absolutist who felt it was his duty to challenge the midcentury American regime of moral censorship, he courted controversy, lawsuits, and even death threats by publishing "obscene" books like *Lady Chatterley's Lover*, *Tropic of Cancer*, and *Naked Lunch*. He also published Beckett, Genet, and Ionesco along with Che Guevara, Ho Chi Minh, and Malcolm X. His taste was viscerally contrarian and he trusted his instincts completely. A 1969 *Life* magazine profile observed, "He does everything by impulse and then figures out afterward whether he's made a smart move or was just kidding." Rosset may have only been half-Jewish, but we proudly claim the Jewish half.

What all this ultimately suggests is that in twentieth century New York, you didn't have to publish Jewish books to be considered a Jewish publisher. It was as much a social identity as anything else—a matter of belonging to the family. Nor was it simply a reflection of your stated editorial priorities, but of your sensibility and methods as a publisher.

With this in mind, let's return to the question I raised earlier: can one really say that a Jewish book is any book that a Jew wants to read? Now that I've had thirty years to think about it, I have finally arrived at an answer. And the answer is yes.

This assertion obviously requires an explanation. So with all due respect to my late mentors—hardheaded Jewish realists who would undoubtedly regard it as lamentably postmodern—my explanation goes like this: A Jewish person, whatever their beliefs, affiliations, or sense of connection to Israel, is in possession of a certain form of consciousness, a lens or prism through which they apprehend the world. And that consciousness, no matter how attenuated, remains distinctly Jewish, because it represents the distillation of some three thousand years of Jewish history, culture, beliefs, and experiences passed down by countless conscious and unconscious influences. It may therefore be said that any time a Jew reads a book, that book also becomes Jewish in some sense, because she reads it Jewishly, whether she knows it or not.

One might very well object that this definition is nebulous and overly subjective, or that it produces a weak version of what we might wish to call a robust Jewish identity. It worked for me because my own Jewish identity was almost entirely intellectual and cultural. But it was no less powerful for that.

My Jewish consciousness began with an influential father, the writer Saul Bellow. Famously steeped in the immigrant Jewish experience, he embodied and conveyed to all his sons a profound sense of Jewish identity. But his rise to fame also coincided with a unique Jewish "moment" in American culture. The 1960s saw an explosion of interest in Jewish cultural productions. *Fiddler* was on Broadway. Anne Frank became a household name. Malamud, Singer, and Roth wrote books that broke through to a mainstream audience. All this, plus Israel's lightning victory in the Six-Day War, gave me and other young Jews a powerful sense of Jewish pride.

Clearly the link between consciousness and culture is strong. But now it seems I may have overestimated the power and persistence of my particular *form* of Jewish consciousness. Today there is no equivalent of the robust secular Jewish culture of my youth. The Jews have had their turn, and American culture has moved on to other "moments." As a result, young diaspora Jews feel less pride in being Jewish. Instead, they participate in a general culture that sounds an occasional Jewish note but is, in the main, not representative of Jewish sensibilities and interests.

As a young editor I didn't feel any particular responsibility for building up this Jewish American culture. But today I see it ebbing and receding. What should our priority be, then, if not to foster a strong, well-nourished Jewish consciousness in the next generation of readers?

***

The funny thing about starting a new imprint is that you never really know where you are going until you see what you've been signing. We make decisions book by book, based less on what we think Jews ought to read than on what we believe they will buy. What is emerging is a mix of continuities and differences.

Like our mentors, we are idea-driven publishers who favor strong contrarian arguments on a wide range of topical issues. Unlike them, we publish books specifically by, for, and about Jews. None of these imposing intellectuals would have set up a Jewish imprint: they would have considered it too narrow and parochial. Evidently, we feel quite assimilated enough and wish to go in the other direction, proudly affirming our identity as Jews in the face of rising threats to our security. We have also made it a priority to publish Jewish fiction, an unplanned development that is purely a result of hanging out our shingle and receiving a flood of submissions. These novels don't fit any mold and have nothing in common other than the fact that we fell in love with them and decided they had to be published.

Broadly, then, our sensibility is contemporary, eclectic, and unabashedly commercial. We are not cultural elitists, nor are we in the business of providing Jewish-themed mental wallpaper for an assimilating ethnic middle class. Rather than seeking to educate and uplift, in other words, we aim to provoke and entertain. If this mixed, improvisational approach to Jewish publishing makes us a little postmodern, then so be it. What else would you expect from a house called Wicked Son?

Meanwhile, with every book we sign, we learn more about what stories, ideas, and arguments matter today. And what our acquisitions tell us is that an important change is under way in Jewish life. Even as the once-vibrant American diaspora loses energy, declines, and turns inward, an expansive, confident, outward-looking Israel is undergoing a massive burst of cultural expression. So far, the Hebrew language barrier has prevented much of it from getting out. But over time, we may expect to see a shift from a collection of separate Jewish cultures to a more open and unified global one, drawing content from across the Jewish world. We have therefore made it a priority to nurture and promote this cosmopolitan Jewish culture and provide it with the platform it requires. For in an age of cultural globalism, why shouldn't Jews be represented? Even overrepresented?

Jewish Priorities is our signature effort, the book we hope will put us on the map as an idea-driven publisher with an ambition to engage the full spectrum of Jewish concerns. No one book can possibly encompass every issue or reflect every voice and perspective. But it isn't meant to be the last word in the debate about Jewish priorities, but rather the first word in a global conversation among Jews that we hope will continue and take on a life of its own.

Come what may, we are proud to have assembled a first-rate group of wicked sons and daughters whose priorities may differ, but whose common aim is to provoke, disturb, and if necessary, offend—as long as it gets you to think. As for the age-old question, "What's a Jewish book?"—we'll let you know when we figure that out. But based on the foregoing, a provisional answer might be, "Any book that a Jew wants to publish."

Discuss.

ACKNOWLEDGMENTS

THE AIM OF THIS BOOK is not to encapsulate the entirety of Jewish public opinion—which would be both impossible and tedious—but to provide a kind of representative snapshot of the creative thinking of a people, looking to the future, at a particular moment in history.

Even this goal seemed pretty daunting when I started working on it during the pandemic doldrums of 2021.

I knew I would need help. The process took more than a year and a half, and the result was a collection that included not only writers I knew personally but also many I'd long admired from afar, as well as a few previously unknown to me. Their essays, I believe, can form the backbone of a new discourse about the collective future of our people. I am deeply grateful to each and every one of the contributors to this volume.

Building the roster involved a lot of conversations and networking, via both potential authors and well-connected friends. I'm particularly grateful to Sally Abrams, David L. Bernstein, Mark Charendoff, Harry Cohen, Shira Dicker, Seth Frantzman, Daniella Greenbaum Davis, Rabbi Shai Held, Rabbi Ammiel Hirsch, Tal Keinan, Yossi Klein Halevi, Rabbi Irwin Kula, Yehuda Kurtzer, Liel Leibovitz, Gregg Mashberg, Avi Mayer, Hen Mazzig, David Miller, Rabbi John Moscowitz, Carly Pildis, Noah Pollak, Roz Rothstein, Jodi Rudoren, Brian Schrauger, Joe Schwartz, Dan Senor, Laura Shaw Frank, Tanya Singer, James Snyder, Andrés Spokoiny, Bret Stephens, David Suissa, Gil Troy, Elisha Wiesel, Einat Wilf, and Rabbi David Wolpe—all of whom offered encouragement and wisdom, many of whom made introductions of consequence, and some of whom contributed essays as well.

The list of confirmed contributors began to grow, and at a certain point it became clear that such a project would require not only professional and moral support, but also material help. I am deeply indebted to those who believed in this project at the earliest stages and provided crucial support: Above all, to Michael Steinhardt, along with his wife Judy Steinhardt and daughter Sara Bloom, who jumped in first and helped turn an ambitious idea into reality. The President and CEO of the Steinhardt Foundation for Jewish Life, Rabbi David Gedzelman, provided many hours of support, introductions, and great ideas. Phil Darivoff also believed in this project from the beginning, and offered help in many forms. Further thanks go to Mark Gerson, Marty Peretz, and Randy Levitt, as well as additional supporters whose preference for anonymity I have reluctantly respected.

In addition to deserving credit for the initial idea behind this volume, Adam Bellow, publisher of Wicked Son, has been an invaluable mentor and guide. His partner, David S. Bernstein, offered encouragement and wisdom throughout the process.

Above all, I am deeply grateful to my beloved wife Dikla, who tolerated my repeated trips abroad and late nights of work, the Zoom calls scheduled when I was supposed to be putting the girls to bed, and the general state of usually-but-not-always-stifled panic to which I subjected her for the better part of two years. At any point she could have said, "Really? You talk about priorities?" Instead, she offered only heartfelt encouragement, patience, and love.

ABOUT THE AUTHOR

DAVID HAZONY is an award-winning editor, translator, and author. He is the former editor-in-chief of the journal Azure and was the founding editor of The-Tower.org. His book *The Ten Commandments* (Scribner, 2010) was a finalist for the National Jewish Book Award. His translation of Uri Bar-Joseph's *The Angel* (HarperCollins, 2016) was a winner of the National Jewish Book Award. He has edited two previous anthologies: *Essential Essays on Judaism* by Eliezer Berkovits (Shalem, 2002), and, with Yoram Hazony and Michael B. Oren, *New Essays on Zionism* (Shalem, 2007). He has a Ph.D. in Jewish Philosophy from the Hebrew University and lives in Jerusalem.